What's New in This Edition

In this edition of *Teach Yourself Access 97 in 14 Days*, you'll find the following valuable additions:

- [ ] Full examples show you how to use Microsoft's new ActiveX controls to add often amazing features to your Access projects. Currently available ActiveX controls include everything from a calendar to a stock ticker tape that gets its data from the Internet. Chapter 27, "ActiveX: The Next Generation of OLE Controls," is wholly devoted to ActiveX controls.

- [ ] Access for Windows 97 is fully Internet-enabled. You can include links to various sites, including the World Wide Web, in your forms or as data in your databases. Chapter 28, "Access and the World Wide Web," shows you how.

- [ ] Added sidebars, tips, and hints throughout the book help you apply your new knowledge of Access to your real-world problems. Add your "book knowledge" to those hints, tips, and sidebars, and then stir in your problems; you'll end up with solutions!

- [ ] Access for Windows 97, Version 8, brims with new wizards. See the most interesting of these wizards in action as you move through the exercises in *Teach Yourself Access 97 in 14 Days*.

- [ ] Access for Windows 97, Version 8, has among its new add-ins a Switch-board Manager. See this timesaver in action in Chapter 23, "Introduction to Macros."

- [ ] Access for Windows 97, Version 8, includes the new Office Assistant, an artificial intelligence (AI) help system that can answer your questions about various Access operations. Chapter 2, "Wizards, the Office Assis-tant, and Help," gives you a head start for using this new system.

- [ ] Access for Windows 97, Version 8, can end relational theory confusion! See how to automatically normalize (set relationships) using the Table Analyzer Wizard shown in Chapter 4, "Table Field Properties."

About This Book

This book starts where you are likely to start—at the point when you first start Microsoft Access, and a whole new world opens up before your eyes. You might be in a state of panic, shock, or total excitement.

This book provides hands-on tutorials, useful tips, and technical information to get you started and keep you going with Access. It takes you from the most basic and elementary database tasks, such as setting up tables and printing quick reports, to advanced techniques such as sophisticated queries and linked-table databases.

You'll see the following specific features throughout the book:

☐ **Do/Don't boxes:** These give you guidance on what to do and what to avoid doing in specific Access database tasks.

☐ **Notes:** These provide essential background information so that you can not only do things with Access, but have a good understanding of what you're doing and why.

☐ **Access Jargon:** These explain database jargon in plain English, so you can impress your friends at parties when the conversation turns to database management.

☐ **The Access Way sidebars:** These give tips, tricks, and warnings specific to Access 97.

Who Should Read This Book

Whether you just need help with a specific database task or want a step-by-step tutorial on every aspect of the program, you will find what you need in this book. For beginners, there's coverage of the basic concepts of database management and the basic techniques of using Access. For readers who are more technically advanced, there's reference information about various aspects of using the program. And for people who just need to "dip into" the book and learn about a specific topic, the clear organization of the sections and lessons makes it fast and easy for them to find what they need.

Conventions

The most notable conventions in the book are

- ☐ Access commands, which are in code listings or embedded in regular text, appear in a monospace font. For example, "Enter the expression `=DatePart("d",[Date of Record])` on the first row of the Sorting and Grouping box" contains a command in monospace.

- ☐ Access menu choices are indicated by the name of the menu, followed by a vertical slash character (|), then the name of the menu choice.

Throughout the book, the emphasis has been on providing useful information in a way that is fast, easy, and fun.

Teach
Yourself
ACCESS 97
in 14 days,
Fourth Edition

Teach Yourself
ACCESS 97
in 14 days, Fourth Edition

Paul Cassel

SAMS
PUBLISHING

201 West 103rd Street
Indianapolis, Indiana 46290

This book is dedicated to my daughter, Tirilee Cassel, who got it all together on Saint Patrick's Day. May her unquenchable thirst for knowledge never cease.

Copyright © 1996 by Sams Publishing

FOURTH EDITION

International Standard Book Number: 0-672-30969-6

Library of Congress Catalog Card Number: 96-69054

99 98 97 96   4 3 2 1

Interpretation of the printing code: the rightmost double-digit number is the year of the book's printing; the rightmost single-digit, the number of the book's printing. For example, a printing code of 96-1 shows that the first printing of the book occurred in 1996.

Composed in Agaramond and MCPdigital by Macmillan Computer Publishing

Printed in the United States of America

Trademarks

Publisher and President: Richard K. Swadley
Publishing Manager: Rosemarie Graham
Director of Editorial Services: Cindy Morrow
Assistant Marketing Managers: Kristina Perry
Rachel Wolfe

Acquisitions Editor
Corrine Wire

Development Editors
Kristi Asher
Todd Bumbalough

Production Editor
Carolyn Linn

Copy Editor
Lisa Lord

Indexer
Erika Millen

Technical Reviewers
Robert Bogue
Kelly Held

Editorial Coordinator
Katie Wise

Technical Edit Coordinator
Lorraine Schaffer

Resource Coordinator
Deborah Frisby

Editorial Assistants
Carol Ackerman
Andi Richter
Rhonda Tinch-Mize

Cover Designer
Tim Amrhein

Book Designer
Gary Adair

Copy Writer
Peter Fuller

Production Team Supervisor
Brad Chinn

Production
Paula Lowell
Mark Mathews
Carl Pierce
Shawn Ring
Ian Smith

Overview

		Foreword	xx
		Introduction	xxv

Day 1

	AM 1	A Short Access Tour	3
	PM 2	Wizards, the Office Assistant, and Help	17

Day 2

	AM 3	Entering Data into Tables	37
	PM 4	Table Field Properties	49

Day 3

	AM 5	Modifying Table Properties	73
	PM 6	Data Types and Validation	91

Day 4

	AM 7	An Introduction to Forms and Form Controls	111
	PM 8	A Look into Queries	143

Day 5

	AM 9	Multitable Queries	167
	PM 10	Basic Reports	183

Day 6

	AM 11	Intermediate Reports	205
	PM 12	Intermediate Forms	223

Day 7

	AM 13	More Intermediate Forms	251
	PM 14	Manipulating Dates and Using Expressions in Queries	267

Day 8

	AM 15	Intermediate to Advanced Queries	289
	PM 16	More Advanced Queries	307

Day 9

AM 17   Forms with Subforms   353

PM 18   Form Control Properties   375

Day 10

AM 19   Instantly Smarter Forms   399

PM 20   Fancy Form Layout   417

Day 11

AM 21   Expressions in Reports and Queries   445

PM 22   Complex Reports   469

Day 12

AM 23   Introduction to Macros   495

PM 24   More Macro Magic   517

Day 13

AM 25   Everything You Need to Know About Programming   547

PM 26   Programming Made Easy with Visual Basic   567

Day 14

AM 27   ActiveX: The Next Generation of OLE Controls   595

PM 28   Access and the World Wide Web   613

Appendixes

A   Quiz Answers   637

B   Exercise Guide/Quick Reference   643

C   The Toolbox Illustrated   653

D   Access Toolbars   657

E   The Sample Data   667

Glossary   683

Index   687

Contents

Introduction   **xxv**

Day 1

AM 1   **A Short Access Tour**   **3**

Installing Access 4
Launching Access from Windows 7
The Parts of the Access 97 User Interface 8
Arranging Toolbars 10
    Sitting on the Dock of the Access Bay 12
Customizing Access Toolbars 13
Morning Summary 15

PM 2   **Wizards, the Office Assistant, and Help**   **17**

Office Assistant 18
Wizards 21
Enter the Wizard 24
Using Help 28
Day Summary 32
Q&A 32
Workshop 33
    Quiz 33
    Put Access into Action 33

Day 2

AM 3   **Entering Data into Tables**   **37**

The Database Project 38
Planning the Database 38
Before the First Table 40
The First Table 42
A Look at Field Types and Properties 46
Data Types 46
Morning Summary 48

PM 4   **Table Field Properties**   **49**

Modifying a Table 50
Adding Fields 52
Creating a New Table Manually 55
Creating the Table 56
The "Why" of a Relationship 61
Making the Link or Relationship 62

A Third Way to Table Creation 64
Day Summary 67
Q&A 68
Workshop 69
    Quiz 69
    Put Access into Action 70

Day 3

AM 5   **Modifying Table Properties**   **73**
Getting Started 74
Quality Assurance, Data-Entry Style 77
Trying Out the Input Mask 80
Changing Field Order 82
    Moving a Field 82
    Changing the Apparent Field Order 83
Changing Field Widths and Row Heights 85
Combo and List Boxes in Tables 87
Morning Summary 90

PM 6   **Data Types and Validation**   **91**
More on Field Properties 92
It's Default of Access 98
Data Validation 101
    The Required Property 104
    A Date-Specific Property 104
    Two Number-Specific Properties 104
Day Summary 105
Q&A 106
Workshop 107
    Quiz 107
    Put Access into Action 107

Day 4

AM 7   **An Introduction to Forms and Form Controls**   **111**
What's a Form? 112
Making a Form 112
Looking Over the Form 114
    Moving to New Records 115
    Some Alternative Navigation Methods 116
Making a Form by Using a Wizard 119
Adding Data Through a Form 122
Form Control Properties 123
Introduction to Form Controls 127
    Bound and Unbound Controls 127
    Moving and Sizing 127

Choosing Multiple Controls 136
Adding and Deleting Controls 138
Changing Appearances 140
Morning Summary 142

PM 8   A Look into Queries   143

A Simple Query 144
Criteria in Queries 151
Some Criteria Variations 152
Using OR and AND Criteria 156
Day Summary 159
Q&A 159
Workshop 161
    Quiz 161
    Put Access into Action 162
    For the Adventurous 163

Day 5

AM 9   Multitable Queries   167

Looking at a Wizard 168
A Simple Multitable Query 169
Removing a Field from a Query 174
Adding Another Table 176
Morning Summary 180

PM 10   Basic Reports   183

Report Concepts 184
Altering the Wizard's Output 187
Mailing Labels 194
A Look Ahead 199
Day Summary 199
Q&A 200
Workshop 201
    Quiz 201
    Put Access into Action 202
    For the Adventurous in Spirit 202

Day 6

AM 11   Intermediate Reports   205

Looking at Report Expressions 205
How Did That Work? 212
Groups 214
Morning Summary 221

PM 12 Intermediate Forms 223

Using List or Combo Boxes in Forms 224
Auto Expanding 231
Manual Combo or List Box Programming 232
How It Worked 236
Finishing Up 238
The Tabbed Form 239
The Image Control 244
Day Summary 246
Q&A 247
Workshop 248
    Quiz 248
    Put Access into Action 248

Day 7

AM 13 More Intermediate Forms 251

The Option Group 251
What's It Good For? 253
What Good Are Numbers? 260
Images as Part of Data Within Databases 262
Morning Summary 265

PM 14 Manipulating Dates and Using Expressions in Queries 267

Dates in Queries 276
Date Arithmetic and Developer-Defined Fields 279
Day Summary 283
Q&A 283
Workshop 284
    Quiz 284
    Put Access into Action 285

Day 8

AM 15 Intermediate to Advanced Queries 289

Parameter Queries 289
The Parameter Query 292
Range Parameter Queries 296
Action Queries 301
Morning Summary 306

PM 16 More Advanced Queries 307

Delete and Append Queries 308
Compacting the Database 314
The Append Action Query 316
Top Queries 324
    The Secret Behind the Top 328

Two Sophisticated Queries 329
   Update Queries 329
   The Crosstab Query 335
Day Summary 345
Q&A 346
Workshop 348
   Quiz 348
   Put Access into Action 349

Day 9

AM 17 Forms with Subforms   **353**

Why You Need Forms with Subforms 354
Preparing for the Form 355
The Form with Subform 360
Dragging and Dropping Your Way
   to Subforms 370
Morning Summary 373

PM 18 Form Control Properties   **375**

Control Properties 375
A Working Example 377
Enabled and Locked 383
Searching About 386
   Filtering Records by Selection 391
Day Summary 394
Q&A 395
Workshop 396
   Quiz 396
   Put Access into Action 396

Day 10

AM 19 Instantly Smarter Forms   **399**

The First Programmed Command Button 400
A Complementary Command Button 405
Event Properties 407
   Context-Sensitive Help to the Rescue 408
   Back to the Event Procedure 410
Don't Worry 412
Pretty Pictures on Buttons 412
Morning Summary 414

PM 20 Fancy Form Layout   **417**

Your Own Tools 418
Tab Order 420
Modifying Subforms 424

Graphic Elements in Forms 428
Page Layout Considerations 433
Further Fancy Forms 434
    Sinking and Rising 436
    AutoFormatting 438
Day Summary 439
Q&A 439
Workshop 440
    Quiz 440
    Put Access into Action 440

Day 11

AM 21   Expressions in Reports and Queries   445

The Situation 446
Joins 463
Morning Summary 467

PM 22   Complex Reports   469

Calculations in Reports 470
A Few Handy Expressions 481
How Access Evaluates Arithmetic Expressions 481
Layouts for Reports 482
Dynamic Controls on Reports 485
Day Summary 489
Q&A 489
Workshop 491
    Quiz 491
    Put Access into Action 492

Day 12

AM 23   Introduction to Macros   495

Macros 496
Access's Three Programming Languages 496
Using SQL 500
Looking at Macros 501
A Switchboard Form 506
The Macros 509
Putting It All Together 512
Morning Summary 515

PM 24   More Macro Magic   517

Conditional Branching in Macros 518
    Prepare to Use the Macro 522
    Macros in Action 525
Macros That Alter Properties 527
Placing the Macros on the Form 536

Access Identifiers 540
Dots and Bangs 540
Day Summary 541
Q&A 541
Workshop 542
　　Quiz 542
　　Put Access into Action 542
　　For the Adventurous 543

Day 13

AM 25　Everything You Need to Know About Programming　547

Reacting to an Event.. 548
　　Is That It? 550
　　How Can I Learn All These Keywords? 551
Functions, or General Procedures 552
　　Using the Function 557
　　Making a Function Summary 561
Error Trapping 562
　　Error-Trapping Summary 564
Morning Summary 565

PM 26　Programming Made Easy with Visual Basic　567

When To Use Visual Basic 568
　　Custom Functions 569
　　Complex Input 569
　　Conditional Loops 569
The Event-Driven Model 570
　　What's the Difference? 570
　　You've Already Done One 570
　　Identifiers 571
　　Annotating Code 571
A Question of Style 572
Functions, Declarations, and Subs 573
　　What's This Implicit/Explicit Business All About? 574
　　Function Procedures 575
　　Sub Procedures 575
A Simple First Code Example 576
　　A Place to Show Off 579
Passing Variable Parameters 583
　　Defining a Global Type 583
　　How It Worked 588
Day Summary 588
Q&A 590
Workshop 591
　　Quiz 591
　　Put Access into Action 592

Day 14

AM 27 ActiveX: The Next Generation of OLE Controls   595

Using OLE Controls 596
Registering ActiveX Controls 597
Using OLE to Link or Embed
    Office Documents 598
        Live Links 603
Using ActiveX Controls 607
    ActiveX Properties 609
Older Controls and Performance Considerations 611
Morning Summary 612

PM 28 Access and the World Wide Web   613

How the World Wide Web Works 614
    How Do I Get There? 614
    What Is a Web Page? 616
    How Can I Do That? 617
Converting a Table/Query to an HTML Document 617
Publishing a Form/Report to an HTML Document for Web Viewing ... 623
Hyperlinks to Office Documents or to Web Sites 624
Day Summary 631
Q&A 632
Workshop 632
    Quiz 633
    Put Access into Action 633

Appendixes

A   Quiz Answers   637

Answers for Day 1 638
Answers for Day 2 638
Answers for Day 3 638
Answers for Day 4 638
Answers for Day 5 639
Answers for Day 6 639
Answers for Day 7 639
Answers for Day 8 639
Answers for Day 9 640
Answers for Day 10 640
Answers for Day 11 640
Answers for Day 12 641
Answers for Day 13 641
Answers for Day 14 641

B	Exercise Guide/Quick Reference	643
C	The Toolbox Illustrated	653
D	Access Toolbars	657
E	The Sample Data	667

StudentPersonal 668
AppendMe 672
AvailableClasses 673
CompletedCourses 676
Demo_Crosstab1 678
Fruit Choices 680
Fruits 680
GradeValues 681
StudentStatusLookup 682

Glossary   **683**

Index   **687**

Foreword

Well, here you are. You've got Microsoft Access up and running and you're anxious to begin building successful applications. You'll be happy to learn that you've joined the company of *millions* of Access users. Microsoft has already shipped more than 14,000,000 copies of Access in all its different versions. Microsoft Access has been the runaway success story in desktop databases since its introduction, surpassing the sales of all other desktop database systems since its initial release in 1992. The Microsoft Access success story is more than justified by its outstanding combination of powerful features and easy-to-use user interface.

These millions of Access users share a single goal: They're all looking for the best solution to their information management needs. All businesses rely on the information that feeds the product development, customer lists, and sales efforts necessary for continued success. Many people use Access to organize their personal and family information, as well. I'm quite sure your situation is no different. However you came to install Microsoft Access and began to tinker with building your own applications, you are driven by the need to manage all that data floating around you.

By their very nature, databases are more complex and more difficult to learn than most word processors and spreadsheets. Not only do you have to know *how* to build Access tables and queries, you've got to understand *why* you're supposed to build them a particular way. Unlike learning to use a word processor, it's hard to learn a sophisticated database system like Microsoft Access by trial and error. Access 97 only complicates the picture with its wealth of sophisticated new features. The new wizards and Internet capabilities boggle the mind of even experienced Access developers. Everyone using Access 97 for the first time is going to need a strong, capable guide to navigate this advanced database development system.

Rest assured you have a valuable resource at your disposal. Designed to walk you through each step of learning Microsoft Access, *Teach Yourself Access 97 in 14 Days* contains everything you need to know to get up to speed. The hands-on approach utilized in this book is the easiest and most rewarding way to learn how to use Access.

Through his many years working with users at all levels of sophistication, Paul Cassel is tuned in to the issues and questions you face as you begin building Access applications. He's taken the daunting task of learning how to use Microsoft Access 97 and broken it down into manageable, logical lessons, each designed to take you less than a day to complete. Having

Teach Yourself Access 97 in 14 Days at your side is like having a *friend* (who just happens to be a genuine Access guru) patiently explaining each step of building Access applications. This is a truly powerful approach to learning Microsoft Access.

Paul takes pride in the fact that he's helped many hundreds of people overcome hurdles as they work with Access. With this book, Paul is sharing his outstanding skills with many thousands of people at the same time. Having known Paul Cassel for several years, I am sure he is pleased to be playing a significant part in your Access education. When you complete this book, you'll be proud of your newly acquired skills as an Access developer!

Michael Groh, Editor, Access-Visual Basic Advisor

Acknowledgments

While this book bears my name as author, it couldn't have come about without a collaborative effort from many people. Whatever mention I can make of them here cannot match their true contribution.

First of all, I'd like to thank Corrine Wire, an acquisitions editor who bossed this project to an astonishingly fast conclusion. Kristi Asher and Todd Bumbalough, the development editors, held this project together and on course. Kelly Held and Robert Bogue, the technical editors, caught and corrected the numerous technical errors and inconsistencies that inevitably find their way into anything I write.

Once again it was Carolyn Linn, the production editor, never hesitating to do what needed to be done, who ended up pulling the all-nighters when the deadlines loomed close.

Nothing is perfect. No doubt this book contains some omissions or inaccuracies. Any of these are wholly my fault. The degree to which this book is complete and accurate is due to the efforts of the above-named people.

About the Author

Paul Cassel has been designing and programming database systems on a wide range of computers for more than 20 years. His clients have included Intel Corp., Los Alamos National Laboratory, Sandia National Laboratories, Pacific Gas & Electric, the Attorney General of New Mexico, federal and state agencies, the Navajo nation, and many small to medium-sized companies. He currently travels nationally giving lectures, teaching seminars, and consulting about numerous small computer topics, including Microsoft Access. He is cohost of the weekly Egghead Software Hour radio show and publishes between 20 and 30 magazine articles a year.

Since 1981, Paul has done PC database development in dBASE, FoxPro, R:Base, Paradox, and most recently, Access, which is his favorite Windows database package. He lives in the high desert of New Mexico with his three-year-old daughter, who regularly outthinks him.

Tell Us What You Think!

As a reader, you are the most important critic and commentator of our books. We value your opinion and want to know what we're doing right, what we could do better, what areas you'd like to see us publish in, and any other words of wisdom you're willing to pass our way. You can help us make strong books that meet your needs and give you the computer guidance you require.

Do you have access to CompuServe or the World Wide Web? Then check out our CompuServe forum by typing **GO SAMS** at any prompt. If you prefer the World Wide Web, check out our site at http://www.mcp.com.

NOTE

> If you have a technical question about this book, call the technical support line at (800) 571-5840, ext. 3668.

As the publishing manager of the group that created this book, I welcome your comments. You can fax, e-mail, or write me directly to let me know what you did or didn't like about this book—as well as what we can do to make our books stronger. Here's the information:

FAX: 317/581-4669

E-mail: enterprise_mgr@sams.mcp.com

Mail: Rosemarie Graham
           Sams Publishing
           201 W. 103rd Street
           Indianapolis, IN 46290

Introduction

Why I Wrote This Book

I wrote *Teach Yourself Access 97 in 14 Days* because I'm crazy about Access. Simply put, I think it's a terrific program.

When Microsoft first introduced Access in the fall of 1992, many people in the Paradox and dBASE developer communities reacted with fear of the new threat on the block. I did, too. But then, I took a serious look at the latest wonder from the wizards of Redmond and realized that Access was truly the first of a new generation of database products.

My opinion was confirmed a few days later when a client called me in to enhance an old dBASE application that was a complete mess. I wondered: "Should I try to clean up what they had, or just start from scratch with totally new dBASE IV code?"

After analyzing the client's needs, I returned to my office to see what I could do about them. Within three hours and without writing a single line of code, I duplicated the client's dBASE IV application and made all the improvements requested.

As you've guessed by now, I did it with Access. It was a very leisurely three hours, too. If I'd worked at it, I could have done the job in an hour and a half.

What This Book Will Do For You

Any database package that gives great results without a lot of work is my kind of program. And that's what Access and this book can do for you. After you've completed this 14-day course, you'll not only be able to create your own database applications, but you could even hang out your shingle as an Access developer—albeit a beginning one. This book covers quite a lot for a two-week course, but it doesn't cover all aspects of Access. There is a lot of database, especially relational database, theory out there. The more you know, the better you'll be. Also, topics needed by a professional-level Access developer are only touched upon or mentioned here. One thing that all computer experts agree on is that their educations never end. Consider this book to be your foundation in Access, not everything you will ever need to know.

What This Book Won't Do For You

This book teaches you much of what you need to know to create solid, powerful database applications. But no book can be a substitute for your own creativity, imagination, and practical experience. As you work with Access, you'll constantly find new ways to do old things. As you do, you can refer to this book for the essential foundations that show you how to turn your new ideas into productive database systems.

Teach Yourself Access 97 in 14 Days doesn't attempt to cover every detail of Access. Instead, it uses specific examples to demonstrate general principles. This book shows you "how to." It doesn't attempt to be a reference work. You can find full reference documentation in the online help system that comes with Access.

How This Book Works

None of the exercises in this book require you to do much data entry. You'll be working as a database manager for a fictional college. The focus is always on learning database concepts and techniques—you didn't buy this book to get some practice typing in data. If you want a fast jump and want to avoid almost all data entry typing, see Appendix E, "The Sample Data," which tells you how to acquire *Teach Yourself Access 97 in 14 Days'* sample data.

The Sample Data and Your Sanity

This is important for your sanity! You can either enter the sample data by hand from Appendix E or download it from CompuServe or the Internet. There isn't any functional reason to use the exact data as printed in Appendix E, however. If you don't have the facilities to download, you can make up your own data as you go.

For example, if the book gives a sample data record using "Tirilee Jones" as a name, you can either use that name or one of your own choosing. You just need to remember that your return will be different from the book's when it uses "Tirilee Jones" in an example.

Why Isn't It Here?

We decided not to include the sample data in a CD-ROM or disk set for this book to keep the price down and because the exact data isn't necessary to get full benefit from the book.

How This Book Is Structured

This book's lessons are presented in 28 chapters, each designed for a half-day session. Each chapter consists of several examples or exercises.

To get the most out of the book, you should complete each lesson before going on to the next. Once you've finished the lessons, of course, you can go back and dip into the book any time you need a quick refresher course on specific points.

But Most of All—HAVE FUN!

I've spent many hours working with Access and enjoyed every hour—well, almost every hour. After going through this book, you'll have the level of expertise needed to create database applications easily with Access—and have fun doing it!

So, enough talk! Let's get started. I hope that you enjoy Access as much as I do and find many productive uses for your newfound database skills. But remember: If you're not having fun, you're missing half the point of doing it!

Database Fundamentals

A *database* is an orderly collection of information. Sales order, personnel, and bookkeeping systems are all examples of databases. A relational database system like Access categorizes its information into logical groups. These logical groups are physically represented in the database by linked tables. Each table holds a particular category of data.

OK, What's a Table?

A *table* is a grid. The grid's rows correspond to data *records*, and the columns correspond to data *fields*. As an example, a particular table in a personnel database might have fields for SSN, last name, first name, street address, and so on. A record is all the fields for a row in a database table. Figure IN.1 is a table in Access.

Figure IN.1.

One table from a registration system created using Access.

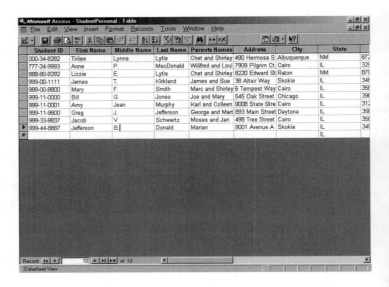

Putting It in Action

Consider a personnel system of about 1,000 employees. Think of all the information such a system must contain and organize. There's personal information along with data about each employee's benefits, department, supervisor, salary history, credentials, reviews, and so on.

When you organize all that information into a relational model, you break down the entire mass into logical categories. One table might contain an employee's name, address, and personal information; another one the employee's salary history; another one department and supervisor information; another the employee's benefit package; and so on until all the information has been categorized.

You might be wondering why you should bother to fragment your information like this. The reason is efficiency. Any database system can manipulate and locate information faster if it's in small chunks. For example, Access, like any database management system, can sort, or order, a table much faster if it operates on a table with three fields rather than thirty.

A relational database can use data from any number of tables; therefore, any data existing in one table should never appear in another. The relational model makes any data duplication unnecessary. This is an important element to keep in mind when designing your database. The process of logically categorizing a mass of data into a relational model is called *normalization*. If that term confuses you, you're not alone. Normalization has nothing to do with being common, but is derived from the mathematical term *normal*. It doesn't translate very well. Nobody ever claimed database terminology made sense.

The potential problem with breaking data into smaller chunks is loss of synchronization. If a person's name is in one table and his salary history is in another, how do you associate the name with the right salary history? The answer is linking fields that coordinate information in two or more tables. A properly designed relational database contains all the necessary links that permit the database to match records in different tables.

A typical personnel system uses the employee's social security number, or SSN, as a link field. Here's how it works. The record containing personal information has one field containing the SSN for the person represented in that record. In a separate table, a record containing the salary history also contains the SSN of the person whose salary history the record represents. Given this embedded information, a relational database can properly match up the right name and salary history information.

StudentID is acting as a linking field for the tables shown in the relationships diagram in Figure IN.2. When asked to, Access can associate the proper CompleteCourses or StudentCurrentCourses information with the information in the StudentPersonal table, even though the information is in separate tables. The trick is to have the same data for all StudentID fields in each table.

Figure IN.2.
The related tables.

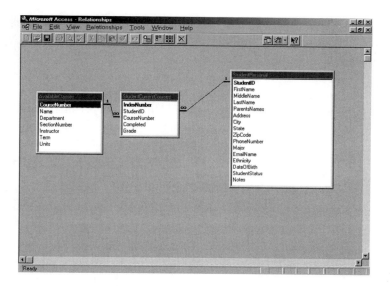

Referential Integrity

One theoretical topic that's important to grasp is *referential integrity*. A student registration system might have one table for student names and another for classes the students signed up to take. One student might sign up for many classes, but any seat in a class can have only one student assigned to it. A link between these tables is called a "one-to-many" link because one student is linked to many classes. Figure IN.3 shows an Access query in which one student has many classes.

Figure IN.3.

An Access query illustrating a one-to-many link.

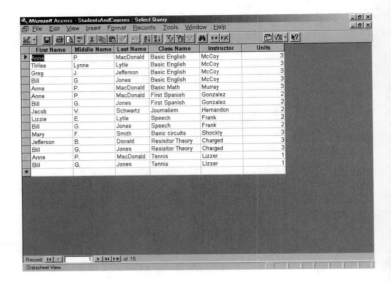

Obviously, class registration information is useful only when it is linked to a particular student. In other words, a person must exist in the system before you can enter any class information. Using Access, you'd first enter a person in the system, and only afterward enter the classes that person's signed up for. The table with the students' personal information is the "one" table. The StudentCurrentCourses table, structurally shown in Figure IN.2, is the "many" table. Using Access, you can protect against adding unlinked class information into the system. This can happen if a data-entry person makes an error typing the StudentID that's supposed to be associated with a class. You can instruct Access to enforce a rule saying you can only enter class information for a StudentID that already exists in the StudentPersonal table.

In traditional PC-based relational database programs, you also need to protect against accidentally erasing linked information in the "one" table because doing so would result in meaningless data being left in table on the "many" side of the relationship. What good is degree information if the person who earned the degree isn't in the system anymore? Access can prevent the creation of this unlinked data or orphan. Referential integrity is a complex way of stating that the system itself guards against unlinked pieces of information.

ACCESS JARGON

referential integrity: The existence of a related value or attribute in a database depends upon another identical value or attribute.

Designing a Database

A database in Access can have any or all of these parts:

- [ ] **Tables** are the basic building blocks of a database. They are where the actual data resides.
- [ ] **Forms** create a framework for presenting or entering data in one or more tables. In Access, forms also have special abilities for manipulating and verifying data not available at the table level.
- [ ] **Queries** search and retrieve data from one or more tables based on entered criteria.
- [ ] **Reports** are a way to output data from tables or queries. Reports can summarize data.
- [ ] **Macros** are a simple way to coordinate operations in Access.
- [ ] **Modules** are functions and procedures programmed through the Visual Basic language.

Design Well

A poorly designed database can bring you years of grief. Professional database designers spend a great deal of time analyzing the entire mass of data they'll be dealing with before actually creating the database. The very nature of Access gives you a great deal of flexibility when organizing your data, but nothing's proof against thoughtless design.

When designing a database, you should categorize your data into the smallest parts consistent with a logically organized structure. Keep in mind one-to-many, one-to-one, and many-to-many relations. For example, if you're creating a database for a hospital, you should consider that one patient has only one bed, but can have many doctors; doctors can have many patients; one patient can have many procedures; a particular prescription should go to only one patient, but many patients might have identical prescriptions; and so on.

Four Steps in Database Design

Here are the four general steps you should take to design a database:

1. Determine user requirements in terms of output. What is it you want to get out of the system? For example, you might move to a computerized personnel system because government-required reporting overwhelms your paper-based system. In this case you would make sure that your database system could create the needed reports.

2. Do a conceptual model. This should usually be a flow chart but can be a simple word diagram. Do this in a formal way, committing the flow chart or word diagram to paper for later reference.

3. Determine a strategy to implement the design. What resources does the project need and how can you commit them? How do you map the conceptual model from step 2 into the particular database you've chosen for the task? In other words, how do you translate your conceptual flow chart to actual Access tables, forms, and reports? Develop at least a rough map.

4. Working from the map in step 3, physically create the database system.

Initially, this process will take some time and you'll make some false starts. Like so many things, after you've made a few passes over the territory, the process will become almost second nature.

Physically Designing the Computer Database

Once you've run through the four steps in database design, you will have a good idea of what tables you need, what should be in each table, and how the tables should be linked. You also need to determine the internal structure of each table.

A Table's Internal Structure

Each field in a database has two characteristics identifying it. The first is the field ID, or name. A field for last names can and logically should have the ID of LastName. The second characteristic is the data type of the field. The field LastName uses the data type called Text. Here is a list of Access's data types with a brief description of each:

- ☐ Text—Alphanumeric characters.
- ☐ Memo—Up to 32,000 alphanumeric characters; generally contain comments.
- ☐ Number—Numeric values with or without decimal places.
- ☐ Date/Time—Dates and time.

☐ Currency—Money.

☐ AutoNumber—A numeric value that can either automatically increment with each record added or assign a random number to each recorded added.

☐ Yes/No—Logical or Boolean values.

☐ Hyperlink—A URL or UNC address. UNC addresses can include subaddresses (anchors).

☐ OLE Object—Graphics, sounds, or other binary objects created outside of the Access program.

You can attach many properties, such as size and formatting, to each data type. The Text type of data can have a size of up to 255 characters. When specifying how large a text field will be, you don't want to use more space than needed for the actual entries you anticipate. Access reserves the amount of space you specify for the Field Size property. It's a waste of your resources to tell Access to reserve 40 or so spaces for a field that will never hold more than 10 characters. Usually, a field size of 20 characters suffices for LastName, 15 for FirstName, and 30 for Address.

Indexes and Key Fields

There are two more small topics to cover before digging into the program. You can tell Access to index certain fields in a table. When you do, Access orders the data according to the index and also tracks the indexed records. If you often search on a particular field, you should instruct Access to make it an index field.

A key field is a field or set of fields in a table that uniquely identifies each record. Access orders or sorts the database based on the contents of primary key fields, and it works much more efficiently if every table in a database has a key field. When you delve into relational theory more deeply, you'll see that every record must have a primary key field or you can't be sure your database will be fully functional. When possible, use part of your data as a primary key field. This helps you avoid littering up your database with nondata frufru. For example, the SSN field is often a good choice for a key field because each person has a unique social security number.

ACCESS JARGON

primary key field: a field or set of fields in a table that uniquely identifies each record, such as a social security number.

Multiple Field Keys

Sometimes there's no unique field in your database to use for a primary key field. In these cases you can use multiple fields as a key, although most people don't bother and instead use an AutoNumber field that increments for this task. However, using more than one field will work and it wastes no space in your database. Be careful: You wouldn't want to use LastName as a key field because that would only allow one instance of the last name Smith. However, combining the LastName field with a FirstName or Telephone field might work.

Summary

This introduction was short and dry, but very important. Just knowing how to use Access or any database program is only part of what you need to manage your data. Before firing up your computer, you must have a good idea of what your data consists of, have planned a logical structure for it, and developed at least a rough map of how to link the various parts of it together.

Much of the first three stages of database design has been done for you in this book. This is a book about using Access, not a theoretical book on database concepts; therefore, it concentrates on the final stage, step 4. As you work through the next few lessons, the theory behind steps 1 to 3 will become apparent. By the time you're done with this book and ready to design your own applications, you should be able to apply correct design elements to your projects.

DAY 1

A.M.

1 **A Short Access Tour**

P.M.

2 **Wizards, the Office Assistant, and Help**

Chapter 1

A Short Access Tour

This morning you'll learn the following:

☐ How to install Access

☐ The meaning of the various installation dialog boxes and screens

☐ The parts of the Access user interface

☐ How to change the shape and location of toolbars and menus

☐ How to customize toolbars

Installing Access

To install Access 97, all you have to do is run its Setup program and make some simple choices. Figure 1.1 shows the section of Setup specific to the Custom setup option. This particular screen comes from a setup over an existing Office 97, but other than the title bar text, a new installation looks the same.

Figure 1.1.

With the Custom option in Office 97 Setup, you can pick and choose among various Office 97 components.

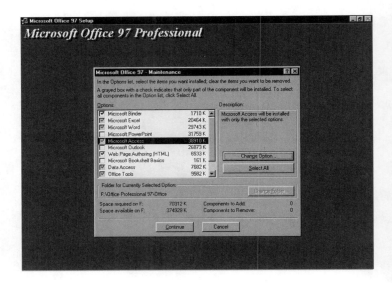

Figure 1.2 shows the options available for Access specifically. You can see these options by clicking on the Change Option button with Microsoft Access chosen in the options list box.

You have options within options. For example, you can choose the help files you want installed (from two to zero) by clicking on the Help Topics choice in Figure 1.2, then clicking on the Change Option button. The result is a screen like Figure 1.3.

Figure 1.2.

*The options specific to
Access 97 within the
Office 97 Professional
Setup.*

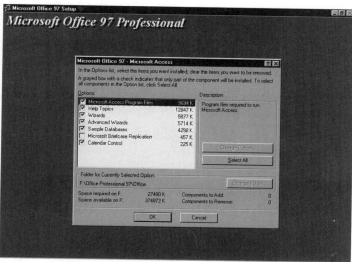

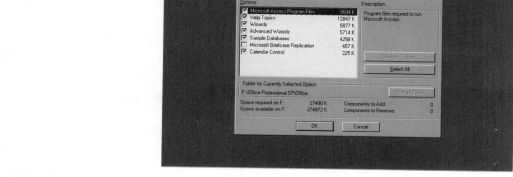

Figure 1.3.

*Setup has options within
options. When it comes to
Access, you can even
choose the number of help
files you wish to install.*

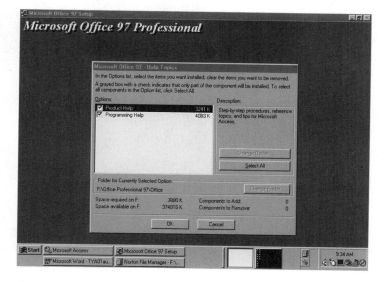

Your own situation will determine which Custom options you choose, or even if you prefer the Custom install option of Setup. You may prefer the Typical install option, which installs those parts of Office 97 that Microsoft believes meet most people's needs. This choice will take up approximately 120MB of space. Setup can't be perfectly specific about the space needed because you might already have some shared components installed, reducing your marginal space needs for Office 97.

If you need to conserve space on your hard drive, you can either choose Microsoft's Compact option or use the Custom option to create your own disk. Setup even enables you to run Office applications from the CD-ROM, which is the most hard disk-conservative of all. It's also a bit pokey in response time since it's dependent on CD throughput instead of hard disk throughput. The CD-ROM option will still use up about 60MB of disk space. If you go all out and choose Custom to install all of Office 97, expect it to eat up roughly 200 MB of disk real estate.

If you are part of a company and on a company network, you might need to consult with your network administrator before installing any software. Your company might also have a special licensing agreement with Microsoft that you need to know about before using Office 97.

Finally, you need to know that certain services you will need in Access aren't part of the options specific to Access. For example, the spell checker and Office Assistant help are options under Office Tools. (See Figure 1.1). Click the Change Option button with Office Tools selected, and you'll see a screen like Figure 1.4.

Figure 1.4.

Some options important to Access 97 are within other options. This screen is the Office Tools option list.

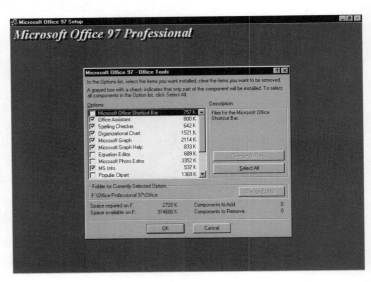

If you're installing on a local hard disk, you'll also have the choice of where to install Office 97 and its components. You don't need to install all of Office's parts on the same volume, but most people do.

After you have run Setup and successfully installed Access, it's time to launch it.

Launching Access from Windows

If you have its group open, launch Access by double-clicking the icon bearing its name; otherwise, from the Start menu, choose Programs and find Microsoft Access. (See Figure 1.5.) The vast majority of Windows 95/97 and Windows NT users launch Access from the Start menu. Just where Access is within that menu depends on how you've customized your Windows interface. Figure 1.5 shows Access as part of an Office group within the Start menu's Programs group. Your screen will probably differ in some details.

Figure 1.5.

Launching Access from Windows 95/97.

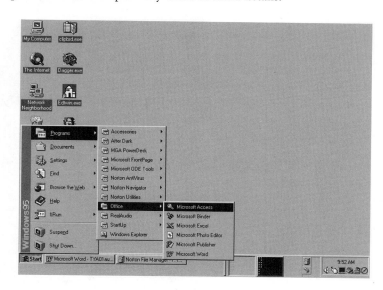

From the opening dialog box, shown in Figure 1.6, you can proceed to the Access interface, manually create a new database, or use a wizard to create a new database. If you're following along, click the Cancel button to move to the Access interface. If you've just set up Access, your list box won't yet contain any databases like those shown in Figure 1.6.

Figure 1.6.

Access's opening dialog box lists recently opened databases plus gives you the options of creating a new blank database or using the Database Wizard to help you make a new one.

The Parts of the Access 97 User Interface

Refer to Figure 1.7—or your actual screen if you have Access launched. The topmost part of the screen has "Microsoft Access" written on it. That part of the screen is called the title bar. Every window, or frame, within Windows has a title bar bearing a name or label. These names usually describe the function of the frame or window.

Figure 1.7.

Access launched without any database loaded.

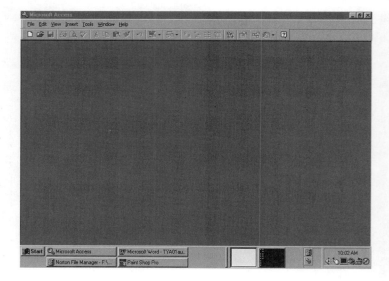

Directly under the title bar is the menu bar, where menu options appear. Which menu options are available to you at any given moment depends on what mode Access is in and whether your Access application has a custom menu system. At this point, Access has nothing loaded.

Below the menu bar is the toolbar. There are many different toolbars in Access. You can also make your own custom ones or customize the ones that come with Access. Toolbars enable you to quickly and easily perform common tasks while using the Access program. You can assign custom buttons on a toolbar to special routines that you've programmed into your applications, but for now, just think of toolbars as shortcuts to commonly performed tasks.

The toolbars in Access 97 are more plentiful and easier to use than in previous Access versions. By default Access will show only a few related toolbars with each "view" of your database. You can modify Access's toolbar behavior from the default, as explained later in this chapter.

If you've never seen the Access toolbar, you probably can't decipher what each button on it does. Even Access veterans occasionally forget the buttons they seldom use. Microsoft, responding to customer demands for easier-to-use toolbars, added tooltips to Access 2. Here's how tooltips work: Move your cursor over the toolbar button on the extreme left of your screen. (That's the button with a white paper icon.) Don't click any mouse buttons. In a second or two, a little balloon will pop up with the caption "New Database." (See Figure 1.8.)

Figure 1.8.

A tooltip in Access.

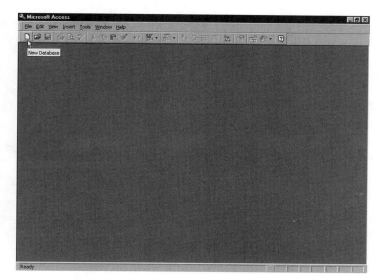

This tells you that the leftmost button will, when clicked, start the process of creating a new database. Also note that the status bar—that's the bar along the bottom of your screen—pops up a slightly expanded explanation for this button's function when you run your cursor over the button or click it.

Without clicking your mouse buttons, move your cursor over some other buttons along the toolbar. Be sure to leave the cursor on each button long enough to evoke the tooltip. Compare the short tooltip with the longer explanation on the status bar. Don't worry if you don't understand what some of these buttons do at this time. In a short while, each button's function will become second nature to you. After you're familiar with how to evoke the tooltips, move on to the next section.

Arranging Toolbars

When Access starts, the toolbar is in a single row right below the menu bar. This works all right for many tasks, but you might prefer a different arrangement. Access is happy to comply with your wishes. Move your cursor to the place on the toolbar with two parallel lines, to the left of the New Database button. Figure 1.9 shows the cursor at this place.

Figure 1.9.

Moving the toolbar.

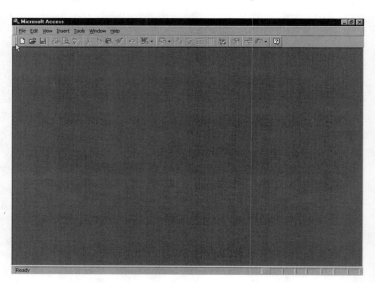

Now click your left mouse button and hold it down. While holding the button down, move the mouse down the screen. In Windows lingo, this is called "dragging." As you drag the toolbar down, it'll detach from the menu bar and change shape, looking more like a square. Release the mouse button to drop the toolbar in a new location. Move your cursor over any

border of the new toolbar. The cursor becomes a double-ended arrow. With the cursor over a border, click your mouse button and drag the toolbar's border. The toolbar changes shape depending on how much and in what direction you drag its border.

Also note that the toolbar, when detached from the menu bar, gains a title bar. The title bar for this toolbar is "Database." This tells you the toolbar you're seeing is the Database toolbar. You can move the newly shaped and sized toolbar by dragging when your cursor is on this title bar. Figure 1.10 contains a moved and shaped Database toolbar.

Figure 1.10.

A moved and resized Database toolbar now floats in the middle of your screen.

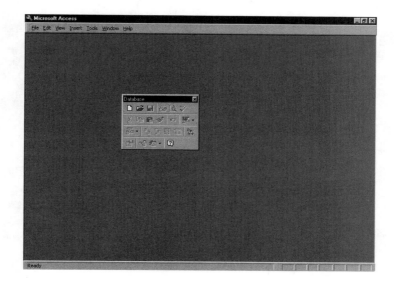

If you want to restore your toolbar to its original place, drag it to just below the menu bar. Shuffle it around until you hit the hotspot that tells Access you wish to replace the toolbar. When you hit this hotspot, the toolbar will get a "ghost" outline showing its original shape. Release the mouse button and the toolbar will snap back to its initial shape and location.

In the same way you can move, resize, and relocate the menu bar. Figure 1.11 shows the menu bar dislocated and floating like the toolbar.

Figure 1.11.

*You can float the menu
bar just as you can the
toolbar.*

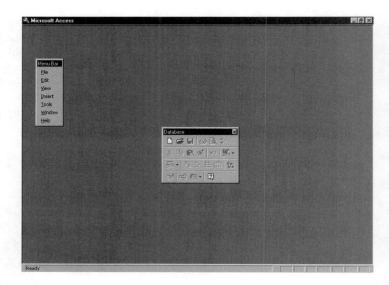

Sitting on the Dock of the Access Bay

You can redock the menu bar and any floating toolbars by dragging them to their hotspots. These spots aren't only at the top of the screen, although that's their traditional place—there are other hotspots in the desktop. Figure 1.12 shows the toolbar and menu bar moved to unconventional docking places. They work just as well. How you arrange your Access screen is a matter of how you like to work and your aesthetic sense. This book uses the Microsoft default locations for all bars.

Figure 1.12.

*You can dock these bars
at any hotspots, not just
Microsoft's standard
locations at the top of the
desktop.*

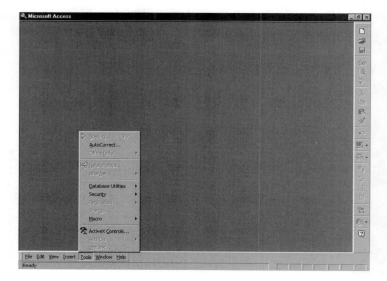

You can also change the toolbars' horizontal aspect by dragging them along their "slot" or perpendicular to the parallel drag bars. Figure 1.13 shows another unconventional arrangement of the bars, with the toolbar dragged to the right and the menu bar under the toolbar.

Figure 1.13.
Another unconventional arrangement of the bars.

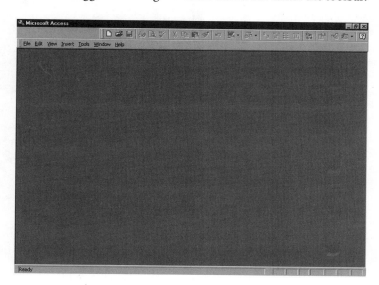

Customizing Access Toolbars

This is a fairly simple topic with many permutations. Once you get the hang of customizing, you will know how to do it all.

Customizing bars, tool or menu, within Access is the same as within other Office 97 applications. The first trick is to get to the dialog box with the customization options. You can do this either by choosing Tools|Toolbars|Customize… from the menus or by right-clicking on any bar and choosing Customize… from the shortcut menu. Figure 1.14 shows the shortcut menu. After you get to the customize menu, you'll see the dialog box shown in Figure 1.15.

Figure 1.14

One Method to get to the Customize option is to use the shortcut menu brought up by a right-click on any toolbar.

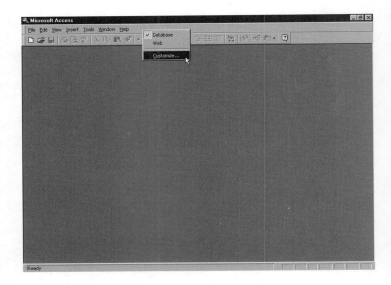

To display a toolbar, click in its check box. For example, Figure 1.15 doesn't show the Web toolbar. In Figure 1.16, the Web toolbar is displayed because its check box has been clicked.

Figure 1.15.

You can use the Customize dialog box to customize menu bars or toolbars to your heart's content.

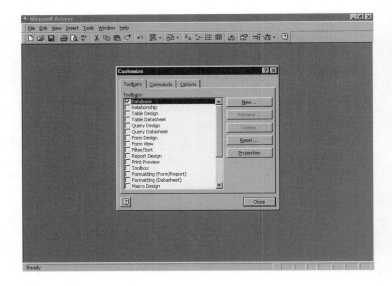

Figure 1.16.

To display a toolbar, click in its check box in this dialog.

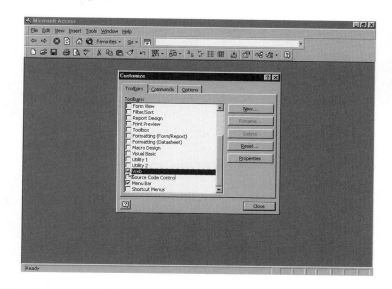

The Access Way

The technique for changing the order of controls in the Tab Order list box is the same as changing the order of almost anything in Access. It is a bit tricky at first, but after you have the hang of it for any function (such as changing column order in a query), you have it made for them all.

Morning Summary

This morning you learned how to install or set up Access. You also saw some options within the Custom option of Setup. Launch Access by clicking on its entry in the Start menu hierarchy. You can use the Customize dialog box to change the shape, location, and contents of the toolbars and menu bars.

Chapter **2**

Wizards, the Office Assistant, and Help

This afternoon you'll learn the following:

- ☐ What the Office Assistant is
- ☐ What wizards are
- ☐ How to use the Office Assistant
- ☐ How to use wizards
- ☐ How to use other online help facilities

Office Assistant

The Office Assistant is Microsoft's attempt to incorporate artificial intelligence into its help systems. This artificial intelligence was first seen in Office 95 as the Answer Wizard. Some people, while enjoying and admiring how well the Office Assistant works, dislike its cute animations. Others enjoy the Assistant's sound effects and animations. You can also get to the information in Access's online help system by selecting the menu choices Help|Content and Index, bypassing the Office Assistant.

As with so many things in a visual apparatus like Access, you can best learn how to use the Office Assistant by trying it out. Exercise 2.1 serves as an introduction.

Exercise 2.1. Introduction to the Office Assistant.

1. Launch Access if you have not already done so. Click Cancel in the opening dialog box to go to the Access interface without opening a database.
2. By default, the Setup routine uses the Office Assistant that looks like a paper clip, and the Office Assistant is active when you start Access. If not, you can activate it by clicking the Office Assistant icon, the rightmost icon on the toolbar just below the menu bar. (It looks like a cartoon's dialog balloon with a question mark in the center.) Alternatively, you can press the F1 key. Click the Office Assistant if you don't see some help text, as shown in Figure 2.1.

Figure 2.1.

The Office Assistant.

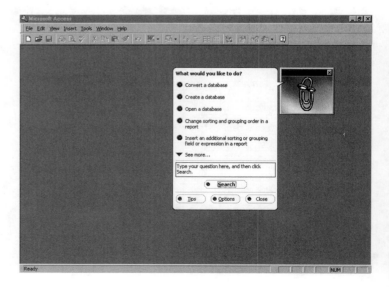

You've just activated the Office Assistant. Here, you can ask the help system questions in natural language. Microsoft's language parser tries to match your question with a topic in the help system.

3. Enter How Do I Make a Table in the box where the Office Assistant has the instructions "Type your question here, and then click Search." Click the Search button. You don't need a question mark. Your screen should look like Figure 2.2.

Figure 2.2.

*The Office
Assistant answers.*

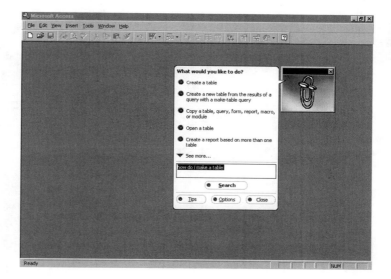

4. Access offers you a quick overview of several topics that relate to your question. Click the button next to Create a table (it should be first topic on your list). The Office Assistant, its job done for the moment, will do a fade and you'll enter into the help system's files at the Create a table page. Your screen should look like Figure 2.3.

5. To see any of these topics, click the >> button just to the left of the topic. Click the first >> button—the one next to the Create a new blank table entry.

6. Access moves on to the next page of instructions, which describes in summary the four ways you can use Access to create a blank or empty table.

If you want to see what any of these choices are, click the >> button for the appropriate topic at the bottom of the help screen. Note that you might have to scroll down to see the jump or >> buttons. Figure 2.4 shows the help screen brought up by clicking the >> button for "Create a new blank table." Note that some of these instructions assume you have a database open, which you do not. Pressing the F11 key at this point won't, for example, switch you to the Database window. With no database open, no such window exists.

Figure 2.3.

Help summoned by the Office Assistant.

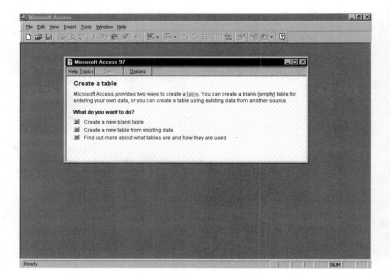

Figure 2.4.

A help screen offering Table Wizard help as one of several help branches. To view any of these topics, click on the >> button to the left of the topic's listing.

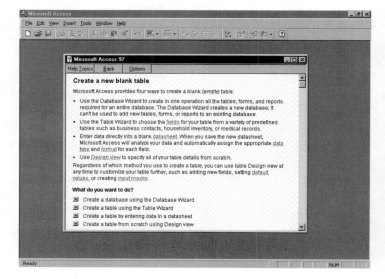

The Office Assistant floats on top of any other Windows object, so you can refer to it as you work. The Office Assistant example you just went through offers only an overview of certain database concepts; the Assistant can step you through actual Access operations. You can also set the help system itself to float on top of Access while you work so you can easily refer to it as you go along. Most other help systems sink when you're in the main program, forcing you to call them back up at each step.

To get the help system itself to float on top of Access (or any other application), click the Options button shown in Figures 2.3 and 2.4. Locate the Keep help on top selection. Highlight that, then choose the On Top option from the pop-up menu. After you set help to be on top, the help windows will float above any windows. If they get in your way, you can always set the On Top property back to the default, or you can minimize the help system so that it appears as an entry on the taskbar.

Do	Don't

DO use the Office Assistant and on top help screens as memory joggers or to lead you through operations with which you don't feel completely familiar.

DON'T forget that you can minimize the on top helps to get them out of the way.

Wizards

The Office Assistant can give you natural language guides to help topics, and the help topics tell you how to do what you want to do, but you need to perform the steps themselves to get results. Wizards take the next logical step in an active help system. They ask you a few questions, and after you and the wizard agree on what needs to be done, the wizard goes out and does it.

Most people use wizards when they are using Access. Even the most highly paid senior-level developers rely on wizards to do some of the grunt work in form and report design. In some areas, such as programming buttons on forms or reports, wizards make the chore so easy that even a fairly naive Access user can make applications that work just like the ones done by experts. True, there's nothing you can do with a wizard that you can't do manually, but ignoring wizards only makes for more work.

Exercise 2.3 uses a wizard to create a table ready for you to add some data to. Before you create a table, you need a database to put it in. Exercise 2.2 shows how to create a new database.

Exercise 2.2. Creating a new database.

1. Launch Access if you have not already done so. Click Cancel to bypass the initial set of choices and move directly to Access. You can create a new database from this initial dialog box, or from the steps in this exercise, or by following along with the Assistant's suggestions. Like so many things in Access, there is more than one path to the goal.

2. Click the New Database button on the toolbar. The New Database button, on the far left, sports an icon of a blank piece of paper. The keystroke for a new database is Ctrl+N (hold down the Control key while pressing the N key). Access will bring up a tabbed dialog box with the Blank Database template on the uppermost tab sheet. Click it to highlight it. Your screen should resemble Figure 2.5. (For this exercise, the Office Assistant has been put away by clicking the close icon (×) in its upper-right corner.)

Figure 2.5.

The blank database.

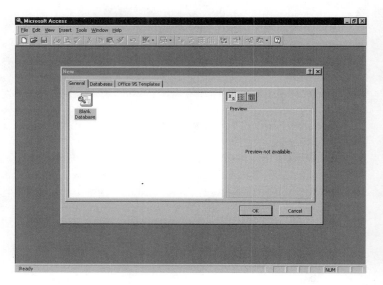

3. Click OK. Access returns with a dialog box inviting you to name your new blank database. Enter myfirst. Your screen should resemble Figure 2.6.

4. Click OK. You've just created a new database called myfirst. The full filename will be myfirst.mdb. Access supplies the .mdb extension unless you force it to use another extension. Click Create to let Access finish the database creation process. When it's done, you'll have a complete but empty database container, as shown in Figure 2.7.

Figure 2.6.

Creating a new database.

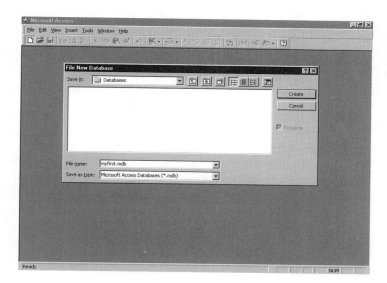

Figure 2.7.

The complete but empty database container.

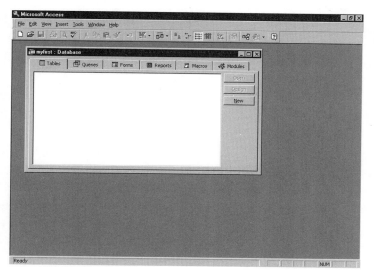

> **Access and Long Filenames**
>
> Access 97 is fully compliant with Windows 95 and subsequent Windows versions. As such it's able to use long filenames. Rather than `myfirst.mdb`, as used in Exercise 2.2, you could have used `My First Access 97 Database.mdb` as a name.

Enter the Wizard

Now you're ready to use a wizard to make a new table. Look at Figure 2.7 again.

The frame or window with myfirst written in the title bar is a container for all the objects you create to use in the myfirst database. Right now it's empty because you've not yet made any objects for myfirst.

> **ACCESS JARGON**
>
> **Database window:** Access's term for a tabbed screen like the one in Figure 2.7, where you can see a database's object collection.

The Database window has several tabs across the top and some buttons on the side. Right now, the only active button is the one with New on it because you can't open or design (modify) something you haven't created yet. Exercise 2.3 shows how to make a table using a wizard.

Exercise 2.3. Using a wizard to make a new table.

1. Click the New button on the right side of the Database window. Click the Table Wizard choice from the next dialog box. Your screen will resemble Figure 2.8.

2. Click OK. Access will grind away for a while, getting its ducks in a row. Click the Personal option button at the lower-left side of the next dialog box.

   Your screen should resemble Figure 2.9.

3. The two option buttons, Business and Personal, specify which of two groups of table types you choose when using this wizard. The list box called Sample Tables lists the tables you can use as templates for your new table. The list box called Sample Fields shows the fields you can use in each sample table.

Click different sample tables and note how the Sample Fields list box changes. This is because each sample table has a specific set of fields in it. When using the Table Wizard, you choose a sample table that contains fields close to what you want in your finished table. Don't worry if the furnished sample tables don't match your needs exactly. Later on you can add to or edit what the wizard does.

Figure 2.8.
Launching the wizard responsible for making a table.

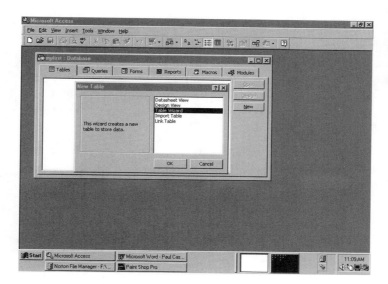

Figure 2.9.
Table Wizard up and running.

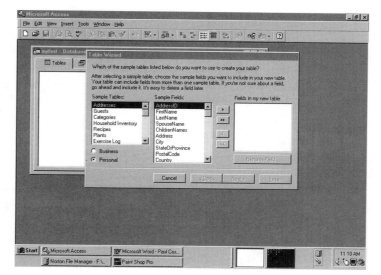

4. After touring around to get an idea of what sort of tables Access's Table Wizard offers, click the Recordings and Recording Artists tables. Note that these two tables can work together, as do some others in each sample data set.

5. Click the Authors sample table. Click the >> button to move all the fields from the sample table to your new table. Your screen should resemble Figure 2.10.

Figure 2.10.
Choosing fields.

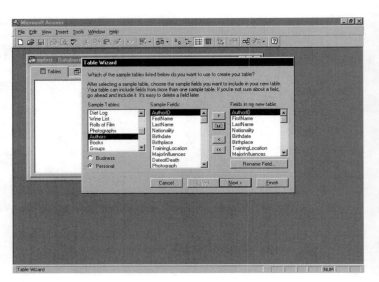

6. You also can choose to add only a few fields from the sample table to your new one. You must add them one at a time. Highlight the field you want to enter and click the > button to move only that field to your new table. You can remove fields from your new table by clicking the < and the << buttons. If you want to change the name of a field, use the Rename Field… button at the lower right of the Table Wizard dialog box.

7. Now that you have all the fields you want in your new table included in the "Fields in my new table" list box, click the Next> button to move on to the next phase of table design.

8. Access suggests the name Authors for your new table. Accept this or choose a name yourself. Access will set the primary key for you. You can manually alter the primary key by clicking on the primary key option button. Leave the primary key at Access's default. Click Next>.

9. Access brings up a screen with a checkered flag, signaling that you're about to finish the wizard process. At this point you have the options of modifying the table's design, opening the table for data entry, or invoking another wizard to create a

form. You can also click the Help check box in the lower center of the dialog box. This will bring up help specific to the context you exit the wizard in.

10. Click "Enter data directly into the table" and click the Finish button. Access creates and opens your new table, Authors. After it's done, your screen should look like Figure 2.11.

Figure 2.11.
The finished table.

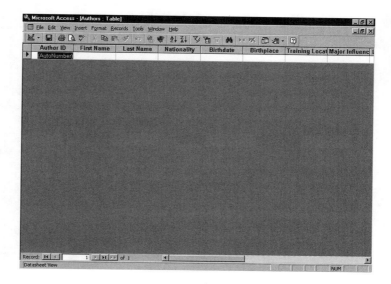

If you want to, tab to the First Name field and enter some data into it. If the mood strikes you, continue on to the balance of the fields. You move between fields in Access either by pressing the Tab key or by pressing Enter. Figure 2.12 is the new Authors table with some sample data entered. Note that you can't enter anything in the Author ID field because that's where Access supplies a set of consecutive numbers to act as field IDs. That's also the primary key for this table. (Don't be concerned if this concept of a primary key isn't familiar to you at this point.)

When you're satisfied, close the table by either double-clicking its Control Menu icon, selecting the File|Close menu choices, or by clicking the × button at the upper right of the table window. If you've altered the width of any fields, Access will ask you whether you want to save your changes. It's up to you whether you save or discard them. You've just created a table in Access and, perhaps, added some data. You're not yet a database expert, but you've made a good start.

Figure 2.12.

Some sample data for the new table.

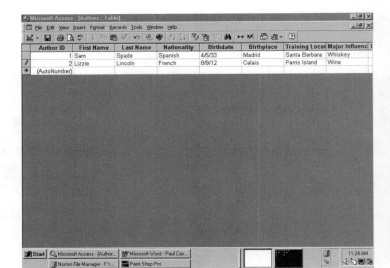

Using Help

Sometimes you'll need help beyond what the Office Assistant or wizards can do. In those cases (such as clarifying the use of a particular function), you'll likely go directly to Access's online help system. Exercise 2.4 steps you through some parts of Access's online help.

Exercise 2.4. Help with Help.

1. Launch Access if you have not already done so. The figures for this section were shot with the database myfirst, from the last exercise, open. If you don't have a database open, your screens will differ at the menu bar.

2. Click the Help entry from the main menu bar.

3. Click Content and Index from the drop-down list. Click Microsoft Access Help (F1) to start or activate the Office Assistant. Your screen should look like Figure 2.13. Since Windows screens can vary depending upon the state of the windows and screen resolution, your actual screens might be slightly different from the ones shown.

4. Click the Find tab at the top of the Help Topics window. Click the top option button to keep your index size to a minimum, then the Next> button. Click Finish to create an indexed list of all help topics. This might take a while depending upon your computer's speed, your RAM, whether this is the first index you created, and how many other tasks you have going on at the same time. After it's done, your screen will resemble Figure 2.14.

Figure 2.13.
The Help Topics section.

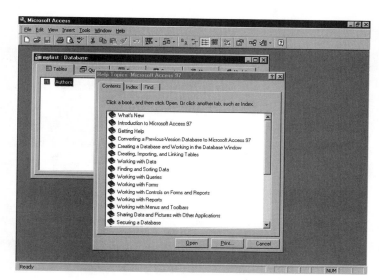

Figure 2.14.
The results of the help index.

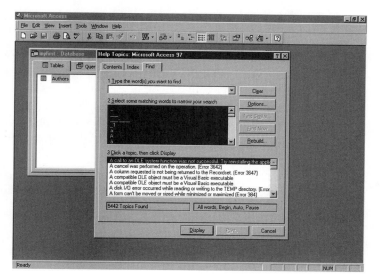

5. What you've done is to create an indexed, or ordered, list of all Access help topics. Study Figure 2.14 and note that there are roughly 5,500 topics to choose from. You'd surely become an Access expert by just going through this list, but in most cases you'll want to locate a specific topic rather than just browse through thousands of topics. Enter the word date at the top of the dialog box to narrow the topics to only those relating to dates. Your screen will resemble Figure 2.15. Note that the topic number is now cut down to fewer than 300—a much more manageable size.

Figure 2.15.

Narrowing help topics.

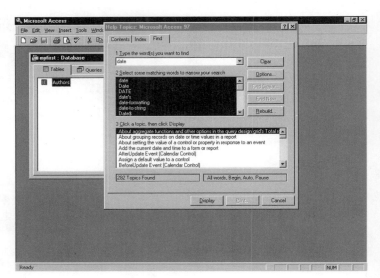

6. Click the Date$ entry in the third dialog space. Click the Display button to bring up the specific help topic matching the highlighted key word.

7. This brings up a help system. If appropriate, the help page you bring up might contain links to other help as shown in Figure 2.16. In the case of the Date$ topic, Access help brought up a page with various string functions, of which Date$ is one. To see the detail information on any of these string functions, click the underlined entry.

8. If the topic you brought up was the one you wanted, you're in luck. If not, you can repeat the search as many times as you wish until you hit on the exact topic and angle you seek.

9. You can also use Access's supplied help index by clicking the Index tab and entering your choice as shown in Figure 2.17. Access's supplied index has the most frequently sought topics, but won't be as complete as your own generated Find index. The down side of using the Find index is that it takes time and eats disk space.

Figure 2.16.

Displaying topics in a successful help search.

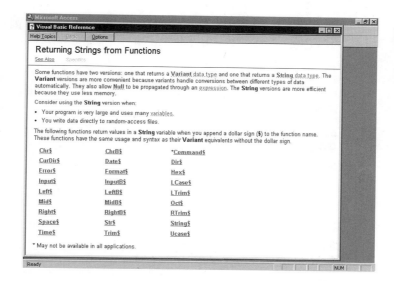

Figure 2.17.

Access has a default index of most help topics.

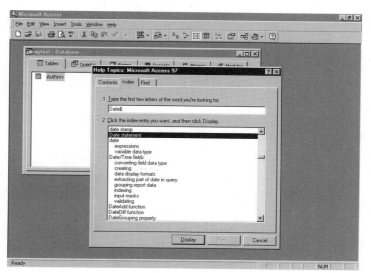

You've just taken the five-cent tour of Access's help system and finished today's lesson. Close Access by either double-clicking its control menu icon or by choosing File|Exit from the menu bar.

Day Summary

Installing Access is as simple as inserting the setup disk or CD-ROM in the appropriate drive and instructing Windows to run Setup from that disk. If you're running Windows 95 or later Windows versions with that interface, you'll likely perform this through Control Panel's Add-Remove program. You'll have to tell Setup where to install Access, which components of Access to install, and what to name the group that will contain Access's icon; at any rate, most of the installation is automatic.

You launch Access by double-clicking its icon. The top three layers of the Access interface are the title bar, the menu bar, and the toolbar. The bottommost strip of the Access interface is the status bar.

You can adjust the shape and location of any Access toolbar by using the mouse to drag the bar to where you want it and adjusting its outline.

Access has three systems in addition to the printed documentation to help you use the program: the Office Assistant, wizards, and online help. The Office Assistant is a special help system with step-by-step instructions for certain operations; wizards interact with you to perform certain functions; online help is (for the most part) a reference system similar to the printed manuals that come with Access.

Q&A

Q Can I adjust the size and location of the menu or status bars the same way I do the toolbars?

A Yes and no. Access only enables custom location of toolbars, of which the menu bar is one. The status bar isn't movable.

Q When should I use the Office Assistant instead of wizards?

A If the output from your wizard isn't close to what you want, you'll have to manually design your database object. If you're unclear about how to do this, the Office Assistant will often help you step through it.

Q Are there dangers if I install Access to a different place than Setup suggests?

A You can install Access wherever you please and have permissions without any adverse consequences. Running Access from network drives can slow it down due to network speed limits.

Workshop

Here's where you can test and apply what you have learned today.

Quiz

Possible answers to these questions are provided in Appendix A.

1. Why should you avoid compact installation routines if at all possible?
2. What shape does the cursor take when it's capable of reshaping a toolbar?
3. How do you launch Access from the Start menu in the Windows interface?
4. What are two clues hinting at or telling you what a button on a toolbar does?
5. Can you move or resize the menu bar?

Put Access into Action

1. Launch Access.
2. Launch the help system.
3. Click the Find tab.
4. After Access brings up the Find dialog, enter average as a word to limit the length of the list. Click any topic that interests you. Read through the topic. Return to the Find dialog box by clicking the Help Topics button in the help topic. When you're satisfied, close the help system.
5. Exit Access.

DAY

2

A.M.

3 Entering Data into Tables

P.M.

4 Table Field Properties

Chapter 3

Entering Data into Tables

This morning you'll learn the following:

☐ What database project this book uses for its examples
☐ How to plan the initial tables for the database
☐ How to use a wizard to create your first working table

The Database Project

As with almost any small computer program, the right way to learn Access is to use it. Rather than go through a series of boring exercises that are unrelated to each other, as you work your way through this book you will devise a solution to a hypothetical problem. Although this particular situation—a student registration and tracking application at a make-believe college—is fictional, you can directly apply the principles you learn to your own particular situation.

Note that the exercises covered in this section have some overlap with what was covered in Chapter 2, "Wizards, the Office Assistant, and Help." This is by design. The focus of this chapter is table and database creation; the previous chapter covered wizards, the Office Assistant, and help in general. If you find yourself on familiar ground at certain places in this chapter, more power to you.

The fictional database must track information such as the students' vital statistics, the courses they take, and the status of their tuition payments. By changing the labels and making a few modifications, this system can also be used for the following:

- [ ] Tracking customer orders and account balances
- [ ] Maintaining a medical or dental practice
- [ ] Tracking retail sales and inventory
- [ ] Keeping a personal inventory
- [ ] Creating a simple accounting system
- [ ] Maintaining a personnel-management system

The principles you learn while building this system can be applied to almost any Access application. Actually, the college-management system you create as you work through this book is more complex than most user-created Access applications. The real problems you'll use Access to solve will probably be much simpler than this sample application.

Planning the Database

Refer back to the introduction to this book if you need a refresher on planning databases and what the relational model is. Remember, in a relational database like Access, you distribute or divide your data into logical groupings of tables. For those needing near perfection, there's a complex mathematical model for performing this process; most people, however, don't need to worry that they've completely optimized their data. As in many other fields, close is good enough for most database work.

3

Close Is Good Enough?

Most Access database projects, even large ones, don't require a laborious design process. Database purists will cringe at that statement, but it's true. Access has the power and the flexibility to let you get away with a rather loose design.

However, the theory behind the relational model is valid for most business-type database projects. The closer you adhere to the relational model, the more efficient your database will be. How much efficiency you require depends on your database size, your desired response time, and your general business goals.

The goal of the relational model is efficiency. Take a look at Figure 3.1, which is the *flat file* (or nonrelational) method to store data for a particular student. Note that for each course this student has taken, the student's name, address, and phone information is duplicated. If you're dealing with only a few records, this duplication isn't a problem. However, today's databases handle thousands or even millions of records. Any database carrying around all that extra baggage would inevitably be bogged down under that extra load.

Figure 3.1.

The flat file database model showing duplicated information.

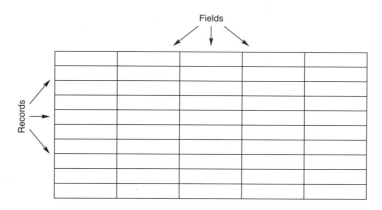

Now take a look at Figure 3.2. This is the same data, but this time it's shown in the relational model. Note that with this model, the data shown in Figure 3.1 is now broken into two tables. One table has the student's personal information, such as student ID or social security number, student name, student address, and phone. The second table doesn't duplicate all this information for each course the student has taken, as in the flat file model shown in Figure 3.1. Instead, the second table contains only the course information for this student plus the student ID for each course. StudentID is the link field that lets Access match the student with the courses taken.

Figure 3.2.
The same information as in Figure 3.1, but shown using the relational model. Note the lack of data duplication.

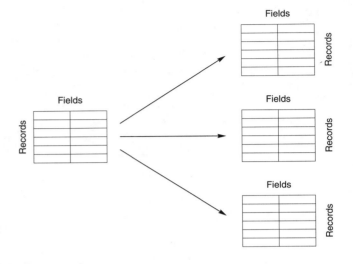

Do	**Don't**

DO organize your data into tables to minimize or eliminate duplication.

DON'T get overly carried away with breaking up your data. After you've organized it to the point of little or no duplication, stop. Breaking up your data any further will lead to inefficiencies.

Before the First Table

Any college database needs a table to store personal information about students, so that will be the first table you add to your database. Before you go further, you need a new database to store your database objects. Exercise 3.1 shows you how to create the new database.

Exercise 3.1. Creating the new database.

1. Launch Access, if you haven't already done so. Select the top option button to create a blank database, as shown in Figure 3.3.

2. If you have Access started, you can shut down and restart it to automatically launch the dialog box shown in Figure 3.3, or you can click the New Database toolbar button, the leftmost one in Figure 3.3.

3. Whichever path you choose, click OK to move to the next dialog box.

Figure 3.3.

Creating a new database.

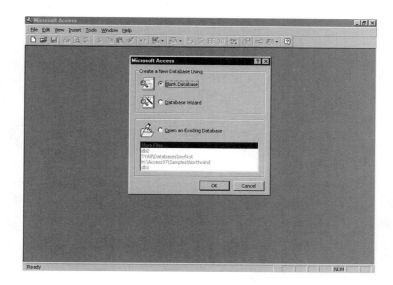

4. Access responds by asking you to name your new database. The program suggests the rather drab db1.mdb as a name. Override Access's suggestion and enter College in the dialog box for the new database's name. You can either include the extension .mdb, or leave it out and let Access attach the file extension automatically. Access uses the file extension .mdb to identify its native format databases.

5. Access will grind away for a while, and after verifying that all's OK with its world, it will create a new database and leave your screen looking like Figure 3.4.

Figure 3.4.

The newly created College database.

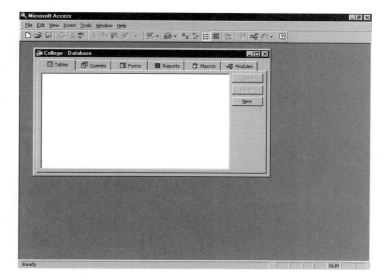

Access 97 and Long Filenames

With Windows 95 and later versions, you can use long filenames if you have this feature enabled. Access 97, being a fully compliant Windows 95 application, can do the same.

This book uses short filenames to accommodate those who don't have long filenames enabled within Windows. This is fairly common at sites with mixed Windows and Windows 3.1 installations. Although Windows 95 has a DOS-equivalent filename, most people don't like seeing `My New College Database.mdb` truncated to `mynewc~1.mdb`. Until the world fully converts to current versions of Windows or their successors, some of us are stuck with the old DOS filename conventions.

The First Table

Right now the College database is empty of any objects. Remember that the first order of business is to make a table to store all the student's personal information. Consider what information is "personal" and, therefore, belongs in this table. Here's where your particular needs must be considered. This application initially stores the following information in the StudentPersonal table:

> Student ID or social security number
> Name (last name, first name, and middle initial)
> Address
> Phone
> Emergency contact and/or parents
> E-mail address
> Major
> Notes

If you were making this database on your own, you might consider more, different, or fewer fields for this table. For example, if you were modifying this model for a customer database, you'd include a company name and a contact person and probably leave out the emergency contact. You'd also need an alternative to the social security number to act as a customer ID.

Now that you've decided on some of the fields you need for the first table, it's time to go ahead and create it.

Exercise 3.2. Creating the StudentPersonal table.

1. Make sure the Tables tab, the leftmost one in the Database window, is selected. (Figure 3.4 shows the tab correctly selected.)

2. Click the New button in the Database box. It's over at the far right of the Database window—the only button that's enabled at this time.

3. Access responds by giving you a blizzard of choices. The first two, Datasheet View and Design View, are manual options for creating a table. The last two, Import Table Wizard and Link Table Wizard, are wizards to help you move existing external tables into your database or link to them, respectively. For this exercise, you need the middle choice, so click on the Table Wizard selection, then click OK. Access responds with a screen that looks like Figure 3.5.

Figure 3.5.

The Table Wizard, again in action.

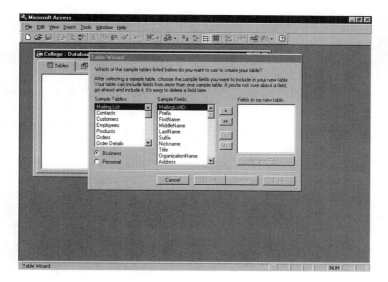

4. Make sure the option button Business, in the lower-left corner, is selected. Use your mouse to scroll through the Sample Tables list; when you find the sample table called Students, click on it.

5. Access is making it easy for you. Look at the Sample Fields list box (shown in Figure 3.6) and note that almost all the fields you want are included in this sample table.

6. Click the >> button just to the right of the Sample Fields list box to include all the sample fields in your new table. Since all the projected students will come from the United States, click the PostalCode field, then click Rename. Change the Postal-Code field to read ZipCode, as shown in Figure 3.6. Click OK to accept this name. Use this same procedure to change the StateOrProvince field to read State.

Do	Don't

DO check to see whether Access comes up with a sample or solution that closely fits your needs. It's not necessary to reinvent the wheel.

DON'T force a fit. If you can't find a sample or solution that's close to your needs, don't be afraid of creating your own from scratch. Later on in the book, you'll learn how easy it is to create your own tables without help from the wizard.

Figure 3.6.
Altering field names within the wizard.

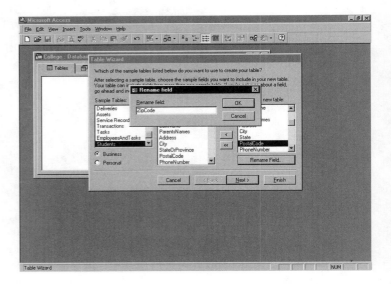

7. Click the Next> button, right next to the Finish button, at the lower-right portion of the Table Wizard dialog box. Access prompts you for a name for this table and suggests "Students." Override Access's suggestion and name your table StudentPersonal.

8. Move to the middle of the wizard dialog box and change the choice from having Access set the primary key for you to "No, I'll Set The Primary Key." In this case, Access's choice for a primary key would do nicely, but it's a good exercise to learn how to set keys manually, so you'll do that later on. Click Next> to move to the next dialog box.

9. The StudentID will be unique to each record because you'll be using the students' social security numbers as student IDs. If a student doesn't have a social security number, you'll have to substitute another value that's unique to each student. Although a person being allowed to walk around today without a social security number is as likely as a flying pig, preserving this option will come in handy later. Therefore, leave Access's choice of StudentID as the field that's unique to each record, but select the bottom option button from the selections in the middle of the dialog box to tell Access that StudentID will be numbers or letters added when you add new records. Your screen should now look like Figure 3.7.

Figure 3.7.

Identifying the unique field for the Table Wizard.

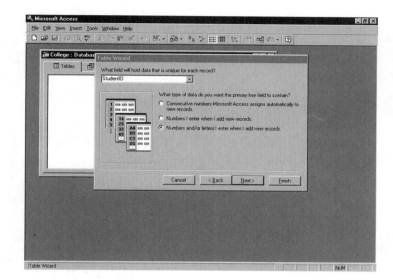

10. Click the Next> button. Access gives you three final choices and signals you're at the end of this wizard by showing you the checkered-flag symbol. If the top option button isn't selected, click on it to tell Access that at the end of the wizard you want to modify the table's design, then click Finish. Remember that at any time prior to finishing you can review and alter the options for a wizard by clicking the <Back buttons. Access will trundle around a bit, create the new table, and leave you in table Design View. Your screen should look like Figure 3.8.

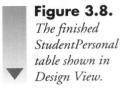

Figure 3.8.
*The finished
StudentPersonal
table shown in
Design View.*

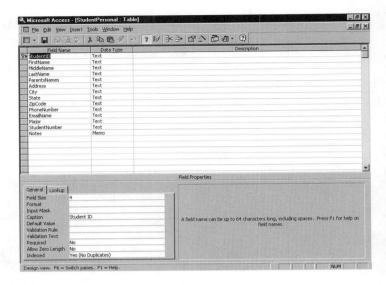

A Look at Field Types and Properties

Refer to Figure 3.8 or your screen. The top part of the table design window shows a list of the field names and their data types. The bottom part of the window has a section labeled Field Properties with two tabs, General and Lookup. Each field in an Access table has three elements: the field name, such as StudentID; a field type, such as Text; and a set of properties. It's important that you set each field in your database to an appropriate field type. It's generally less important, but still a matter of concern, that your table fields have their properties set correctly.

Data Types

The data type for a field tells Access what type of data, or information, you plan on entering in that field. Access allows the following data types:

Text: Also known as Alphanumeric. This data type accepts any normal characters and is limited to a field length of 255 characters.

Number: This data type accepts numbers. You can specify the level of precision for a Number data type. Use the Number data type when you plan on applying arithmetical operations on a field or fields.

Date/Time: A specialized form of Number data type, for entering date or time information. Like the standard Number data type, the Date/Time data type allows you to perform arithmetical operations. For example, you can find the number of days between two dates if they're entered as Date/Time data types. (If you entered date or time information in a Text data type field, Access would accept the entry, but you couldn't perform arithmetical operations on the entries.)

Currency: This is another specialized Number data type, which fixes a certain number of decimal places. It's useful for entering monetary information.

AutoNumber: When you make a field an AutoNumber data type, Access automatically applies sequential numbers to records as you enter them if you have the Field Property New Number set to `Increment`. If you have it set to `Random`, Access automatically generates random numbers for each new record.

When set to `Increment`, Access starts the numbering at 1. Incrementing or random fields work for primary keys because Access never reuses a number after it has been assigned to a record in a table. Ironically, using these fields unnecessarily violates relational theory because it can bulk up a database with unneeded information. Use AutoNumber fields for primary key fields only if no other primary key seems reasonable.

When using AutoNumber for a primary key, most people use Increment. The Random New Number property is a special case, used when the Increment property might result in creating a duplicate primary key as data is entered at two or more locations.

Yes/No: Accepts only two values—`Yes` or `No`.

Lookup Wizard: Looks up values you can enter in another database object. For example, if you want to allow only entry of data that's been previously entered in another table, you'd set this field to look up data in that table. You'll see examples of this later on in this book.

Hyperlink: A table entry that has either a Universal Naming Convention (UNC) entry, which has the form `\\servername\directory\file`, or a Universal Resource Location (URL), such as `http://www.microsoft.com/sitebuilder/`.

OLE Object: Enables you to either link or embed an object created in another program that can act as an OLE server program.

Memo: A field for adding notes or memoranda to a record.

Keep in mind that you can't index on either the Memo, Hyperlink, or OLE fields. Generally speaking, use the Text data type unless you're sure either that all your data will conform to one of the less flexible data types or that you'll need to perform math on a field's data. You can't do math on a Text field, even if that field contains only numbers.

Do   **Don't**

DO try to get your data types correct the first time.

DON'T despair if you defined a data type incorrectly. In most cases, you can change data types even after you've entered data into the table. In some cases, you might lose some entered data, but Access will warn you if this could happen.

Morning Summary

This morning, you learned how to create a new database and add a table to it by using a wizard. You also were introduced to the various data types Access uses.

Chapter **4**

Table Field Properties

This afternoon, you'll learn how to do the following:

- ☐ Modify a wizard-created table
- ☐ Manually create a table
- ☐ Create a simple two-table relationship

Modifying a Table

Access enables you to modify almost any aspect of an existing table, whether it's made manually or by using a wizard. In almost every case, a wizard-based table needs some sort of customizing. You saw this in Exercise 3.2 when you renamed two fields supplied in the sample table.

Many times you'll design a table and then realize that a particular field's data type is wrong, or you included a field you shouldn't have, or you left one out that you need. In all these cases, you would need to modify an existing table design.

The StudentPersonal table was fairly close to what you needed when it came out of the wizard. It needs only three major modifications: adding a field for ethnicity, eliminating the redundant StudentNumber field, and adding a field for a hyperlink to the student's home page. The ethnicity field is necessary for many government reports a college needs to file. Since the school administration will track students by StudentID, the first field, it'll also use that number as a student number.

You change a table's design by clicking in the appropriate area of the table design grid, then making whatever changes you want. Sound simple? It is.

Exercise 4.1. Modifying a table.

1. If you've closed Access, the College database, or the StudentPersonal table, you'll need to reopen them. If necessary, launch Access, and open the College database by using either the opening dialog box or the File|Open menu choices. With the StudentPersonal table highlighted, click the Design button in the Database window. Your screen should look like Figure 3.8.

2. Locate the field called StudentNumber. Move your cursor to the gray area (unless you have a different color scheme) immediately to the left of the field name. The cursor will change to a right-facing arrow. Click your left mouse button to highlight the entire field (row). Your screen should look like Figure 4.1.

3. Press the Delete or Del key, and Access gets rid of the field. Your screen should now look like Figure 4.2.

Figure 4.1.
Highlighting a field before deleting it.

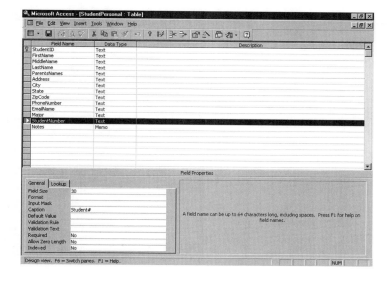

Figure 4.2.
The StudentPersonal table after field deletion.

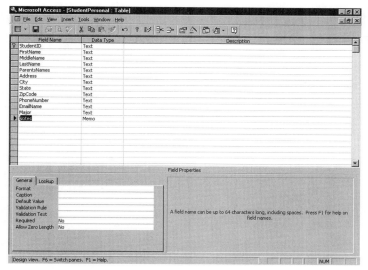

The Access Way

Because of a long-standing database convention, Access wizards use field names lacking white space. This stems from a time when database programs limited their field names to eight characters and couldn't handle white space within those names. Those days are, for the most part, long gone, but many database veterans still get nervous seeing a field name such as First Name, so the designers of Access conceded the point and concatenated First Name to FirstName.

There's a practical side to this as well. Field names without white space export to these older database programs much better. They also work properly with Structured Query Language (SQL), which Access uses. However, feel free to add white space to your field names if you're fairly sure you won't have to contend with older technologies and will use the Access query grid exclusively to create queries. At this point, you probably can't answer these questions, but keep them in mind for later.

Adding Fields

You can easily add a field to an existing Access database. Here's how to add a field called Ethnicity to the StudentPersonal table.

Why the Wasted Effort?

If you're thinking it would have been easier simply to not include the StudentNumber field when in the wizard rather than include it only to eliminate it later, you're right.

You'll also soon realize that it would have been easier to just rename the StudentNumber field to Ethnicity, rather than deleting and then adding. The point of these two exercises isn't to be highly efficient, but to demonstrate how to do different things within Access. After seeing how to do these operations, you should become not only proficient, but efficient in using the program.

Exercise 4.2. Adding a field to an existing table.

1. Your screen should look like Figure 4.2. If not, make the necessary adjustments.

2. If needed, use the vertical scrollbar to scroll down the Field Name list until you can see the field name Major. Move your cursor to the left border of the Field Name

column. Your cursor will change to a right-facing arrow to highlight the row. Click your left mouse button. Your screen should now resemble Figure 4.3.

3. When you click to highlight the entire row, be sure not to move the mouse cursor from the little gray square just to the left of the Major field. This can be a little tricky and might take you a few tries to get right.

4. With the entire row containing the field name Major highlighted, press the Insert key on your keyboard. Access will insert a new empty row and push the field Major down one row. Your screen should now look like Figure 4.4.

The Access Way

You don't need to highlight an entire row to insert a new field. Just clicking in the Major field, then on the toolbar button Insert Field, will do it. Similarly, you could have deleted a field (row) by clicking in it, then clicking on the Delete Row button in the toolbar.

Figure 4.3.
Getting ready to insert a new field in an existing table.

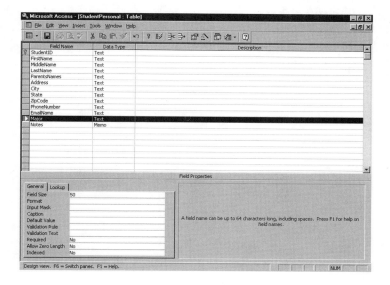

5. Click once in the Field Name column of the highlighted row. The row will lose the highlight and your cursor will be at the extreme left of the Field Name column. Type the word Ethnicity.

6. Tab or press Enter to move your cursor to the Data Type column. Access responds by suggesting the data type Text and also reveals a pull-down tab to the right of the Data Type field. Click to pull down the list. Your screen should now resemble Figure 4.5.

Figure 4.4.

Getting ready to add a new field name to an existing table.

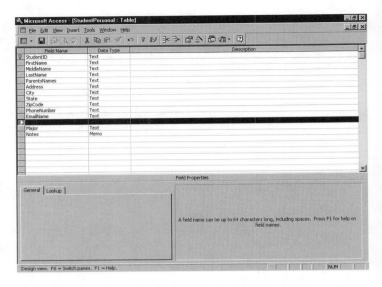

Figure 4.5.

Specifying the data type for Ethnicity field.

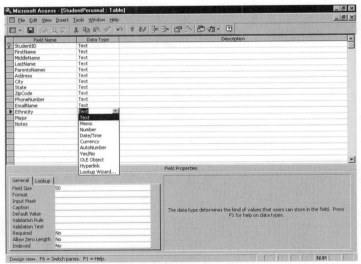

7. Text is the correct data type for the new Ethnicity field, but just to take a look at what else you might choose, click on the down arrow to the right of the data-type entry. Access will drop down the list part of a combo box containing all its data types.

8. In a similar way, add a new field, HomePage, directly below the Ethnicity field. Make its data type Hyperlink. If you want to try something different, try clicking

in the Major field, then clicking on the Insert Row button in the toolbar. The effect will be the same.

Do	**Don't**

DO use whatever keyboard navigation methods you like. For example, you had a choice of pressing the Enter or Tab key after adding the field name Ethnicity to move the cursor to the Data Type column. What you choose to do depends on how you like to work and how you've worked in the past. The point is to get there, not the road you traveled during the journey.

DON'T worry about following the keystrokes in this book precisely. If your preferred method for using Access differs in some minor way from the instructions in this book, use whatever makes you comfortable.

9. You've just added two new fields to the StudentPersonal table. Close the StudentPersonal table either by double-clicking on its control menu icon or by clicking on the × button. When Access asks whether you want to save the changes you made to the table, click OK.

Creating a New Table Manually

Sometimes a table you need doesn't resemble anything in the wizard's samples. In these cases, you'll need to create one from scratch. Many database veterans are reluctant to let wizards take over their work, so they opt for manual design even if a good prototype exists in the wizard. No matter how experienced you are, you should get a feel for manual table design since it's only a matter of time until you will need to use table design skills. Actually, if you've done the two exercises in this chapter, you already have a good idea of what it takes to manually design a table in Access.

> **The Wizard Strikes Again!**
>
> Actually, the Database Wizard has a rather competent sample called Students and Classes.mdz, which is a database similar in function to the one manually created in *Teach Yourself Access 97 in 14 Days*.
>
> After completing this book, you'd be well advised to examine the results of this wizard to see how Microsoft tackled a situation similar to the one posed in this book.

You need a table to store information about student course registrations. This table will have a field for StudentID so that it can be linked to the StudentPersonal table. *Linking* means that you can't add any information into the dependent table if a corresponding record doesn't already exist in the independent table. Specifically, in this case, it means that after you've linked the two tables, you won't be able to register a student for a course until that student's information has been entered in StudentPersonal.

This table will also need fields for course number, an indication as to whether the student finished the course, and the student's grade. Each semester, this table will feed information into another table that will, in effect, be the student's transcript.

NOTE

> This example is a somewhat simplified college registration system. You can assume that all course numbers point to unique courses and that there are no sections to these courses. Although in real life many college courses have sections, adding this complexity to the example would obscure the point of these exercises. If you're working on a real-world college registration system, adding items such as sections will be easy after you learn the basics in these exercises.

Creating the Table

After you close the StudentPersonal table in Exercise 4.2, your screen should look like Figure 4.6. If it doesn't, navigate around Access until it does. Exercise 4.3 shows you how to create a table manually.

Exercise 4.3. Creating a table without a wizard.

1. Click the New button to start the table creation process. When Access offers you blizzards of wizards, choose Design View and click OK. Access will immediately open a blank table design grid, as illustrated in Figure 4.7.

2. Your cursor will be on the first row in the leftmost column of the design grid. This is the column where, as you saw in the exercise where you modified a table, Access stores field names. Take a moment to examine the square in the lower-right corner of the table design grid. Right now, it says, "A field name can be up to 64 characters long including spaces. Press F1 for help on field names." As you use Access, the program helps you along with tips (often valuable) such as this. As you work through this exercise, watch not only the prompts in this box but also those along the status bar at the very bottom of your screen.

Figure 4.6.
Ready to create a new table without a wizard's help.

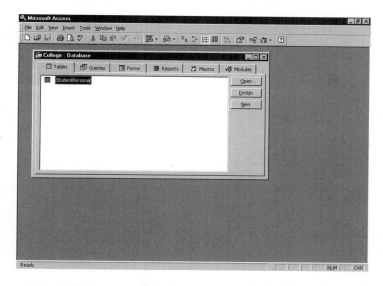

Figure 4.7.
The blank table design grid.

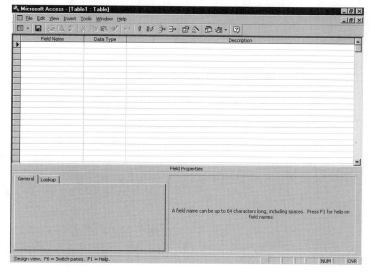

3. Enter the words IndexNumber for the first field name, then press Tab or Enter to move to the Data Type field. Access will suggest the Text data type. Click on the pull-down tab to choose another data type. Locate the AutoNumber data type and click on it. The IndexNumber field will be the key field for this table. Although some people think key fields aren't absolutely necessary, Access operates more efficiently by using tables with key fields, and you'll keep out of trouble by making

sure every table has one, so one is included here. The AutoNumber data type means that Access will automatically add unique numbers to this field for each record you create as you use this table. Look down at the bottom section of the screen and note that the New Values field is set to Increment. This is the default for the AutoNumber data type.

4. The next field you need is StudentID so that you have a common field to link this table with the StudentPersonal table. Press Tab twice to move through the Description field to the second row of the Field Name column.

Unlike Names, Like Data

Link fields need to hold like data, but don't necessarily need to be named identically. However, unless you have a business or functional reason to have different names for link fields, keep them the same to eliminate confusion.

Do   **Don't**

DO comment your tables and other database objects with full descriptions if users will be asked to maintain them. Access shows the contents of the field description column in the status bar during data entry for a table.

DON'T be cryptic or overly cute when commenting. The comments or descriptions you think are clever today might come back to haunt you tomorrow.

---

5. Enter StudentID, then move to the Data Type field. Accept Access's default of Text type and tab twice to move to the next row. Keep in mind that the StudentID field in the StudentPersonal table is a Text data type; that's why the StudentID field is also a Text data type.

6. After moving to the next row, enter CourseNumber. Again move to the Data Type column and accept Access's default by tabbing twice to move to the fourth row in the Field Name column. Your screen should now look like Figure 4.8.

The field CourseNumber was left at the default Text data type even though the field will contain only numbers. This is because no math will ever be performed on this field and, surprisingly, Access handles Text fields more efficiently than Number ones.

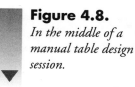

Figure 4.8.

In the middle of a manual table design session.

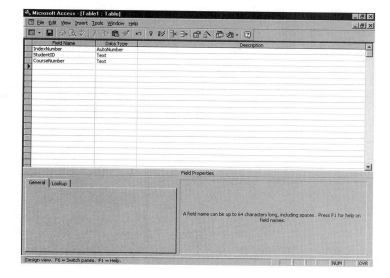

7. Enter `Completed` as the next field name and choose Yes/No as its data type. Move to the next Field Name row.

The Access Way

When your cursor enters the Data Type field, press the *Y* key. Access autoscrolls to the Yes/No data type. Pressing the *A* key would scroll to AutoNumber data type, and so on. As you move through Access, you'll discover dozens of little ways its design speeds and simplifies your database chores.

---

8. Finish this table's field names and data types by entering `Grade` and leaving the data type as Text. Don't tab away from the Data Type column just yet.

9. Since a grade won't ever take up the 50 spaces Access allows for a field size, click on the Field Size row in the Field Properties section of the table design grid. Change the default value of `50` to `2`. Your screen should now look like Figure 4.9.

10. The only thing left to do is to tell Access you want the IndexNumber field to be the key field. A *key field* in Access contains unique data for each record. Access indexes or orders the table primarily on that key.

11. Click on the first row in the first column of the table design grid; that is, click on the field name IndexNumber. Look at the toolbar until you find a button with a small down-pointing key on it. Move your cursor over this button and you should

see the balloon help "Primary Key" appear. Click this button. A little key will appear just to the left of the IndexNumber field name, indicating that you've just set IndexNumber to be the primary key field for this table. Your screen should now resemble Figure 4.10.

Figure 4.9.

Changing a field size.

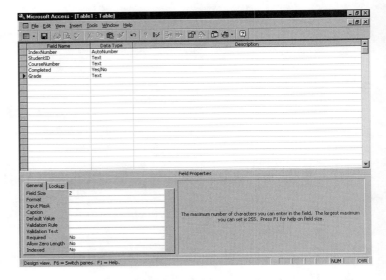

Figure 4.10.

Defining the primary key field for the finished table.

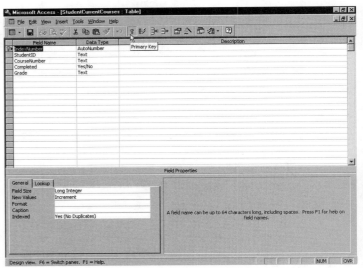

12. Save and name this table. Click the menu item File and choose Close. Access will respond with a dialog box asking you whether you want to save the changes to Table1. Click Yes. When prompted for a table name, enter StudentCurrentCourses, then click OK. Access will save the table and return you to the Database window that now contains two tables: StudentPersonal and StudentCurrentCourses.

Taking the Long Way Around

Before closing the StudentCurrentCourses table, you could have moved your cursor to the StudentID field, clicked on the Lookup tab in the Field Properties section, and told Access to look up values in the StudentPersonal table for use in this table.

This book treats linking as a separate topic in the next section. Although this is the long way to perform the task, it shows an alternative method that visually demonstrates link fields. After you have a feel for table links, choose the make link method you're most comfortable using.

The "Why" of a Relationship

Take a look at the functions of the StudentCurrentCourses table. You wouldn't want any entries in this table for non-students or anybody the system doesn't have already entered in it. You also want to be able to match the courses taken with the appropriate students. In a relational database such as Access, links serve both these functions.

The Access Way

Most people believe that the proper way to design a database is to separately code each type of database object. For example, tables might bear the prefix *tbl*; queries, *qry*; forms, *frm*; and so on.

This is a good idea, but one not followed in this book for the sake of simplicity. Essentially, the number of database objects in College won't grow large enough to force using a naming convention.

However, when working on your own, consider a standard naming convention not only for your database objects, but also for everything down to code variables. What naming convention you use depends on which you prefer, but decide on one and use it.

4

> Naming conventions come in handy when you're modifying reports or forms. Knowing that a form, for example, is based on a database object called "tblStudents" immediately tips you off that the object is a table and not a query.

You need to establish a link between the StudentPersonal table and the StudentCurrentCourses table so you can do two things: validation and matching. *Validation* means you want to make sure you don't get any erroneous data in StudentCurrentCourses; for example, you don't want data for a course being taken without a student attached to it. Therefore, you should make sure a record exists for a student in StudentPersonal before you try to make an entry for that student in StudentCurrentCourses.

You also want to make sure you can enter many records for any one student in Student-CurrentCourses, since one student can take many courses during a semester. A relationship in which one record can be linked to many others is called, not surprisingly, a *one-to-many relationship*. Making sure a record exists in the table on the "one" side before any records can be entered in the "many" side is called *referential integrity*.

Matching means you'll be able to match up information in the StudentPersonal table with the information in StudentCurrentCourses. The link tells Access which fields match up to which in the two tables.

If this seems complicated, don't worry about it for now. After you establish the link this afternoon, enter some data tomorrow, and continue to work with this database later on, the ways in which these elements fit together will become clear.

Making the Link or Relationship

Your screen should now be at the Database window, as it was when you finished Exercise 4.3. If it's not, navigate there before you start Exercise 4.4.

Exercise 4.4. Creating a one-to-many link.

1. Click the menu item called Tools and then click Relationships at the middle of the drop-down list.
2. Highlight each table in turn, then click the Add button to add each table to the Relationships window.
3. Click the Close button in the Add Table dialog box. Your screen should now look like Figure 4.11.
4. Note that the two fields, IndexNumber in the StudentCurrentCourses and StudentID in StudentPersonal, are shown in boldface to indicate that these fields are the primary key fields for their respective tables.

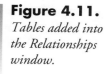

Figure 4.11.

*Tables added into
the Relationships
window.*

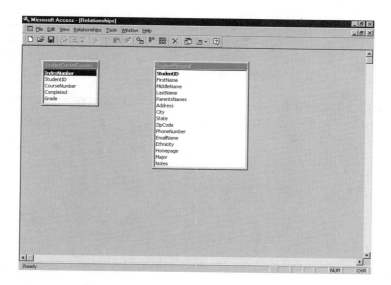

5. Now for some tricky mouse work. Establish a link between tables by dragging your
   mouse from table to table within the Relationships window. Here's how to do it:

   Move your mouse cursor to the entry called StudentID in the StudentPersonal list
   box. Click the left mouse button and hold it while you drag the cursor into the
   StudentCurrentCourses list box. Still holding the mouse button down, move the
   cursor over the StudentID field in the second list box and then let go. Access
   responds with a dialog box, shown in Figure 4.12.

Figure 4.12.

*The Relationships
dialog box.*

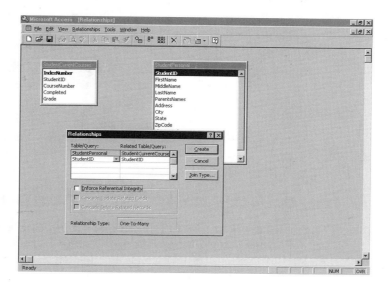

4

6. Click the check box labeled Enforce Referential Integrity. This prevents you from making an entry in StudentCurrentCourses unless a previous entry exists in StudentPersonal. Click the Create button, and Access will respond with a screen like the one in Figure 4.13.

Figure 4.13.
The finished table link.

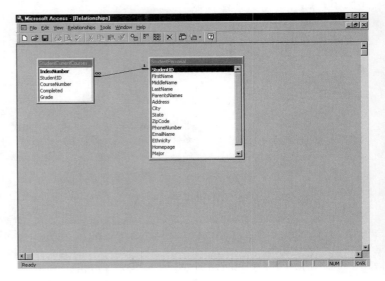

Note that Access indicates a one-to-many link pictorially. Near the point where the link line enters the StudentPersonal list box, you can see a number 1. This means that the StudentPersonal table is the one side of the one-to-many relationship. Near where the link line enters the StudentCurrentCourses list box is a "lazy eight" sign representing infinity. This shows that the StudentCurrentCourses table holds down the many side of the one-to-many relationship.

Again, don't be concerned at this point if linking and relationships are difficult concepts for you. Chapter 5, "Modifying Table Properties," will help to clarify these issues.

7. Click on the menu items File|Close. Access will ask if you want to save the Relationships window changes. Click Yes, which takes you back to the Database window.

A Third Way to Table Creation

There's a third way to create a new table—by using the Datasheet View. The following section illustrates how this works, but there's no formal exercise. Now that you have a feel for manual table design, making a table by using the Datasheet View should be fairly easy, if you want to use this technique instead of Design View or a wizard.

To make a new table with the Datasheet View, make sure the Tables table is selected in Database View. Click the New button, then choose Datasheet View from the list box. (See Figure 4.14.)

Figure 4.14.

Making a new table with the Datasheet View technique.

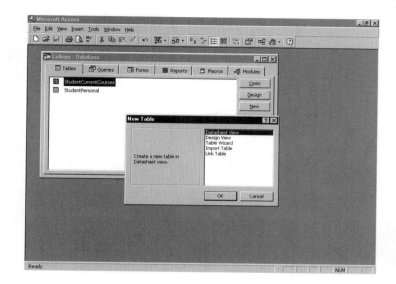

Access will grind away for a while and return with a blank datasheet, as shown in Figure 4.15.

Figure 4.15.

The Datasheet View in design phase.

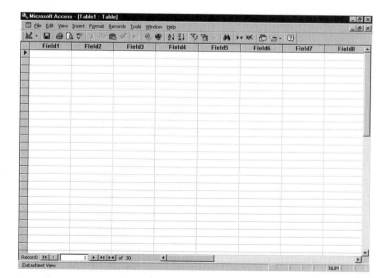

Defining fields is as easy as entering data in each field. Access will make a good guess as to the data type you want for each field, based on your initial entries. To name the fields, double-click on the field headings—the places that now say Field1, Field2, and so on. You have 20 columns to work with at first. If you need more, choose Column from the Insert menu. When you're done, click the Save icon in the toolbar or choose File|Save from the menu.

Access will ask whether you want it to add a primary key field to the table. If you haven't included a field appropriate for a primary key, you ought to take Access up on its offer. Otherwise, decline and then move to Design View and set the primary key there, as you learned in the previous exercise.

Figure 4.16 shows the table from Figure 4.15 with some data entered and the field names altered. Figure 4.17 shows the table in Design View. Note that Access dropped the columns without data and correctly assigned the data type to the fields.

Figure 4.16.

The table with data added to the fields and appropriate field names based on the contents.

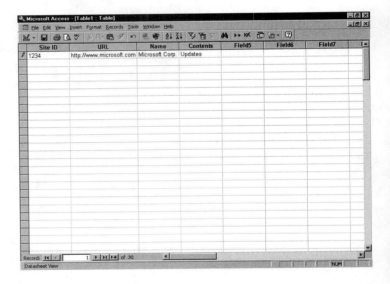

Figure 4.17.

The table from Figure 4.16 in Design View, showing how Access automatically assigned the right data type to each field.

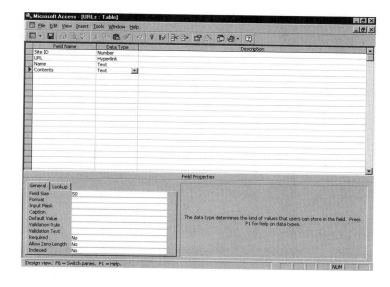

Day Summary

The ongoing project you're doing in this book is a student tracking-and-registration system for a hypothetical college. Today you created two tables for this database. You created the first table, StudentPersonal, by using a New Table wizard. Since a good prototype apparently didn't exist (or at least, we pretended it didn't), you created the second table, StudentCurrentCourses, manually.

Often you'll need to change some elements of a wizard-created table. You can easily do this from the table design grid. For example, to change a field name, just double-click it to select it, then type in the new field name.

It's important to set the right data type for fields. Access defaults to the Text data type, which, generally speaking, is appropriate for most fields. However, Access also has several less flexible data types, such as Number, and specialized number types, such as Currency. Use one of the Number or Date/Time data types for fields in which you'll need to perform math. If you won't be doing any calculations on a field, the safe approach is to leave it as a Text data type—even if you anticipate that all its entries will be numbers.

4

Each field also has a set of properties. These properties, such as field size, vary with the data type. Key fields always have the Indexed property set to Yes (No duplicates) because the nature of key fields is that the data for any record can appear only once in a table, and Access indexes (or orders) a table primarily on the key field's entries.

Creating a table manually is the same operation as altering the entries in a wizard-created table. You can also create a table in Datasheet View.

You create a link, or relationship, between two tables by first choosing Tools|Relationships from the menu in the Database window. Then add the tables you want to add to the link structure by highlighting them in the Show Table dialog box and clicking the Add button. You create the links themselves by dragging the mouse cursor from one table's list box to another. Finally, you finish the linking process by choosing options for the link in the Relationships dialog box.

Q&A

Q While browsing around in Access 97, I noticed several sample tables with names like Classes and StudentsAndClasses in another wizard. Why didn't we use those tables instead of making one from scratch?

A You've got sharp eyes. Actually, you could have used the Access-supplied sample tables for the second table you made today, but I had you do it manually for practice.

Q I noticed many other field properties in the table design grid. When do you set these?

A The most efficient time to set these properties is during the initial design, but you lose nothing but a little time if you skip this at first and come back to it later. Most of the properties were skipped during today's exercises to focus on basic table-design methods. When you're familiar with Access and making your own applications, try to set as many field properties as you can anticipate during the initial design phase.

Q I created a field with the Text data type. It accepted date entries such as September 2, 1994, just fine. Why should I bother with the Date/Time data type?

A Date/Time is a specialized number format, which means you can perform math on fields with this data type. Say you have a database with tables tracking loans, and you have fields for the starting and ending dates of those loans. If the data type is Text, you won't be able to use Access to calculate the time between these dates. If the data type is set to Date/Time, performing these calculations is simple. Later in this book, you'll see how handy the Date/Time data type is for this purpose.

Q Yikes! My Access came without wizards.

A If you chose to install Access in certain configurations, Setup won't install your wizards, so you need to rerun Setup and choose a fuller installation. (See Question 1 after Day 1 for a related answer.)

Q Why use the Text data type for the numbers-only Zip field?

A A Number data type field cannot start with a zero, since in a Number data type, zeros on the left are meaningless and Access will drop them. If you enter the number 010 into a Number data type field, Access will strip the left zero and enter just 10. Some ZIP codes begin with a zero, so you need to specify the Text data type. Even if no ZIP codes started with a zero, Text is the appropriate data type to use here, since you don't do math on ZIP code fields.

Workshop

Here's where you can test and apply the lessons you learned today.

Quiz

Possible answers to these questions are given in Appendix A.

1. What's the first step in creating a new Access table?

2. You have an order-entry sales system that has two linked tables: Customers and Sales to Customers. Which table do you suppose is the "many" in this one-to-many link?

3. Why use a wizard when making a table?

4. What's the maximum size of a field with the data type set to Text?

5. What is the maximum number of characters (including spaces) for a field name in an Access table?

6. Say you're going to export a table called A List of My Friends to an old database system that can't handle white space in table names. What do you suppose will happen when you try to use this table in the older database system?

Put Access into Action

1. During Exercise 3.2, you altered the field name PostalCode in the StudentPersonal table to ZipCode. However, the field property Field Size was left at 20. Open the StudentPersonal table in Design View and change the Field Size property for the ZipCode field to 11.

2. Add a field called DateofBirth to the StudentPersonal table. Have the new field appear just below the Ethnicity field. Set the data-type format to Date/Time.

3. To get your StudentPersonal table back into sync with this book, delete the DateofBirth field from StudentPersonal. Hint: To do this, highlight the entire row containing the field and press the Delete key. If you accidentally delete the wrong field, press Ctrl+Z or choose Edit|Undo from the menu.

4. Close the StudentPersonal table, discarding all changes. This is to keep in sync with this book's sample data. If you prefer, you can keep the table in the altered form.

DAY

3

A.M.

5 **Modifying Table Properties**

P.M.

6 **Data Types and Validation**

Chapter 5

Modifying Table Properties

Yesterday was devoted to basic table-making, with an introduction to table field properties. Today's lesson builds directly on that foundation. This morning, you'll learn about the following:

- ☐ Adding data directly into a table
- ☐ Using an input mask
- ☐ The Field Size property
- ☐ Basic data-validation and default methods
- ☐ Rearranging field order in a table
- ☐ Altering the apparent size of a field
- ☐ List and combo boxes in tables

This might seem like a lot of territory to cover, but each new technique follows logically from the one that precedes it. The material about data validation, defaults, and input masks directly addresses the integrity of your data, so pay particular attention to those sections—especially if you're planning on creating a database application for others to use. Keep in mind that although much of this is rather dry, it's important.

Getting Started

The tables you made yesterday are empty storage units for the information you want to keep in an orderly fashion. Tables in and of themselves do nothing—it's the data they can store that's the heart of your database project. Entering data into a table is as simple as typing it in. Exercise 5.1 guides you through creating your first record with Access.

Exercise 5.1. Entering data directly into a table.

1. Launch Access, if you haven't already done so.

2. Open the College database by choosing File|Open from the menu, by choosing it as Access opens, or by clicking the Open Database button on the toolbar. (The Open Database button has an open folder as its icon.)

   When Access opens College, the Database window should be on the Table objects and the highlight on one of the tables. By default, Access shows database objects in alphabetical order at the Database window. If you want a particular table to appear at the end of the Database window's list, start its name with a *zz*. You can also hide a table from a casual user's view by prefacing the table name with *usys*. This hides the table unless a user changes Show System Objects to Yes in the Options menu.

   You can change the order of objects in the Database window by clicking the Details button in the toolbar, then selecting one of the other detail heads as the order in which to present the objects. Figure 5.1 shows the Database window with the Details button selected and the objects (in this case, the two tables) ordered by the date they were created. You can also see the Table Properties dialog box, where you can enter a description of any database object in the Database window. The Properties dialog box has a place to enter a description and also a check box to hide the database objects. To see the Properties box, right-click the object and choose Properties from the menu.

3. Highlight the StudentPersonal table. Click the Design button to open the table in Design View. Make sure the StudentID field has room for at least 11 characters; if not, modify it. Switch to Datasheet View by clicking the leftmost button in the toolbar, the one with the View tooltip. Datasheet View is the working view of a table. It means that the table's ready for data entry, editing, or viewing (as opposed to Design View, in which a table's open to modify its design). Your screen should resemble Figure 5.2.

Figure 5.1.

Details and properties of database objects.

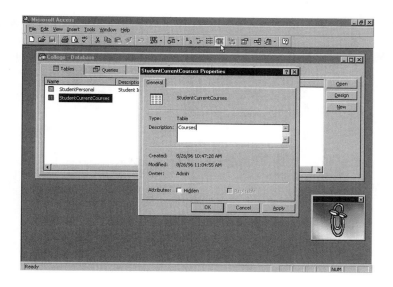

The next steps are easier if you click the maximize button in the StudentPersonal table's window. That's the middle button in the upper-right corner with a single window on it. If your middle button has two windows, your table's child window is already maximized.

Figure 5.2.

A table shown in Datasheet View.

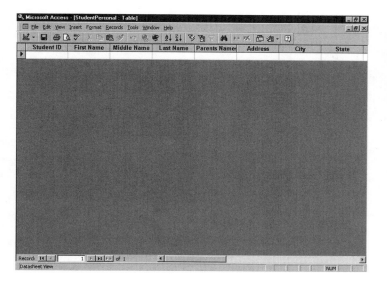

4. Your cursor will be in the first field, StudentID. Enter 999-11-0000 as the student ID for this record. The college has a policy of using a student's social security number as a student ID number. (The case of a student without a social security number is considered later in this chapter.)

5. After entering the student ID, press Tab or Enter to move on to the FirstName field and enter Bill.

In a similar manner, continue entering the following information for this record:

Table 5.1. Data for StudentPersonal table.

Field	Data
MiddleName	G.
LastName	Jones
ParentsNames	Joe and Mary
Address	545 Oak Street
City	Chicago
State	IL
ZipCode	39844
PhoneNumber	(317) 555-9873
EmailName	billg@speedy.fictional.edu
HomePage	http://www.fictional.edu/billg3.htm
Ethnicity	Anglo
Major	English
Note	Hobbies include woodworking and skiing

Entering data directly into a table is as easy as typing it in. However, doing it this way is, to say the least, inconvenient, and there's currently no way to make sure you're entering valid data. You also might have noticed that Access formatted several fields for you as you entered data. When the wizard created this table, it also formatted those fields—ZipCode and PhoneNumber—it knew would hold known data that use standard formatting. Since you specified Hyperlink as the field type for the HomePage field, Access created a link when you entered the URL for Jones's home page in the table.

Quality Assurance, Data-Entry Style

If the only thing you want Access to do is store raw data, you need go no further, but it's capable of much more. One of the ways in which an electronic storage system such as Access is superior to a paper-based system is that the electronic system can examine input and then, based on rules you supply, accept or reject it.

You can edit data in an Access table in much the same way you edit field names during the table design phase. Edit Bill Jones's StudentID by clicking in the StudentID field just to the right of the last zero. Drag the cursor all the way to the left of the StudentID number to highlight the entire field. Enter `Hello World!` and tab to the FirstName field. The text Hello World! replaced Bill's StudentID. Hello World! isn't anywhere close to a valid social security number or a student ID, but Access permitted it.

The reason Access accepted Hello World! as a StudentID is because you didn't tell it not to. Also, although each StudentID will follow the form of ###-##-#### (with data substituted for the # characters), you had to manually insert the dashes. You can solve the problems of having to insert dashes manually and of inappropriate entries at the same time. Before moving on, edit Bill's StudentID back to `999-11-0000`.

ACCESS JARGON

view: Access heavily utilizes the word *view*, which replaces the more descriptive term *mode* for many Access activities. So although you might think you are in Table Design *mode*, Access's term for this is Table Design *View*. This terminology seems to fit with Microsoft's corporate leadership in visual tools such as Visual Basic and Visual C++. The term *view* is certainly overused in Access, but once you get used to it…well, you'll be used to it.

ACCESS JARGON

input mask: Also called a field template, this is a set of literals and placeholders that control the data entered into a field. For example, the input mask that appears (###)###-#### uses the ( ) and the – characters as literals. The # is a placeholder for a number. As you likely can see, this input mask limits entry into this field to U.S.-style phone numbers.

Exercise 5.2 shows how to add an input mask.

Exercise 5.2. Adding an input mask.

1. Locate the Design or Datasheet View button on the toolbar (the button to the far left). When you're in Datasheet View, as now, this button has a pencil and a triangle on it. (See Figure 5.2.) When you're in Design View, it has a representation of a datasheet on it. At any time, you can click down this button's pull-down list to see all your current view options.

2. Click the Design View button to switch you from the table's Datasheet View to Design View. After the switch, your screen should look like Figure 5.3.

3. Click on the field name StudentID because you'll initially be setting a field property for this field. Clicking in the row with a field name tells Access to bring up the properties for this field.

4. Examine the Field Properties list box at the lower part of the table design grid. One of the properties is called Input Mask. Click in the now empty field just to the right of the Input Mask property label.

Figure 5.3.

The table returned to Design View.

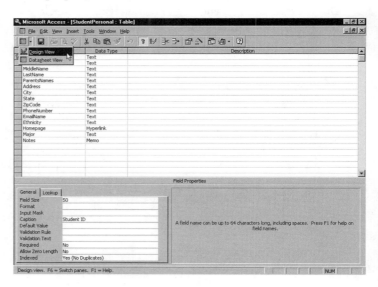

Note that when you clicked on the field for Input Mask, a button with three dots appeared to the right of the field. This is a *builder button*, and there are many of them scattered throughout Access. Clicking a builder button brings up an appropriate builder or wizard. At this point, clicking this button or the toolbar's build button brings up an Input Mask Builder Wizard. This exercise creates an input mask manually—even though the exact mask you'll build is available for the price of a few simple clicks in a wizard.

5. Enter `AAA-AA-AAAA;1;" "` for an input mask. The *A*'s in the input mask are place-holders indicating that you must enter a total of nine alphanumeric characters for this field. Press Tab to move to the next field. Access adds two backslashes before each dash, but otherwise accepts the entry.

Access Input Masks

Access input masks have three parts. The first part is the look of the mask. Entering `??-??` enables the acceptance of any four characters but separates them with a dash. Access added the backslash before each dash in Exercise 5.2 because the backslash indicates to Access that the next character should be literally interpreted. If you had an input mask such as `?\??`, Access would accept any two characters separated by a question mark.

The second part of the input mask comes after the semicolon. This can be blank, a numeral `1`, or a `0` (a zero). A blank or a `1` in this space tells Access to store only the field's data; a `0` tells Access to store not only the input data, but also the formatting characters.

The third and final part of an input mask tells Access what character to use as a placeholder. This example uses `" "`, or white space, to tell Access that you want blanks as placeholders.

After entering your input mask, your screen should resemble Figure 5.4.

Figure 5.4.

An input mask after Access inserts the literal characters.

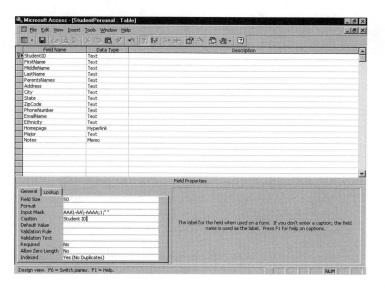

Trying Out the Input Mask

Return to Datasheet View by either clicking the Datasheet View button in the toolbar—it's the one second from the left—or choosing View|Datasheet from the menu. Access will tell you that you must save your changes before entering Datasheet View. Since that's what you want, click Yes.

Click on the StudentID field on row two of the table to get ready to enter a new record. Try to enter Hello World! Two things then happen. First, Access adds dashes after Hel and lo, and second, it refuses to accept the entire text. The input mask told Access to insert a dash after the third and fifth character and not to accept more than nine characters for this field.

You could have told Access to accept only numbers for this field, but that would have caused a problem with students (such as visiting exchange students) who don't have a social security number. For those students, the college generates a student ID based on the student's birthday and last name.

Here's how the college system works for students without a social security number: The college creates a student ID using the student's birth date in the form DDMMYY and the first three letters of the student's last name. For example, a student born on July 12, 1972, with the last name Johnson would have the StudentID of 071272JOH. A student born on May 5, 1967, having a last name of Smith would have a student ID of 050567SMI, and so on. Since alphabetic characters such as JOH and SMI might be included in the StudentID field, the input mask accepts letters as well as numbers.

Press Esc to cancel this record's data entry. Click back on the StudentID field for row two, enter the incomplete student ID 99998098, then press Tab or Enter. Access displays one of its standard message boxes telling you that your entry doesn't meet the requirement of the input mask you've defined. Click OK to acknowledge this message. Access refuses to accept a StudentID entry shorter than the input mask.

Press Esc to cancel data entry and return to Design View. Click on the PhoneNumber field to examine its Input-mask Field property. You will see !\(999") "000\-0000. The big difference between this and the previous input mask is that here Access has 9 and 0 as placeholders. The 9 means entry is optional, but must be numeric; the 0 means entry is mandatory and numeric. Unlike StudentID, this field won't accept alphabetic characters in the phone number, so it accepts phone numbers like (317) 555-1234, but not (317) KL5-1234. Return to Datasheet View. The ! tells Access to fill this field from right to left. This means that if you add a phone number without an area code, you'll get 555-1234 rather than (555) 123-4 as the entry for the field. The ! can appear anywhere in an input mask, but by convention usually appears first.

Add a second record to this table, using the data shown in Table 5.2.

Table 5.2. Data for StudentPersonal table.

Field	Data
StudentID	999-00-9800 (remember, don't add dashes)
FirstName	Mary
MiddleName	F.
LastName	Smith
ParentsNames	Marc and Shirley
Address	6 Tempest Way
City	Cairo
State	IL
Zip (PostalCode)	35854
PhoneNumber	(317) 555-9038
EmailName	`99955.495@compuserve.com`
HomePage	`http://www.fictional.edu/marysm34.htm`
Ethnicity	Indian
Major	Mathematics
Note	On full scholarship

Note how much easier it is to enter data when an input mask exists. At this point, the first record contains the literal dashes as part of the data, but the second doesn't. To make both records the same, delete the information for StudentID in the first record, then re-enter it the same way; however, this time Access will use the input mask you've made.

5

Ex Post Facto Input Masks

Input masks will operate only on newly added data. They won't go back and affect previously entered values.

Do   **Don't**

DO use input masks, especially in applications where you expect a lot of data entry, since they make data-entry chores much easier.

DON'T ignore the second part of the input-mask field. Generally speaking, you don't want to embed input-mask literals in your data, but if you do, you must tell Access specifically that you do.

Changing Field Order

Changing the order of fields in a table is something you might want to do from time to time. Keep in mind that the order in which fields appear in the design grid doesn't force you to have fields in the same order in Datasheet View, forms, or reports.

Moving a Field

Click the Design View button to bring up the table design grid. Exercise 5.3 moves the Major field to just under the PhoneNumber.

Exercise 5.3. Changing the field order of a table.

1. Click on the gray border just to the left of the field called Major. Access highlights the entire row, just as it did when you inserted or deleted a field. Your screen should now look like Figure 5.5.

Figure 5.5.

Getting ready to move a field.

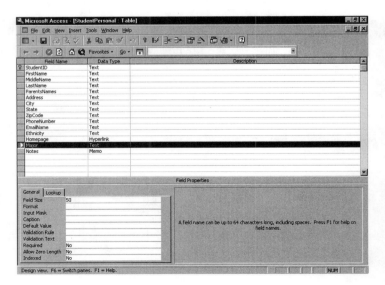

2. Release your mouse button, then move the cursor back to the gray area you clicked on to highlight the row. Make sure you've maneuvered the mouse so its cursor looks like a slightly left-leaning arrow.

3. Click your mouse again and hold. You should see a small "ghost" rectangle below the mouse cursor. This rectangle means you can now move the field. Keep the mouse button pressed down and drag the cursor up until the moving dark line appears just below the PhoneNumber field.

4. Release the mouse button to drop the Major field to the space below PhoneNumber. Your screen should now look like Figure 5.6.

5. Return to Datasheet View, telling Access it's OK when it reminds you that you must save changes before changing view.

6. Scroll over so you can see the PhoneNumber and the field just to its right. The field to the right of PhoneNumber is now Major rather than EmailName.

Figure 5.6.

A field moved and dropped to a new location.

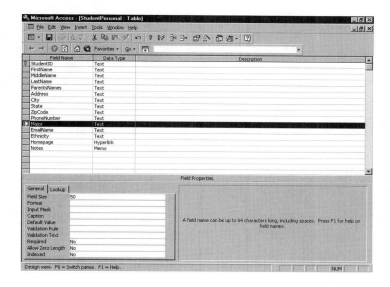

Changing the Apparent Field Order

When you change the field order in the field design grid, you also change the order in which the fields appear in Datasheet View. However, you can make changes in Datasheet View that won't change the field order in Database Design View, as Exercise 5.4 illustrates.

Exercise 5.4. Changing the apparent field order.

1. If you're not in Datasheet View, click on the toolbar or use the menu selections in the View menu to make that view current.

2. Click on the gray area just above the LastName field. This gray area has the label "LastName" in it. The entire LastName column will then be selected. (See Figure 5.7.)

Figure 5.7.

Getting ready to move a column in Datasheet View.

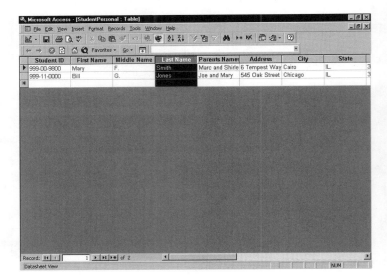

3. Move your cursor over the selected gray area again. You've hit the appropriate place when the cursor changes to look like a left-leaning arrow. Click again without moving the mouse, but this time hold the mouse button down. You'll get a "ghost" rectangle at the base of the cursor. Drag the cursor to the left until a black line appears between the fields StudentID and FirstName, then release the mouse.

   The LastName field now appears just to the right of the StudentID field. Your screen should look like Figure 5.8.

4. Switch to Design View. Note that the LastName field remains below the MiddleName field, just as it did before you moved it in the Datasheet View.

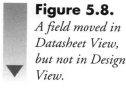

Figure 5.8.

A field moved in Datasheet View, but not in Design View.

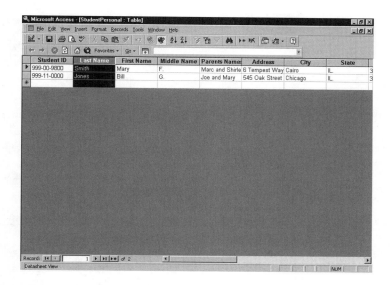

The Access Way

LastName or Last Name? You might wonder at Access's display of the LastName field as "Last Name" in the column head. The name of this field is LastName without spaces. The Caption property of the LastName field is Last Name with a space. Check it out yourself by switching to Design View for StudentPersonal, then examining the Caption property setting.

The Caption property tells Access how to display a field's name in tables and queries or by default in reports and forms.

When referring to this field in queries, reports, forms, code, or macros, use the real name of the field, LastName. The Caption property is only for show, not go.

Changing field locations or widths in the Datasheet View *does not* change their location in Design View, but changing field locations in Design View *does* change field locations in the Datasheet View.

Changing Field Widths and Row Heights

The Field Size property for Text fields determines the capacity of the fields but doesn't affect how wide they appear in the Datasheet View. Naturally, that leaves some fields looking too small and others too wide in the default Datasheet View. Changing apparent field sizes from Access's default in the Datasheet View is quite simple, as Exercise 5.5 demonstrates.

Exercise 5.5. Changing apparent field widths and height.

1. Return to Datasheet View, if you haven't already done so.

2. Most street addresses are longer than the default size Access has allowed for fields in the StudentPersonal table, so the next step shows you how to make this field look a bit wider.

   Move your cursor into the gray area where field names appear. Now move the cursor to a point between the Address and City fields. The cursor changes to a wide vertical beam with left- and right-facing arrows. (See Figure 5.9.)

Figure 5.9.

Getting ready to alter a field's width.

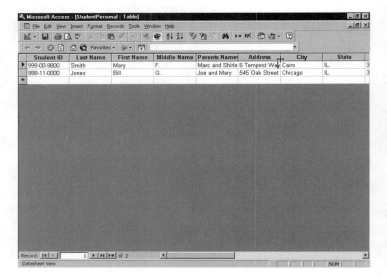

3. Click and hold the mouse button. Keeping the mouse button pressed down, drag the cursor to the right to widen the Address field. When it's roughly one-and-a-half times larger, release the mouse button. The field is now wide enough for most street addresses. (See Figure 5.10.)

   That's all there is to making a field wider. To make a field *deeper*—to increase row height—use the preceding steps, except move your cursor to the gray area left of the leftmost field. Then move the cursor between two rows until the cursor becomes a horizontal bar with up- and down-facing arrows. Click and drag the row to its new height.

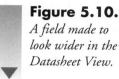

Figure 5.10.
A field made to look wider in the Datasheet View.

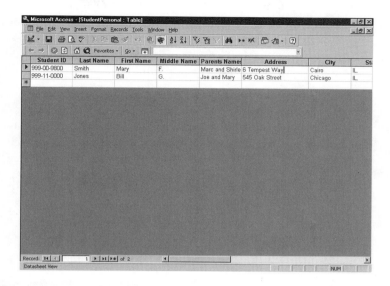

Access calls these appearance changes *layout changes*. When you close a table, Access asks whether you want to save these layout changes to field width and height. This gives you the freedom to make layout changes for a session, then discard them when closing the table. You can also accept Access's offer and make the changes permanent until the next datasheet session, when you again have the option to alter the layout.

You might wonder why you'd ever want to change a row height in a datasheet, but there are two common uses for greater row height. If you store pictures in a database, the standard row height won't show them very well, so increasing it is just the ticket. Also, if you have long Text or Memo field entries, trying to view those entries in one long text row is impractical. If you change the row height to accommodate more than one line, Access wraps the long text entry to fit in as many lines as you want.

Well, that's it for now. Close the StudentPersonal table. When Access asks whether you want to save the layout changes, click No.

Combo and List Boxes in Tables

It's easier and safer to add or edit table data through forms, but Microsoft responded to user requests and has, in Access 95 and now repeated in Access 97, made entering data directly into tables easier. The reasons to use forms for data entry or editing are discussed in the chapters that address forms, but if you're determined to manipulate tables directly, here are a few things to make your life easier.

In addition to input masks and other data-validation services covered this morning, you'll see how Access 97 enables you to look up existing data in another table when entering data directly into a table. Here's a quick look at how this works. Although this isn't an "official" exercise, feel free to follow along with these steps.

You don't want to add data in the StudentCurrentCourses table for a nonexistent student—that is, one not already entered in the StudentPersonal table. When you established a link between the StudentPersonal and StudentCurrentCourses tables in Exercise 4.4, you made sure this couldn't occur because you checked the Enforce Referential Integrity check box.

However, looking up the right StudentID when entering data in StudentCurrentCourses can be a royal pain. Again, these chores should be handled only through forms, but here's how to simplify the task using only tables.

1. Open the StudentCurrentCourses table in Design View. If you're at the Database window, highlight (click on) the StudentCurrentCourses table and click the Design button. Your screen should look like Figure 5.11.

Figure 5.11.

Adding lookup ability in tables in the Design View.

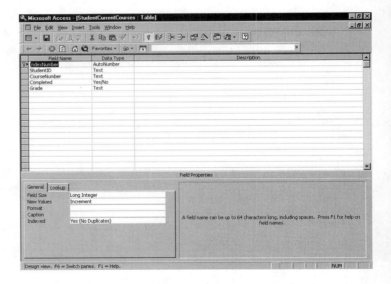

2. Click in the StudentID field, then click the Lookup tab in the Field Properties section. Click the pull-down icon in the Display Control field and select Combo Box. The screen then changes to accommodate the needs of a combo box in a table.

The Access Way

Several fields in this and other Properties list boxes are toggles—fields with a few possible entries. These entries are often limited to two: Yes and No. To change a Yes/No entry in a Properties list box from one to the other, double-click in the field where the Yes/No entry is.

3. Change the properties for the Lookup tab to match Figure 5.12.

Figure 5.12.

Setting the properties for a table combo box.

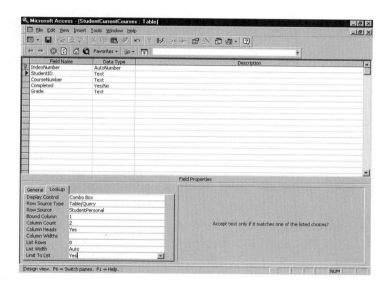

4. Switch to Datasheet View, saving the changes. Widen the StudentID field to about twice its default size, then move to the StudentID field. Note that a pull-down icon appears when the field has the focus. Click on this icon to see all the StudentIDs currently in StudentPersonal, along with the first names of the students for each StudentID. (See Figure 5.13.) Naturally, if you wanted to use this feature for real data entry, you'd arrange StudentPersonal to show the LastName field next to StudentID rather than the FirstName one.

5. Return to Design View and undo the Lookup properties set in the previous four steps to get your database back in sync with the book's. The easiest way to do this is to change the Display Control property back to Text Box.

Figure 5.13.

A combo box in a table.

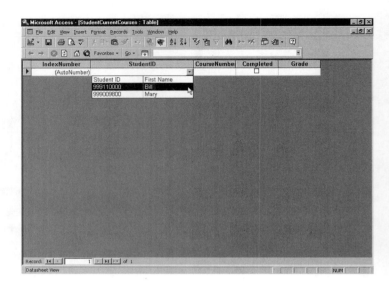

Morning Summary

This morning you reviewed how to enter data directly into tables, how to create an input mask to format data's appearance, and how to change the look of tables by altering the order and width of columns or the height of rows.

5

Chapter **6**

Data Types and Validation

This afternoon's lesson delves deeper into the important subject of table field properties. Specifically, it covers the following:

- ☐ The field properties for different data types
- ☐ Setting a default value for a field
- ☐ The differences in the Field Size property for Number and Text data type fields
- ☐ The Format property
- ☐ The Validation Data property
- ☐ The Validation Text property

More on Field Properties

This morning, you saw how adding an input mask to a field can make data entry easier and help make sure the data entered into that field is appropriate. The term *data integrity* is database jargon for ensuring that data entered into a database is correct not only for the field and table, but also for the database in general. There are several other field property settings that can make your data entry easier and/or ensure your data's integrity. Take a look at these properties by doing this: Open the StudentPersonal table in Design View, click on the FirstName field, and look at the Field Properties list box. If you maximize the design grid window, your screen should resemble Figure 6.1.

Figure 6.1.

The properties for a field with the data type Text.

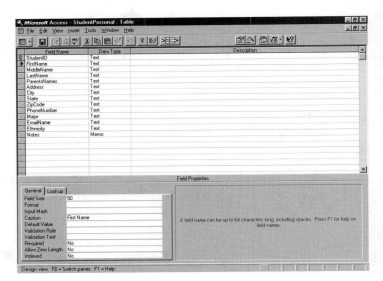

Now click on the field called Notes. The Properties list box changes to list only those field properties that a Memo field can have. Click on the field called State, and the list box switches back to Text data type properties.

Each data type has a particular set of properties associated with it. The Notes field lacks an Index property because you can't index a field with the data type Memo. Figures 6.2 through 6.10 show the field properties associated with the different field types in Access.

6

Figure 6.2.

*The field properties of a
Text data type.*

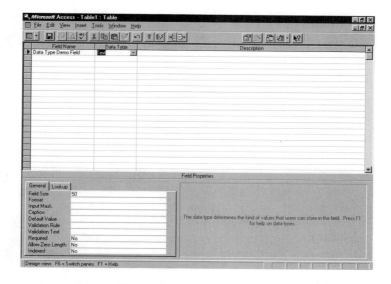

Figure 6.3.

*The field properties of a
Memo data type.*

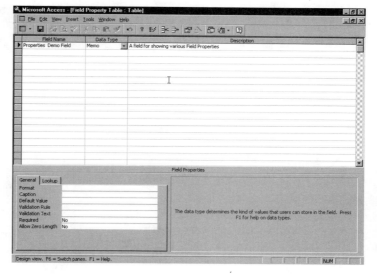

Figure 6.4.

*The field properties of a
Number data type.*

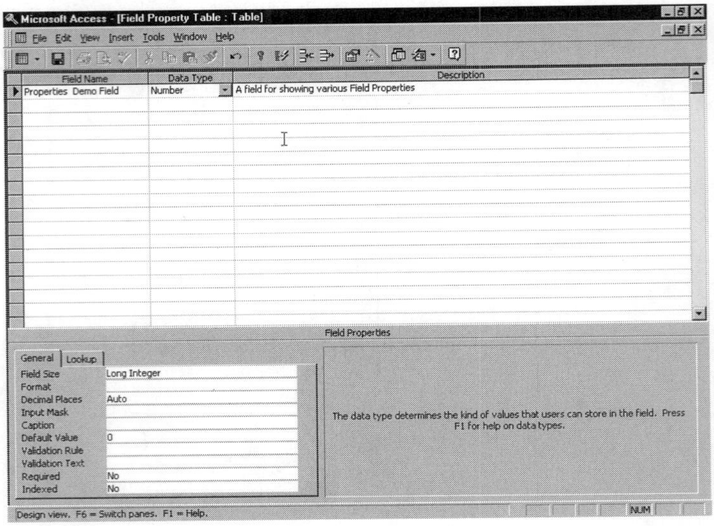

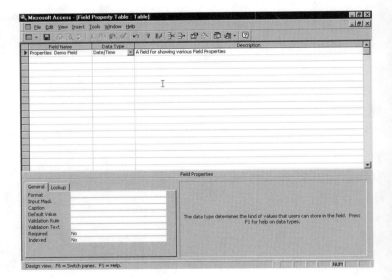

Figure 6.5.

*The field properties of a
Date/Time data type.*

Figure 6.6.

The field properties of a Currency data type.

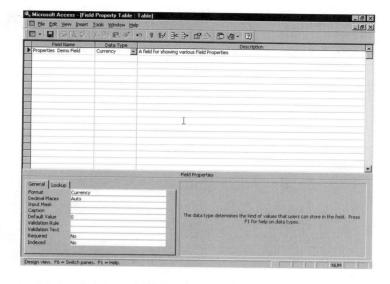

Figure 6.7.

The field properties of an AutoNumber data type.

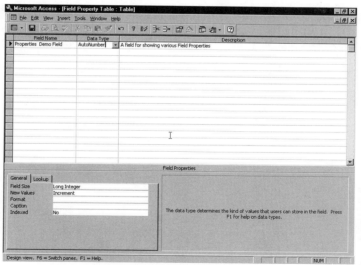

Figure 6.8.

The field properties of a Yes/No data type.

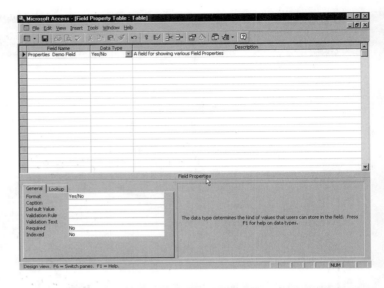

Figure 6.9.

The field properties of an OLE data type.

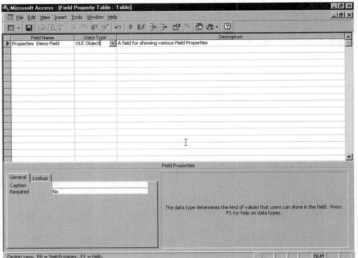

Figure 6.10.

The field properties of a Hyperlink data type.

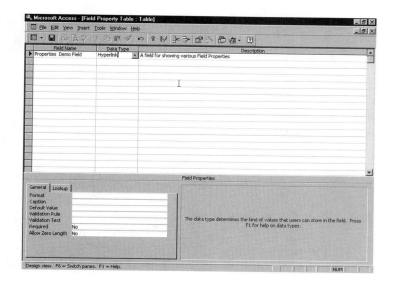

The last entry in the Data Type list, Lookup Wizard, isn't strictly a data type; it's a wizard used to have a field look up data existing in another table.

Most of the field properties for each data type are at least somewhat self-explanatory from their labels, but one isn't. In a Text data type, the field size means the amount of space that Access allows for an entry. Therefore, a text field with a field size of 5 can't hold the 11-space text entry "Hello World!" (The blank and the exclamation point each take one space, too.)

Take a look at Figure 6.4, which shows the field properties for a Number data type. There's an entry for field size there too, but in the case of a Number data type, field size has a completely different meaning than it does for a Text data type. Field size in a Number data type means number precision. The various field sizes for a Number data type are as follows:

Byte: Whole numbers from 0 to 255.

Integer: Whole numbers from -32,768 to 32,767.

Long Integer: Whole numbers from -2,147,483,648 to 2,147,483,647.

Double: Decimal numbers with 10 places of precision.

Replication ID: A very long number used to uniquely identify a record. The length of this number should prevent another record from having the identical number. The common name for a Replication ID is GUID, for Globally Unique Identifier.

Single: Decimal numbers with 8 places of precision.

6

Each of these field sizes requires a different amount of storage in your computer. For example, Access reserves eight bytes of space for a number with a field size of "double," but only a single byte for a number with the field size of "byte."

The reason for having large field-size type numbers, such as single and double, is to ensure precision in calculations. The more precisely a number is stored in Access, the more precise the calculations using that number will be. This is particularly important in repeating calculations (or more precisely, recursive calculations), in which the results of one calculation are fed back in for further iterations. The most common recursive calculations are interest calculations, which add a period's interest to the principal to form the basis of the principal for the next period's calculation.

It's Default of Access

The default value for a field is a handy property; when you specify one, Access automatically supplies that value during data entry. One helpful feature of default values is that you can override them, so setting defaults causes no penalty in your application.

Do	Don't

DO assign default values liberally in your applications. Even if you override them most of the time, you'll end up saving time overall.

DON'T be concerned about potential penalties or "gotchas" that a default field value might create. There are none.

This example's fictional college is in southern Illinois, and most of the students are from Illinois. Therefore, it makes sense to set the default value to IL for the State field in the StudentPersonal table. Exercise 6.1 shows how it's done.

Exercise 6.1. Setting a Default Field property.

1. Make sure the StudentPersonal table is open in Design View.
2. Click on the State field in the Field Name column.
3. Click in the Default Value area of the Field Properties list box.
4. Enter IL for a value. (See Figure 6.11.)

   It's that easy. Note that Access surrounds IL with quotation marks after you leave the field.

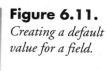

Figure 6.11.
Creating a default value for a field.

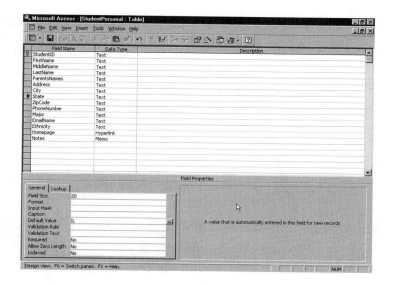

5. Now switch back to Datasheet View, saving the changes when Access reminds you that you must. Enter a record with the following data:

Table 6.1. Data for StudentPersonal table.

Field	Data
StudentID	999-11-9800
FirstName	Greg
MiddleName	J.
LastName	Jefferson
ParentsNames	George and Martha
Address	893 Main Street
City	Daytona
State	IL
ZipCode	35888
PhoneNumber	(317) 555-2983
Major	Speech
EmailName	gregj@speedy.fictional.edu
HomePage	http://www.fictional.edu/gregger.htm
Ethnicity	Black
Note	Honor society candidate

Did you notice that before you got to the State field, Access not only filled in this field for Jefferson's record but subsequent records as well? Look at Figure 6.12, which shows how Access is now supplying a default value for the State field.

6. Here's how to use a field with a default value. If the record you're entering uses the default value, just tab or hit Enter when you get into this field. If you need to change the default value to another, just tab into the field with the default value and enter the right data.

Figure 6.12.

The Default Field property in action.

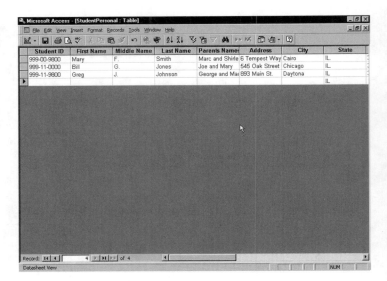

ACCESS JARGON

default: If you're bothered by the term *default* for a value that's automatically assigned by Access to a field, you're not alone. Default, which means "failing in an obligation" to most English speakers, is standard computerese for any automatically assigned value. This is one term that the Access team didn't make up. It's borrowed from a long-standing computer tradition.

Data Validation

In many cases, you'll want to limit field entries to one or a specific group of selections. One way to do this in Access is to set the Data Validation field property. The exercise that follows isn't an optimal use of the Data Validation property—it was chosen for its simplicity—but working through it and reviewing the table of data-validation examples will give you a good idea of this field property's use.

Exercise 6.2. Setting the Data Validation field property.

This exercise limits the possible entries for the Ethnicity field to ensure data consistency. A data-entry person might enter any of the following for the ethnicity Anglo:

> White
>
> white
>
> Caucasian
>
> Anglo
>
> European extraction

When the college makes certain government reports, it must group students by ethnicity. If data-entry people are free to enter their own terms for identifying ethnicity, extracting and grouping this data will be an enormous chore, since you'll have to tell Access to extract any possible values for all the possible ethnic labels data-entry people might use. So for this table, confine the permissible entries to the following: Anglo for all non-Hispanics of European heritage, Hispanic for those of Spanish heritage, Black for those of African heritage, Asian for those of Asian heritage, and Indian for those of Native American heritage. This system doesn't pretend to meet actual government-reporting criteria; it simply illustrates how to set a Data Validation field property.

1. Get the StudentPersonal table to Design View, if it isn't there already.
2. Click on the Ethnicity field to let Access know you want to set a field property for this field.
3. Click the Validation Rule property.
4. Enter one of the following: `Anglo Hispanic`, `Black`, `Indian`, or `Asian`.
5. Tab to move away from this field.

Access will alter the Validation Rule to proper syntax, which in this case is `"Anglo"` or `"Hispanic"` or `"Black"` or `"Indian"` or `"Asian"`. When Access checks for these validations, the check is not case-sensitive. (See Figure 6.13.)

Figure 6.13.

Adding Validation Rule properties to a table.

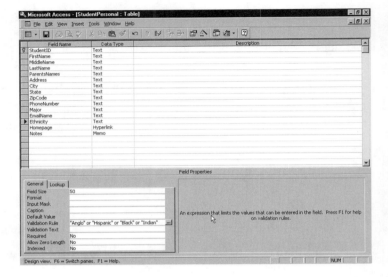

6. Return to Datasheet View, saving the changes when Access reminds you that you haven't. Access displays an additional message box reminding you that data-validation rules have changed, and some previously entered data might not meet the new criteria. It asks permission to search previous field entries to see whether they meet the new criteria. Click No, then move to and double-click on the Ethnicity field for Jefferson. Edit this field to read `White`.

7. Try to tab away from this field. Access gives a slightly rude and oddly worded, but informative, message box saying that the new entry violates the data-validation rule for this field. Click OK, and then press Esc to return this value to its original entry.

In Exercise 6.3, you'll change the error message from Access's choice to a custom one.

Exercise 6.3. Making a data validation error message.

1. Return to Design View, click on Ethnicity, then click on the field property Validation Text.

2. Enter `Please enter one of these values: Anglo, Black, Hispanic, Asian, or Indian for this field.`

3. If it bothers you that you can't see all the text you're entering, press Shift+F2 to enter the Zoom view. This gives you a large editing area for entering this message. When you're done editing and entering your new message, just click OK to exit Zoom view.

4. When you're through entering the validation text, return to Datasheet View. Click OK when Access gives you the save reminder.

5. Repeat the procedure you used when trying to change Jefferson's Ethnicity value from `Black` to `White`. Access still won't accept the entry because it violates the validation rule you set, but this time it gives you your custom message-box message. Click OK to close the message box, then press Esc to return Jefferson's Ethnicity field to its original value.

The following table lists some additional examples of validation rules for table fields.

Table 6.2. Validation Rule examples.

Example	Meaning
=5	Must be 5.
Between 1 and 5	Between 1 and 5 inclusive.
Between #2/3/90# AND #1/31/92#	Any date from February 3, 1990 to January 31, 1992, inclusive.
Like "A[a-z]B"	Must begin with the letter *A*, contain any letter from *a* to *z* as the second letter, and end with *B*.
Like "V####"	Must start with *V* followed by four digits. Valid entries are V5888, V9023, or V0000, for example.
="USA"	Must be USA.
In ("Arizona", "New Mexico")	Can be either New Mexico or Arizona.
Not "New York"	Any entry that's not New York.
Not Between 1 and 10	Any number not between 1 and 10 inclusive.

The Required Property

The Required property is another field property you'll use extensively. This field property extends for all field types. It's somewhat self-explanatory. Access won't accept a record without an entry in the field or fields where this property is set to Yes.

A Date-Specific Property

The Date/Time data type has several predefined Format properties. Figure 6.14 is a sample table in Design View with the Format property combo box pulled down to show the different predefined formats along with their examples.

All data types have a Format property, and the Date/Time data type has several predefined formats. These are as many as most people need, but you can create your own formats. For information on this, search online help using "Format" as a search criteria.

Figure 6.14.

The formats for the Date/Time data type.

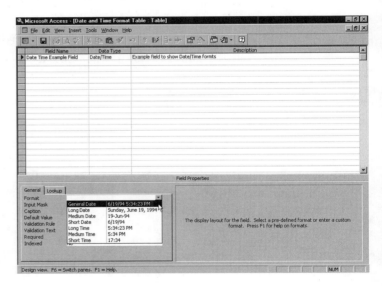

Two Number-Specific Properties

As discussed previously, the Number data type has the Field Size property, which is different from the Field Size for Text fields. If left to default, Access will choose Long Integer for the field size of a number. This is the most commonly used Number field size and is fairly economical in database resources. If you're sure all your numerical data for a particular number field will be whole (that is, nondecimal numbers), specify Byte or Integer or leave things at Long Integer for this property. If you need decimal precision, use Single or Double, depending on how much precision you need.

There's one caution here: When you're going to relate two fields and the key field on the "one" side of a one-to-many relationship is an AutoNumber data type set to Increment, the matching field in that case is Long Integer. Therefore, if your primary field in a relationship is AutoNumber-Increment, make the data type and format of its link field a data type Number with Field Size Long Integer.

The other special property for Number fields, one that they share with the Currency data type, is the Decimal Places property. Access defaults to Auto for a Decimal Places field property. Auto means that the format for the field (that is, what it looks like) determines the number of decimal places shown. Keep in mind that the number of decimal places shown doesn't change the precision of the number. A number with the field size Double will double the precision no matter what the Decimal Place property is set to.

That's it for the discussion of field properties. This is a vital part of Access since tables hold the data for any of your applications. Because of this, any topics relating to tables will have far-reaching ramifications in an Access project.

Day Summary

Changing the location of a field in the table design grid changes its location in the Datasheet View. You can also change a field's location and size in the Datasheet View, but doing so won't affect either the field's position in the design grid or the Field Size property.

Access has many settings for different field properties. You can specify a default value for a field that you can override or a validation rule that you can't. Access gives you an informative (but abrupt) error message if you try to enter a value in a table that violates data validation rules. You can change this message to one of your own choosing by adding a Validation Text property.

One of the most commonly used field properties is the Required property. If you set this property to Yes, Access requires an entry in this field before accepting a record. Key fields have their Required property set to Yes by inference.

Fields with the Number data type use the property called Field Size to specify how much precision they have. This directly affects the amount of data storage space Access reserves for entries in this field. Although Double is the most precise field size for the Number data type, letting all your number fields remain at the default Long Integer size isn't right for all occasions, even though it's commonly used. Try to use the most economical field size for your numbers consistent with your need for precision.

6

NOTE

> Past versions of Access used Double as the default Number data type. If you've used Access in the past, watch out for this "gotcha."

The Number and Currency data types share the property called Decimal Places. This controls how the data appears, not the underlying precision of the field.

Finally, the Date/Time data type has some unique format properties predefined. You can show data in Access by using these predefined format types or you can define your own.

Q&A

Q If I change the size and location of a field in Datasheet View, will Access preserve those changes?

A When you close the datasheet, Access asks whether you want to save your layout changes. If you click Yes, those changes will be preserved; otherwise, they'll be discarded.

Q Can I enter decimal numbers in a field with the data type Integer?

A You can enter them, but Access rounds them off to the next highest whole number.

Q Can I enter fractions, such as 1/2, in a number field?

A Access has no native way to accept fractions in a number field. You can enter 1/2 in a Text field as a text entry, but you can't use it in calculations since it's a text value. However, you can enter the value 1/2 in a Number field by entering its decimal equivalent, .5.

Q Can I change data type for a field after I've already entered some values?

A Yes, but you might lose data. For example, consider a Text data type field containing numbers for all records except one that reads Sam. Converting the data type from Text to Number will cause you to lose the Sam entry. Access gives plenty of warnings before it discards any of your data, but if you insist, it will go ahead with the conversion.

Q How can I delete a record from a table?

A Click to the left of the leftmost column in the gray area. This is called the *record selector section*. The record next to which you clicked is then selected. Press the Del or Delete key to delete this record. If you want to delete a series of records, you can click and drag on the record selector to choose many records. If you want to delete records according to a criterion (such as all records with a date older than 2/3/94), you'll need to perform a Delete action query. This topic is covered in Chapter 16, "More Advanced Queries."

Workshop

Here's where you can test and apply the lessons you learned today.

Quiz

Possible answers to these questions are given in Appendix A. If you need to research any of these answers, try online help or ask the Office Assistant.

1. You're in Datasheet View. How can you tell when your cursor is located in the correct position to change a field's apparent width? Apparent height?

2. Will moving a field in Datasheet View change that field's position in the table design grid?

3. Will the validation rule "A#" accept the value A1?

4. If you set a Default property for a field, can you override it during normal data entry? If not, what must you do to override the default value?

5. Will the validation rule "Between #1/2/90# and #2/1/90#" accept the value 1/5/91?

6. Why bother making input masks?

Put Access into Action

1. Open the StudentPersonal table in Design View.

2. Change the default value for City from blank to Chicago.

3. Try entering a record using data of your own. Did the default value work? Delete this record by clicking on the gray area just to the left of the record (the record selector) and pressing the Delete key. Confirm with Access that you want to delete this record.

4. (This one is a toughie.) Return to Design View. Using the following bits of information, design an input mask that allows up to 12 letters for any entry in the FirstName field, capitalizes the first letter of the name automatically, and enters the rest of the name in lowercase. The following are some characters used in input masks and their meanings:

   > means what follows in the mask is uppercase

   L means you must enter a letter

   < means what follows is lowercase

   ? means any character or space including blanks

   If you need to, search the online help system, using the key words "input mask," or ask the Office Assistant for a hint.

6

5. Delete the input mask for the FirstName field. (Optional.)

6. Close the StudentPersonal table, saving or discarding changes (depending on what you chose to do in step 6). Exit Access.

DAY 4

A.M.

7 An Introduction to Forms and Form Controls

P.M.

8 A Look into Queries

Chapter **7**

An Introduction to Forms and Form Controls

This morning's subject—an introduction to forms and form controls—is a lot more interesting and just plain more fun than what came yesterday. Forms are, primarily, attractive ways to show, edit, or enter data. Beyond that, forms have intrinsic properties that help in database administration by making forms the right way to enter data into tables. Today is a long day, but the topic is light and enjoyable.

This morning, you'll learn the following:

☐ What a form is

☐ How to make a quick form

☐ How to navigate in Form and Datasheet Views

☐ How to use a Form Wizard

☐ How to add data to the new form

□ What form control properties are
□ The meaning of bound and unbound controls
□ How to manipulate form controls
□ How to select more than one control at a time
□ How to add a control to a form
□ How to delete form controls
□ How to change the appearance of form controls

What's a Form?

A *form* is an array of controls you use to view, add, or edit data in Access. You've seen that you can view, add, or edit data in Datasheet View, so you might wonder why you should bother with forms if they only shadow what can be done without them. There are two fundamental reasons to use forms:

1. They make the job of editing, adding, and viewing data easier.
2. They add many features and capacities beyond what a datasheet can do when it comes to adding, editing, or viewing data.

When you see all the features you can add to your database by using forms, you'll want to use them in even your simplest database applications.

ACCESS JARGON

controls: Controls are objects on forms or reports that enable you to access data or manage the form or report. Examples of form controls are text boxes, combo boxes, check boxes, and command (push) buttons.

Making a Form

In the bad old days of B.A.—Before Access—creating database forms was something of a chore. It has been said that compared to other database systems, Access requires a lot of computer horsepower to run. That's true, but the reason Access requires so much computer power is that, compared to lesser products, you can do many more things with it. Form design is one of those areas where Access shines, partly because of its excellent design and partly because it's a native Windows application.

You paid a lot of money for a computer that could run Access well; now you're about to reap some benefits from that investment. Watch how easily Access handles the job of making a simple data-entry form in Exercise 7.1.

Exercise 7.1. An instant form.

EXERCISE

1. Launch Access and open the College database.
2. Open the StudentPersonal table in Datasheet View.
3. Locate the New Object button on the toolbar. See Figure 7.1 for help if you have trouble finding it. Pull down this button's list and select AutoForm.

Figure 7.1.

Starting an instant form from the Datasheet View.

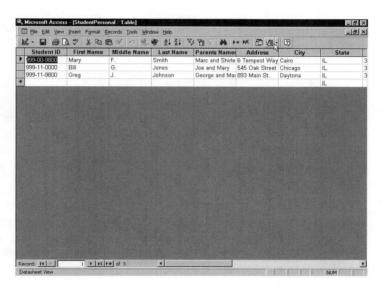

4. Click on the AutoForm choice. Access takes some time to process your request. When it's done, your screen should resemble Figure 7.2. If your screen varies somewhat, try maximizing it by using the button in the upper-right corner of the form's window.

7

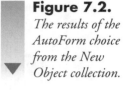

Figure 7.2.

The results of the AutoForm choice from the New Object collection.

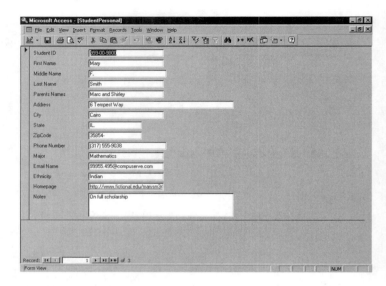

Does Your Screen Look Different?

The screens shown in this book have all been shot at the common super-VGA resolution of 800×600. Your video adapter might be set to any of several other resolutions, such as 640×480 or 1024×768. The numbers in these resolutions represent the number of dots your screen shows horizontally and vertically, so a 640×480 screen has 640 dots along the horizontal plane and 480 dots along the vertical.

If your screen shows more or less than the standard screens in this book, your displays will differ, perhaps significantly, from those shown. Most displays today use the standard VGA or higher. Windows 95 itself seems sized to look best at 800×600, which is the reason these screens were shot at this resolution. If your screen has a higher resolution than standard, it'll hold more information and in effect, you'll have a wider view of Access than what's shown in the figures.

That's it. You've just created your first form in Access.

Looking Over the Form

Using the AutoForm button in the toolbar is the same as using the Auto option in Form Wizard. (You'll learn about interacting with the wizard a little later.) Refer to Figure 7.2 or your screen. You might recognize the data shown in the new form as the first record in the

StudentPersonal table. If your screen has less real estate than the one used for this book, not all the fields might be shown because the AutoForm button simply stacks fields and doesn't try to fit them all on one screen.

In this form's case, the EmailName, Ethnicity, HomePage, and Note fields might be wholly or partially below the form's "horizon" if you're using a screen of less than 800×600. Figure 7.3 has been artificially manipulated to show this case. If you have any fields below the form's horizon, click near the bottom on the vertical scrollbar to the extreme right of the display. Access moves the thumb button on the scrollbar down and reveals the last three fields—but at the cost of hiding the first four, this time above the horizon. Your scrolled screen should now reveal the bottom fields.

Figure 7.3.

The form in 800×600 resolution with several fields below the bottom of the screen.

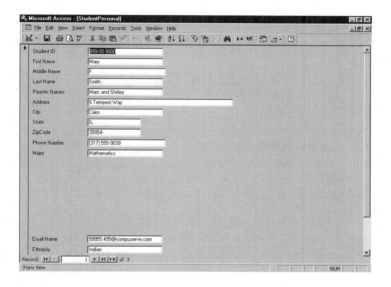

You use the scrollbars in Access to navigate around a form within a particular record. Click toward the top of the vertical scrollbar and Access moves the form upward; click the bottom and it moves the form downward.

Moving to New Records

Although you can navigate through your records in Access forms in several different ways, the simplest method is using the VCR buttons at the bottom of the screen, right above the status line. These VCR buttons, or record navigation buttons, are to the right and left of the specific record count box. In Figures 7.2 and 7.3, the specific record box tells you that you're at Record 1 of 3. This means the record set supplying the data for this form has three records and you're looking at the first one.

Clicking the inner-right VCR button, the one just to the right of the numeral 3, moves you one record down in the record set. Try it yourself. After you click this button, your screen will bring up the record for Mary Smith, and the specific record count box will read "Record 2 of 3." This is the "move one record forward" button. Its equivalent for moving one record back is to the left of the numeral 1 and looks the same (except it faces in the opposite direction).

The VCR button to the right looks like the "move one forward" button, except that it has a vertical bar added to its graphic. This is the "jump to the last record" button. Similarly, there's an opposite-facing button to the left that moves you to the first record. Try clicking the button that moves you to the end of your records, then click the left button to move to the first record. Your screen should again look like Figure 7.2. The navigation button to the far right, the one with the asterisk (star), is a "jump to new record" button. Clicking this button takes you to a blank record, ready for new data entry.

Some Alternative Navigation Methods

To navigate quickly around a form, you can use the keyboard, the menus, or the toolbar.

Keyboard Shortcut

If you know the record number you want to get to, Access has an express train you can ride to it. Press the F5 key and you'll find yourself in the Record box with the current record highlighted, as shown in Figure 7.4.

Notice two things. First, the number 1 in the notation "Record: 1 of 3" has the highlight. Second, the status bar directly under this section of the screen reads "Enter New Value." Enter a number from 1 to 3, press Enter, and Access will immediately jump to that record.

Menu Shortcut

Under the Edit menu, click on the menu choice Go To. (See Figure 7.5.) Clicking on the different choices from this pop-up menu enables you to move through your records almost instantly.

Figure 7.4.

Speeding to a record number.

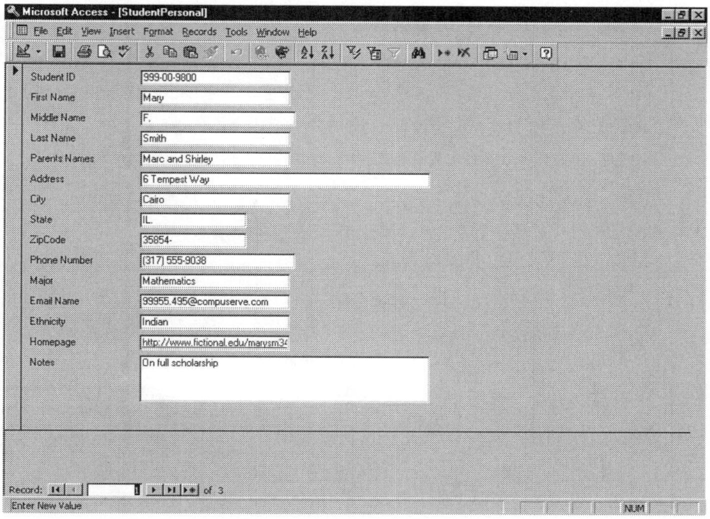

Figure 7.5.

Using the menu to navigate through records.

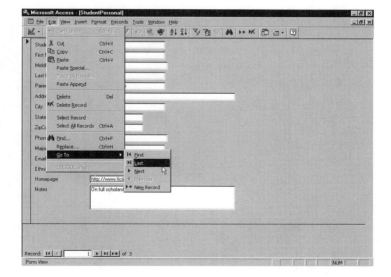

Toolbar Shortcut

The standard toolbar for forms has two buttons used for record navigation. The "move to new record" button is the one with a right-facing triangle and an asterisk; when you click that button, Access moves you to a new blank record. You can enter data in this new blank record just as you can on a blank line in the Datasheet View.

The leftmost toolbar button is the View Selection button. The choices on the pull-down menu for this button vary, depending on where you are in Access. When in Form View, you can quickly switch to Datasheet View by pulling down this button, then clicking on the Datasheet View choice. Figure 7.6 shows the results of clicking the Datasheet View button while viewing Record 2 of 3 in the StudentPersonal table's form.

Figure 7.6.

The jump to Datasheet View from the Form View.

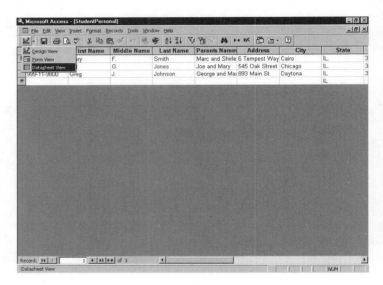

Note that Access kept track of where you were when jumping to that new view. If you were on Record 2 of StudentPersonal, you remained there after the jump to Datasheet View. Click on the StudentID field in the last record, the one for Greg Johnson.

Do	Don't

DO use whatever navigating method you prefer to move around your records.

DON'T think there's an absolute right or wrong way. The right way for you is the way you like; the wrong way is the way you dislike.

Now pull down the selector and click the Form View choice. Access returns you to Form View, but with Johnson's record (Record 3) now the current one. (See Figure 7.7.)

Figure 7.7.

Jumping back from Datasheet to Form View.

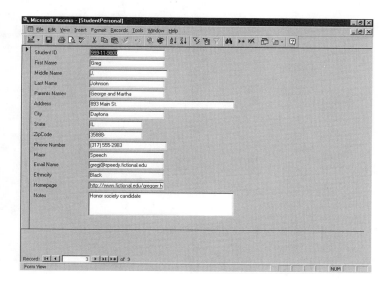

Making a Form by Using a Wizard

Close the AutoForm either by choosing File|Close from the menu or by double-clicking on the form's Control menu icon or the × button. When Access asks whether you want to save the form, click No. Close the StudentPersonal table if it's open.

Back at the Database View, click on the Form tab, the one that's third in the Database View. Click the New button to start a new form, which launches the form-making process.

Exercise 7.2 shows how to use a wizard to make a form.

Exercise 7.2. Using a wizard to make a form.

EXERCISE

1. Pull down the Select A Table/Query combo box toward the bottom of the dialog box and click on StudentPersonal, then click on Form Wizard. Your screen should look like Figure 7.8.

2. Click the OK button to start the wizard process for a form based on the StudentPersonal table. The Form Wizard choice is a general-purpose wizard with more flexibility than the different AutoForm choices. Your first choice is what fields to include in the form. You have the option of including fields from more than one table or query. At this point, if the term *query* is unfamiliar to you, don't worry. You'll get an introduction to queries this afternoon.

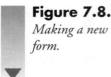

Figure 7.8.
Making a new form.

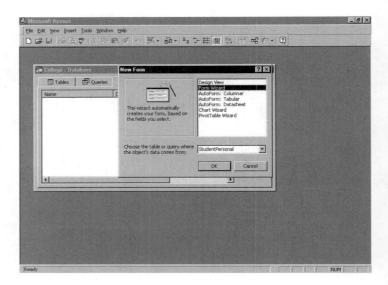

The Access Way

There are design and cosmetic differences between the forms made by using the AutoForm toolbar button and those made by choosing any of the AutoForm choices from the Form|New menu selection. However, the AutoForms function similarly no matter how they are created.

3. Forms don't have to include all the fields from the table or query on which they're based (bound). In some cases, you should restrict the fields on a form because you don't want unauthorized viewing of certain fields in a table. You'll be using this form for entering and editing records in all fields, so click the >> button to add all the fields from StudentPersonal to this new form.

4. Click the Next> button to move on.

5. This next dialog box gives you choices about the form's layout. Experiment by clicking on the various option buttons in this dialog box to see what they mean. When you're satisfied as to what each choice will give you, click the Columnar option button, then click the Next> button to move on.

6. The next dialog box gives you some options as to the look of your form (this example uses International). Click the Next> button and edit the suggested name for this form to read Student Personal Data. Make sure you've chosen or left the top option button selected. Your screen should look like Figure 7.9.

7. Click the Finish button. When Access finally displays a form, your screen should resemble Figure 7.10.

Making a basic form by using a wizard is just that simple. Consider yourself a master of the simple Form Wizard.

Figure 7.9.

The final dialog box for a Form Wizard.

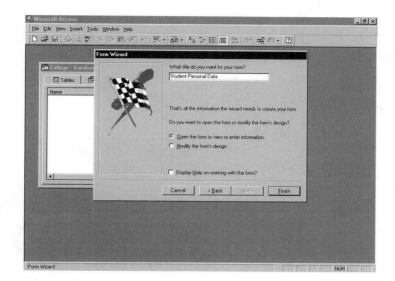

Figure 7.10.

The finished form. Your results will vary, based on your screen resolution and the choice you made for a background.

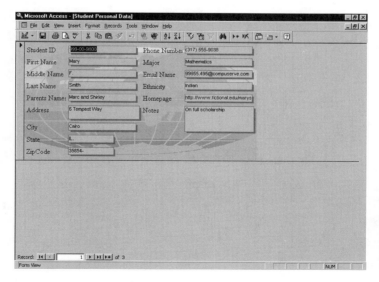

Adding Data Through a Form

Click on the menu choice, toolbar, or navigation button to move to a new (blank) record, using the navigation method you prefer. Enter the record shown in Figure 7.11. After you've entered the data for a field, you can move to the next empty field by hitting either the Tab key or Enter.

Notice that Access preserved the input mask for both the Phone Number and StudentID fields. Also note the scrollbars that appear when you enter either the Address or Notes field.

Try editing Ogur's Ethnicity field to Chinese. Access will give you the same error message it would if you tried doing this in the Datasheet View. Press Esc to return her Ethnicity field to Anglo.

Figure 7.11.

A new record entered through a form.

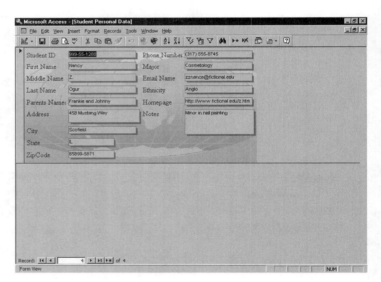

The Access Way

Access preserves your table's field properties when you use the table in a Form View. You also can add many other properties exclusive to a particular form. These form properties are in addition to the underlying properties you already set when designing your table.

7

Form Control Properties

Just as you can manually design a table, you can manually design a form. The selector button on the far left of the toolbar pulls down in Form View just as in the other views you've seen. Click that button now to pull down the list and then choose Design View. (See Figure 7.12.)

Your screen might differ in two basic ways from that of Figure 7.12. Your toolbox—that's the toolbar on the far left shown in a vertical orientation—might be below the menu bar and across the top of your screen. Additionally, you might have one or more floating property list boxes open. The figure has one floating box, the Properties box, open at the bottom right of the screen. If your toolbox isn't oriented as in Figure 7.12, you can click on its title bar and drag it to the left side of the screen. Like other toolbars, it'll snap into place as soon as you get it fairly close to the side, top, or bottom of a screen.

Figure 7.12.

The Form Design View.

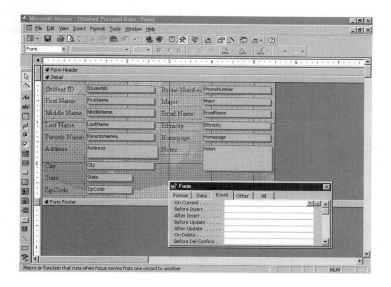

Feel free to close any floating list boxes at this time. Figure 7.13 shows the screen in Figure 7.12 with the addition of another floating list box.

Close these boxes by either clicking their × icons or clicking their toggle buttons on the horizontal toolbar.

Figure 7.13.

*Floating property
list boxes.*

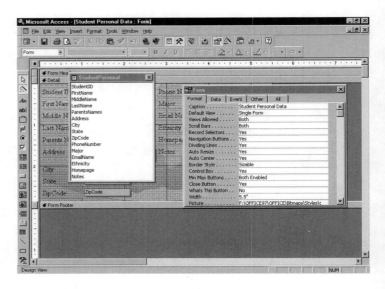

DO check the figures from time to time to make sure you're following along with the exercises.

DON'T worry if your screen gets out of sync with this book. Some variances can't be helped. As long as you're not lost, you're doing all right.

Each element of a form is a *control* (or, as some prefer to say, a form object). Just like fields in a table, each form control has a set of properties that vary from one control to another.

The form in Figure 7.12 is quite simple. It has only one type of control, the Text Box. To get a feel for other types of form controls, run your mouse cursor down the buttons in the toolbox (the toolbar to the far left). Pause over each button long enough for the tooltip to pop up. You'll come across controls such as Label, Text Box, Option Group, Toggle Button, and so on. Each of these controls has a different set of properties, but shares at least a few properties with other controls. The last button in the toolbox is the More… button that brings up a further selection of form controls.

Take a look at Figure 7.14. It displays a partial list of all the properties for a Text Box control; the properties shown pertain only to formatting the text box.

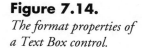

Figure 7.14.

The format properties of a Text Box control.

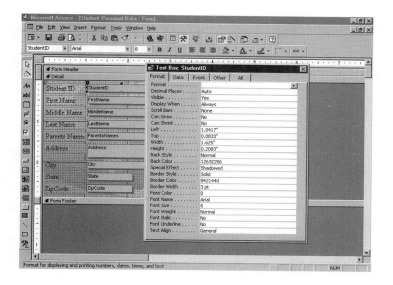

That's a pretty imposing list, isn't it? Memorizing all those properties for all the controls and all their options would be a daunting task. Luckily, Access makes it fairly easy by doing two basic things.

First, you can categorize your properties according to function, so you're not overwhelmed with choices. You do this by clicking on the appropriate tab at the top of the Properties list box, thus choosing one of the categories. Figure 7.15 shows the Text Box control's properties limited to those that affect how the control reacts to events. Look at the top of the list box; you'll see that you've told Access not to show Format Properties, as in Figure 7.14, but Event Properties. If you want to see all properties at one time, click the All tab.

The second thing Access does to help you manage form control properties is offer you "point and shoot" choices. Look at Figure 7.16—it shows your choices for setting the Special Effect property in a Text Box control.

You get these choices just as you did in table design—by clicking next to the property you want to examine or alter and pulling down the list when Access indicates it has a list from which to choose. Later on, you'll learn some other ways Access helps you when you are setting properties.

7

Figure 7.15.

Text Box control properties that apply to events.

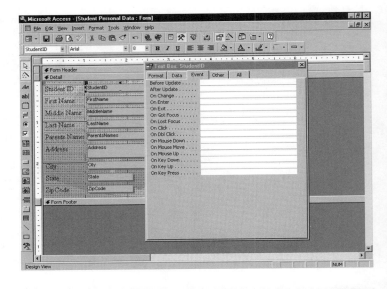

Figure 7.16.

Choosing a property from a list.

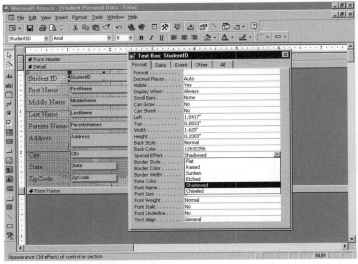

In many cases, Access automatically sets properties for you as a consequence of another choice you made during form design.

Close the form either by double-clicking its Control menu icon or choosing File|Close.

Introduction to Form Controls

The elements of form design presented in this section are the basis for many operations you'll perform in Access.

Bound and Unbound Controls

There are two general categories of controls in Access forms: bound and unbound. A *bound control* is one that's tied to some underlying element; in Access, this usually means a query or table. A Hyperlink control is bound to a file or URL, and OLE controls—currently known as ActiveX controls—can be bound to something external to Access.

An example of a bound control is the StudentID field in the StudentPersonal data form you created by in Exercise 7.2 using the wizard. That field is tied to the StudentID field in the StudentPersonal table. The control shows whatever information is in the StudentID field for the current record.

Unbound controls aren't tied to anything; they are generally used for information display, calculations, manipulating or decorating forms, and (as you'll see later in the book) reports. The label StudentID: to the left of the StudentID bound field shown in Figure 7.2 acts as a label, informing you that the text field is showing the StudentID information. For example, an unbound control on a form might calculate the sum of several bound controls on that form.

Moving and Sizing

When Access inserts Text Box controls into a form through a wizard, it makes a guess based on the Field Size property to determine how wide to make that field. Take a look at Figure 7.2 again. The StudentID field is much bigger than it needs to be to hold any possible student ID information. Also, both of the forms made with the AutoForm button and the wizard don't quite fit on one standard VGA screen. The following exercises address both these issues.

Sizing

To make all the fields or form controls fit on one screen or just to make them the right size for the intended data, you need to both alter the size of overly wide ones and move some of them up from the bottom of the form. Keep in mind that the terms *field* and *form control*, or just *control*, refer to the same thing. A *form control* is the way to show a field on a form.

Exercise 7.3. shows how to resize a form control.

7

EXERCISE

Exercise 7.3. Resizing a form control.

1. Launch Access and open the College database, if you haven't already done so.
2. Click on the Form tab in the Database View.
3. Click the Design button to open the Student Personal Data form in Design View. (See Figure 7.17.)

Figure 7.17.

A form opened in Design View.

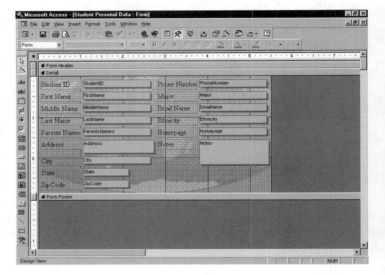

4. If your screen has some floating list boxes in it, close them by either clicking on their × icons or clicking their toggle buttons on the horizontal toolbar. Figure 7.17 shows the toolbox docked at the leftmost side of the screen.

5. Click on the StudentID field in the text control where the StudentID data is displayed when this form is in Form View. (See Figure 7.18.)

   When you click a control, you highlight it. Take a close look at your screen or Figure 7.18. A highlighted control gains a series of squares around its periphery, indicating that it's selected. Drag your cursor over the highlighted field. When the cursor changes shape to look like a hand, you can click and move the field.

6. You don't want to move this control, just resize it. The smaller squares around the control's periphery are "hotspots" for resizing controls. Move your cursor to the center square at the right side of the StudentID control—the one pointed to by the cursor in Figure 7.19. Your cursor then changes shape to look like a two-sided arrow.

Figure 7.18.
*Highlighting a
form control.*

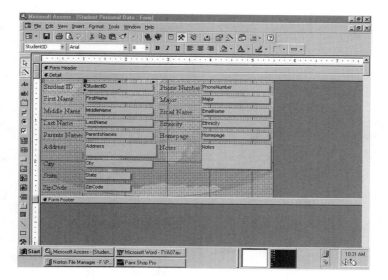

Figure 7.19.
*The cursor
changing to
indicate it's now in
resizing mode.*

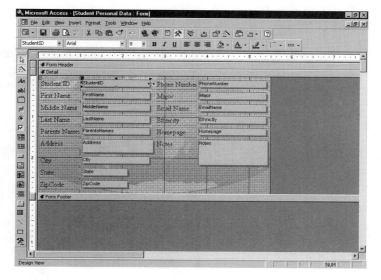

7. Keeping your cursor over this hotspot, click and hold your mouse. Drag the cursor to the left until the StudentID field is a little over an inch long. Refer to Figure 7.20, which shows the field during the sizing operation. Note the ruler on the top of the form design grid, which indicates the length of the field and the position of the cursor.

Do	Don't

DO proceed slowly and carefully through this and the following sections, especially if you're not comfortable or familiar with mouse actions. Highlighting fields without inadvertently moving them, hitting the right hotspots, and dragging are all difficult for those who are less than expert in mouse operations.

DON'T become discouraged if you feel clumsy exercising your form design skills with a mouse. Skill will come in time. Meanwhile, keep in mind the Access "undo" facility. If you accidentally move, size, or delete a form control, you can undo it either by pressing Ctrl+Z or choosing the menu items Edit|Undo. Almost everybody uses this feature when learning about Access form design.

Figure 7.20.
Resizing a field.

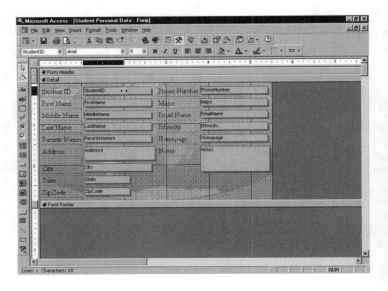

8. Release your mouse button and the field snaps into its new size, looking like Figure 7.21.

Figure 7.21.

The resized field.

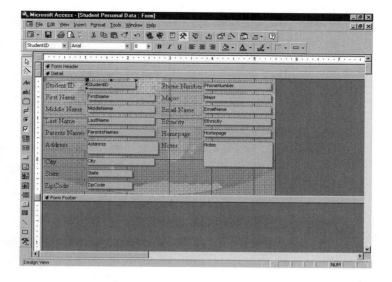

9. Using this same technique, resize the PhoneNumber field so that it's roughly the same size as the ZipCode field.

The Access Way

You might find that you can't finely adjust the size of your fields because Access snaps them to certain points. Access has the options Grid and Snap To Grid. The *grid* is a series of virtual points in the Design View. You can control how fine this grid is by setting the relevant form properties. When Access is set to Snap To Grid, each control on the form must locate and size to one of these points. When doing this exercise, it makes no difference if your Snap To Grid is on or off. It's not that important to size and locate the controls exactly.

That's all there is to sizing controls. The only other thing to bear in mind is that the other hotspots for resizing work differently. For example, the two hotspots in the lengthwise middle of the controls act to size them vertically, not horizontally like the one you just used.

The Access Way

The two large squares in the upper-left corner of both the control and the field label are not hotspots for sizing; rather, they give you a way to move a control independently of its label or to move a label independently of its control.

Controls on the Move

You can move controls either with or independently of their field labels. If you moved your cursor around the control in the last exercise, you saw your cursor change to a hand shape, indicating you can now move a field with its label. The following exercise moves two controls with their labels so that the entire form fits on one screen.

Exercise 7.4. Moving form controls.

1. If necessary, click toward the bottom of the vertical scrollbar to reveal the bottom of the form. You'll probably have to do this if your screen resolution is less than this book's 800×600. If you can see all the controls on your form, this step is unneeded. Figure 7.22 simulates the need to scroll the form by placing some controls at the bottom rather than on the side.

Figure 7.22.

When form controls are off the screen, Access displays a scrollbar so you can move down to them.

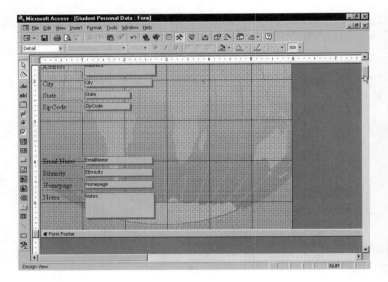

2. Click in the Notes control, in the area where the form displays notes information when it's in Form View. Your cursor should change to look like a hand. Continue to hold your mouse button down; if you let go, click again when the cursor looks like a hand. Your screen should look like Figure 7.23.

3. If you missed—that is, if you find yourself clicking around in the field, unable to get the hand cursor back again—click away from the control. (Anywhere else on the form will do.) Then try clicking back on the Ethnicity control, but this time click and hold. Getting your hand cursor should be easy with this technique.

4. Continue to hold the mouse button down. Drag the Notes field to a place directly to the right of the ZipCode field, then release the mouse button. (See Figure 7.24.)

Figure 7.23.

A form control ready to move.

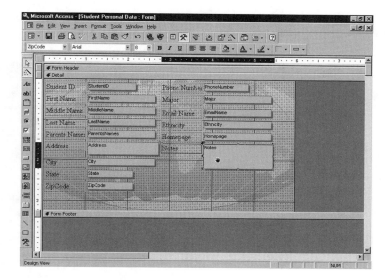

Figure 7.24.

The form control after a move.

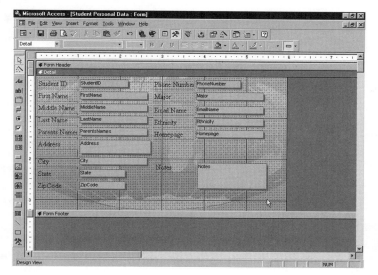

7

5. Experiment with moving other controls around until you have a good feel for how this works. Arrange and resize the controls until you think you have a pleasing arrangement. If you need more form territory, move your cursor to the sides of the form. It'll change to to look like a double-facing arrow. After the cursor changes, you can drag the form to a new size.

Figure 7.25.

Resizing the form itself.

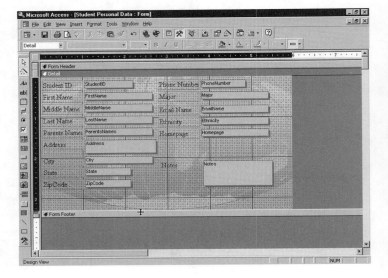

Note that the form itself resizes to accommodate field movements. You don't need to manually resize a form before moving a field, but many people like doing so.

6. Locate your cursor over the large square in the label part of the Notes control. The label for the Notes field is the box that says "Notes" in it, not the place where the Notes data appears. When you move your cursor over the large black square, it changes to a hand with an upraised finger. Click and drag. You'll be able to move the label independently of its control. Similarly, by moving your cursor over the large square in the control, you can move it independently of its label. Return the Notes label to its former spot.

7. Resize the field using the techniques you learned in Exercise 7.3 to make it accommodate more information for notes. You can see this book's example of moved and resized form controls with a moved control label in Figure 7.26. If you have trouble locating the hotspot that controls the vertical control size, examine Figure 7.26. The cursor in that figure points to the hotspot you need. Naturally, your screen will look different if you chose to design the form to your tastes.

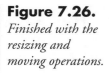

Figure 7.26.

Finished with the resizing and moving operations.

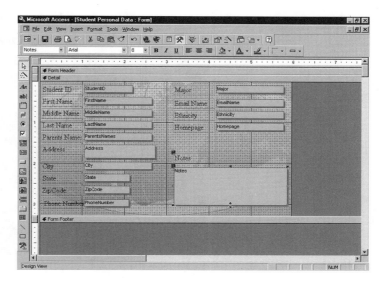

The Access Way

There are many global options you can set in Access, and some of them affect how Access works. Some, if set differently from their defaults, will put your copy of Access at odds with the configuration used for these exercises.

The next exercise requires you to have the Selection Behavior option set to `Partially Enclosed`. To make sure it is, choose Tools|Options from the menu. Access gives you a tabbed dialog box with several choices. Click on Forms/Reports and look at the options that follow. Locate the property Selection Behavior and, if necessary, change its option to `Partially Enclosed`. Your screen should now look like Figure 7.27.

Click OK to exit this dialog box.

Do   **Don't**

DO check your global options if your version of Access seems to be behaving differently from the book's.

DON'T be overly worried about experimenting with global options. Most are self-explanatory. It's difficult to get into trouble by altering these options. Feel free to configure Access so it works the way you prefer.

7

Figure 7.27.

Setting global options.

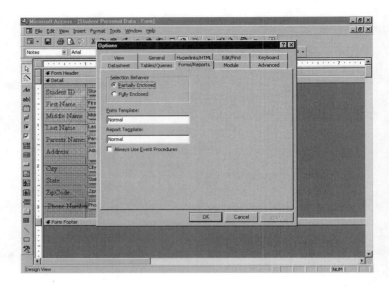

Choosing Multiple Controls

Often, you'll want to act on several controls at once. You can choose several controls quickly and easily by using a marquee selection. Exercise 7.5. shows you how.

Exercise 7.5. Marquee selections.

1. With your screen as you left it after the last exercise, move your mouse cursor to the left of and slightly above any field. This exercise uses the group of controls that start with Major and end with the Homepage fields, as shown in Figure 7.26. If your screen looks different, use any two or more fields for this exercise.

2. Click and hold your mouse button, then drag the mouse down and to the right. You'll see a contrasting "rubber band" rectangle that grows as you move your mouse. (See Figure 7.28.) Note that because of the background, the rubber band selection marquee doesn't show up too well in this shot.

3. Continue dragging the rubber-band box until it covers at least part or all the form controls you've chosen to include for this exercise. Now release the mouse button. All the fields you had covered with the rubber-band box now are highlighted. Your screen should look like Figure 7.29.

Figure 7.28.
Creating a marquee selection.

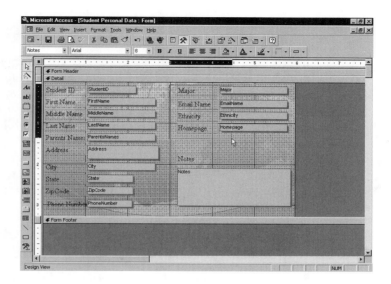

4. Move your cursor into any of the highlighted areas. It'll turn into a hand, as shown in Figure 7.29. If you click and drag now, you'll move all these fields at once. This preserves their positions in relation to each other, but not to the form in general or to any other non-highlighted controls. Try dragging this group of controls around. After you're satisfied with how this works, return them to their former location, or if you prefer, drop them anywhere, then choose Edit|Undo from the menu and Access will snap them back to their original positions.

Figure 7.29.
The finished marquee highlight.

> **The Access Way**
>
> You set control properties by first selecting a control or controls, then altering the
> relevant properties. You can set the properties for all of a form's controls at the
> same time by choosing Edit|Select All from the menu or by pressing Ctrl+A. You
> can affect several adjacent controls by using marquee selections. Finally, you can
> select any number of nonadjacent controls by holding down the Shift key as you
> click on the controls.

5. Click anywhere outside the areas having the highlight to remove the highlight from
   these controls.

Adding and Deleting Controls

You can delete a control from a form by selecting it, then either pressing the Delete key or
choosing the menu selections Edit|Cut. Click on the First Name field to highlight it. When
you press the Delete key, Access removes the field from your form.

Click the Form View button in the toolbar to move your form into Form View. (See Figure
7.30.) Then click the Datasheet View button in the toolbar. Note that Access has eliminated
the First Name field from this view also. Return to Design View.

Figure 7.30.

The Form View.

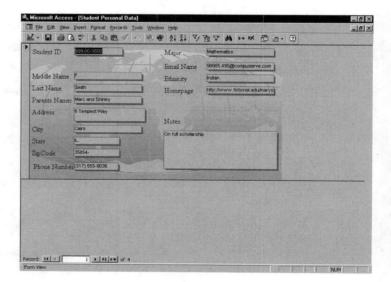

Click the Field List button in the toolbar. Refer to Figure 7.31 if you need help finding it.

Figure 7.31.

Opening the Field list box.

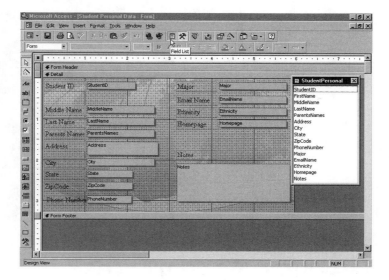

Click the Text Box control in the toolbox, which is the vertically oriented toolbar shown docked at the far left side. The Text Box control is the button with an "ab|" on it. When in doubt about any tool in the toolbox, let your cursor linger over it for a second or two until the tooltip pops up. Click and hold on the FirstName field in the StudentPersonal list box—the box you opened when you clicked on the Field List button.

Without releasing the mouse button, drag the FirstName field onto the form, juggling it around until it's in the same position as the field you deleted. Release the mouse button. Your screen should look like Figure 7.32.

If you have Snap To Grid on, you might not be able to align this field in its former position. If this is the case, choose Format|Snap To Grid from the menu to turn off grid-snapping. Place the FirstName control precisely where you want it, then choose Format|Snap To Grid again to reactivate grid-snapping.

The Access Way

If you highlight several controls, you can group-align them by choosing Format|Align and then one of the options. This is a tremendous time saver compared to manually aligning several controls.

Figure 7.32.
Manually placing a field in a form.

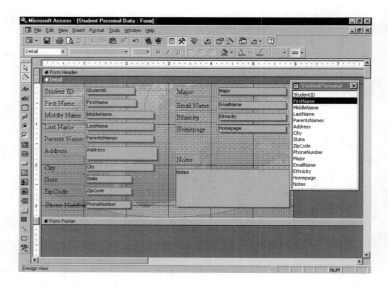

Changing Appearances

This morning's final topic is how to change the appearance of form elements. This is generally done with the Formatting toolbar, but you can alter these elements, depending on what's happening in an Access application, by using macros or Visual Basic.

Remember how the AutoForm's controls had a sunken look? Exercise 7.6. shows how Access did that.

Exercise 7.6. Using the Formatting toolbar.

1. Start with your form just as you left it after Exercise 7.5.
2. Press Ctrl+A to select all the controls on this form.
3. Close the Field list box by clicking its button in the toolbar or clicking its × icon.
4. Make sure the Formatting toolbar is active. This is the toolbar that, by default, lies just below the Form Design toolbar. Figure 7.33 shows the Formatting toolbar pulled from its anchor at the top of the screen to show you which one it is. If you don't see it, right-click on the Form Design toolbar, then drag down to the Formatting entry and click on it to make it visible again.

EXERCISE

Figure 7.33.

The Formatting toolbar.

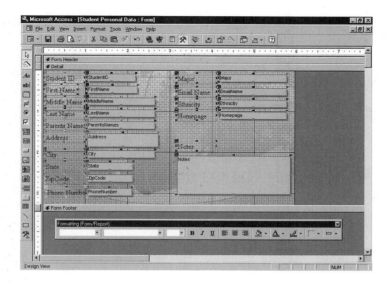

5. The Sunken option is on a pull-down button called Special Effects. This button is at the far right on the toolbar if you have the standard toolbar. (Refer to Figure 7.34.)

Figure 7.34.

The Sunken option.

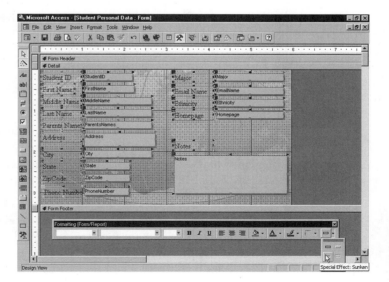

7

6. Click the Form View button and note that now all the fields or controls on your form have a sunken look.

7. Return to Design View and experiment with changing the color and the look of different controls until you develop a good feel for how the Formatting toolbar works. When you're done, manipulate the form to resemble Figure 7.34 and close it, saving your changes.

That's it for this morning. More exciting adventures await you this afternoon!

Morning Summary

A form is an attractive way to enter, edit, or view data stored in tables. There are several ways to create one: You can click the AutoForm button in the toolbar when in Datasheet View, use a wizard, or manually generate one from scratch.

Once you have a form, you can navigate through records by using menu choices, the VCR navigation keys, or direct jumps to record numbers. The Page Up and Page Down keys work as well, but they aren't as convenient, especially if your form takes up more than one vertical screen.

Adding data to a table by using a form can be the same as adding it directly through a table, but keep in mind that there are properties for form fields that can alter data entry with the form. The real power of forms is that they can hide the underlying tables' structures, so that data can be easily entered across multiple tables.

Forms maintain the properties of the underlying tables, plus they can add properties of their own. Forms can contain bound and/or unbound controls. Bound controls are tied to some underlying item, usually inside Access (although in the case of some controls, you can link to applications outside Access).

Forms have three views: Design, Form, and Datasheet. You can design your form in Design View, but the other two views give you access to your data. You change a control in a form by first selecting it, then applying whatever modifications you want. You can select several controls at once by holding down the Shift key as you click, by using a marquee selection, or by pressing Ctrl+A to choose all form elements.

You delete form controls by selecting those you want to delete and then pressing the Delete key, or you can choose Edit|Cut from the menu to cut controls from a form. You add bound controls to the form by dragging the fields from the Field list box to the Form Design grid. The Formatting toolbar lets you set the initial display attributes for your form controls. You'll learn later on that you can change certain of these attributes by using macros, Visual Basic, or a combination of the two.

Chapter 8

A Look into Queries

Queries perform many functions in Access. Relational databases, such as Access, work best when the data they contain is broken into small chunks that are logically grouped. Queries rejoin those small chunks when needed. Primarily, queries in Access perform the following functions:

- ☐ Extracting data according to criteria you set (for example, everybody born after a certain date)
- ☐ Performing actions on extracted data, such as deleting or updating table information
- ☐ Linking several tables or queries to present data the way you want to view it
- ☐ Grouping, sorting, and calculating data from tables and other queries

Queries in Access is a large topic, but one that's not particularly difficult to master if taken one step at a time. In short, you use queries to ask Access about your data or tell Access to manipulate it.

NOTE

> Starting with this chapter, *Teach Yourself Access 97 in 14 Days* relies on the book's sample data for the examples shown. The exercises start with the sample data and then build on it for more complex examples. Details on how you can get this sample data can be found in Appendix E, "The Sample Data."

A Simple Query

You can construct a simple query by telling Access you want to create a new query, then telling it what fields to include. Exercise 8.1 shows you how to construct a simple query.

Exercise 8.1. The simple query.

1. Launch Access and open the College database, if you need to. Click on the second tab, the one labeled Query, in the Database window, then click the New button to start a new query. Click on Design View (if necessary) to bypass the wizards for this exercise, then click OK. Your screen should look like Figure 8.1.

> **Different Screens**
>
> For the sake of simplicity, this chapter shows only those tables and queries relevant to the exercises. Your screens might differ from the book's examples if you have more of the sample data added to your College database. It's important that you have at least the sample data or the equivalent shown in this chapter so you can follow along with these exercises. You can safely ignore any extra data or database objects, either from the sample data or from your own working with Access.

2. Click the StudentPersonal table shown in the Show Table list box, then click the Add button. This tells Access that you want to query the StudentPersonal table. Because this is the only table you want to query at this time, click the Close button. Your screen should look like Figure 8.2.

   Right now, Access knows you want to query the StudentPersonal table, but doesn't

know which fields you want to query. To tell Access that, you must place fields in the query design grid by dragging fields from the Field list box to the query design grid.

Figure 8.1.
Ready to construct a new query.

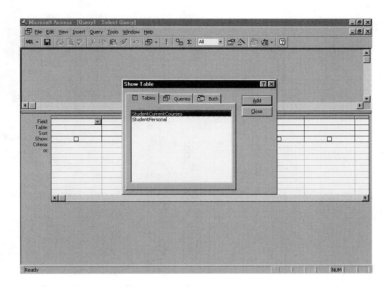

Figure 8.2.
The query design grid with one table added.

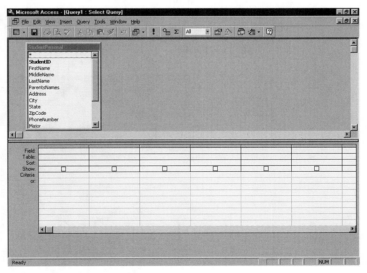

3. Click and hold down the mouse button on the FirstName field in the StudentPersonal list box. Drag the field from the list box to the first row of the first column of the query design grid. Release the mouse button as soon as your mouse

cursor enters the first row of the first column. After you release the mouse button, your screen will look like Figure 8.3.

Figure 8.3.

A field inserted in the query design grid.

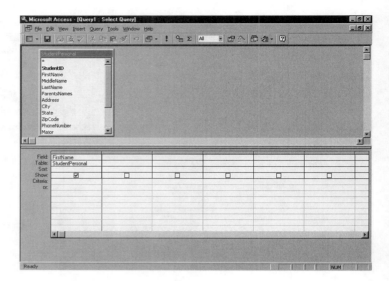

4. Using the same technique, add the LastName and City fields to the first row of columns two and three. You might have to scroll the list box containing the fields of the StudentPersonal table to find the City field. When you're finished, your screen should look like Figure 8.4.

Figure 8.4.

A multifield query.

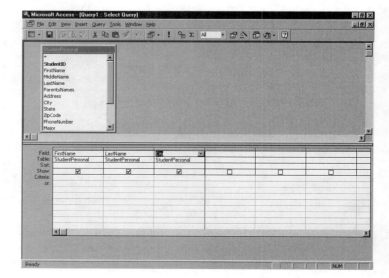

The Access Way

You can resize and arrange the query design grid to suit your needs and tastes. Move your cursor around the query design grid and see how at certain hotspots the cursor changes its shape to indicate it can now manipulate the size or shape of the windows that make up the grid. Figures 8.2 through 8.5 are examples of how the grid can be changed to make working with this query easier. How you work with Access is up to you.

Figure 8.5.

The cursor changes to a new shape when it's on a hotspot to change the look of the query design grid. This shot shows the bottom half of the grid being enlarged.

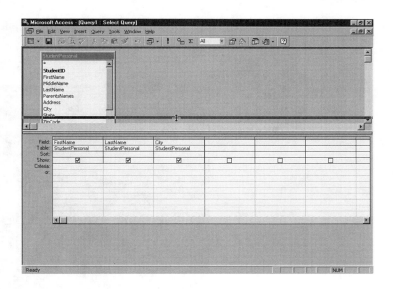

5. Click the Run button, the one with the exclamation point, in the toolbar. Access then runs the query, resulting in a screen similar to Figure 8.6.

Pat yourself on the back—you've just constructed and successfully run an Access query!

The Access Way

Access queries are "live." Changes made to them are reflected in underlying tables or queries. Look at Figure 8.6. If you were to edit the name Nancy Ogur to Ogre in the query, you'd also change the entry Ogur in the StudentPersonal table to Ogre.

This is in contrast to most other PC database programs, where queries are dumped into dead tables. Edits into dead tables don't affect the underlying data. If you're used to this type of database, keep the concept of Access's live data queries in mind when editing queries in the Datasheet View.

Also, if you're used to dead table queries you might, at first glance, feel Access's live queries are a dangerous feature, but it's actually as safe as you make it. It can also greatly increase Access's power and flexibility over those programs that dump queries into dead tables. You'll see examples of Access queries' power and flexibility as you pursue the subject of queries.

Keep in mind that keeping your computer well backed up is part of having a computer. Many of the changes Access queries make will be permanent.

Figure 8.6.

Running the simple query.

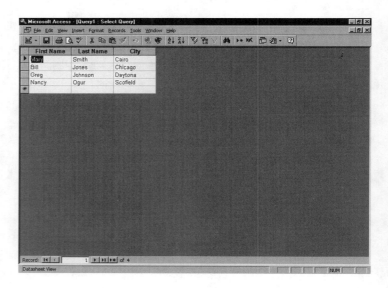

Well, that was easy—but it wasn't particularly useful. This query just takes some of the fields in an Access table and shows all the records for those fields. Access can do much more.

Return to Design View by clicking the Design View button on the far left in the toolbar.

Exercise 8.2 demonstrates sorting in a query.

Do   Don't

DO remember that queries keep live links to their underlying tables.

DON'T forget how handy that can be when you need to edit data in more than one table at the same time.

Exercise 8.2. Sorting in a query.

1. Locate the Sort row in the query design grid. It's the third from the top in Figure 8.5.

2. Click in the first column of the grid in the Sort row. Access returns a down arrow indicating that this field is a combo box with a pull-down list. Click on the down arrow. Your screen should look like Figure 8.7.

Figure 8.7.

Telling Access to show the query in a different sort order than the underlying table.

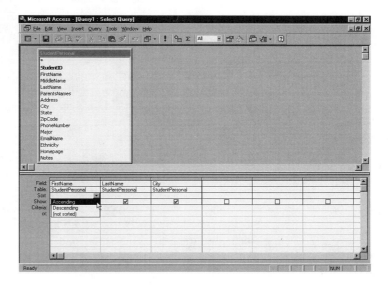

3. Click on Ascending. You've just told Access to present your data in an ascending sort based on the data in the FirstName field. Choose File|Save from the menu and save this query as Temp. Run the query by clicking the Run button. (See Figure 8.8.)

Figure 8.8.

*A query can use a
different sort order
than the table it's
based on.*

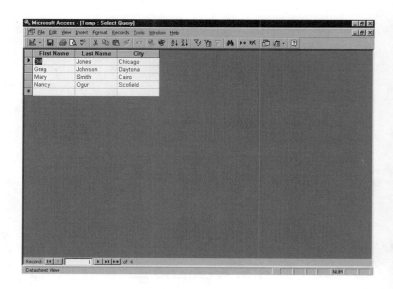

NOTE

Compare Figure 8.8 to Figure 8.6. Note that 8.6 shows the record for
Mary Smith of Cairo because Smith's record comes first in the
StudentPersonal table. Also remember that the StudentPersonal table
uses StudentID as a key field, so Access orders records on that field. In
the sample data, Smith's StudentID has the least value and so is
ordered first.

When you told Access to order the query according to first name, the
name Nancy was last alphabetically; to put it another way, it had the
greatest value, so it came last, as shown in Figure 8.8. Note also that
Access has the smarts to keep records together. In both Figures 8.6 and
8.8, Access has the LastName field Smith and City field Chicago
attached to the Mary FirstName field.

The Access Way

There's an important difference between edits made to Access queries and sorts
performed in them. Altering the sort order for fields in an Access query doesn't
alter the order of the data in the underlying table.

Occasionally, you'll want to view your data in varying orders. The easiest way to do this is to construct a query for each different sort view you want. Access allows multiple queries on the same table, and each query can have its own criteria and sort order.

Criteria in Queries

Access queries also perform the important function of extracting subsets of your data. If, for example, you want to view all the records in a table for which the City field is Cairo, you can easily do so. Exercise 8.3 shows how to convert the general query made in Exercises 8.1 and 8.2 into one with a criterion.

Exercise 8.3. A criteria query.

1. Starting from where you left off in Exercise 8.2, return to Design View.
2. Choose File|Save from the menu, or, if you prefer, click the Save icon in the toolbar. The Save icon looks like a 3 1/2 inch floppy disk.
3. Locate the Criteria row in the query design grid. It's the fourth row down from the top. Enter Cairo in the Criteria row under the City field column, then press Enter. Access adds quote marks to your specified criterion. (See Figure 8.9.)

Figure 8.9.

Constructing a criteria query.

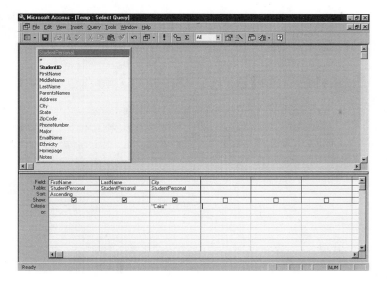

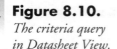

4. Run the query by clicking the Run button in the toolbar. Your screen should look like Figure 8.10.

Figure 8.10.

The criteria query in Datasheet View.

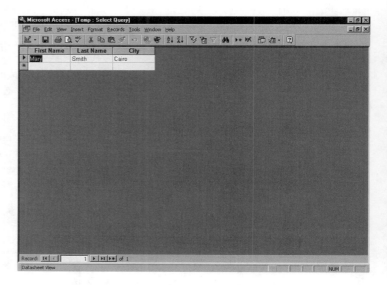

Access ran the query as before, but this time extracted only those records in which the City field matched the criteria of Cairo. In this example, only one record had Cairo in the City field, so Access returned only one record when you ran the query. If your StudentPersonal table has more records in it, your query might have returned more records. The important thing to concentrate on here is that all records returned, whether one or a million, have Cairo as the city.

Some Criteria Variations

Access allows you wide latitude when it comes to criteria you can enter into a query. Using a little imagination and some knowledge, you can extract your data in almost any manner you can think of. Exercise 8.4 goes into some variations on the criteria theme.

8

Exercise 8.4. Variations of criteria.

1. Click the Design View button to return to Design View for this query.

2. Edit the criteria Cairo to read `C*`. Press return. Access modifies your criteria to the proper Access syntax of `Like "C*"`.

Do   **Don't**

DO experiment with different criteria entries, determining which ones work the way you expect them to and which ones yield unexpected results. Access is unusual when compared with most computer programs because it tries to do what you mean, not just what you say. Therefore, when you enter the criterion `C*`, Access correctly interprets this to mean you want to extract all records that "Start with a C."

DON'T assume Access can figure out what you want all the time. Like any machine intelligence, Access has its limits. Until you're sure you understand query criteria, carefully check Access's output to make sure you got what you expected.

---

3. Run the query. Your screen should resemble Figure 8.11. Note that Access returns more records than from the data set used earlier in this chapter because the book uses an expanded data set, which is included in the sample data. (Instructions for getting the sample data are in Appendix E.)

   If you're familiar with DOS commands, you probably figured out what happened. Access, following DOS conventions, accepted the wildcard asterisk to mean "accept whatever" in this space. So by entering `C*`, you told Access to extract all those records starting with the letter *C* and anything that follows.

4. Return to Design mode. Edit the criterion `C*` to read `Ch*`, then run the query again. (See Figure 8.12.)

5. Here's a way people get wrong data when making criteria queries. Return to Design View and modify the criteria `Ch*` to `Ch`. Press Enter, and Access returns your criterion as `Like "Ch"`. Run the query. Your screen should resemble Figure 8.13.

Figure 8.11.
A wildcard query criterion.

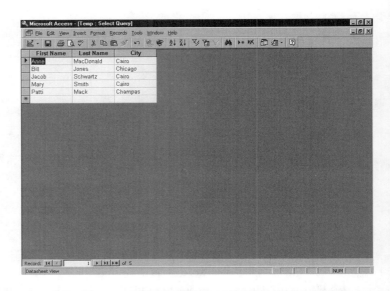

Figure 8.12.
A modified wildcard criterion.

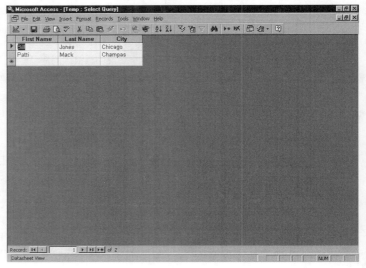

Figure 8.13.

A criteria query giving unexpected results.

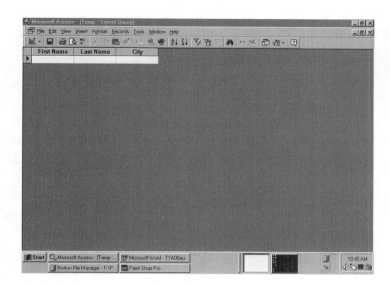

What happened? Your criteria now tells Access to return any records in which the City field is Like "Ch", rather than any city beginning with *Ch*, as the criterion "Ch*" instructs Access. You've modified your wildcard criteria query to a literal request to locate cities named Ch in your database. Naturally, there is no such city.

Table 8.1 gives a few examples of other query criteria. Note that criteria expressions closely resemble table validation expressions. In Chapter 18, "Form Control Properties," you'll encounter filter expressions, and the expression examples in Table 8.1 work there, too.

Table 8.1. Some criteria examples.

Criteria	Return
"Cairo"	Field must match Cairo.
"Cairo" or "Chicago"	Field can match either Cairo or Chicago.
=#2/20/85#	Matching the data February 20, 1985. Note that when entering data criteria in Access, you must surround the date with two number signs (#) so Access can recognize you're entering a date rather than the literal. In most cases, Access is smart enough to supply its own # marks, but look to be sure.
Between #1/3/84# And #6/7/85#	Anything between January 3, 1984, and June 7, 1985, inclusive.

continues

Table 8.1. continued

Criteria	Return
In ("Cairo", "Chicago")	Another way to match either Cairo or Chicago. A syntactical alternative to or.
Not "Cairo"	Any record that's not Cairo. The opposite of "Cairo".
< Date()- 30	Dates more than 30 days old for this field.
Year([Order Date])=1988	Records that have the Order Date field in 1988.
Like "C*"	Starts with C; anything else following.
Like "*a"	Starts with anything; ends with a.
Like "[J-M]*"	Starts with J through M inclusive and ends with anything.
Left([City], 1)="O"	Anything with O in the leftmost position.

Using OR and AND Criteria

Suppose you wanted to see all your company's files for customers who live in either Chicago or Cairo; you would ask your assistant to "Get me those files where the customer lives in Cairo and Chicago." This makes sense in human speech, but the relentless logic of computers interprets this request as "Get me those files where the customer lives in BOTH Cairo and Chicago." This clearly isn't what you wanted.

Logically speaking, you should have asked for those files with a customer who lives in Cairo *or* Chicago. This is one important area in which Access does what you tell it to do, rather than what you might mean for it to do. Exercise 8.5 illustrates the distinction.

Exercise 8.5. ORs and ANDs in criteria.

1. Return to Design View from the failed query in Exercise 8.4. Edit the City criterion back to Like "C*" to return all records in which the city begins with the letter C. Run the query to make sure you return the records in which the city begins with the letter C.

2. Return to Design View and edit the first Criteria row under the FirstName column to read Like "J*". (See Figure 8.14.)

Figure 8.14.

Starting the AND
criterion query.

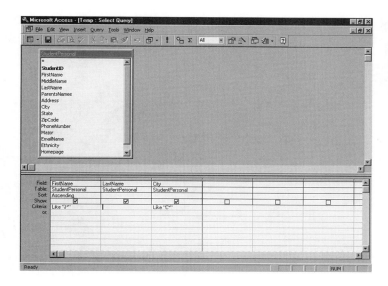

3. Run the query. Your screen should resemble Figure 8.15.

   You told Access to extract all those records in which the City field starts with *C* and the First Name starts with *J*. Only one record in the sample database now meets these criteria. Look what happens when you make a slight change to make this an OR criterion.

4. Return to Design View. Click and drag to highlight the criterion Like "J*" under the FirstName field.

Figure 8.15.

Running the AND
query.

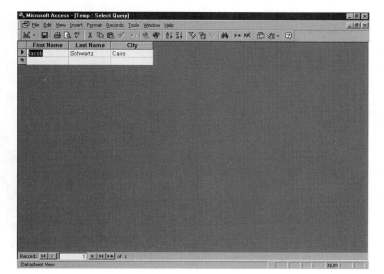

5. Press Ctrl+X to cut this criteria expression to the Clipboard. Click on the second line of the Criteria grid under the FirstName column next to the word *or*. Press Ctrl+V to paste your criteria to the new row. Your screen should look like Figure 8.16.

Figure 8.16.
Constructing the
OR *criteria.*

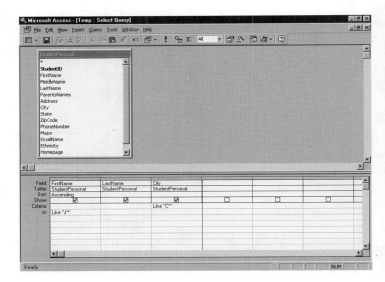

6. Now run the query. Your screen should resemble Figure 8.17.

Figure 8.17.
The OR *query's*
return.

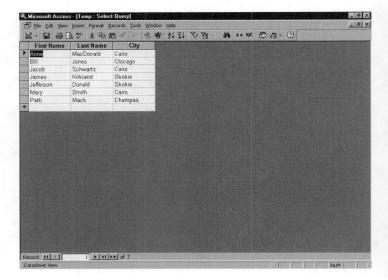

Note the difference between the query results shown in Figure 8.15 and Figure 8.17. In the criteria entered for Figure 8.15, you told Access to show you all the records in which the city begins with the letter *C* AND the first name begins with the letter *J*. Access returns only those records that match *both* criteria.

When you changed the criteria to be on two rows, you told Access to extract all those records in which the FirstName field begins with *J* OR those records in which the city name begins with *C*. This query returned all those records for which either criterion was valid, so you also got Jefferson Donald's and James Kirkland's records, even though their cities are Skokie.

Day Summary

The morning lesson was an especially long introduction to forms. Forms are a way to view, edit, or enter data into a table or a query. You can create a form by clicking the AutoForm selection in the toolbar's New Object button's pull-down when the table or query you want to create the form for is active. You can also create forms by using several wizards that give you a great deal of variety in what your form looks like and, most important, what fields appear on the form.

Forms can have their own validation and formatting. They, as well as queries, do preserve the underlying table's validation and similar "rules" for data entry and editing. Objects on forms are called *controls*. You can specify which controls you add, including field type controls, by using the toolbox. Forms and their controls can be resized by grabbing their "handles" with your mouse cursor and dragging. Forms themselves can be resized by using the "handles" at their margins when you're in Design View.

This afternoon you got a good introduction to queries, used in Access to extract sets of data from tables or other queries. You can include as many fields as you want in a query. and you can also use criteria in queries to extract records meeting this criteria.

The only tricky thing about this afternoon's material is the way Access interprets AND and OR query criteria. By placing multiple criteria on one line, you're telling Access you want to use an AND set of criteria; by putting multiple criteria on multiple rows, you're telling Access you want an OR extraction.

Q&A

Q **The text implies you can change a control's display when the form's open in Form View. Why would you want to do this?**

A When you review a form's layout properties, you'll see many items you might want to alter, depending on the state of the form or its data. For example, one property that a control has is called Visible. You might want to make some controls visible or not, depending on the current data or the state of another control.

Q Why doesn't Access show a field in Form Datasheet View if that field's not on the form?

A The reason is security. Say you have a form with restricted information. You might clear people to see that form because it lacks the fields containing sensitive data from the underlying table. The way Access works, users of this limited form could not violate security by choosing the Datasheet View. You can also limit the Datasheet View by setting the appropriate form property.

Q Is there any difference between adding, editing, or deleting data through a form rather than doing it directly into a table?

A There can be—not in the data, but in how a person can address it. Remember, each control on a form has a slew of properties that act in addition to the properties of the fields in a table and the table's properties. You might not, for example, have any data validation set at the table level, but you might at the form level. This would have the effect of no data validation when entering data directly into a table. Instead, that validation would be effective only when using the form.

One reason to do this is so you can vary the data validation depending on which form is used to enter data into the table. Many forms can be bound to one table. As you'll see later on, one form can contain several tables as well.

Q Forms look to me like rearranged table fields. Can they do more than that?

A Forms can be very powerful tools in organizing and displaying your data. This chapter covered only the basics. Later you'll learn about other form controls, such as check boxes, option groups, and command buttons, which, when used correctly, greatly enhance your applications.

Q Is there a rule of thumb saying when to use a form for data entry and when to do it through the Datasheet View directly?

A There's no real rule of thumb, but since most people find data entry to be much easier in Form View than in Datasheet View, why not use forms all the time? Even if you ask Access to generate an AutoForm for each data entry session, then discard the form, you'll probably save time by using a form for data entry. As you learn more about forms, you'll see that they can do many things that are impossible (or at least very awkward) to do from a datasheet.

Q You can edit queries, so why bother having tables?

A You need to base a query on either a table or another query, which in turn is based eventually on an underlying table. You can't query nothing. You don't need data entered in a table to base a query on it, but you need some final structure for your data to reside in.

Q I have a table with three entries: Smith, Jones, and Jenkins. I want to return only Smith's and Jones's records. Is it better to make a query with criteria Smith OR Jones, or should I use NOT Jenkins as the criteria?

A Access doesn't care, so use whichever you prefer. The advantage of using Smith OR Jones is that your return will definitely give you only Smith or Jones. NOT Jenkins would also include Jensen, for example, if you were wrong and your table had a fourth entry.

Q The sample data in these exercises seems a little simplistic. Why would I use a computer to manipulate such small amounts of data?

A The data-entry requirements for these examples are intentionally kept small for those readers who have to enter the data manually. The principles apply to any data amount—either the tiny examples used in this book or the thousands of records a real college would use. Also, the complexity of the data relationships is kept low because this is intended as a book for novices. The data structure shown here would have to be expanded on several levels to operate a real college's student and class system.

Q What if I want an OR criteria for a single field?

A Just enter the two criteria separated by the word OR. For example, if you want to modify the Temp query to return records only for those students with the first name Jacob or Greg, edit the first criteria row under the FirstName column to read Jacob OR Greg, then run the query.

Workshop

Here's where you can test and apply the lessons you learned today. Because of the length of today's lesson, the query projects will come at the end of tomorrow's lesson.

Quiz

Possible answers to these questions are given in Appendix A.

1. How do you know when a form control is highlighted—in other words, has focus?

2. What visual indication does Access give you so you know when you can move a form control?

3. What does the mouse cursor look like when it's over a hotspot and able to size a field or control on a form?

4. If you delete a field from a form in Form Design View, can you see that field when you switch to Form Datasheet View?

5. How can you select (or highlight) two noncontiguous controls on a form?

6. How can you select (or highlight) four contiguous controls on a form?

Put Access into Action

1. Launch Access and open the College database, if you haven't already done so.

2. Open the StudentCurrentCourses table in Datasheet View.

3. Create a form by using the AutoForm choice of the toolbar's New Object button. Your screen might resemble Figure 8.18. Exactly how your AutoForm turns out depends on Access's condition and your Windows setup. The control layout should be similar.

Figure 8.18.

Using AutoForm to create a form.

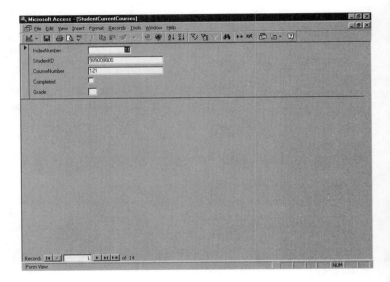

4. Change to Design View. Rearrange and resize the controls on this form to look like Figure 8.19, which shows the rearranged controls in Form View. Hint: The size of the form itself was shortened vertically. Move your cursor to the bottom of the form and it'll take on the shape you saw when resizing table fields. Click and drag to resize the form itself.

Figure 8.19.

The reworked AutoForm.

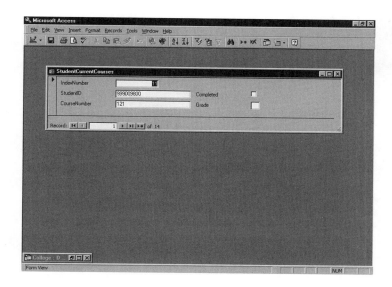

5. Return to Form Design View and select the Completed check box control. Open up the Properties list box and find the Default Value property either by scrolling through the All Properties list or choosing Data Properties. Enter Yes for a default property, then return to Form View. What change do you see in the Completed check box? Scroll through all the records to see any changes. Now move to a new (blank) record. Does the default value kick in? Did it kick in with existing records? Move on to the next section, if you want; if not, close this form, discarding any changes.

For the Adventurous

From Form View, try adding a record to the StudentCurrentCourses table through the form from the preceding section. Tab away from the (AutoNumber) field, enter a StudentID that's *not* in the StudentPersonal table, and enter any data you want for the rest of the fields. When you try leaving the Grade field, does Access accept your data?

Remember that this table is linked to the StudentPersonal table. If the error message box is obvious to you, click OK to close it, then press Esc to void this entry. If the message box didn't make sense to you, click the Help button and read Access's explanation for why it entered an error condition.

In either case, after you're done, press Esc to void this entry, then close the form and discard the changes.

DAY 5

A.M.

9 Multitable Queries

P.M.

10 Basic Reports

Chapter 9

Multitable Queries

This morning you'll learn

- ☐ How to construct queries using multiple tables
- ☐ How links work in queries
- ☐ How to use criteria in multitable queries

Breaking your data into logical chunks makes it much easier for Access to manipulate, but on many occasions you'll want to reconstruct or rearrange your data into larger pieces. For example, the College database stores students' names in the StudentPersonal table, course information in the AvailableClasses table, and courses the students are currently signed up for in the StudentCurrentCourses table.

What if you want to see a class list? The information is all in the College database but scattered throughout these three tables. The way to join all this data into a coherent whole is through a query.

NOTE

> Continuing with this chapter, *Teach Yourself Access 97 in 14 Days* relies on the book's sample data for the examples shown. The book uses the sample data to build more complex examples. Details on how you can get this sample data can be found in Appendix E, "The Sample Data."

Before moving on to this topic, however, this chapter introduces query wizards. I skipped this step in the previous lesson to give you some hands-on experience with queries. Unlike some other wizards, Access supplies query wizards only for the most complex type queries.

Looking at a Wizard

If your query's still open from yesterday's lesson, close it, discarding changes. You can save the Temp query for later experimentation if you like, but this book won't use it for subsequent exercises. (It is part of the sample data.)

Navigate to the Database window either by clicking around, closing everything, or by pressing F11. Click the Query tab if you're not at the query window. Click New. Your screen should resemble Figure 9.1.

Access not only has wizards for some complex queries, but a simple one too. There's a wizard for doing a simple query like the one you did yesterday afternoon. Now is a good time to experiment by running through the Simple Query Wizard on your own. The work you did yesterday will serve to familiarize you with the wizard's steps. The scope of what the more complex wizards do is beyond this chapter's scope, but Figure 9.1 shows you some of the interesting and useful query wizards in Access 97.

If you feel adventurous, by all means try your hand at any of these more complex wizards, but to move on to this morning's lesson, click Design View to bypass all wizards.

9

Figure 9.1.

New Query dialog box showing the different query wizards.

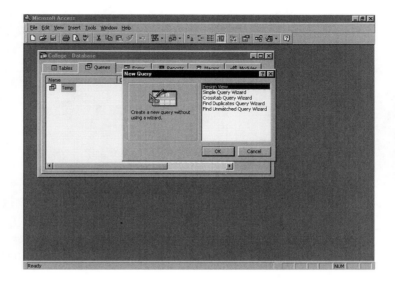

A Simple Multitable Query

The first exercise this morning shows you how to manually construct a simple two-table query. Depending on how you like to work, you might prefer, when using Access for your own data, to use a wizard for even the simplest queries. However, the right way to learn is to do. After Exercise 9.1 is completed, you'll add another table and enter some criteria to construct a rather sophisticated query.

Exercise 9.1. A two-table query.

1. If you're at the Database window, click the Query tab if necessary. Click the New button. Click the Design View selection to skip the wizards. Click OK. Your screen should resemble Figure 9.2.

2. Click the StudentPersonal table in the Show Table list box. Click the Add button.

3. Click the StudentCurrentCourses table in the Show Table list box. Click the Add button.

Figure 9.2.

Selecting a table for the two-table query from the Show Table list box.

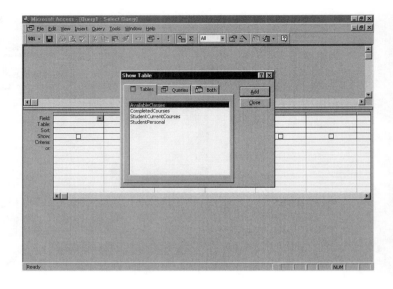

4. Click Close to close the Show Table list box. (See Figure 9.3.)

Figure 9.3.

Starting the two-table query.

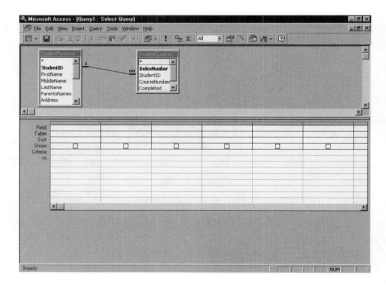

Access remembers that there's a link between these tables and proves to you that it remembers by drawing a line between the tables, illustrating what fields are the link fields as well as which side of the link is the one side and which is the many side. Remember that you established this link in the Relationships windows earlier. Access also remembers that the relationship is a one to many, with the StudentPersonal being on the one side of the relationship.

Optional: Adjust your query design grid and the list boxes to look like Figure 9.4. This simplifies creating the following queries, but isn't required to complete the exercises.

Figure 9.4.

The query design grid adjusted for clarity.

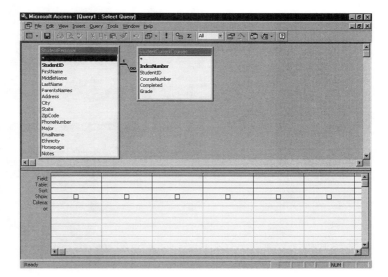

5. You want to tell Access to show you the classes students are currently taking. Drag the following fields from StudentPersonal into the query design grid, starting with column one: StudentID, FirstName, MiddleName, LastName. Your screen should resemble Figure 9.5.

6. Now you're ready to add the courses these students are signed up for. Click in the StudentCurrentCourses list box on the CourseNumber field and drag that into the first empty column. (See Figure 9.6.)

Figure 9.5.
Starting the multitable query construction.

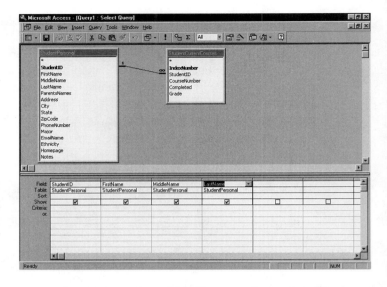

Figure 9.6.
Fields from two tables in the query design grid.

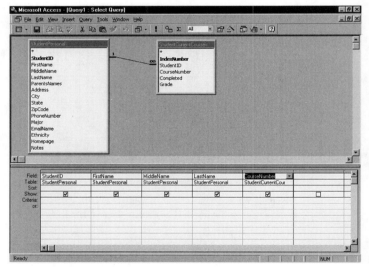

7. Click the Run button in the toolbar. Access evaluates the query design grid and returns the results shown in Figure 9.7.

Figure 9.7.
The multitable query running.

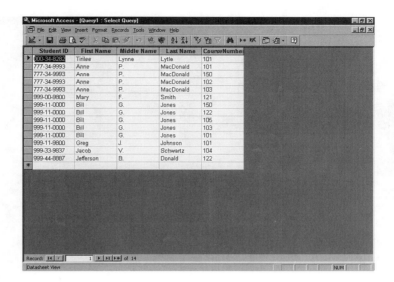

Well, that's all right, but not terribly useful as it sits. For one thing, you wanted only the students' names, but you also have the StudentIDs. For another, the class number information is the number of the class, but that doesn't really tell us anything about the name of the class, the section, or the credit hours.

Note that although the StudentID field is in the StudentCurrentCourses table, it's not included in the query. Even without the link field, Access has the smarts to link up the right student with his or her courses.

The first modification is to eliminate the StudentID field from the query's display. Return to Design mode and click the Show check box under the StudentID field. Your screen should resemble Figure 9.8.

Run the query again. Your screen should look like Figure 9.9.

Figure 9.8.

Suppressing a field's display in a query.

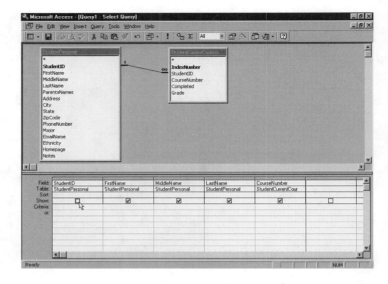

Figure 9.9.

The results of suppressing a field's display in a query.

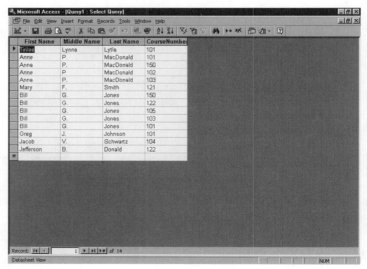

Removing a Field from a Query

The only reason to include a field in a query while suppressing its display is if you want to include some criteria for that field for a query's return, but you don't want to display the field. You don't want to enter a criterion for StudentID in this query, so you can safely delete it from the query design grid. Save this query by selecting File|Save As from the menu, giving it the name Temp if it doesn't conflict with the previous optional query that you may have saved. If it does conflict, make up a name for this query.

Do   **Don't**

DO include only those fields in queries for which you want to either display or enter criteria.

DON'T bother to litter up your query design grid with extraneous fields just for the sake of links. Access links all right with these fields left out.

Return to Design View. Move to the StudentID column in the query design grid. Move your cursor to right above the name StudentID in the design grid. The cursor switches to a down-facing arrow. Click to highlight the entire column. (See Figure 9.10.)

Figure 9.10.

Getting ready to delete a field from a query.

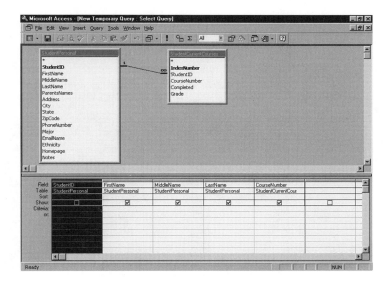

Press Delete or Del to clip this field from the query design grid. Run the query to see that Access still returns the same results even with no StudentID field anywhere in the query. If it doesn't, return your copy of Access and demand your money back.

The Access Way

Access doesn't need the inclusion of link fields in a query to know how to link tables in queries. It's smart enough to understand the underlying relationships even with the link fields excluded.

Adding Another Table

This query is shaping up, but it still doesn't include the information about course title and credit hours that you want. This information is in the AvailableClasses table, which isn't yet part of this query.(The AvailableClasses table is included in the sample data; see Appendix E.) Exercise 9.2 adds the AvailableClasses table to the query.

Exercise 9.2. The three-table query.

1. Return to Design View. Locate the Show Table button in the toolbar and click it. (It's the button with a table and a plus symbol.) Refer to Figure 9.11.

   Access brings up the Show Table list box. Click the AvailableClasses table, then click the Add button. Click Close.

   Notice that Access remembers the link between StudentCurrentCourses and AvailableClasses. This link was established during the creation of the sample database. If you manually generated your sample data, you'll have to establish the link yourself. To do this, close the query, saving changes. Click the Tables tab in the Database window, then choose Tools|Relationships from the menu. If necessary, add the AvailableClasses to the Relationships window by clicking the Show Table button in the toolbar and dragging AvailableClasses to the window. (The Show Table button in the Relationships window is the same as the one in the Query design grid, shown in Figure 9.11.) Drag your cursor from the CourseNumber field in AvailableClasses to the CourseNumber field in StudentCurrentClasses. Your screen should resemble Figure 9.12. To return to the exercise, close the Relationships window, then click the Query tab. Click the saved query to open it, then switch to Design View.

   Return to the exercise at the point where you add the AvailableClasses table to the query design grid. Arrange the new table's list box so that your screen resembles Figure 9.13.

2. Click the Show check box in the CourseNumber column to suppress its display in the final query. Now drag the following fields from the AvailableClasses table to the query design grid and place them in the next available empty columns: CourseNumber, Name, Instructor, Units. (You might have to scroll horizontally to find empty columns.) This query would have worked all right with only one CourseNumber field in it. The second one was left for the sake of instructional clarity and to demonstrate that you can sort on nondisplayed data.

Figure 9.11.
*Adding a table
to a query.*

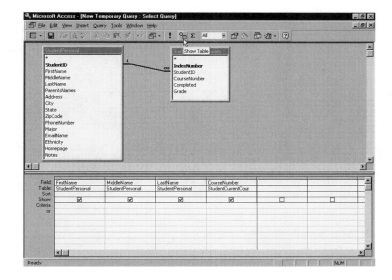

Figure 9.12.
*Establishing a
relationship.*

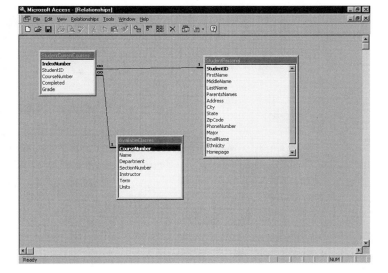

Figure 9.13.
*Adding the third
table to the query
design grid.*

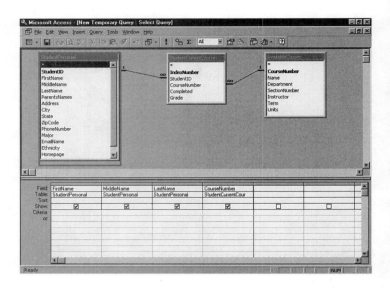

The Access Way

Access enables you to dump one field on top of an occupied column and automatically shifts the new field to a new column. This works all right, but it's confusing when you see it for the first time.

---

3. After you've dragged the fields into the query design grid, click the Run button. Adjust the widths of the fields in the Datasheet View like you adjusted the column widths in a table. Your screen should resemble Figure 9.14.

That's more like it. This is getting to be a useful set of information. The only thing that's lacking is that the query is in student order. This might be all right for some purposes, but not all.

4. Return to Design mode. Click the Sort row in the nondisplayed CourseNumber field—the one from the StudentCurrentCourses table. Pull down the combo box and click Ascending. (See Figure 9.15.)

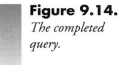

Figure 9.14.
The completed query.

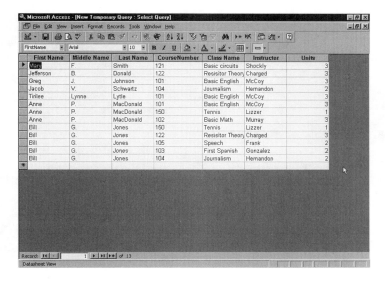

Figure 9.15.
Adding a sort to a nondisplayed field.

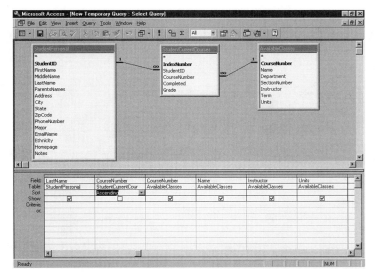

5. Click the Run button. Your screen should resemble Figure 9.16, which is the desired query.

Figure 9.16.

The finished three-table query.

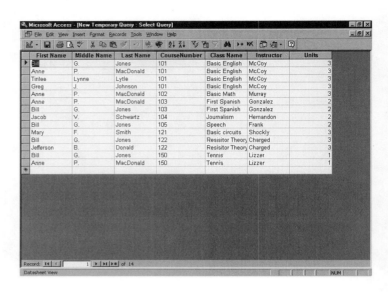

This query shows all the students and their courses, along with course information grouped by course. Save this query, using the name StudentsAndCourses, for later work.

Morning Summary

NOTE

For the sake of continuity, this summary includes some material covered yesterday afternoon.

You start new queries just like you start creating other Access objects. Move to the Database window, click the Query tab, then click the New button. You can manually construct your queries or call in a wizard. You'll probably want to use wizards for the more complex queries—at least until you get a feel for how Access puts these together.

You add tables or other queries to your new query by highlighting the table or query you want to add in the Show Table list box and clicking the Add button.

After you've added the tables you want into your query, click the Close button in the Show Table list box and start dragging fields from the list boxes to the query design grid. After they're in the query design grid, you can treat fields several ways. You can extract data according to criteria expressions such as Like "Ch*", you can sort on a field's data, and you can choose to display or suppress a field from the final query.

Keep in mind the difference between natural language and computer syntax when creating criteria using the operatives OR and AND. OR tells a computer to widen the criteria; AND tells the computer to narrow the criteria. People generally use AND like the computer's OR.

Finally, until you're comfortable with Access query methods, carefully check what Access returns to you. The expression Like "C*" returns Cairo and Chicago. The expression Like "C" won't return either.

Chapter **10**

Basic Reports

This afternoon's lesson covers the following:

☐ What reports are

☐ How to use the general Report Wizard for quick results

☐ How to customize reports

Report Concepts

Reports are very similar to forms. The main difference between them, as far as application goes, is that reports work much better for data output, especially to printers. Also, Access 97 can present data for viewing over the World Wide Web, and reports perform a vital function in presenting data for this purpose. The primary mission of forms is data entry and display, and the main mission of reports is data output.

Like forms, reports are bound to underlying tables or queries. Access can do much with unbound forms, but most people see little sense to an unbound report, although Access enables you to create one through the Design View option when you tell Access you want to create a new report.

Exercise 10.1 makes a sample report using the StudentPersonal table. This report prints out students' names and addresses. Exercise 10.3 takes you through the report again to illustrate how easy it is for Access to create the same data, but on mailing labels.

Exercise 10.1. The basic report.

1. If necessary, launch Access and open the College database. Click the Report tab. Click New. Pull down the combo box and click the StudentPersonal table to choose it as the basis of this report. This step is called binding the table to this report.

2. Click the Report Wizards option in the list box. Your screen should resemble Figure 10.1.

The Access Way

Note that when you pull down the combo box to bind a query or table, Access doesn't segregate the two types of objects as it does during query design. This is a good illustration of why a naming convention would be useful. For example, if you prefixed all tables with *tbl* and queries with *qry*, you could, at a glance, see that you have three tables and one query to choose from for this report.

---

3. Click OK to tell Access you're ready to go.

4. Access opens up the StudentPersonal table and examines it, determining what fields are available. Click the field names, then click the > button for the following fields: FirstName, MiddleName, LastName, Address, City, State, and ZipCode. This operation tells Access that these are the fields you want for this report. Your screen should look like Figure 10.2.

Figure 10.1.

The Report Wizard just starting out.

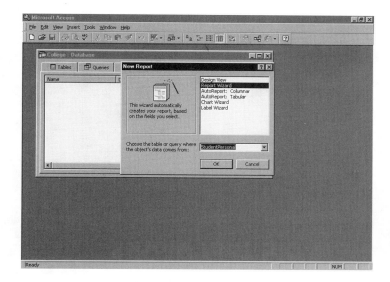

Figure 10.2.

Using the Report Wizard to include the fields you want in your report.

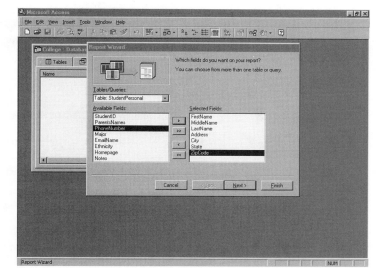

5. Click Next>. There aren't any groups (collections) germane to this report, so click Next> again. Pull down the combo box and choose LastName as a sorting order. Click Next> to move on. Accept Access's defaults for this report, which should be Portrait orientation, a Tabular layout, and Auto adjustments to fit all fields on one page.

6. Click Next>. Click the Compact layout option if it's not already chosen by Access and click Next> to move on.

7. You're almost done now. Edit Access's suggestion for a report title to read: `Students' Names and Addresses`. Your screen should resemble Figure 10.3. Make sure you've chosen the option button "Preview the report."

Figure 10.3.
The last wizard screen.

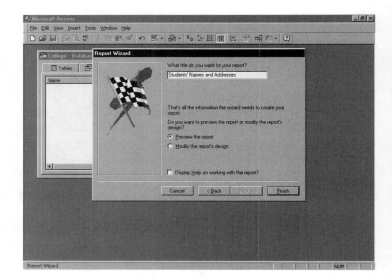

8. Click the Finish button. Access displays the finished report. (See Figure 10.4.)

Figure 10.4.
The finished report from a wizard.

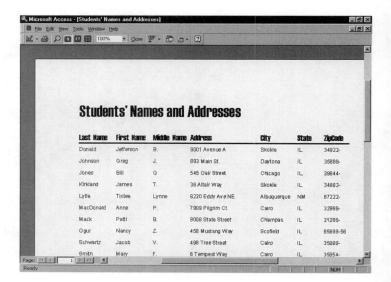

Scroll through this report. If you like, click the Print button in the toolbar to see a printed version of it. All the data is included. There's nothing wrong with this report, but it's not perfect, either.

Altering the Wizard's Output

For most purposes, this report is just fine. Note that all the field labels read all right except for ZipCode. Access uses the Caption property for field labels when making forms or reports. Each field in this table, except for ZipCode, has a name and a different Caption. For example, the field named LastName has a Caption property Last Name. This gives us the best of both worlds. You can use LastName for manipulating data (as in queries) where a space might pose problems, but the field displays as Last Name (that is, in good human terms) in forms and reports. However, without a Caption property set for ZipCode, Access has to fall back on the actual field name for a label.

Exercise 10.2 shows how to change a report.

Exercise 10.2. Modifying a report.

1. Click the Close Window button in the toolbar. This is the button with the word Close on it (some stuff is almost too easy). This button pretty well corresponds in function to the Design View buttons in other Access modules. Your screen should look like Figure 10.5, showing the wizard-created report in Design View.

Figure 10.5.
Report Design View.

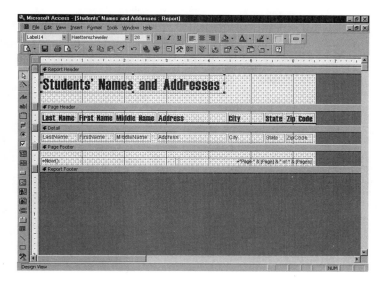

The view you have now is very similar to form Design View. Operating in it is also very similar. You rearrange fields by selecting them and dragging them just as you did in form design. This report is a bit more complex than a simple form because the wizard has left both the report header and footer and the page header and footer sections open.

The Access Way

A *page header* is a section printed at the top of each page. *Page footers* appear at the bottom of each page. Access also can have headers or footers for groups and whole reports. A band is the place in report design where you enter what's to be placed in a header, footer, or the detail section of a report.

In the example shown in Figure 10.5, the words Students' Names and Addresses are in the Report Header band. These words appear at the top the entire report. The Report Header band is a place you put things you want to appear at the top of an entire report and only once. Footers, both page and report, appear at the bottom of each page and report respectively.

This Page Header band has entries for the report labels. Use the Page Header or Footer bands to show information (not just labels) you want to appear at the top and bottom of each page respectively.

2. Click the label with ZipCode on it to highlight it. (See Figure 10.6.) Move your cursor inside the field and it'll become an I-beam cursor, indicating that you're in Edit mode. Move to the place just to the left of the *C* in ZipCode, and press your spacebar. Access will stretch ZipCode into two words. The edited field is shown in Figure 10.7.

The Access Way

A persistent problem people have with visual design program such as Access is selection of individual objects. The problem isn't so much selection as selecting without moving the object at the same time. Access solves this problem quite neatly. Take a look at the Formatting toolbar in Figure 10.5. That's the second or lower toolbar.

The leftmost combo box has the word Report in it. That means that at this time the entire report is selected. Pull down the combo box and you'll see all the objects that are on this report. To select one, just choose it from the pull-down list and Access will highlight it.

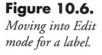

Figure 10.6.
Moving into Edit mode for a label.

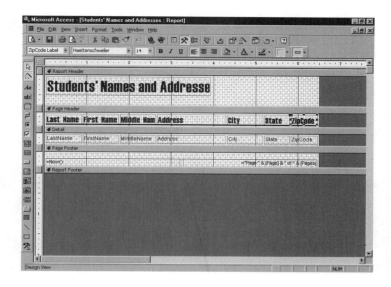

The Access Way

The Page Footer band also has the entry Now() in a text box. This is an Access built-in function that prints the system date or time. The advantage of using a function like Now() in this place is the report picks up the computer's date and time whenever you run this report and places it in the page header.

If you entered a date such as June 1, 1997 for the date field, you'd have to edit the report design each time you ran the report to get the right date in this field. Using the Now() function performs this automatically. You can tell Now() is a function because it ends with the open and closed parentheses [()]. You'll learn more about functions, both built-in and of your own design, later in *Teach Yourself Access 97 in 14 Days*. Built-in functions are discussed in several chapters. Chapter 26, "Programming Made Easy with Visual Basic," shows you how to create custom functions. Don't be concerned if the operation and meaning of Now() isn't fully clear to you at this time.

Figure 10.7.
The edited label.

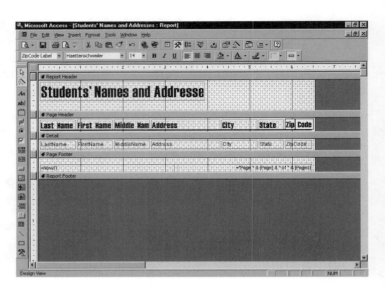

3. To leave Edit mode for the ZipCode field, click anywhere on your screen away
   from the label being edited. You can also resize or move fields or labels just as you
   did with forms. Select the State field. Move to a sizing square and decrease the size
   of this field until it's roughly three-fourths-inch long. Do the same for its label.
   Figure 10.8 shows these fields after they have been resized.

Figure 10.8.
*Resizing report
fields and labels.*

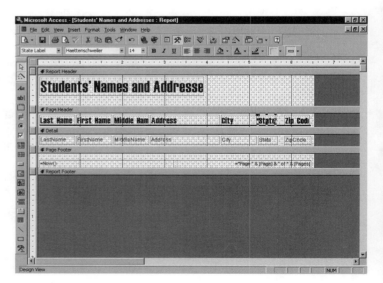

Remember that you can resize a field when the cursor changes to look like a double arrow. You move a field when the cursor looks like a hand. These operations work in report design just as they did in form design.

4. Experiment moving fields around and resizing them. The example moved the Street and City fields to the right so the Middle Name field label could be expanded sufficiently to show the entire word *Name*. Figure 10.9 shows the finished version of the sample report in Design View. Figure 10.10 shows the sample report in Print Preview.

As you change your report around, occasionally click the leftmost button to switch into Report View. If you don't want to chance ruining this report, save and close it now, then rerun the wizard to make a clone to experiment with. You might also want to experiment with other wizard options. For example, Figure 10.11 shows the results of running the wizard with one option change. The layout is specified as justified instead of tabular. What a difference one option can make!

Figure 10.9.

The modified report in Design View.

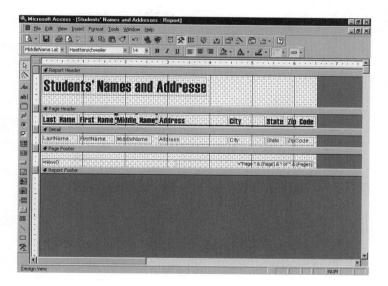

Figure 10.10.

The modified report in Print Preview.

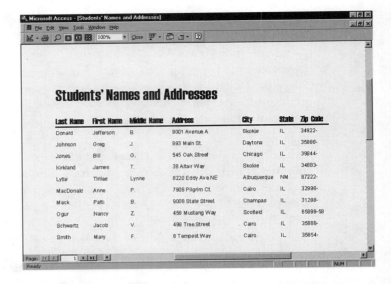

Figure 10.11.

The report from Figure 10.10 shown as justified layout rather than tabular.

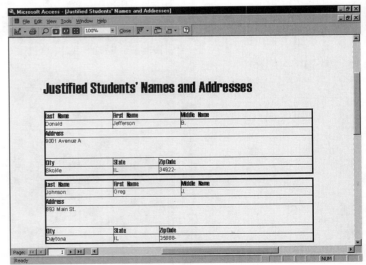

The Access Way

You might find it easier to align your report's fields to look like the example's if you alter the default grid and keep Snap to Grid on. This exercise used the Snap to Grid with a grid set at 10×12.

To change the default grid spacing from 20×24 to a more practical 10×12, pull down the Edit menu and choose Select Report. This selects the entire report rather than just one object or section.

Click the Properties button in the toolbar. Locate the Grid X and Grid Y properties in the Properties list box. Enter 10 for Grid X and 12 for Grid Y. Close the Properties list box by clicking on its button. That's all there is to it.

5. If necessary, reload the Students' Names and Addresses report by returning to the Database window, highlighting that report, and clicking Design. Click the Print Preview button in the toolbar. It's the one first on the left. When you run your cursor over this button, Access responds with the tooltip "View." Click the one-page button, third from the left. Now pull down the combo box that reads "Fit" or shows a percentage from 10 percent to 200 percent in it. This combo box lies two buttons to the right of the one-page button—it's the fifth toolbar object from the left. Experiment with other zoom levels in this box. Zooming at 75 percent is a good compromise for the report at an 800×600 screen resolution. This is shown in Figure 10.12.

Figure 10.12.

A 75 percent zoom of the report from Figure 10.10.

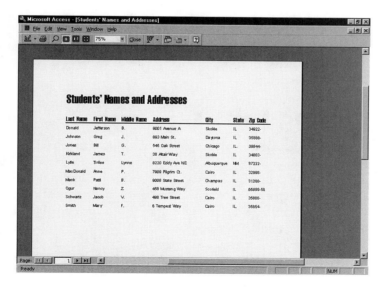

The Access Way

Your report will look different from the screen shots shown here because of screen resolution and font availability. Access chose the Haettenschweiler font for this report's labels and Arial for the report data. If you don't have those fonts your report will, naturally, vary from the examples shown.

This is serviceable, but still a bit away from what you'd want to give your bosses or clients. You'll come back to this report later and spiff it up even more. For now, pull down the File menu and click Close. Save or discard changes as appropriate if you're prompted. Your finished report should, when saved, resemble Figure 10.12.

Do   **Don't**

DO use Report Wizards to rough out your reports.

DON'T be disappointed if a wizard's output isn't exactly what you desire. That's what manual design is for. In many cases a report should be laid out according to the qualitative content of your database. Access wizards, at least in the current version, aren't capable of making value judgments on your data, so they use general rules to lay out your reports. General rules applied to a specific case often come close, but very rarely hit a bull's-eye.

Mailing Labels

Since most printers do a poor job of handling envelopes, creating mailing labels from the information in a database is a common and often annoying job. Making these labels poses two problems: getting the text in the center of the individual labels and preventing label creep. Label creep happens when the text prints right on the first set of labels, but then creeps up or down until it starts printing off the labels and onto the space in between them. The truly annoying thing about label creep is that when it occurs, you often have to do much of the printing job over again, wasting a lot of time and materials.

Access has a wizard aimed at making the label printing job quite a bit easier than it would be if you did it manually. The best part of the wizard is that it has programmed into it the most popular label sizes and layouts cataloged by label number. This way you can just tell Access what type of label you're planning to use and the program does the proper layout. No more do you have to calculate how many 2 3/8-inch labels plus header, footer, and interlabel spaces fit on a page. The makers of the Label Report Wizard have done all the tedious work for you.

Another difference between the Label Wizard and the standard Report Wizard is the former creates report expressions as you supply it field and punctuation information. This distinction doesn't seem apparent now perhaps, but Exercise 10.3 illustrates the differences.

Exercise 10.3. Making mailing labels.

1. You should be at the Database window with the Report tab clicked. If you're not, navigate back to that place. Click the New button to start a new report.

2. Click the pull-down list part of the combo box and select StudentPersonal as the bound table for this set of mailing labels.

3. Click the Label Wizard. Click OK. Choose Avery 5163 as the label type at the next screen, as shown in Figure 10.13. If your label selection doesn't show a large variety of labels, click the Show Custom Labels check box to deselect it. Click Next>. Leave the next screen at the defaults, which for this example are Arial font, 8-point type size, and light font weight, black in color. Click Next>.

   Refer to Figure 10.14. This is where you not only tell Access what fields to include in your mailing labels, but format the labels as you see fit to create a prototype label.

Figure 10.13.

Choosing a label type.

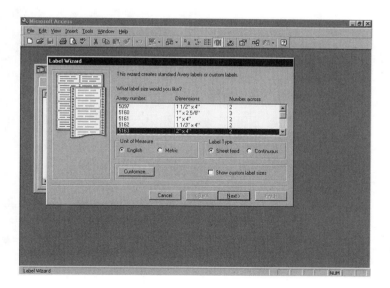

4. Double-click on the FirstName field in the left-hand box. Access inserts the FirstName field between curly braces ({}) to indicate that the data from the FirstName field will be inserted in the labels rather than the word FirstName. Press the spacebar to insert a space between the first and last name. Click on the LastName field, then click the > button to insert the LastName field in the label. Your screen should resemble Figure 10.14.

5. You're ready to move on to the next line, so click where you think a new line should appear on the label—that is, right below the {FirstName} {LastName} line. Access moves the focus down to the second line of your label template.

6. Scroll down the left-hand box until the Address, City, State, and ZipCode fields come into view, if necessary. Add the Address field to the second line of the label. This is the only entry on the second line, so click to make a new line.

Figure 10.14.

Designing the mailing label.

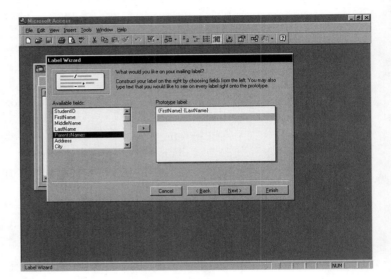

7. Add the City field, a comma, a space, the State field, a space, and finally the ZipCode field to the mailing label's third line. Your screen should resemble Figure 10.15.

The Access Way

You can add literals to mailing labels just like field data. The comma after the City field is a literal, for example. If you want such an entry, such as the word ATTN:, enter it wherever you want it to appear on the label. Access is happy to accommodate you.

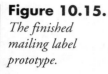

Figure 10.15.
*The finished
mailing label
prototype.*

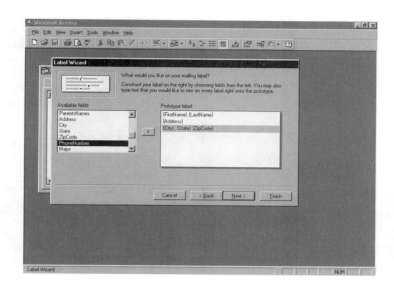

8. Click the Next> button and choose the LastName field to sort or order this label
   report on as shown in Figure 10.16.

Figure 10.16.
*Specifying a field
to sort on for
the report.*

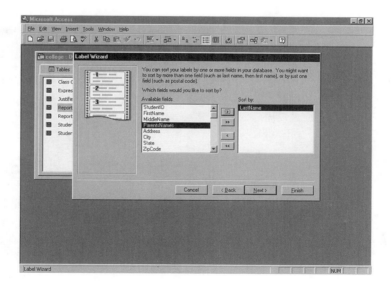

9. Click the Next> button. Here's where you give a name for your label report.
   Edit Access's choice to Student Mailing Labels. Your screen should resemble
   Figure 10.17.

Figure 10.17.
*Naming the
label report.*

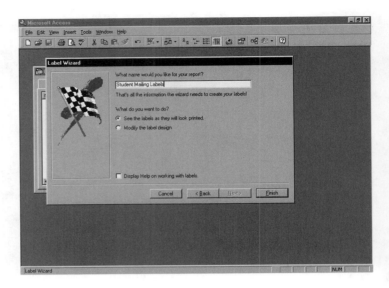

10. Make sure you have the "See the labels as they will look printed" option button
    checked. Click the Finish button to move to Print Preview mode. (See Figure
    10.18.)

Figure 10.18.
*The mailing labels.
Note the sort order
works across, then
down.*

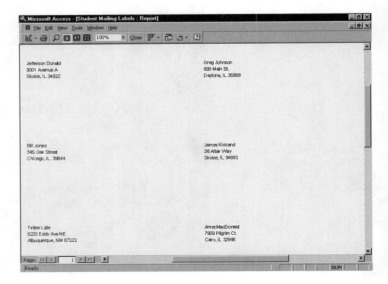

Figure 10.19 shows the Mailing Label Wizard's work in Design View. If you wanted to print these labels for a mailing, you'd only need to tell Access to print this report and feed Avery 5163 or equivalent labels to your printer. Access makes the tedious and often frustrating job of printing mailing labels as simple as using a wizard.

Figure 10.19.

The finished mailing label report in Design View.

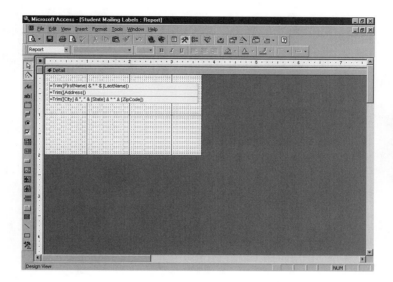

A Look Ahead

Before closing up shop for this afternoon, let's take a look at what's to come tomorrow. Examine Figure 10.19 and note that the expression `=Trim([FirstName] & " " & [LastName])` makes up the first line of this label.

Everything included in this label is an expression. You made these expressions when you instructed the wizard in the Prototype label dialog box, as shown in Figure 10.14.

Examine this label in Design View to get an idea how the wizard interpreted your instructions. Tomorrow you'll learn how to do this wizard trick on your own. Save this report and close it.

Day Summary

This morning you learned how to construct multitable queries and how to use criteria in multitable queries.

This afternoon you learned how to use the general Report Wizard and how to modify some aspects of the wizard's output. You also got a good run at using the Mailing Label Wizard to design mailing or other labels. Keep in mind that the Label Wizard is good not only for mailing labels, but also for other labels such as folder, record, and book labels. The Mailing Label Wizard can be an enormous time and mood saver. Use it whenever you need to put data precisely on standard size labels or cards.

Q&A

Q **I'm making a mailing label, but don't want to output to an Avery brand label. Can I create my own label size?**

A Yes. If none of the predefined labels meets your needs, you can create your label either manually or using the wizard. After you're in Design View for the label, choose File|Page Setup from the menu. This brings up a tabbed dialog box that enables you to create labels (or other page-related information) to your liking. You can see this dialog box in Figure 10.20.

Figure 10.20.

The Page Setup dialog box in report Design View.

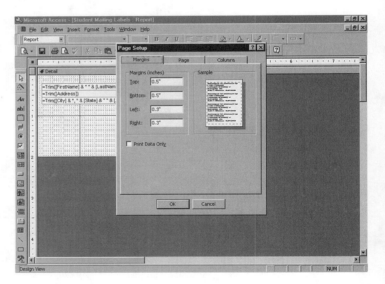

Q **Can I make monster queries with 50 tables and thousands of columns?**

A The monstrous part is something for your judgment. However, Access does put limits on the number of objects in and size of a query. You can put no more than 32 objects in a query nor can that query exceed 255 columns.

Q **What about putting unrelated tables into a query?**

A This does have some limited use, mostly for displaying concatenated information. Technically, this describes something called a "Cartesian product." Unless the parts of the product have some reasonable selection criteria that give them a "relation-ship" of a sort, this product has little if any use.

Q Can I set a display of the running sum in a report?

A Yes, and you are getting a little ahead of where we are. Quickly, you include a running sum by including a bound text box or an unbound text box with an expression in the band where you want the sum to apply to. You then set the Running Sum property for that text box to the sum type you wish to calculate.

Q I tried printing a mailing label report. The report seems to work all right, but the labels came off in my laser printer. This could have caused real damage. Luckily, none was done. What good is making a mailing label report if I can't use my printer to do output?

A You need to buy mailing labels specifically made for laser printers. These work much better than general-purpose labels. Also, if your printer has the option of using a straight paper path, opt for doing the printing that way even if you have to position a tray to catch the output.

Workshop

Here's where you can test and apply what you have learned today.

Quiz

Possible answers to these questions are provided in Appendix A.

1. What is concatenation?
2. Will the expression =Ltrim(Rtrim([FirstName])) yield the same output as =Trim([FirstName])?
3. How often will a label in the Report Header band appear?
4. If you want a footer on each page, where should you put the label when in Design View?
5. Can a mailing label report be based in a query if that query has expressions in-cluded in it? What will the adverse consequences of doing this be?
6. What properties control the grid spacing in the report design grid? (The same properties control the grid spacing in the form design grid.)
7. If you include two tables in a query, what design changes will occur to the table on the *right* side of the query?

10

Put Access into Action

1. Start a new query. Bind the StudentPersonal table to this query.
2. Include the fields for parents' names, addresses, cities, states and ZIP codes in the query.
3. Add a criterion that selects for only those records in which the city name starts with a C.
4. Save the query using a name of your choosing.
5. Create a mailing label report based on this query. Use any predefined label type appropriate to this task.
6. Check your output by using the View button.
7. You may save this report if you want to. This book will not refer to it again.

For the Adventurous

If you feel spunky, try doing a mail merge with Word. From the Database window, highlight an object such as the query you made in steps 1–4 of "Put Access into Action." Choose the Office Links toolbar button. Then choose the Word option and follow your nose. You might prefer to review the online help for the steps before you set off on this adventure.

DAY 6

A.M.

11 Intermediate Reports

P.M.

12 Intermediate Forms

Chapter **11**

Intermediate Reports

This morning you'll learn how to

☐ Create expressions in reports

☐ Group report data

Looking at Report Expressions

Yesterday you saw how you can include fields in reports. Although Exercise 10.1 uses the general Report Wizard, you can also drag fields into reports from a field list box using the same method you did to drag fields into forms.

Fields dropped into forms work well, but as you might imagine, the finished report designed this way can leave a bit to be desired. Although the report at the end of Exercise 10.2 is serviceable, some might not consider it attractive or professional looking because a few fields don't exactly fit the data that went into them. The end of the exercise explains how to adjust field sizes or labels to make them fit better.

In some reports, the field length left by the wizard-generated reports results in rather amateurish-looking output. The fixed-length fields such as those in Exercise 10.2 must be large enough to show all the data that could possibly be entered into them, but then they are too large for some of the entries. If you were to shrink down the fields so that small entries looked good, the longer entries would be truncated, or chopped off.

Here's an example. Fields large enough to show the entire name Constance Jacqueline Fortesque show the name Tom J. Doe like this:

```
Tom          J          Doe
```

Size the fields to fit Tom J. Doe correctly, and Constance Jacqueline Fortesque looks like this:

```
Con J For
```

Neither size compromise is satisfactory. Using expressions based on the fields instead of the fields themselves solves the field size dilemma in this type of report. In this case, an expression is a series of fields, punctuation marks, and spaces that may or may not include some Access-specific instructions. You saw an example of expressions in the Mailing Label Wizard's output. Exercise 11.1 shows how to modify the report from Exercise 10.3 to include field expressions.

The Access Way

Field expressions are only one type of expression you can use in Access. You've already seen some Access expressions in queries, the label report, and in tables. The expressions used in Exercise 11.1 show only a few tricks you can do with expressions.

Exercise 11.1. Field expressions in reports.

This exercise modifies the wizard-generated report to include variable length field sizes. You might not like the result in this report, but the point of this exercise is instruction, not making a perfect report. This technique is very useful for a variety of other reporting tasks.

1. Launch Access if necessary and load the College database. Click the Report tab. Highlight the Students' Names and Addresses report and click the Design button to open this report in Design View. Your screen should resemble Figure 11.1.

Figure 11.1.

The report in
Design View.

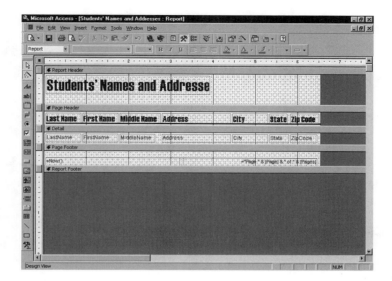

2. Delete the FirstName, MiddleName, and LastName fields from the first line of the
   Detail band of the report design grid. This example used a marquee selection to
   first highlight all the fields, then the Delete or Del key to cut them from the report.
   Use this technique or one you prefer.

The Access Way

You might find selecting fields in this narrow Detail band to be tedious or difficult.
You can increase the size of the Detail band by moving your cursor to the bottom
or top of it, then dragging. If you do this, be sure to return the band back to its
original size before running the report, or the report's spacing will look a bit odd.

If you find using the marquee selection awkward, you can also select several fields
by Shift+clicking them. Shift+click is Access talk for "extend selection."

After you've cut the fields from your report, your screen should resemble
Figure 11.2.

11

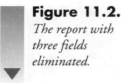

Figure 11.2.

The report with three fields eliminated.

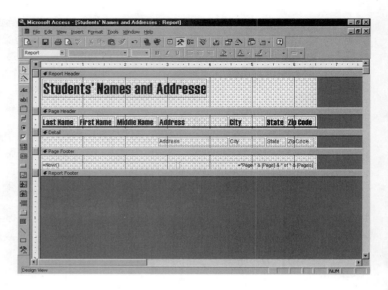

3. Now you need a container for your expression. Initially, this will be an unbound text box. You'll bind the text box to the fields later on. Click the Text Box tool in the toolbox. This is the tool with *ab|* on it. Click in the report's design grid in the Detail band and drag a text box field to be roughly the same size as the Address field next to it. Figure 11.3 shows this operation underway.

4. Click away from the new field to remove the highlight. Click only on the label part of this field and delete it. The label part of the new field will have text in it saying something like "Text 19." You now have a report with a text field to the left of the Street field. The new text field has the word Unbound in it.

5. It's now time to use an expression to bind this field to the underlying table. Click the Properties button in the toolbar. Click the new text box to bring up its properties in the Properties list box. That's the button with a white square and a hand on it over toward the right. Click the Data tab. Locate the Control Source property. Your screen should resemble Figure 11.4, although the name for your text box (in the Properties list box title bar) might be different from that shown in Figure 11.4. The text box's name is unimportant for the purposes of this example.

11

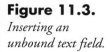

Figure 11.3.
Inserting an unbound text field.

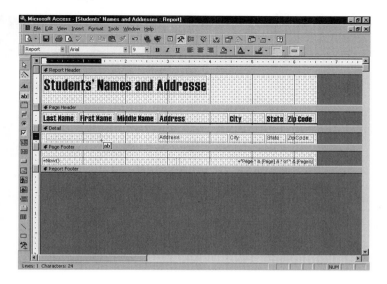

Figure 11.4.
The Control Source property controls what Access displays in a text box.

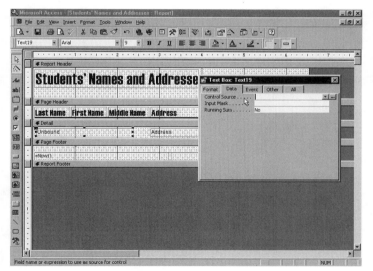

6. Click in the empty row to the right of the Control Source label. Press Shift+F2 to zoom into an editing box. This last step isn't necessary to enter an expression, but it makes your job much easier. Your screen should look like Figure 11.5.

Figure 11.5.
Zoom mode for entering expressions.

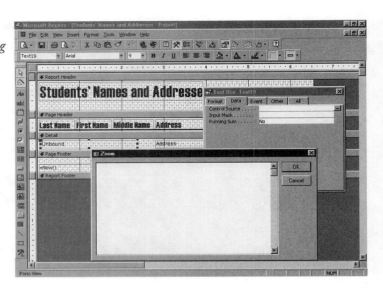

7. Enter the expression: =Trim([FirstName]&" "&[MiddleName]&" "&[LastName]) in the Zoom box. (See Figure 11.6.)

Figure 11.6.
The expression for student name.

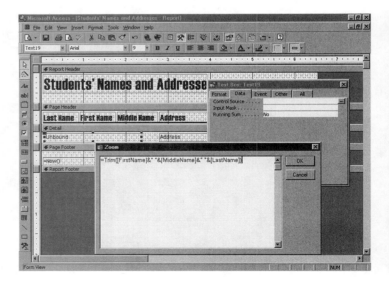

8. Click OK to close the Zoom box. Access will insert the Zoom box's text into the Control Source property. Click the Layout View button to see your results. The first line of your report detail should look like the first lines of the entries in Figure 11.7. Note the differences between this report and the wizard's output from the last chapter.

Figure 11.7.

The report's output after the inclusion of an expression.

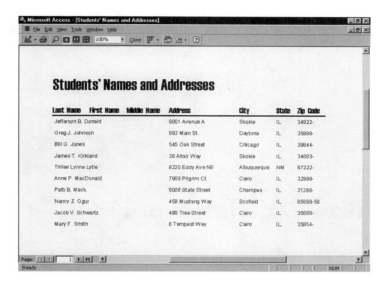

9. Return to Design mode. Delete the City, State and ZipCode fields (not the labels at this point). Insert an unbound text box just as you did for the first line of this report. Delete its label. Highlight the now unbound control. Locate the Control Source entry area for this text box and press Shift+F2. Enter the expression

   `=Trim([City] & ",  " & [State] & " " & [ZipCode])`

   (See Figure 11.8.)

10. Click the Layout View button in the toolbar. Access runs the report. If you've made no typing errors, you'll see your report now automatically sizes the first and third fields to fit the data. The Address field is single, so it doesn't need this treatment. At this point, delete all the labels from the Page Header band because they are out of touch with the body of the report. You could also suppress the display of the Page Header band by shrinking it to zero height.

Figure 11.8.

The expression to concatenate the City, State, ZipCode fields in the report.

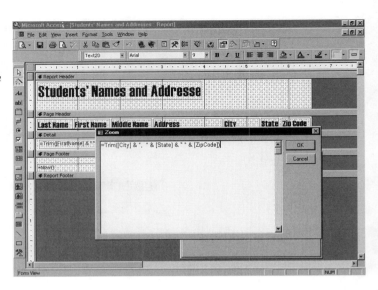

How Did That Work?

Back when you started this report, you told Access to bind the StudentPersonal table to it. This is a key element in how these expressions worked. Return to Design View for this report if you're not there now. Click the Address field to highlight it. Look in the Properties list box to see the control source property for this control. It's set to Address.

A Control Source is the source of what appears as contents for that control when outside of Design View. In the case of the Address control, the contents of the Address field in the StudentPersonal table is what appears when you print or preview this report. Access knows to look in StudentPersonal for the Address field because during the initial phase of the Report Wizard, you told Access that StudentPersonal is the table bound to this report.

When you enter an equals sign (=) at the beginning of a Control Source, you're telling Access you'll be entering an expression—the same as with Excel. You could edit the Control Source for the Address text box to read =[Address], which gives you the same results as you have now with this control, but it would serve no practical purpose.

The expressions you added to the unbound text controls for the Name and the last part of the address are more complex than that. They contain not only the field contents for more than one field, but spaces and a comma.

The Access Way

Access, like many computer programs, interprets the space character as the end of a string of characters—or a delimiter. It is unusual in that it'll let you enter field names containing spaces. These spaces are a problem in expressions because Access has no way of knowing when it hits a space whether you mean that as an end to the name or a part of the field name.

You can use field names containing spaces by enclosing them in square brackets ([ ]) within expressions. It's a good habit to always enter field names within square brackets even if they have one-word names such as Address. That way you'll get into good habits and won't hit baffling "gotchas" later on.

Look at the expression in the first row of this report's Detail band. It reads

```
=Trim([FirstName] & " " & [MiddleName] & " " & [LastName])
```

Let's take it apart to see how it works. The first character is the equals sign (=). This indicates to Access that what follows is an expression.

The second element is the word Trim. `Trim()` is a built-in Access function that strips white spaces from the right and left side of a string of characters. Access has two related functions, `Ltrim()` and `Rtrim()`, which only strip spaces from the left and right of a character string, respectively.

The parentheses that functions come with and are identified by are for function parameters. Parameters are things the functions operate on. In this case, `Trim()`'s parameters are the whole expression. This tells `Trim()` that you want the spaces stripped from the right and left of the whole expression.

The Access Way

You can use `Ltrim()` and `Rtrim()` together with results identical to just `Trim()`. In other words, `=Ltrim(Rtrim([Name]))` results in the same output as `=Trim([Name])`. Access programmers are apparently a wild and crazy bunch.

The third element is the field FirstName in square brackets `[FirstName]`. The StudentPersonal table's field names don't contain spaces, so there's no requirement to include the field name in brackets, but as the sidebar says, it's good practice. There's no penalty for using brackets for field names and two advantages to always doing so: You'll never have an expression with a space misfire due to lack of brackets, and you'll be able to differentiate field names from other elements in expressions.

11

After [FirstName] comes the &, or ampersand operator. This tells Access to concatenate, or join, two elements in a string expression. This first & joins the [FirstName] field to the " ", which is an open quote, a space, and a close quote. If you didn't include this space in the string at this place, the FirstName field would be jammed up against the MiddleName field. The spaces here and after MiddleName prevent Greg J. Jefferson from looking like GregJ.Jefferson.

The rest of the expression follows the first part. The last element is the closed parentheses, indicating the end of the string expression the Trim() function applies to.

The City, State, ZIP Code expression is almost identical to the first except the first space also has a comma (,) inserted. This gives us the comma after the City field in the third line. Anything enclosed in double quotation marks in an Access expression appears as a literal. So if you modified the first row to read as follows:

```
=Trim([FirstName] & " Hi! " & [MiddleName] & " " & [LastName])
```

the report would come out:

```
Greg Hi! J. Jefferson
Bill Hi! G. Jones
```

and so on.

Do	Don't

DO use expressions liberally in your reports. In many cases, they look much better than just fields.

DON'T neglect to enclose all your field names in square brackets even if Access allows you to get away with skipping this step. Good programming practice always pays off.

Groups

Think back to the query done in Exercise 9.2. This showed students' names and courses sorted or ordered by course number. One logical thing you can derive from this query is a report creating student enrollment cards showing all the courses a student is signed up to take for a semester.

Close the report created in Exercise 11.1, saving any changes. The report is part of the sample data using the name Expression Students' Names and Addresses. The point of the next exercise is to create a report showing all the courses all the students are signed up for, plus add up the course load to see the total credit hours for each student. This is a lot simpler to do than to say, as you'll soon see. Exercise 11.2 bypasses the wizard process. Access includes a wizard that sorts and groups well, but using it will disguise the underlying principles this exercise is supposed to demonstrate. At this point you should be comfortable enough manipulating Access that you won't have a problem following along with the comparatively faster pace of this exercise.

Exercise 11.2. A grouped and totaled report.

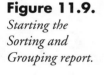

1. At the Database window, click the New button to start a new report. Scroll through the list of queries and tables Access gives you to locate the three-table query done in Chapter 9, "Multitable Queries." If you followed the book's examples exactly, this query is called StudentsAndCourses. (This query is part of the sample data.) Click the query's name, then click the Design View option, then OK.

2. Click the Sorting and Grouping button on the toolbar to open up the combination list box shown in Figure 11.9.

Figure 11.9.

Starting the Sorting and Grouping report.

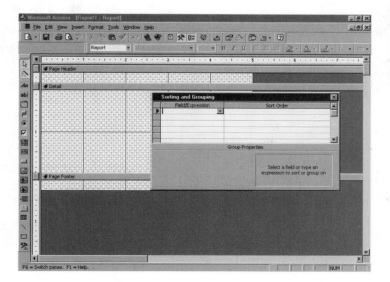

3. Pull down the Field/Expression combo box and click LastName to tell Access you want to group on the LastName field. Access will default to Ascending order. Leave that as it is.

4. Pull down the combo box for Group Header in the Group Properties section and change that to Yes. You can also double-click this field to toggle it. Access will add another band to the report.

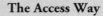

The Access Way

LastName works for this example because our tiny database has no duplication of names. In a live application, you wouldn't want to group on the LastName field because duplicate names can easily exist in your data. Instead, you'd use the key field for the StudentPersonal table, which is StudentID. While this report and query work with the sample data, grouping on a field that might contain duplicate entries isn't good practice.

5. Open the Field list box by clicking on its button on the toolbar. That's the button with a plain piece of paper on it as shown in Figure 11.10. If your screen is too cluttered for your tastes, close the Sorting and Grouping box by clicking on its toolbar or × icon. At this point your screen should resemble Figure 11.10.

Figure 11.10.

Setting up to add fields for the Sorting and Grouping report.

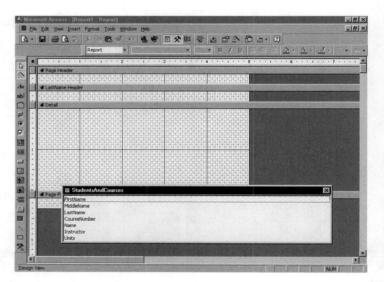

6. Click the LastName field in the field list box. Drag it to the LastName Header band. Click away from the LastName field, then click its label only. Press Delete to remove the field label from this field.

7. Click and drag the Name (this is the course name) to the detail section of the report. Do likewise with the Number, Instructor, and Units fields.

8. This next step isn't really tricky, but it's tedious. You need to move the labels, and only the labels of all the fields in the Detail section, from the Detail section to the Group Header section. The Group Header section, or band, is the band labeled

LastName Header where you dragged the LastName field earlier. You will probably
have to enlarge this band to accommodate the new field labels. The easiest way to
remove and insert the labels is to click on the report away from any fields, then
click a field label. Hold down the Shift key and click the other three labels. Press
Ctrl+X to cut the labels to the clipboard. Click in the Group Header section and
press Ctrl+V to paste the labels there.

9. Arrange the report to look like Figure 11.11. Don't be overly concerned about
    aligning fields to look good. The focus of this exercise is grouping, not aligning.
    You can always prettify your reports after you have the basics down.

Figure 11.11.

*The arranged
report.*

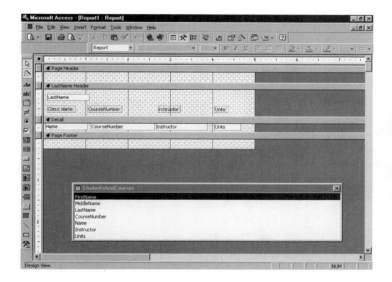

10. Click the Layout View button on the toolbar. Your report should perform like the
    one shown in Figure 11.12 even if it doesn't look exactly like it.

Even the book's example isn't terribly neat looking, but it works and that's the important
thing. The only two elements missing are a label for the students' last names and some detail
to show the current course load for each student. Exercise 11.3 shows you how to add these.

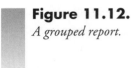

Figure 11.12.
A grouped report.

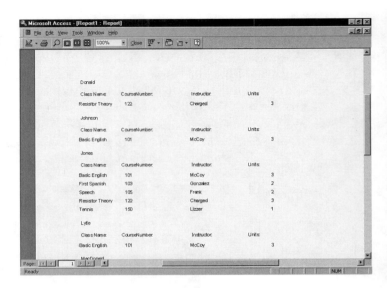

Exercise 11.3. Adding report elements.

1. Return to Design View for this report, if necessary, by clicking the Close button in Print Preview. Open up the Sorting and Grouping box if you closed it last exercise. Locate the Group Footer pull-down field in the Sorting and Grouping box. Double-click this to change its entry to Yes and open up a Group Footer band. Close the Sorting and Grouping box if you choose.

2. Locate the Text Box control in the toolbox. This is the same as the Text Box control for forms. Click it and drag a text box in the LastName Group Footer band right under the Units field. Open the Properties list box and locate the Control Source for this unbound text box. Enter =Sum([Units]) as a control source for this text box. Edit this control's label to read Total.

   Keep in mind that you can edit the label's entry by either clicking within it, then editing the contents, or by locating the Caption property in its Properties list box (labels have them too) and editing the entry there.

3. Locate the Label control in the toolbox. That's the control with the large A on it. Click it and drag to add a label just above the LastName field. Enter Student Name: in this label. This example also changed the font size from 8 to 11 and made it bold for both the label and the LastName field. Your screen should resemble Figure 11.13. This is a bit redundant, as you could have edited the original label, but this exercise shows what you can do. You can decide later how you want to do things.

4. Run the report by clicking on the Layout or Print Preview button. Then save it (File|Save As) under the name Class Cards. When running, your results should look like Figure 11.14, although your alignment probably won't be the same. The important things to focus on are

☐ Is your report grouping on the students' last names?

☐ Are your unit totals correct?

Figure 11.13.

Design View of a slightly complex report.

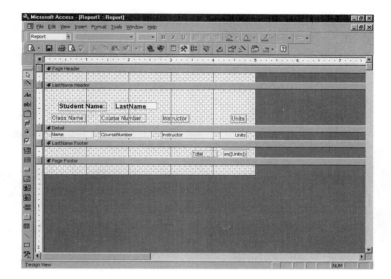

This report doesn't look very good, but it could if you changed the fonts and font sizes using the Formatting toolbar, added a few lines or boxes from the toolbox, and generally aligned the fields better. If you tell Access to break each page on the group by adding a page break, you have a report that prints out a class card for each student on a new piece of paper. You've seen the fundamentals this morning. Adding the frills can be time-consuming, but isn't technically difficult. Figure 11.15 shows the same report with some added lines and formatting. It took about three minutes for an experienced Access user to go from Figure 11.14 to Figure 11.15.

Figure 11.14.
Print Preview of a slightly complex report.

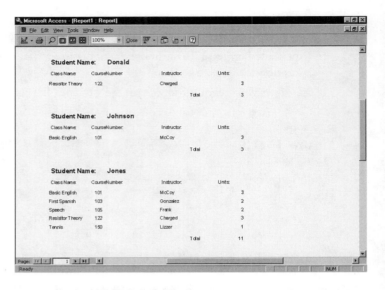

Figure 11.15.
The report with a few added frills.

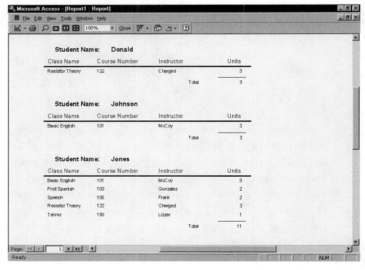

Morning Summary

Reports present data much as forms do. The biggest difference between forms and reports is that forms work best on the screen while reports work best printed. You can view report data on the screen, and you can print forms, but neither is optimal.

Access contains report wizards that work much like form wizards. Two extremely handy report wizards are the Mailing Label and Sorting and Grouping options in the standard Report Wizard. Both save you a great deal of time. You didn't see the Sorting and Grouping Wizard in this chapter because it's rather self-explanatory. Instead, you reproduced the work of the wizard manually.

The Mailing Label Wizard has memorized the dimensions of just about all the labels you're likely to encounter, so it'll save you a great deal of layout frustration, too.

Chapter **12**

Intermediate Forms

This afternoon's material covers these topics:

- ☐ Using list or combo boxes in forms
- ☐ Binding combo boxes to lists
- ☐ The TabControl for forms
- ☐ Adding graphics with Image Control
- ☐ Dynamic indexing in combo boxes

Using List or Combo Boxes in Forms

Think about the data entered in the StudentCurrentCourses table. It contains information related (linked) to two additional tables: StudentPersonal, which holds the student IDs; and AvailableClasses, which holds course number information. You wouldn't want even the possibility of entering an incorrect student ID or course number into this form.

The StudentCurrentCourses table is linked to both AvailableClasses and StudentPersonal, and Access has been told to enforce referential integrity in these links. In this context, referential integrity means that when you enter, for example, a StudentID in the StudentCurrentCourses table, Access will look in StudentPersonal to make sure that StudentID really exists. The same rule exists for entering a Course Number in StudentCurrentCourses because it's linked on that field to the AvailableClasses table.

Referential integrity enforcement does prevent entry of wrong or nonexistent student IDs or course numbers. It does nothing to assist the data-entry person in finding the right values for these fields.

Primitive data-entry systems gave data-processing people a paper list of valid entries as a reference. This worked, but wasn't particularly efficient. What would be much better is to have Access look up correct values from within a data-entry form bound to StudentCurrentCourses. This eliminates the need for paper references and greatly speeds up the data-entry process. It also goes a long way toward preventing data-entry people from entering a valid, but wrong, value for either of these fields.

Like so many things in personal computers, getting a feeling for how this works is easier when seen than explained. The exercises that follow create a form for entering data into StudentCurrentCourses. Two of the controls on this form look up existing values from previously entered data.

All the controls on the forms shown so far in this book have been text or memo boxes. You can do data entry and basic editing within them. List and combo boxes are also handy controls for data entry. A list box shows a list of values you can scroll through. A combo box, a combination of a list box and a text box, has a place to enter data and a drop-down list that works exactly like the list box. Exercise 12.1 shows you how to create a form with a combo box. The administration will use this form at the end of the semester to record student grades.

Exercise 12.1. A form with combo boxes.

1. If necessary, launch Access and open the College database. Click the Form tab and click the New button to create a new form. Pull down the combo box; scroll to the StudentCurrentCourses table and click it. Your screen should resemble Figure 12.1.

EXERCISE

12

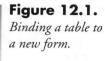

Figure 12.1.

*Binding a table to
a new form.*

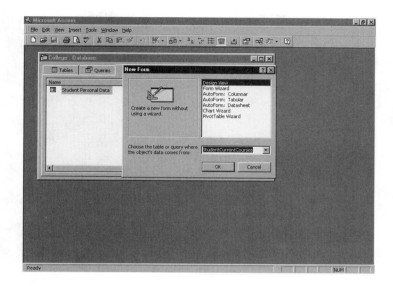

2. Be sure to select (or leave selected) the Design View option to bypass the wizards.

The Access Way

This will be a simple form with some fancy controls—combo boxes for two fields.
There's no way to tell Access to use combo boxes rather than text boxes during a
simple wizard form operation. In this case, using the wizard, then undoing what
the wizard left us, would be more work than just going directly to manual design.
You could, though, run the wizard, then have Access change the control type from
text box to combo box. However, manual design teaches techniques better than
running a wizard, and learning the technique is the real point of this exercise.

3. After you click OK, your screen should resemble Figure 12.2. Note that in this
figure, the toolbox has been reshaped to be vertically docked at the left of the
screen, and the screen is maximized. Your actual screen might vary from this figure.
If your screen doesn't show the StudentCurrentCourses Field list box, click the
Field List button in the toolbar. If your screen is more complex than the screen in
Figure 12.2 because it has, for example, the Properties list box or the Formatting
toolbar showing, you can either keep them or close them by clicking the appropriate toolbar button.

12

Figure 12.2.

The form design grid.

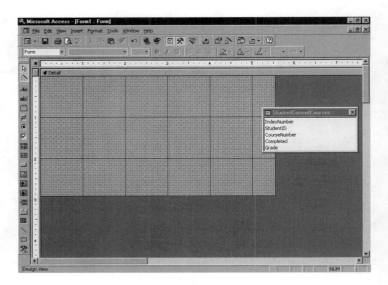

4. The StudentCurrentCourses table has a key field (IndexNumber) that sports the data type AutoNumber-Increment. Since Access increments this field automatically when you enter records, you don't need to include that in this form. The only fields you need to include on a form are those you enter data into or those that have information you need to view. You can safely skip IndexNumber because it meets neither of these criteria. Click the StudentID field to select it for placing on the form.

Do   **Don't**

DO include only those fields on your forms you need to view, edit, or make entries into.

DON'T litter up your forms with unnecessary fields. Doing so serves no useful purpose and will only confuse your users.

5. Examine the toolbox in Figure 12.2. Note that the magic wandlike tool is selected, indicating Control Wizards are on. Click your Control Wizard toggle, if necessary, to turn it on, too.

6. The first field you'll place on this form is StudentID. You'll use a combo box for this and let a wizard do most of the work. Click the Combo Box tool in the toolbox. This tells Access that you want to use this control type for the previously selected StudentID field. Click the StudentID field in the StudentCurrentCourses

list box. Hold down the mouse button and drag the StudentID field to the form design grid. Release the mouse button. Access will automatically start up the Combo Box Wizard. Your screen should resemble Figure 12.3.

7. Of course you want the combo box to look up values for you, so leave the top option box checked and click the Next> button.

Figure 12.3.

Inserting a combo box in a form.

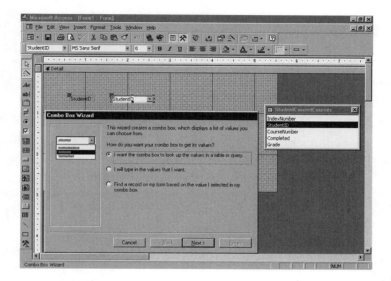

8. The values for the StudentID field you want to look up are located in the StudentPersonal table because the purpose of this exercise is to make sure that no record is added to StudentCurrentCourses for a student not previously entered in StudentPersonal. Highlight StudentPersonal in the next list box. Your screen should resemble Figure 12.4. Click the Next> button. Like the Show Table list box in query design, this dialog box gives you the option of showing tables, queries, or both. Keep in mind that you can look up values in queries as well as tables.

9. You could have only the StudentID field appear in this combo box, but most people find it easier to search a list for text values such as a person's name than to look for an arbitrary set of numbers and letters such as the StudentID. Click the > button four times to include not only the StudentID, but the FirstName, MiddleName, and LastName fields. Your screen should resemble Figure 12.5.

12

Figure 12.4.
Binding a combo box to a table.

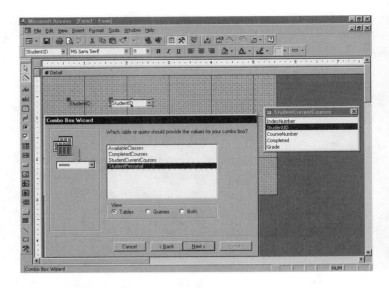

Figure 12.5.
Including fields in a combo box.

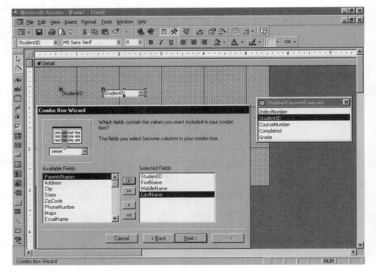

10. Click the Next> button to move to a dialog where you can adjust the field widths that will be shown in this combo box. Be sure there's no check in the Hide Key column (recommended) choice. This example left the field widths at their defaults as shown in Figure 12.6. You can change the width of the drop-down combo box's

fields at this screen by clicking between the fields and dragging, just as you can adjust apparent field widths in Datasheet View. You can also hide the key field. Users will look up data both by name and by asking for the StudentID number, so deselect this check box if it has a checkmark in it. Click the Next> button.

Figure 12.6.

Adjusting the field widths in a combo box.

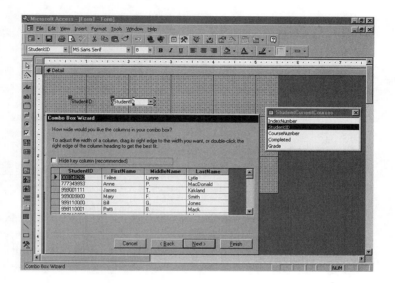

11. At this point Access will ask you for the field that uniquely identifies the record. In this case it's the StudentID field, so leave it selected, and click Next> to move on. In the next dialog box, tell Access what to do with the value looked up. Because you want to enter the value in the StudentID field of the bound table, StudentCurrentCourses, leave the default option button. Store that value in this field, selected as in Figure 12.7. Click the Next> button.

12. Don't modify the label for this field, as is your option in this dialog box. Click the Finish button to see your results. Access grinds around a bit and ends up placing the now programmed combo box on your form. Click the Form View button to see how this control works. Click this combo box's down arrow. (See Figure 12.8.) If your combo box is too small to show all the fields, open up the Properties list box. Find the List Width property in the Format tab and enter 4. This tells Access to make the entire drop-down box 4 inches in width. Save the form, giving it the name Student Enrollment.

12

Figure 12.7.

Telling Access how to handle a looked-up value.

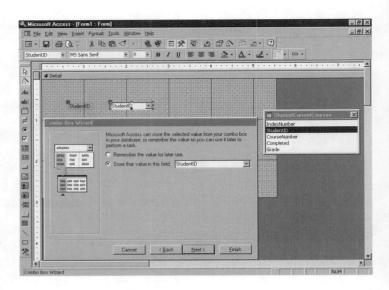

Now entering correct values in this form for the StudentID field is as simple as pulling down the combo box and clicking on the value you want from the supplied list. This list has the added advantage of showing not only the StudentID field, but also the FirstName, Middle-Name, and LastName fields, so a data-entry person can locate a record on these values, not just StudentID.

Figure 12.8.

The programmed combo box.

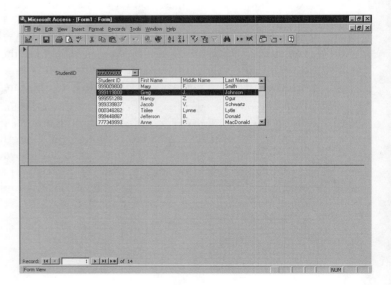

A multicolumn combo box can be an important option if you create applications that serve the public. Have you ever been annoyed that someone you're doing business with required that you remember your customer identification number before you could be located in the business's records? A multicolumn combo box enables you to locate people by various fields in their records.

Auto Expanding

Access will try to locate values already in a combo box list as you make an entry into the text portion of the combo box. Using the partly completed form created in the preceding exercise, move to a new record (if necessary) by clicking on the New button in the toolbar, then try this: Pull down the combo box to show the list portion of the combo box. Enter 8. Access immediately knows that there's only one value in the list that begins with the number 8, and it not only goes to that value in the list portion, but fills in the text section of the combo box with this value for you. (See Figure 12.9.)

Figure 12.9.

Auto Expand in action.

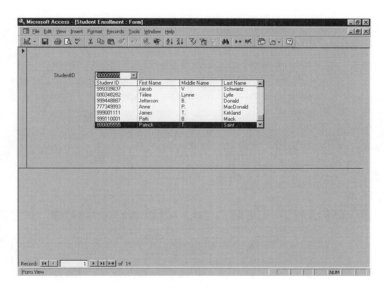

Try the same procedure, but enter 9 instead of 8. Access immediately moves to the top of the section where StudentIDs start with a 9 and fills the text portion of the combo box with the value located there. Enter two more 9s. This still doesn't give Access any more limiting information because all the StudentIDs starting with a single 9 also start with three 9s. Now enter 0. Access immediately knows you must mean the StudentID 999009800 because that's the only one that starts with three 9s followed by a 0.

Combo box Auto Expand (or auto index) works the same with text as with numbers. If you have the values Tom, Thomas, and Tirilee in your combo box's list section, entering *T* takes you to the top of the *T*s and fills in the value Tirilee in the text portion of the combo box. Entering an *o* or an *h* next lets Access move your selection to the single right one if it's not Tirilee. The property that controls whether Access auto expands (or auto indexes if you prefer) is the Auto Expand property under the Data tab in the Properties list box.

The Access Way

If you set the Limit to List (next to Auto Expand in the list box) property to Yes, you're telling Access to limit the entries in a field to those entries already entered in the field specified as a Row Source.

Return to Design View after you're satisfied that you are familiar with combo box operations.

The Access Way

If you change the Limit to List property to No, you can alter the data in the StudentID field on this form for an existing record. If after experimenting with this control you find your actual data is out of sync with the book's, you probably modified existing data rather than experimenting with a new record. You can continue on with slightly modified data or edit your data back to the book's by comparing your data with the unmodified sample data.

Manual Combo or List Box Programming

The wizard works fine for programming list or combo boxes, but the reason for the wizard's actions is important to learn also. Just as you should use a calculator only after you know how to add, you should know what a wizard is doing with these controls before you use it. Exercise 12.2 shows how to manually program a combo or list box.

You use the same method for programming both a combo box and a list box. Whether you use a list or combo box depends on your aesthetic sense and your specific application. List boxes remain full size—there's no pulling them down. List boxes work well when you want to show a value selection all the time or when you don't want a pull-down control. Figure 12.10 shows the CourseNumber field as it would appear on this form in a list box.

Figure 12.10.

A list box on a form.

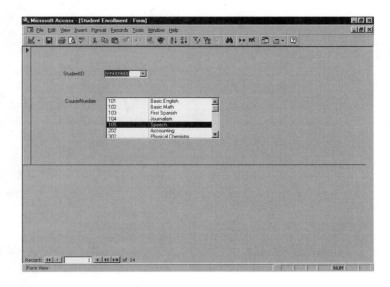

Exercise 12.2 creates a combo box for the CourseNumber field. If you prefer the list box, you could use that for this application as well.

Exercise 12.2. Manual combo box programming.

1. Return to Design View for the form started in Exercise 12.1. Click the Control Wizards button in the toolbox to turn off Control Wizards. Move your cursor to the bottom of the form design grid until it's on the border. Your cursor changes to a bar with an up- and down-facing arrow. Click and drag the form down to resize it to resemble the form in Figure 12.11.

2. Click the Combo Box control in the toolbox, then click the CourseNumber field in the Field list box and drag the CourseNumber field onto the form just under the StudentID field. (See Figure 12.12.)

   This time Access didn't start up a Combo Box Wizard because you turned off these wizards by toggling the Wizard control in the toolbox earlier in the exercise. If you failed to do this and the wizard started anyway, just click the Cancel button to end the wizard's participation in this exercise.

EXERCISE

12

Figure 12.11.
Resizing a form.

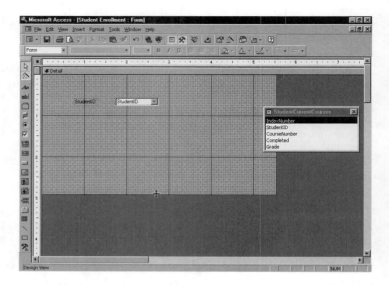

Figure 12.12.
Placing a new combo box on a form.

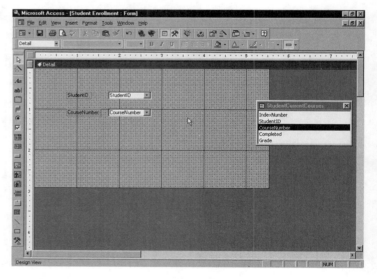

3. Programming this combo box amounts to setting certain properties for it in the Properties list box. You can use an SQL (Structured Query Language) statement to set these properties, or you can use the method shown in this exercise.

   Click the Properties list box button—the button with the icon showing a hand holding a white square. Find the Row Source property (it's in the Data tab section), and click its row. Pull down this property's combo box, and click the AvailableClasses table. Remember, the values you want to look up for this field reside in the AvailableClasses table. Your screen should resemble Figure 12.13. When you dragged the field from the Field list box, you told Access where to store the looked-up value (in the CourseNumber field within the StudentCurrentCourses table).

Figure 12.13.

Binding the combo box to a table; in other words, telling it where to look up its values.

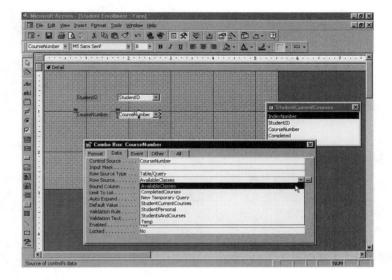

The Access Way

Access, by default, binds the first column of a table or query specified in the Row Source property of a list or combo box. In this case, Access binds to the CourseNumber field in AvailableClasses. This is right for our purposes. It's not as if Access were suddenly able to read our minds, but rather that the CourseNumber field is first in the AvailableClasses table.

12

4. Modify the combo box's Format properties to match the list box in Figure 12.14. This example changed the Column Count, Column Heads, Column Widths, and List Width properties. Also check to make sure Limit to List and Auto Expand properties under the Data tab are set to Yes.

5. Click the Form View button and then pull down the combo box to see the operation of this control. Your screen should resemble Figure 12.15. This example also added the input mask of AAA\-AA\-AAAA to the StudentID field. The Input Mask property is under the Data tab of the StudentID's Properties list box.

Figure 12.14.
Programming the combo box.

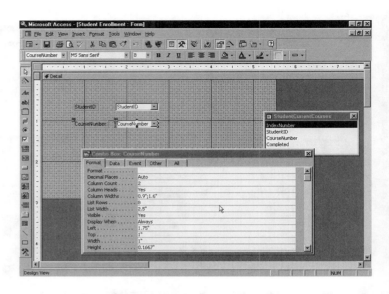

Figure 12.15.
The finished combo box.

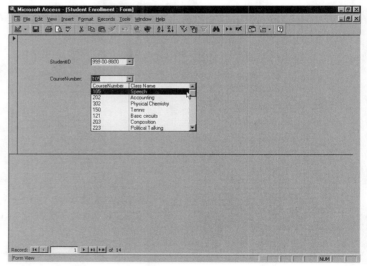

How It Worked

Table 12.1 lists the control's properties you altered and provides an explanation of what the modifications did.

Table 12.1. The Course Number combo box.

Property	Value	Meaning
Column Count	2	Show the first 2 columns of the AvailableClasses table.
Column Widths	.9";1.6"	Set these widths for columns 1 and 2, respectively.
List Width	2.5"	Make the entire list portion (the thing that drops down) of the combo box 2.5 inches.

The Access Way

You can activate a combo or list box by pointing and clicking as in the preceding example. However, Access is a program firmly based on SQL, and many prefer to perform lookups using this language, which also forms the underpinnings of Access queries.

SQL is a subject worthy of its own book, and there's not room enough in this chapter for even a primer on this language. Later on you'll get a small introduction to it. SQL is really just plain English (although a bit stilted) and not all that tough to pick up.

To get a quick course in SQL, create a few queries, pull down the combo box attached to the leftmost button, and choose SQL View. Access will respond by showing you the underlying SQL statement that forms the query.

Another good idea is to let the Combo Box Wizard or List Box Wizard run a few times and examine the SQL statement it constructs for a Row Source property. For example, if you wanted to manually create a SQL statement for a Row Source to do what you did in the preceding exercise, you'd enter

```
SELECT DISTINCTROW [AvailableClasses].[CourseNumber],
[AvailableClasses].[Name] FROM [AvailableClasses];
```

and that would do it. Remember, when you are addressing fields in Access tables you use the field's name, not its Caption property. If you pull down the combo box you made manually, you'll see the Caption property for column heads, not the actual field names. That's why the second field in the SQL statement appears as Name when its column head appears as Course Name.

12

Finishing Up

Finishing this form takes little more effort. Return to Design View. Click the Check Box control in the toolbox. Drag the Completed field to the form so it occupies a place on the form similar to that shown in Figure 12.16. Click the Text control and drag the Grade field to the form so it also occupies a place on the form similar to that shown in Figure 12.16. You'll probably have to rearrange your fields somewhat to make your form look like Figure 12.16.

The only thing left is to enter a label for this form. Click the View menu. Click the Form Header/Footer selection to show this section of the form design grid. Click the Label control in the toolbox. Click in the Form Header band and enter the label: Student Enrollment Form. Press Enter to leave Edit mode. While in Edit mode, your screen should resemble Figure 12.17.

Pull down the Font Size combo box and select 18 as the point size for this label. Click the Bold button to change the font to bold. Resize the label box to accommodate the new size and style font. Click the Form View button. Your screen should resemble Figure 12.18.

Save this form as Student Enrollment if you didn't already do so.

Figure 12.16.
Finishing up the form.

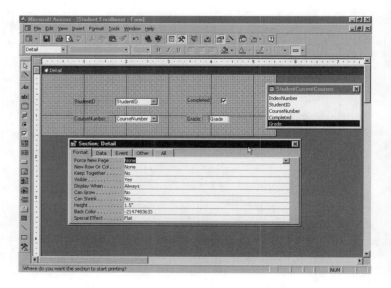

Figure 12.17.

Placing a label on a form.

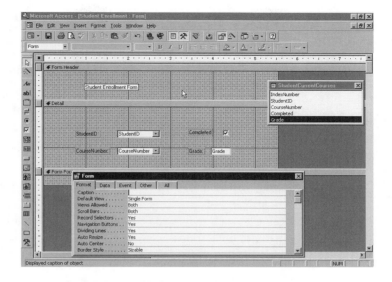

Figure 12.18.

A functionally finished form.

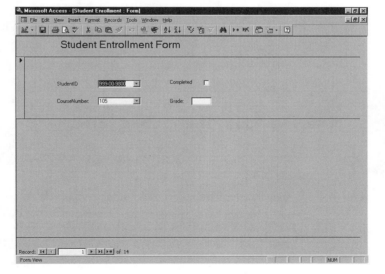

The Tabbed Form

Access 97 includes a TabControl as one of the tools in the toolbox. The TabControl makes it possible for you to use one form for several views using a format identical to what Microsoft uses in its complex dialog boxes.

The Database window is an example of a tabbed form. Each tab has on it a different selection of objects. The advantages of such a tabbed form are

☐ You can stack data in the z axis as well as the x and y axes as on usual forms, so you can include more data on a form.

☐ You can group data or form controls according to some logic you wish to include in your application.

☐ You can give your application a sophisticated look that matches what users will see in Microsoft applications.

Using a TabControl is fairly simple. You add a TabControl from the toolbox to the form, add the controls you want, then do some simple formatting to make the tabbed form look as you wish. You can also use macros or Visual Basic for Applications to manipulate TabControls. This example sticks to the basics. Once you see how to use macros and Visual Basic in your applications, you'll have no difficulty applying those skills to TabControls.

Exercise 12.3 shows you how to create a tabbed form for StudentPersonal data. The exercise creates a form with two pages—one for home information and one for school information.

Exercise 12.3. The tabbed form.

1. Open Access if necessary. Click the Forms tab, then click New. Bind the form to the StudentPersonal table, then click OK. Your screen should resemble Figure 12.19.

2. Locate the TabControl in the toolbox—that's the control that looks like two stacked manila folders—and click it. Note that the tooltip for the TabControl is "Tab Control." Click in the Detail area of the form. Your screen should look like Figure 12.20.

3. You'll need a larger TabControl to accommodate all the controls, so increase the size of the TabControl to roughly the size of the entire form. Open the Field list box by clicking its icon in the toolbar.

EXERCISE

12

Figure 12.19.
Starting the tabbed form.

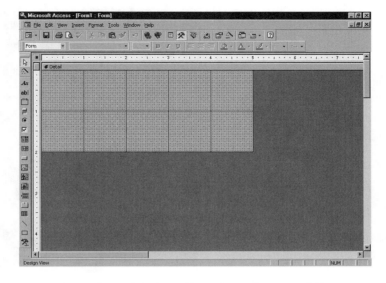

Figure 12.20.
Adding a TabControl to a form.

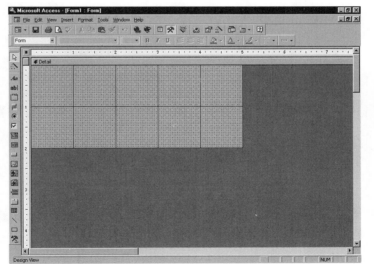

12

4. Drag all the fields, starting with StudentID and ending with PhoneNumber, onto the first page of the TabControl. You choose which page of a TabControl is active by clicking on the page or its tab. Arrange your fields in any manner you like, or follow the book's example as shown in Figure 12.21.

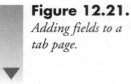

Figure 12.21.

Adding fields to a tab page.

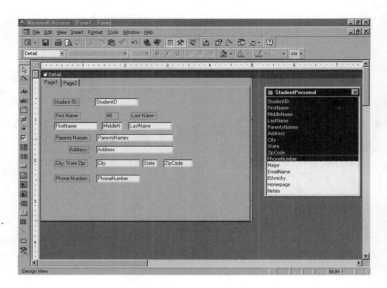

5. Click the tab that says Page2 to activate page 2 of the TabControl. Now drag the rest of the fields to this page, arranging them as you see fit. Figure 12.22 shows the book's arrangement.

Figure 12.22.

Adding fields to a tab page.

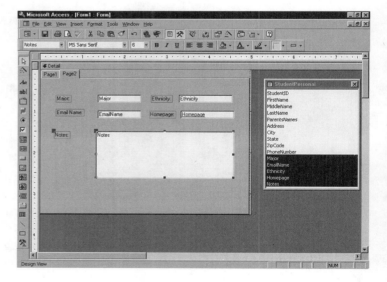

6. The form is almost finished. The only thing left is to add meaningful captions (labels) to the tabs. To do this, open up the Properties list box. Click the Format tab in the Properties list box. Click the tab that now says Page2. Locate the Caption property (it's first) and enter School Information as a caption for this page. Press Enter or tab away from this field, and Access will add the new caption to the TabControl. (See Figure 12.23.)

Figure 12.23.

Changing the caption for a tab page.

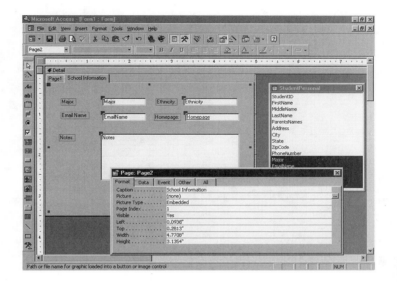

7. Now use the same method to change the caption for Page1 of the form to read Home Information. That's it— you're done. Save this form as TabbedStudentPersonal.

Switch to Form View. Try clicking on each tab to see the different views of your data. Figure 12.24 shows how the sample form turned out.

If you want to add or remove pages to or from your tabbed form, right-click the last tab, then choose Delete Page or Insert Page, depending on what you want to do.

The Access Way

You can add any kind of control to a TabControl page except another TabControl.

Figure 12.24.

The tabbed form in action.

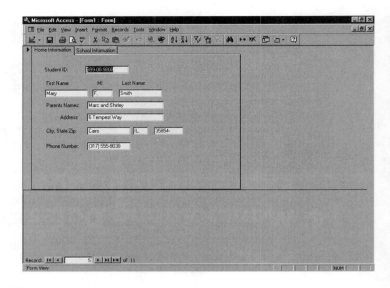

The Image Control

Access 97 includes a control that makes it very easy to include graphics on forms and reports. Using this control is quite simple, as the following example illustrates. While this isn't a formal exercise, you can treat it as such.

This demonstration adds the graphic fictional.bmp (part of the sample data found in Appendix E) to the TabbedStudentPersonal form.

Figure 12.25 shows the TabbedStudentPersonal form opened in Design View. The fields have been moved around some to accommodate the image.

Click the Image control in the toolbox. Click anywhere on the first page of the tabbed form. Access will bring up a dialog box asking you which graphic file to open. If you're following along, your screen should resemble Figure 12.26.

Locate the graphic you wish to include in the form. Move the graphic to a reasonable location where it doesn't cover the fields. Figure 12.27 shows the finished form in Form View.

Figure 12.25.

The tabbed form ready to get a graphic.

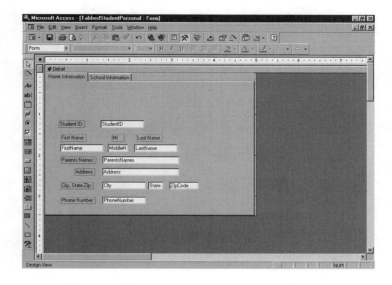

Figure 12.26.

Telling Access which graphics file to include on the form using the Image control.

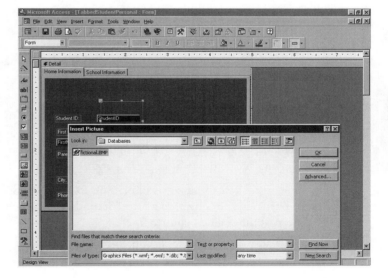

Figure 12.27.

The tabbed form with a graphic added.

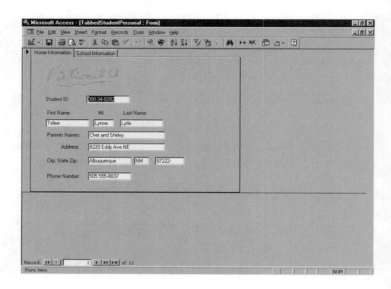

Day Summary

Combo and list boxes show a list of data. Although these controls have a variety of uses, most often Access developers use them to look up existing data to make data entry easier or to help in data validation. You can insert and program these controls both manually and with a wizard.

The trick to making these controls work properly is to bind their Row Source property to a proper source. This source can be an entered list or a previously existing query or table. After you've set this property to point to the right source, all that remains of the list or combo box programming is to improve its aesthetics or its ease of use.

The TabControl can add a z-axis dimension to your forms. There are three steps in this process. First, add the control to a form. Second, add the controls to the individual pages. Third, format the pages as you see fit.

Using the Image control, you can easily include existing graphics files in reports and forms. Simply add the control to a form or report, then tell Access which graphic to use for that control.

12

Q&A

Q **How do you show the Report and Page Header and Footer bands? I need to open these bands before I can enter data into them.**

A In report Design View, click the Layout View menu, then select either Report Header/Footer or Page Header/Footer.

Q **Why can't Access be smart enough to know when field names end and begin without my bothering with square brackets?**

A Look at the following: Last Name Street Address. What are the field names? They might be Last Name and Street Address, or there might be three fields here—Last Name, Street, and Address. Placing brackets—[Last Name][Street Address]— removes any ambiguity.

Q **I don't like the manila file look of the TabControl, but I like its function. Can I change the appearance of this control?**

A You can to some extent. The TabControl has a Style property (under Format) which will allow you to substitute buttons for tabs in this control.

Q **Why not just apply the `Trim()` function to the fields themselves rather than construct an expression?**

A Following your idea, you'd need three `Trim()`s, and although Access allows this, you wouldn't get your desired result. Look at the Mailing Label Example report's second line. It reads =Trim([Address]). The reason your idea won't work is fields start and end at specific places. If the fields could shift around to make room for nonspace characters and squeeze back for trimmed spaces, your technique would be all right. You wouldn't want to do it anyway. It would actually be more effort than just making an expression because you'd need to edit three fields.

Q **What's the difference between Row Source and Control Source in a combo box?**

A Row Source is the source for the data in the list portion of a combo or list box. Control Source is where the data entered in this form will end up in the bound table or query.

Q **Can I use OLE to edit pictures in the Image control?**

A No. You need to edit the picture outside of the Image control.

12

Workshop

Here's where you can test and apply what you have learned today.

Quiz

Possible answers to these questions are provided in Appendix A.

1. What first character tells Access an entry in the Control Source property list box is an expression?
2. Why bother with brackets ([]) for field names?
3. What built-in function does Access have that totals number fields in a group or a report? Hint: Look at the Class Cards report in Design View.
5. Can you bind a report to another report? To a table? To a query?
6. What two controls make up a combo box?
7. If you place an Image control image on page (or tab) 3 of a tabbed form, will you be able to see that image on page (or tab) 1?

Put Access into Action

1. Use the Sorting and Grouping options in the Report Wizard to create a report similar to the Class Cards report, but bind it to the AvailableClasses table. Have the report include all the fields from the table grouped on Department and totaled on hours only.

   You can keep this report for later experimentation or delete it; *Teach Yourself Access 97 in 14 Days* won't refer back to it.

2. If you have the sample data, examine the Class Cards report in Design View. Look at the Page Footer band. Note the entry =[page]. What do you suppose that does? Run the report in Print Preview and see if your supposition was right. Will this entry work similarly in the Page Header band?

3. If you have a printer, print the first page of the Class Cards report. (When you go to print, Access brings up a dialog box where you can instruct it to only print one page.)

4. Return to Design View. Open, or make visible, the Formatting toolbar, and color the Detail section of the report dark gray. Print page one of this report again. Did you like the effect?

5. Optional step: Include a graphic on this report using the Image control.

6. Close this report, discarding changes.

12

Day 7

A.M.

13 More Intermediate Forms

P.M.

14 Manipulating Dates and Using Expressions in Queries

Chapter **13**

More Intermediate Forms

The material this morning combines the fairly complex topic of option groups with the simple and often useful placement of bound graphics objects in forms. You'll learn the following:

☐ What an option group is

☐ How to modify a table to accept the option group's output

☐ How to place an option group in a form

☐ How to include a bound OLE graphics object in a form

The Option Group

An option group is a set of option buttons, toggle buttons, or check boxes in which one control *must* be selected, and no more than one control in a group *can* be selected.

To quickly get a feel for option groups, start a new form. When Access asks you for a binding table or query, leave the combo box blank and click the Form Design option, then OK. (See Figure 13.1.)

Figure 13.1.

The option group demo form, which is blank and unbound.

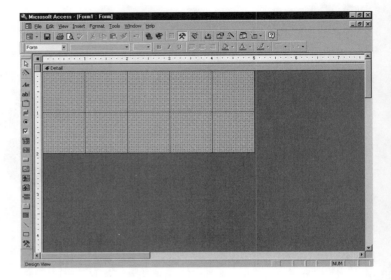

Locate these two controls in the toolbox: the Option Button and the Option Group. The Option Group icon is a square with the letters *XYZ* on the top. The Option Button is a solid circle within another circle. Click the Option Group and click somewhere on the form to place an option group on it.

Click the Option Button tool, then click in the option group box. Repeat until you have two or three option buttons inside the option group and two or three option buttons outside the group. Your screen should resemble Figure 13.2. Note that the form in Figure 13.2 has been saved with the name Option Demo, as you can see in the title bar. Don't be concerned if your form objects have different label numbers than the ones shown here.

Click the Form View button. Try choosing more than one option button in the option group. Try making no button in the option group selected. Now try the same thing with the buttons outside of the group.

Your form might open with no option group buttons selected, but the minute you do select one, you won't be able to return the group to having none selected. The option buttons outside of an option group can toggle on and off unrelated to their neighbors.

13

Figure 13.2.

The option group demo form with buttons added.

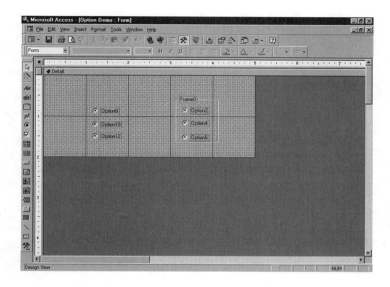

What's It Good For?

In many cases you'll want to give your application users a choice from several options. Option buttons work well for this. If you want to force a choice of one from a group of selections, the option group is the easiest way. Take a look at Figure 13.3. This is the form from Figure 13.2 with labels, showing how you might use option buttons in and out of an option group.

Figure 13.3.

A practical use for an option group.

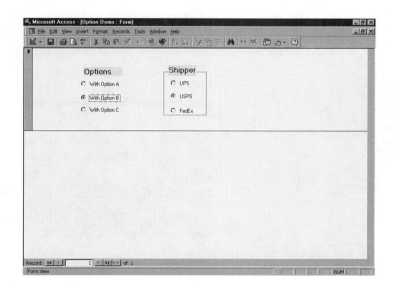

This is another fictional example—for a mail order company where management needs to ship all sales. Each shipment might include Option A, B, or C, but doesn't have to include any of these options. These choices appear outside of an option group. However, all orders need to be shipped via some carrier, so the Shipper option buttons are in an option group.

Our fictional college has three types of student status: full-time, part-time, and visiting scholar. Each student must be one of these, and none can be more than one. This is a great application for an option group.

The value for student status will be stored in the StudentPersonal table. The first thing you need to do is modify the table to accept this new data. Exercise 13.1 simply adds a new field to StudentPersonal to store a 1, 2, or 3 corresponding to a student status.

Exercise 13.1. Modifying an existing table.

1. Close the Option Demo form, discarding changes, as the book does not return to it. The Option Demo form as shown in Figure 13.3 is part of the sample data.

2. Back at the Database window, click the Tables tab. Highlight the StudentPersonal table and click the Design button to enter Design View for this table.

3. Locate the Note field and click just to the left of it to highlight the entire row. Press the Ins or Insert button on your keyboard to insert a blank row just above the Note field. Your screen should resemble Figure 13.4.

Figure 13.4.

Inserting a new row in a table's design grid.

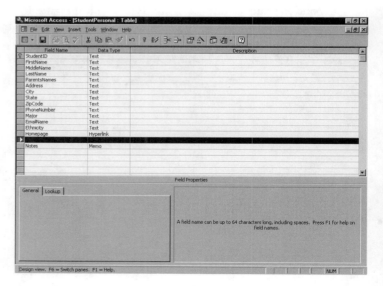

4. Click in the Field Name column of the blank row and enter StudentStatus as a field name. Move to the Data Type column and enter Number as a data type. Move to the Field Properties section of the table design grid and change the field size to Byte. Finally, change the Default Value property to 1. Your screen should resemble Figure 13.5.

> **The Access Way**
>
> The values in the StudentStatus field will be limited to 1, 2, or 3, as you'll soon see. The Number data type with field size Byte is a very efficient way to store information in Access; however, entries in this type of field are limited to positive integers no greater than 255. This fits our projected data perfectly.
>
> The general rule of using a Text data type field unless you're sure you'll be doing math on a field's contents was overridden here for the sake of efficiency and in the sure knowledge that no text will ever be entered in this field.

5. Close this table, saving changes.

Figure 13.5.

The new field for StudentPersonal.

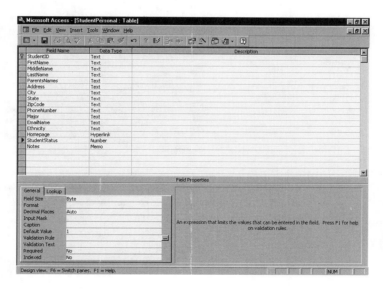

You need a form to place the option group in. As luck would have it, you saved the TabbedStudentPersonal form earlier. This form in its completed state is part of the sample data.

Exercise 13.2 makes room on the TabbedStudentPersonal form for the new option group and then installs the option group on it.

Exercise 13.2. Creating and programming the option group.

1. At the Database window, click the Form tab. Click the TabbedStudentPersonal form, then open it in Design View. Your screen should resemble Figure 13.6.

2. Click the School Information tab to activate page 2 of the tab control. Resize and rearrange the fields until your form resembles Figure 13.7. Don't worry if your form doesn't look identical to Figure 13.7. Close is good enough here.

Figure 13.6.

TabbedStudentPersonal in Design View.

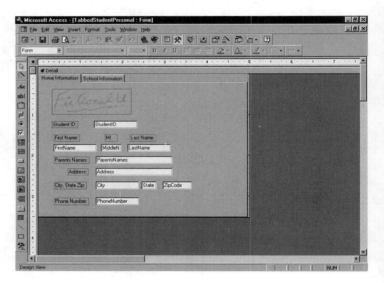

3. Make sure the Wizard button in the toolbox isn't selected. Click the Option Group button in the toolbox. Click in the lower-right portion of the form to insert the option group there. (See Figure 13.8.) You will need to resize and manipulate the default option group's shape if you want your screen to resemble Figure 13.8.

The Access Way

Making an option group is easier if you use a wizard. This exercise avoids the wizard to show you the underlying principles of an option group. You might want to redo the exercise using a wizard to see how Microsoft has automated the process for you. When using Access for production chores, you'll probably use the Option Group Wizard rather than bothering to do these tasks manually.

Figure 13.7.

The rearranged form ready for the option group.

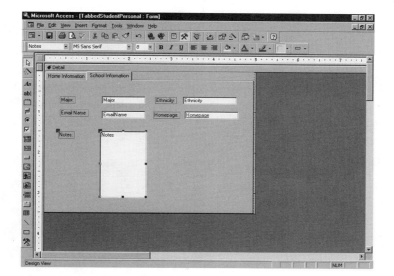

Figure 13.8.

Inserting an option group on a tab form.

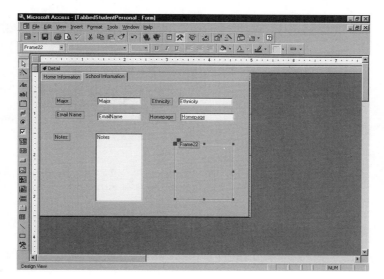

4. Insert three option buttons in the option group box, as shown in Figure 13.9. Remember that you can drag a control and its label separately by dragging on the large square in the upper-left corner of the control or label when the control is highlighted.

Don't be concerned if your controls are numbered differently than the example's. You'll take care of that next.

5. Click the Properties button in the toolbar to open up the Properties list box. Click the top option button in the option group. Make sure the option button and not its label is highlighted.

6. Locate the Option Value property in the Data tab for this control. If necessary, edit it to 1. If this is the first option button you added to the form, it should already have this value. Figure 13.10 shows this control and its Properties list box with the proper value entered for the Option Value.

Figure 13.9.

The option buttons placed in the Option Group box.

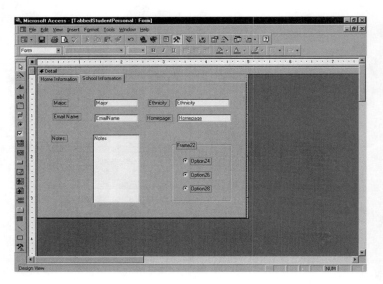

7. Highlight the label for this option button and enter F/T for its Caption property. (You edit the label for this control either directly on the form or by changing its Caption property on the Format tab of the Properties list box.) The first option button now identifies this option button as F/T for full-time. If you want to, you can resize the label box to accommodate this new value for its caption.

8. Similarly, set the Option Value property for the middle option button at 2 and the right one at 3. You should find that Access has anticipated your needs and set these values for you when you placed the option buttons within the group. Set their labels' caption properties to P/T and Visiting, respectively. (See Figure 13.11.)

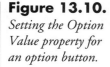

Figure 13.10.
Setting the Option Value property for an option button.

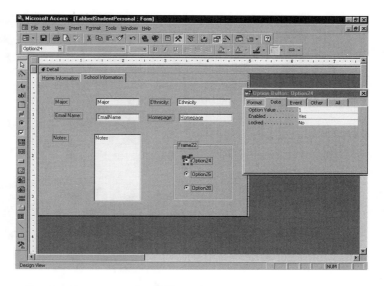

Figure 13.11.
Finishing up the option group.

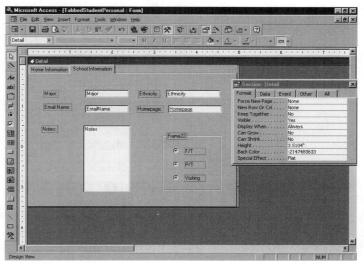

13

9. Finally, bind this option group to the StudentStatus field in the StudentPersonal table. Click the option group itself. Look in the Properties list box for the Control Source property. Either pull down the combo box and click StudentStatus, or enter StudentStatus for this property. Edit the label for this option group to read Student Status. (See Figure 13.12.)

10. Switch to Form View. The current record showing should be Tirilee Lytle. Click the F/T option button for this student. Scroll through the records one by one, clicking on the F/T option button until you hit Mary Smith. Click P/T for her record and the next. You'll have to change tabs to know where you are— a down side to tabbed forms. Move to the next record and set Visiting for the last and next-to-last records.

11. Close the form, saving changes. Click the Tables tab and open the StudentPersonal table in Datasheet View. Scroll to the StudentStatus column and note the values you entered at the option group are reflected here.

Figure 13.12.

Binding the option group.

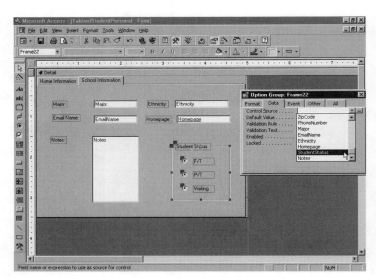

What Good Are Numbers?

Option values must be numbers. Because you want to know if a student's full-time, part-time, or visiting, not what the number is, you have to do a final step. Construct a table with two fields: StudentStatus Number and StudentStatus. This table, StudentStatusLookup, is shown in Figure 13.13 and is part of the sample data.

The next thing to do is construct a simple query linking the StudentStatus field's data in StudentPersonal with the StudentStatusLookup table. The design of this demonstration query is shown in Figure 13.13. Figure 13.14 is the StudentStatusQuery in Design View showing the relationship links between the two tables of the query. Figure 13.15 shows this query in action. This query is called ShowStudentStatus and is part of the sample data.

Figure 13.13.

The StudentStatusLookup table.

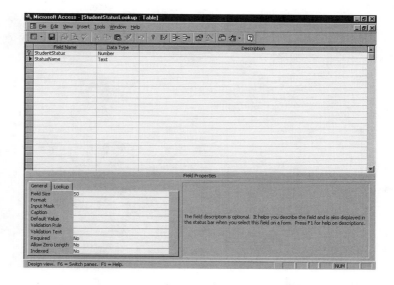

Figure 13.14.

The Design View of the ShowStudentStatus query.

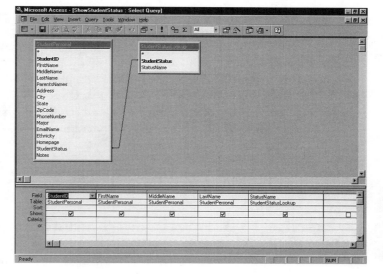

Figure 13.15.

The results of running the ShowStudentStatus query.

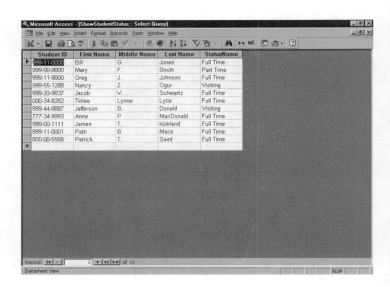

Images as Part of Data Within Databases

The last thing to cover this morning is how to embed graphics images in forms and reports when those images are part of the data. Yesterday you saw how easy it is to include decorative graphics in a form or a report using the Image control. Access can include graphic objects, such as photographs of students, as part of its dataset. Such data are called bound OLE objects. The next exercise shows you how to embed this type graphic in your form. The same principles apply to including graphics in both forms and reports.

Our fictional college had decided to take photographs of its students at registration time and include those pictures as part of the computer record. Exercise 13.3 creates a simplified form with a picture control to demonstrate the concept of bound OLE objects within the dataset.

Exercise 13.3. Embedding a graphic in a form.

1. The first step is to have a place in a table to put a picture. This type of field has the data type OLE Object. The table, StudentPersonalPicture (part of the sample data), has such a field included. This table contains a subset of the records in StudentPersonal, but also has the additional field, Picture, with a picture file inserted for each record. If you want to experiment with including pictures in your tables, add a field with the data type OLE Object.

   In Datasheet View, right-click the new field and choose Insert Object. Select one of the supplied bitmaps or use your own. The bitmaps in the sample data have been converted to device-independent bitmaps to save resources. To convert an existing image within a datasheet, right-click it in Datasheet View, then choose Bitmap

Image Object. Choose Convert, then the DIB option. Figure 13.16 shows the StudentPersonalPictures table in Design View. Figure 13.17 is the same table in Datasheet View.

Figure 13.16.

A table with an OLE Object field in Design View.

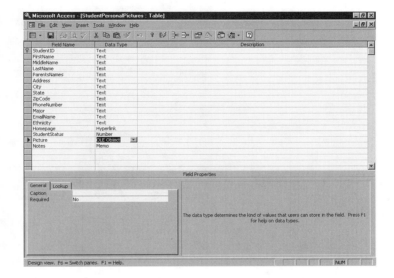

Figure 13.17.

The table from Figure 13.16 in Datasheet View. Note that the Picture field has been moved to the left in this layout.

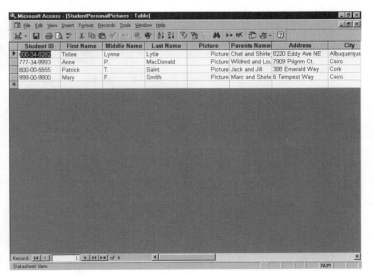

13

2. Close the StudentPersonalPictures table if it's open. Click the New Object AutoForm button in the toolbar. Access responds by creating and opening a new form, as shown in Figure 13.18. Your screen might vary from the example's, but should be fairly close.

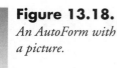

Figure 13.18.
An AutoForm with a picture.

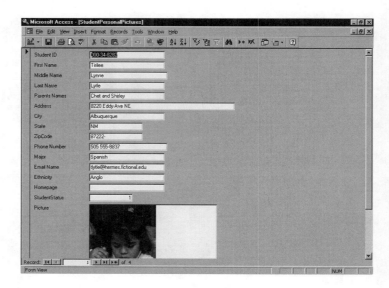

3. Move to Design View for this form. Each bitmap picture supplied as part of the sample data is 150 pixels wide. Alter the size of the picture frame to that size, which is about 1.5 inches. Figure 13.19 shows the AutoForm slightly rearranged with the picture frame resized in Design View. Figure 13.20 is the same form in Form View.

Figure 13.19.
Rearranging the AutoForm's output for a more pleasing form layout.

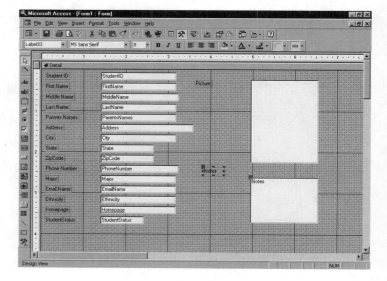

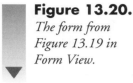

Figure 13.20.

*The form from
Figure 13.19 in
Form View.*

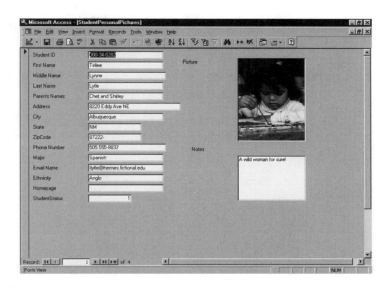

Do	**Don't**

DO use OLE to use the tools of other applications you may have, such as Excel or Word 8, in your Access databases. You can have a lot of fun and make a much more effective database using OLE, especially on a multimedia machine.

DON'T try using OLE on a marginal system, that is, a computer with less than 16MB. Although it works, you'll be disappointed in the performance.

---

4. While in Form View, scroll through the records. You'll see that the picture changes for each record. (The Image control graphic from yesterday stayed the same for each record.) Close this form, saving it as PictureStudentPersonal if you created it yourself. That's the name of the finished form in the sample data.

Morning Summary

Option groups are boxes containing check boxes, option buttons, or toggle buttons. The distinguishing characteristics of an option group are that only one control in the group can be selected and one must be selected. If you wish to use many unrelated option buttons, check boxes, or toggle buttons on your form, you can do so, but don't place them within an option group.

Access stores graphics, sounds, or other OLE type objects as data in a database. These objects are called bound objects. You can show unbound objects in forms and reports as decorative items. With Access you can either create objects at the time you insert them into a form or report, as the exercise this morning demonstrated, or use a preexisting file such as a bitmap.

13

Chapter 14

Manipulating Dates and Using Expressions in Queries

This afternoon's material covers the following topics:

- ☐ Expression (developer-defined) fields in queries
- ☐ How Access handles date information
- ☐ Date formats
- ☐ Date arithmetic

In many ways, queries form the heart of Access or any other relational database system. Access can take information from one or more query fields, operate on that information, and then create a new field for the output of the operation.

Dates are an important part of most databases. Think of all you could do with an information system, even if you could only query it by date. Here are a few examples of questions you could find answers to:

> How many and which customers have ordered in the past month?
>
> How many customers haven't bought anything in the past year?
>
> What patients haven't been in for their yearly checkup?
>
> How old are your accounts receivable?
>
> How many of your employees have been here long enough to be vested?
>
> What was your sales volume for each month in 1997?
>
> What products sold the greatest quantity in each month of 1996?

You can imagine that extracting such information from a paper-based filing system would be a great chore. With Access, however, each of those questions could be answered in a few seconds using queries.

Before moving on to dates in queries, this chapter shows you how Access records dates in databases, how it displays dates, and what underlying magic it has to let it perform date-based queries.

One item still missing from the StudentPersonal table is a place for date of birth. Exercise 14.1 adds a Date field to the StudentPersonal table and examines how Access can present date information.

Exercise 14.1. Adding a Date field to a table.

1. Launch Access and open the College database if necessary. Click the StudentPersonal table to highlight it, then click the Design button to open this table in Design View. Locate the StudentStatus field; click just to the left of it to highlight the entire StudentStatus row. Press the Ins or Insert key. Your screen should resemble Figure 14.1. (The sample data uses the name StudentPersonalDOB for this table.) You can also insert a row in this table by choosing Insert|Row from the menu.

2. Click in the Field Name column. Enter DateOfBirth as a label for this field. Tab to the Data Type column and enter a d. Date's the only data type beginning with a *d*, so Access auto fills in the rest of the column's entry. (See Figure 14.2.)

14

Figure 14.1.
Making room for the DateofBirth field.

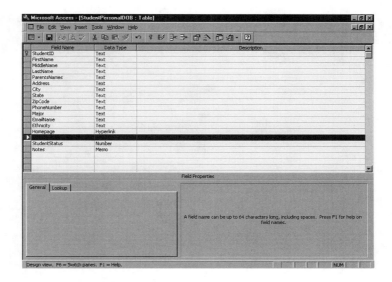

Figure 14.2.
Access uses auto fill to set the data type for a field.

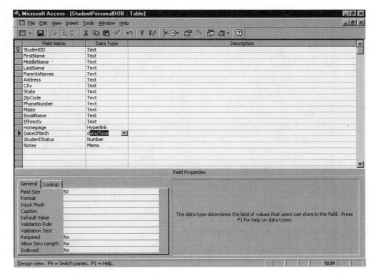

3. Tab away from this field. Access changes the Field Properties section to one appropriate for Date data types. (See Figure 14.3.)

14

Figure 14.3.
Field properties for the data type.

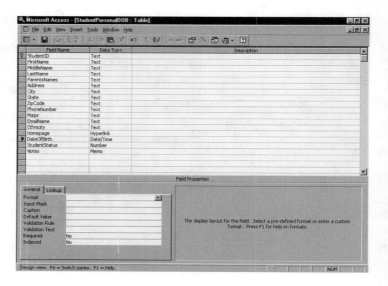

4. Most of these properties are old friends. The one new property to consider in this section is Format, which is first on the list. Click in the Format property to give this field the focus. Press F4 to drop down the list section of this combo box. Pressing F4 in a combo box has the same effect as clicking on the down arrow. Your screen should resemble Figure 14.4.

The Access Way

Access stores data in Date/Time data type fields uniformly. The Format property for this data type only affects the display of the data, not its value.

---

5. Choose Long Date for the Format. Edit the Caption property for this field to read Date of Birth.

   Click the Datasheet View button to leave Design View. Click OK when Access reminds you that you must save your table before leaving Design View.

   Move the newly designed table's DateofBirth field next to the LastName field. (See Figure 14.5.) This move is a temporary one; data entry for each student is easier with this field near the name fields.

Figure 14.4.

The types of formats for the Date/Time data type.

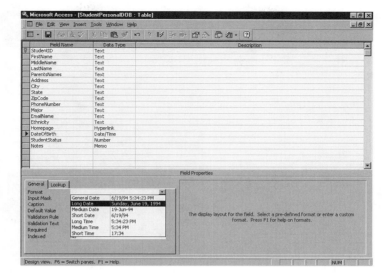

Figure 14.5.

The new DateOfBirth field moved next to the LastName field.

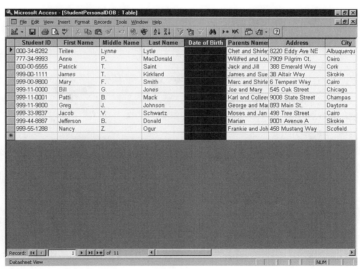

Remember, to move a column in Datasheet View, first click its header, the place in the column showing its field name, to highlight the column. Release the mouse button, and click the header again. Access responds by showing a rectangle at the base of the cursor arrow. This signifies you're in Move mode and you can drag the column to any new position you want.

Enter 12/1/74 as the Date of Birth for Tirilee, as shown in Figure 14.6.

14

Figure 14.6.

Entering a date in Access.

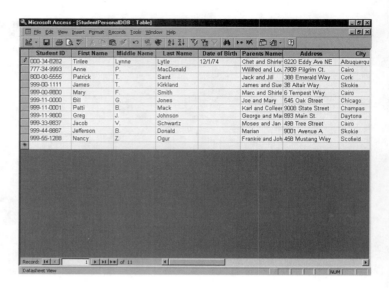

Tab out of this field. As soon as you do, Access changes this field to the Long Date format as shown in Figure 14.7. Note that the Date of Birth column in this figure has been slightly widened to show all the detail of this field.

Figure 14.7.

Access automatically changes the date to Long Date format.

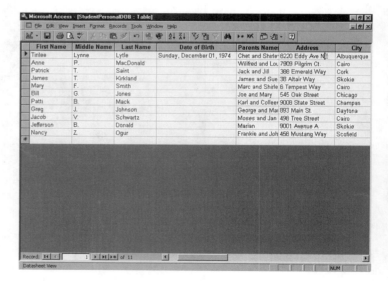

Even though you didn't enter the day of week information, Access was able to return the right day of the week for Tirilee's birth. Move down to the next record in the Date of Birth column, the one for MacDonald. Enter 2/30/75 for Anne's birthday. Press Tab. Your screen should resemble Figure 14.8.

Access is smart enough to know that there is no February 30 in 1975, or any other year for that matter. It won't accept dates that make no sense in date fields. You are free to enter wrong dates that are valid, but not obviously invalid entries such as 2/30/75. Click OK to clear the message box. Edit MacDonald's date of birth to 2/3/75. Access will now accept your entry, as shown in Figure 14.9.

Figure 14.8.

Access refuses to accept incorrect date information.

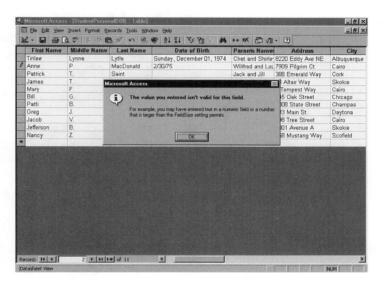

Within certain limits, Access doesn't care how you enter dates. The next student, Patrick Saint, was born July 8, 1974. You can enter that date as you've done before, 7/8/74, or in its full format, July 8, 1974. This date is a Monday, but Access won't accept day of week data. It insists on supplying that itself. Finish entering the dates for the students in this table with the data in Figure 14.10.

If you want, experiment entering dates in different formats. Access accepts 7 Jul 74, July 7, 1974, and Jul 7, 74, to give you an idea.

14

Figure 14.9.

Corrected Date field for date of birth.

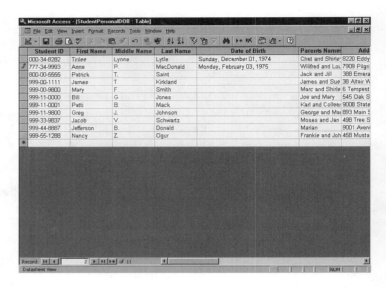

Figure 14.10.

The rest of the birth dates.

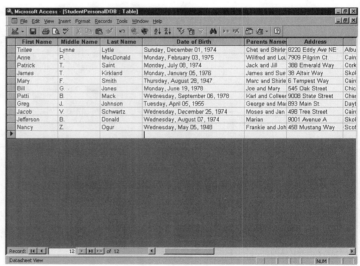

Return to Design View. Click in the DateofBirth field to show the field properties for this field. Change the Format property from Long Date to Medium Date. Return to Datasheet View. Click OK when Access asks you if you want to save your changes. Your screen should resemble Figure 14.11.

Figure 14.11.

The effect of changing the Date Format property. Once again the DateOfBirth field has been moved next to the LastName field for clarity.

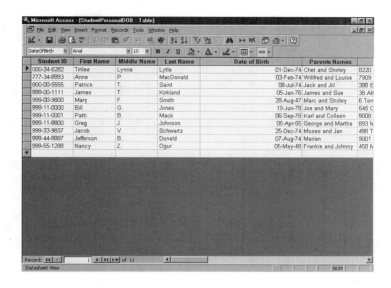

The Access Way

Changing the format of a date doesn't change the value of the date. If you changed the Format property for the DateofBirth field to a time format, Access would have changed all Date of Birth displays to 12:00 A.M., but would still have kept the right data for each record stored in the field.

Close this table. Tell Access you don't want to save layout changes if you rearranged your columns like the book did after Exercise 14.1.

The Access Way

Even though you told Access to discard changes to the table's layout, Access kept the edits you did to this table. That is, discarding layout changes did not cause you to lose the data you entered for date of birth for the students.

Access writes data to disk as soon as you leave the last field if the data's valid and in a valid record. Discarding layout changes has nothing to do with the data entered in the table.

14

Dates in Queries

Internally, Access stores dates as double precision numbers. The whole part of the number, the part to the left of the decimal place, is for the date. The fractional part of the number is the time. Access dates start with the number 1 for December 31, 1899, and go up to the year 9999. Dates prior to December 31, 1899, are negative. Thus, the number 2.0000 represents January 1, 1900, in Access's method; January 11, 1900, is day 12.0000; and so forth. Each date is really a number.

In human expression, subtracting 1/2/31 from 4/5/65 is a mind-boggling job. Since these dates are reduced to simple numbers internally within Access, the program can do all sorts of manipulations on them quite easily, as you shall see.

Exercise 14.2 shows how you can use dates as criteria for queries.

Exercise 14.2. Date criteria.

1. From the Database window, click the Queries tab. Click New. Click the Design View option to bypass the wizard. Click OK. Click the StudentPersonal table from the Show Table list box if you modified the original table. If you're using the sample data, choose the StudentPersonalDOB table. Click Add to add this table to the new query. (See Figure 14.12.)

2. Click Close to close the Show Table list box. If you want to, adjust your screen to resemble the layout in Figure 14.12.

3. Click and drag the FirstName, MiddleName, LastName, and DateOfBirth fields from the Field list box to columns 1–4 in the query design grid. (See Figure 14.13.)

4. Click the Run button in the toolbar. (See Figure 14.14.)

5. No surprises here. This query simply extracts all the records for the selected fields. Return to Design View. Enter <1/1/74 in the criteria row for the DateofBirth column. Tab away from this column. Your screen should resemble Figure 14.15. Note that Access understands you mean 1/1/74 to be a date and surrounds your criteria with the needed number sign (#) marks.

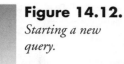

Figure 14.12.
Starting a new query.

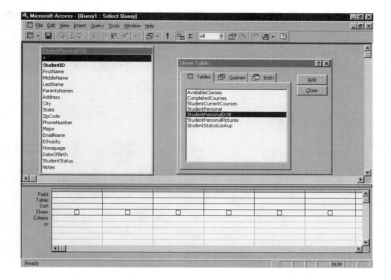

Figure 14.13.
The new query without criteria.

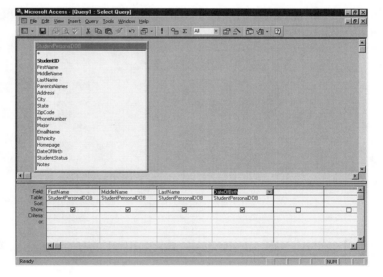

14

Figure 14.14.
The new query running.

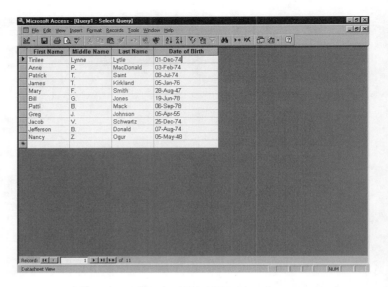

Figure 14.15.
Creating a criterion based on date.

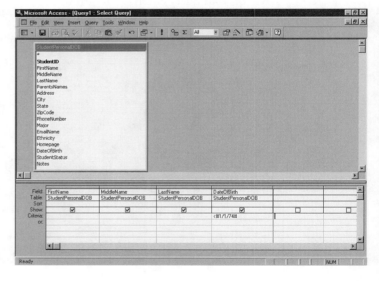

6. Again run the query. Access now only returns those records with birthdays earlier than January 1, 1974.

The Access Way

The expression <1/1/74 reads "less than January 1, 1974" in English. This doesn't sound sensible when used in date or time fields. So, when using date expressions in Access, think of the < operator as "before" and the > operator as "after."

Access can use dates for query criteria the same as it uses text values or numbers. Operators like = (equals), < (less than), and > (greater than) work alike with dates, times, and numbers. You can even combine these operators to read <= (less than or equal to), >= (greater than or equal to), and <> (not equal to, but literally less than and greater than).

Do	**Don't**

DO feel free to use expressions to extract your information in creative ways.

DON'T rely on your query criteria to return what you expect they will. Be sure to try your queries with known data that will yield results in which you can easily spot errors. Don't rely on complex queries until you're absolutely sure they're working correctly.

Date Arithmetic and Developer-Defined Fields

So far, this afternoon's material has been rather tame and obvious. Things are about to pick up speed. Exercise 14.3 shows how to use date math. It dynamically calculates the age of each student in years. Dynamic calculation means the computer fetches the current date and does the age calculation based on that date and the fixed value of the student's birthday.

Exercise 14.3. Date math and expression (developer-defined) fields.

1. Return to Design View for the query you did in Exercise 14.2. Drag your cursor over the criteria for the DateOfBirth field to highlight the entire criteria expression. Press Del or Delete to delete this criteria expression.

2. Click the Field row for the column just to the right of the DateOfBirth column. Press Shift+F2 to enter Zoom mode. Enter

   ```
   Age in Years: DateDiff("yyyy",[DateofBirth],Date())
   ```

   in the Zoom box. Your screen should resemble Figure 14.16.

EXERCISE

14

Figure 14.16.

Entering an expression in the Zoom box.

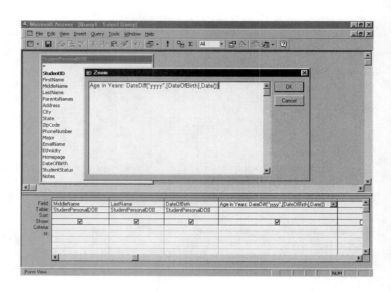

3. Click OK to leave Zoom mode. Click the Run button in the toolbar. Your screen should resemble Figure 14.17.

Figure 14.17.

A field based on a date calculation expression.

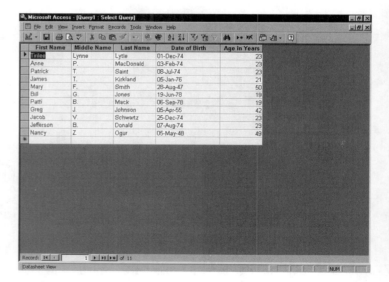

The Access Way

The figures for the Age in Years column will vary depending on your computer's date. This computer's date was set to mid-1997 for this and some other screens. If, for example, your clock is set to early 1998, the students will be shown as one year older—because they are! This is dynamic date calculation in action.

The entire operation of this query depends on the expression

```
Age in Years: DateDiff("yyyy",[DateOfBirth],Date())
```

The first part of this expression is the label for this developer-defined field. Access knows that from the colon to the right of the field. Anything to the left of the colon in a defined field is interpreted by Access as a label for the column.

The second part of this expression is its heart: `Datediff`. `Datediff()` is another built-in function that calculates the difference between two dates. It takes parameters between its parentheses `()`. The parameters for `Datediff` read as follows:

```
interval, date1, date2[,firstweekday][,firstweek]
```

The last two parameters in the square brackets (`[]`) are optional. The interval is how you want the date differences to be expressed. You can enter `"ww"` for weeks, `"d"` for days, `"m"` for month. This example used `"yyyy"` for year interval. Figure 14.18 is the same query edited to return students' ages in months. Figure 14.19 shows the expression that returned the screen in Figure 14.18.

The second element is the first, or earlier, date that figures in the date math expression. In this case you told Access to fetch the data entered into the DateofBirth field to use as the `date1` parameter. You should enter the field DateOfBirth in square brackets even though it's a field name without spaces. It's always a good idea to enclose field names in square brackets because you'll get unpredictable results if your field contains spaces. Not only do the brackets act as insurance in case your field names do contain spaces, but they show you at a glance that the entry `[DateOfBirth]` is a field name and not a function.

The last element of the parameter is the function `date()`. This merely tells Access to use the current system date as `date2`. The two optional functions `[,firstweekday]` and `[,firstweek]` aren't used in this query. You can set the optional parameters `[,firstweekday]` and `[,firstweek]` to count the specific days or weeks in the interval.

14

Figure 14.18.
The datediff()
*function returning
intervals.*

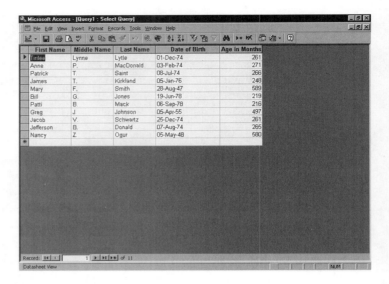

Figure 14.19.
*The expression edit
box that returns
month intervals.*

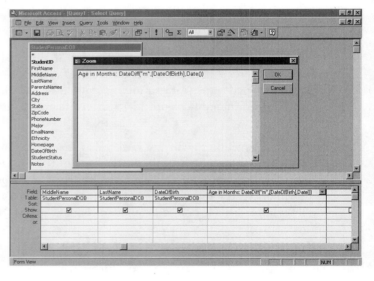

That's about enough for this afternoon. Close this query and save it using the name
StudentAges. This query is part of the sample data.

Day Summary

This afternoon you learned how to include dates in tables, how to format those dates, and how Access stores date information internally. Queries can use dates for criteria, as you saw in Exercise 14.2. Finally, you saw how to create a complex expression to calculate the difference between today's date and the students' dates of birth and return the values in years. Further, you learned how to place the results of this calculation in an artificial field called Age in Years.

This morning you saw how to use option buttons within and outside of option groups. If you prefer, you can use other controls such as toggle buttons or check boxes in option groups. Combining various controls within an option group can greatly extend the usefulness of your application.

Access can include any OLE object as part of the dataset. This morning you saw how you can include a picture for each record. Using the identical technique, you can include other OLE objects such as sound or even OLE documents created by other applications.

Q&A

Q What's an OLE object?

A Certain Windows applications support Object Linking and Embedding (OLE). Applications that allow objects they create to be used by another application are called OLE server programs. Access 97 is an OLE client application. It can use objects created by an OLE server but cannot share objects it creates with another OLE client. For example, take an OLE image embedded in an Access form. Paintbrush can act as an OLE server program and Access the OLE client, so Access can use an object created in Paintbrush for its own purpose. However, Paintbrush cannot use objects created by Access in its applications, in part because Access isn't an OLE server.

Q What other kinds of OLE objects are there?

A There are as many OLE objects as application programs that can act as an OLE server. For example, Word and Excel are OLE servers, so you can embed Word documents and Excel spreadsheets in your Access database. This gives you all the financial and numerical analysis powers of Excel or the editing power of Word in Access. The down side of this is you must own either Word or Excel to use this tool.

14

Windows comes with all the tools you need to play WAV sound files if your computer is sound capable. Using the same techniques as shown in this chapter, you can embed WAV sound files in forms or tables to give your databases some real flair.

Additionally, OLE is resource-demanding. A 386/33 with 12MB of RAM works all right for Access alone. Using OLE on this machine would be slow going indeed.

Q Can I use the `DateDiff()` function to perform time math?

A Yes, it does so whether you ask it to or not. The trick to seeing time intervals between dates is to use *h*, *n*, or *s* for hours, minutes, or seconds. (The *n* for minutes isn't an error. The *m* is reserved for months.)

Q If I know a date is, say, a Sunday, should I enter the date like this: Sunday, [the date] where [the date] is the date that's a Sunday?

A No. Format the field as Long Date to show days of the week. Access won't permit you to make entries looking identical to its Long Date format. It's funny that way.

Q I created a combo box and set the Column Widths property to 1 in; 1 in; 2 in, yet the combo box just stays small, showing part of only one column. Why?

A A combo box will stay the size it is during Design View unless you set the List Width property to the total of what's in your Column Widths property. The List Width property can be as wide as you want, but cannot be smaller than the combo box is during Design View.

Q Why create an unbound form?

A You'll see the use for this later on. Unbound forms work very well for such things as button menu forms (switchboards) which are discussed in Chapter 23, "Introduction to Macros." You can also create an unbound form, then bind it using an SQL statement if you prefer to work this way.

Workshop

Here's where you can test and apply what you have learned today.

Quiz

Possible answers to these questions are provided in Appendix A.

1. What property binds an option group to a table field?

2. You have a form MyForm bound to the table MyTable. You want to enter a combo box, MyCombo, on this form that will look up values in a table called MyLookup. Do you enter MyLookup as the control source or row source for MyCombo?

3. If you have a field in a query with the Data Type set to Date/Time, will a criterion of "January" select for those records in the month of January?

4. What property must be set to Yes to limit the possible entries to those already entered as a row source for the combo box?

5. What does >#1/31/97# mean as a criterion?

Put Access into Action

1. Launch Access and open the College database if necessary.

2. Open the TabbedStudentPersonal in Design View.

3. Add a new option button to the option group on page 2. Label this button N/Degree. You might have to adjust the position of the existing buttons, resize the group, or both. (See Figure 14.20.)

Figure 14.20.

The edited option group.

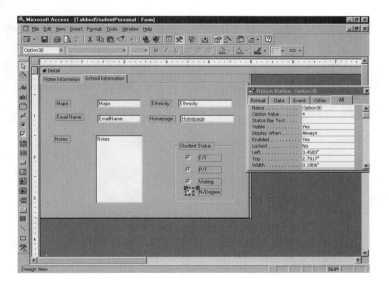

4. Make sure Access has set the Option Value property for this new control to 4.

TIP

You can change the label for a control by either directly editing the label or altering its Caption property from within the Properties list box.

14

5. Close the form, saving changes. Edit the StudentStatusLookup table to add a number 4 for StudentStatus and Non-Degree for StatusName. Your screen should resemble Figure 14.21.

Figure 14.21.

Adding a new value in a lookup table.

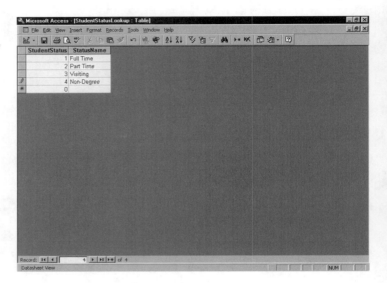

6. Close the table. Access will automatically save the table edits you made.

DAY 8

A.M.

15 Intermediate to Advanced Queries

P.M.

16 More Advanced Queries

Chapter **15**

Intermediate to Advanced Queries

This morning you'll learn how to do the following:

- ☐ Construct a parameter query
- ☐ Use wildcards within parameter queries
- ☐ Construct a parameter query that returns a range of values
- ☐ Create a query that prompts users for criteria
- ☐ Create a new table from a query

Parameter Queries

So far all the queries you've done set the query criteria at the Design View. This isn't always desirable for two reasons. First, you might not know what criteria you will need when you run the query or you might want to quickly change criteria for the same query. The second reason is security. You might want a user to be able to establish a query criterion without getting to the Design View for the query.

The way to enter criteria at the time a query is run, rather than when it's designed, is to convert your query to a parameter query. Access is rather loose when using the words *criteria* and *parameter*. Think of query parameters as criteria entered during the execution of a query.

The first full exercise this morning, 15.2, shows the construction of a simple parameter query. Before trying it, go over Exercise 15.1 to see how the parameter works at the familiar Design View. This exercise shows the parallels between criteria and parameters in queries.

Exercise 15.1. A different criteria demonstration.

EXERCISE

1. Launch Access and open the College database if necessary. From the Database window, click the Query tab. Highlight the StudentAges query. Click Design to open this query in Design View.

2. Locate the Age in Years expression field. Enter: >=21 on the first criteria row for this field. Your screen should resemble Figure 15.1.

3. Click the Run button in the toolbar. Access will run the query and return a screen similar to Figure 15.2. Keep in mind that the return you get will depend on your system date and the specific records you have entered into the data for the StudentPersonal or StudentPersonalDOB table.

4. Return to Design View and delete the criteria from this query.

Figure 15.1.

Entering a criterion for an artificial field.

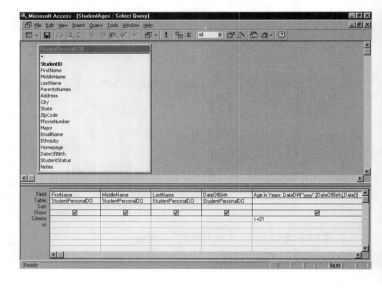

15

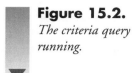

Figure 15.2.
The criteria query running.

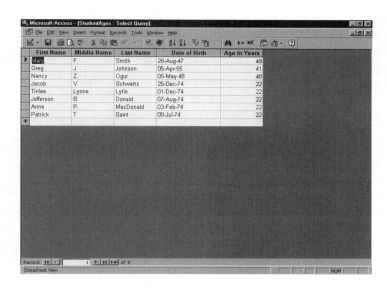

That didn't pack much of a surprise. Access had no problems figuring out that you wanted to select people older than or equal to 21 years of age. The query might have taken a little longer to run than other queries because Access had a two-step problem; first, it had to do the Datediff() calculation, then it had to apply your criteria to filter out the unwanted records. The more you ask an Access query to do, the longer it'll take to run.

The Access Way

The query in Exercise 15.1 might seem almost trivial, but it's one that's widely used in databases. Imagine you're creating an aging of your accounts receivable and you want to find out which accounts are less than 30 days old, which are between 31 and 60 days old, and finally which are more than 60 days old. One way to do this is to use the Datediff() function in three columns, then enter these criteria for the three columns: <=30; Between 31 and 60; and >60.

The beauty of using the Datediff() function is that any time you run this query, you'll be up-to-date aging your receivables because the query's based on the difference between the date entered in the table or query and the current date.

The Parameter Query

Exercise 15.2 shows how to construct a simple parameter query. This query will extract information similar to that extracted in Exercise 15.1, but you'll be able to alter your query criteria without entering Design View.

Exercise 15.2. The parameter query.

1. If you're still in Datasheet View from Exercise 15.1, return to Design View.
2. Enter [Enter First Name:] on the Criteria row for the FirstName column. Your screen should resemble Figure 15.3.
3. Click the Run button. Access responds with the screen shown in Figure 15.4.
4. Enter Tirilee in the dialog box and click OK. Your screen should resemble Figure 15.5.

Figure 15.3.

Constructing a simple parameter query shown in Zoom mode.

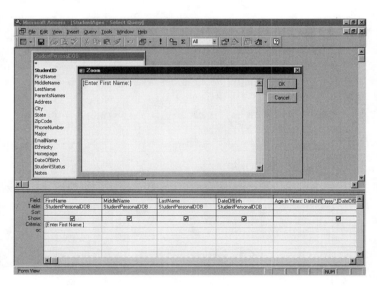

15

Figure 15.4.
When the parameter query is run, this dialog box appears.

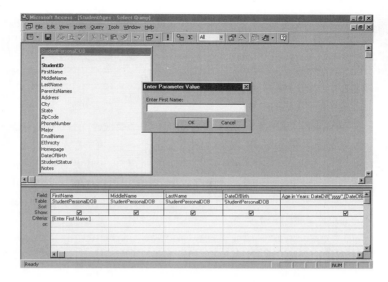

Figure 15.5.
Parameter queries return criteria entered as they are running.

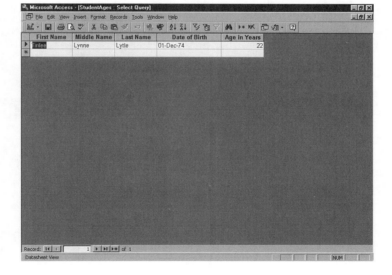

You can't enter wildcards in parameter dialog boxes with the query constructed as in Exercise 15.2. The expression Like "J*" entered as a straight (nonparameter) criterion for the LastName column will, when the query's run, return records for Jones and Jefferson. Entering J* or Like "J*" in the query dialog box for the query done in Exercise 15.2 will yield no records returned. Exercise 15.3 shows how to use wildcards in parameter queries.

Exercise 15.3. Wildcard parameter queries.

1. Starting where you left off in Exercise 15.2, return to Design View. Run this query again. Enter J* for a parameter in the parameter dialog box. (See Figure 15.6.)

   Click OK. The results of running this query are shown in Figure 15.7.

2. Return to Design View. Edit the parameter criterion to read Like [Enter Last Name:] as shown zoomed in Figure 15.8.

3. Run the query again, this time again entering J* for the parameter, as shown in Figure 15.9. Click OK.

   This time things work like you might have anticipated they'd work earlier. Your screen should resemble Figure 15.10.

Figure 15.6.

Entering a wildcard in a conventional parameter dialog box.

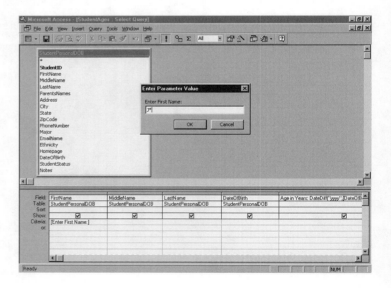

Figure 15.7.

The wildcard parameter surprisingly results in no matched records.

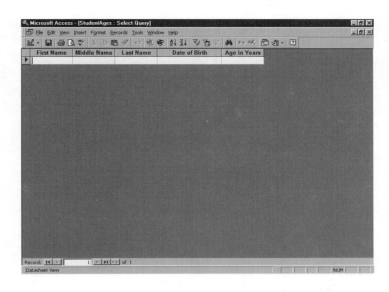

Figure 15.8.

Modifying the parameter criteria to accept wildcards.

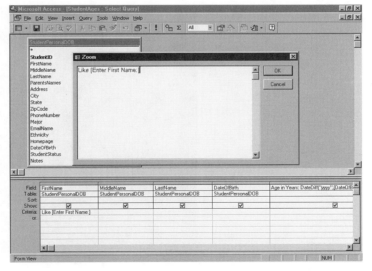

Figure 15.9.

Trying a wildcard parameter in the new query.

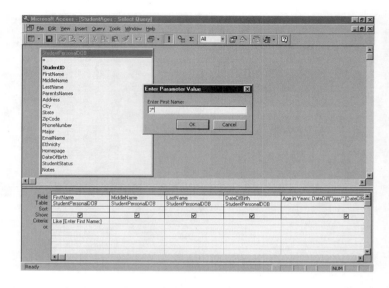

Figure 15.10.

The successful wildcard parameter query.

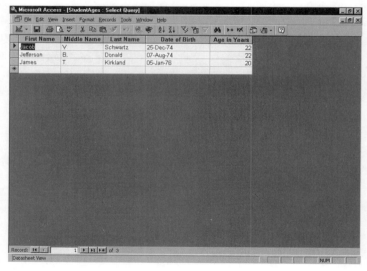

Range Parameter Queries

Sometimes you'll want your query to extract information from a table based on a range of information. Look at Figure 15.11. The criterion for the DateOfBirth field reads

```
Between #1/1/74# AND #12/31/74#.
```

This query looks as if it'll return all records with student birthdays in 1974. It does just that, as shown in Figure 15.12.

This is a rather constrained query. Sure it's useful, but in many cases you'll want to enter the beginning and ending dates at the time you run the query to ask Access to fetch, for example, all your sales for a particular span of time. Access has the built-in capacity to do just this. Exercise 15.4 shows you how to construct a parameter query that returns a range of values.

Figure 15.11.

A criteria expression to return all records from 1974.

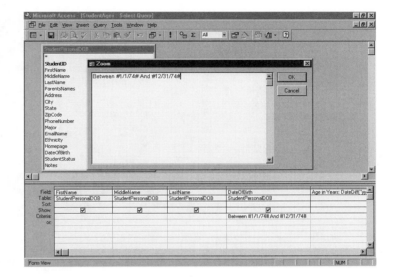

Figure 15.12.

The results of the 1974 query shown in Figure 15.11.

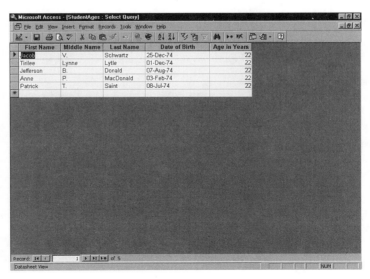

Exercise 15.4. The range parameter query.

1. Return to Design View for the query you constructed in Exercise 15.3. Delete any criteria you might have entered either in the exercise or through your own experimentation. Enter the following on the criteria row for the DateOfBirth column:

   `Between [Enter Earliest Date:] AND [Enter Latest Date:]`

   Your screen should resemble Figure 15.13 if zoomed.

Figure 15.13.

The range parameter query criterion.

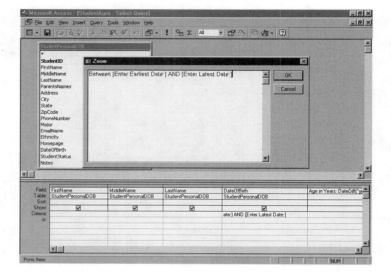

2. You've just told Access that you want two parameter prompts when this query's run. First, Access prompts you with a dialog box saying `Enter Earliest Date:`. When you enter a value and click OK, Access will bring up a second dialog box prompting you with `Enter Latest Date:`.

3. Click the Run button on the toolbar. Access responds with a screen like the one in Figure 15.14.

4. Enter `1/1/33` and click OK. Access responds with the dialog box shown in Figure 15.15.

5. Enter `12/31/65` and click OK. Access runs the query with these parameters and gives you the screen shown in Figure 15.16.

Figure 15.14.

The first range dialog box.

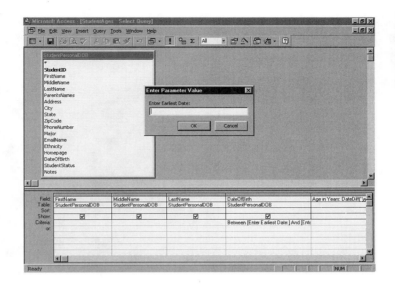

Figure 15.15.

The second range dialog box.

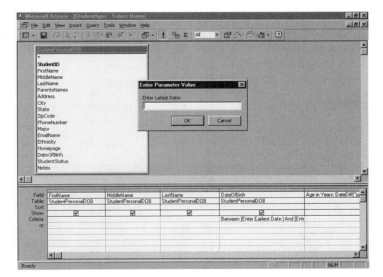

Figure 15.16.

The range parameter query returns the range you specified.

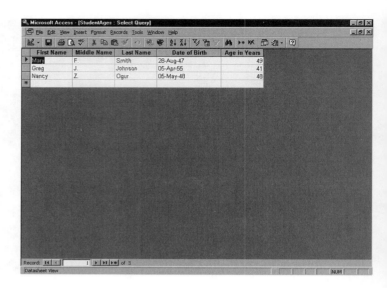

Although the results of this run can be identical to those of the fixed range query shown running in Figure 15.11, the difference is that you can now choose your range of values for the parameters at the query's runtime rather than in its Design View. Try running this query again, but enter 1/1/33 and 03/31/74 as criteria. This time you'll also pick up the record for Anne MacDonald, who was born on February 3, 1974, as shown in Figure 15.17.

Close and save the new query using a different name if you wish to preserve your original query, StudentAges. The book's example saved the query at this stage using the name StudentAgesParameter.

Do	Don't

DO use parameter queries when you don't want to alter the design of a query to change its criteria.

DON'T use a parameter query to construct queries with unchanging criteria such as `older than 30` days. This works technically, but it slows down the flow of work, as you'll have to enter the same criteria over and over again.

15

Figure 15.17.

Expanding the parameter query's range.

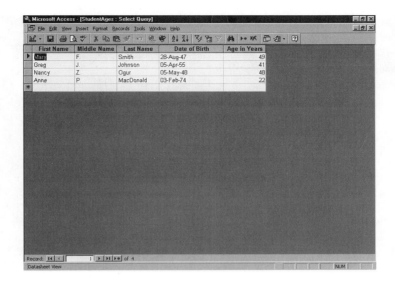

Action Queries

One of Access's most powerful features is the capability to take the results of a query and do something with them. Exercise 15.5 shows how you can take the output of a query and have Access automatically create and enter data into a new table. In this exercise, you convert a select query to a simple action query that creates a new table containing the query's output.

Exercise 15.5. The make table action query.

1. The default type of query Access creates is called a select query because it selects records and fields from a table or another query. To make an action query, first construct a select query in the normal way. It's highly recommended that you run the query in Select mode to make sure it's running as you think it should.

2. Return to Design mode after running the query as in either Figure 15.16 or Figure 15.17. If you're using the sample data and didn't save the query from Exercise 15.4, use the query StudentAgesParameter as a starting point for this exercise. Click the Query menu. Click the Make Table entry. Access responds with a dialog box. Enter `FirstTrial` as a name for your new table. Your screen should resemble Figure 15.18.

Figure 15.18.

Creating a make table query.

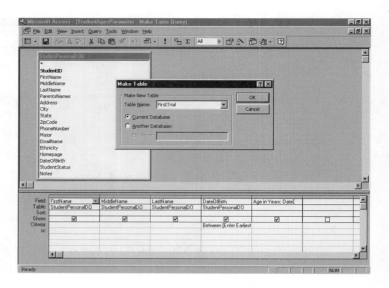

3. Make sure the Current Database option button is selected. Click OK. Now run the query. That's all there is to it. After confirmation from you, Access runs the query and places the contents of it into a new table, FirstTrial.

4. Click the Run button in the toolbar. Access prompts you for two dates. Enter 8/1/72 as the earliest date and 12/31/81 as the latest date, as in Figures 15.19 and 15.20.

   Access will crank around a while and respond with a confirmation message box, as shown in Figure 15.21.

5. Click OK to finish running this query. Nothing apparently occurs. Close this query, saving changes. The sample data saved this query as StudentAgesMakeTable. Back at the Database window, note that this query now has a new icon next to its name in the Database list box, as shown in Figure 15.22. This visually tells you that this query is an action query that will make a new table.

6. Did it work? Click the Tables tab. (See Figure 15.23.)

   Click the Open button for the FirstTrial table. (See Figure 15.24.)

15

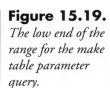

Figure 15.19.
The low end of the range for the make table parameter query.

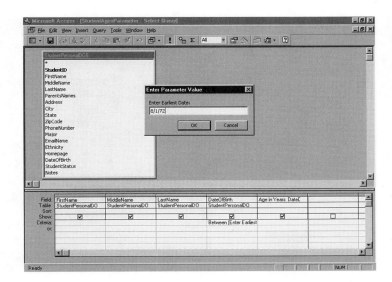

Figure 15.20.
The high end of the range for the make table parameter query.

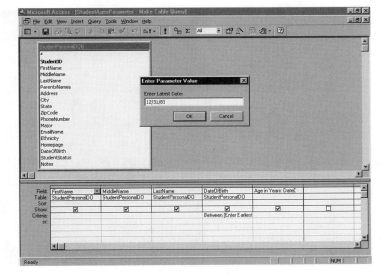

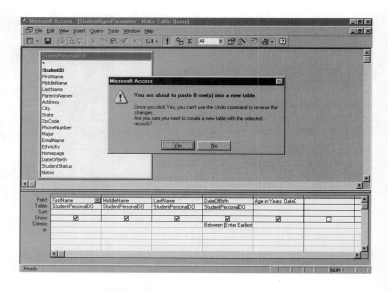

Figure 15.21.
The confirmation message box for the make table query.

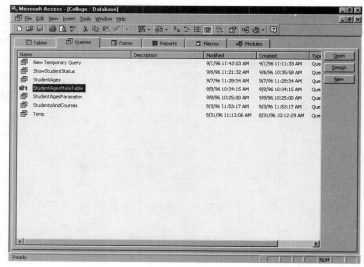

Figure 15.22.
The Database window showing different kinds of queries. Most queries here are select ones, but StudentAgesMakeTable is a make table query and it has a different icon.

15

Figure 15.23.

The new table at the Database window.

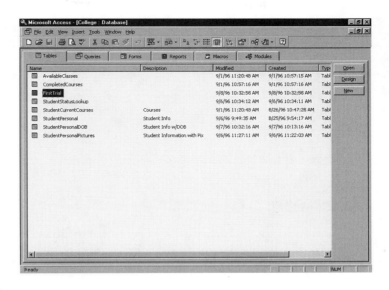

Figure 15.24.

The newly created table showing the records automatically entered after being selected from a parameter query.

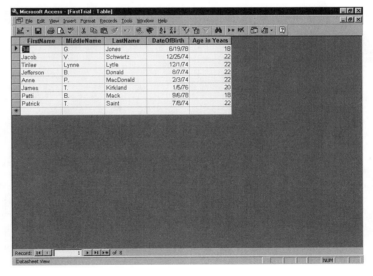

Do   **Don't**

DO make as many action queries as your application requires. This is a very useful Access capability.

DON'T use these queries as action queries until you've reviewed their output as select queries.

It's been a long morning, but one covering a lot of new and important territory.

Morning Summary

Access can prompt for a range of values to extract data. This is called the range parameter query. You use the Between...AND operators to construct such a query.

Access can use the output of a query to perform some action. To have Access create a table using a query's output, change the query type from Select to Make Table and tell Access what the new query's name is to be.

15

Chapter 16

More Advanced Queries

This afternoon you'll learn

- ☐ What append action queries are
- ☐ What delete action queries are
- ☐ How to construct and run these two action queries
- ☐ Why and how to compact databases
- ☐ What top queries are and how to use them
- ☐ What crosstab queries are and how to use them
- ☐ What update queries are and how to use them

Delete and Append Queries

Deleting a single record from a table is quite easy. You open the table in Datasheet View, locate the record you want to eliminate, and click to the left of the row containing the record to be deleted. This highlights the row. Press the Del or Delete key on your keyboard to eliminate the record.

What do you do if you want to eliminate many records, such as all those records older than a particular date? You could go through your table record by record to locate, then delete, these records. You could also create a query, sort on the target date range, then delete the records by highlighting them and pressing the Del key.

The second method might sound ingenious, but it's more cumbersome than just doing a delete query. Take a look at Figure 16.1.

Figure 16.1.

Two tables showing existing records in each.

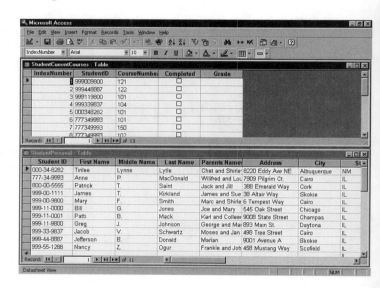

Note that the BeforeStudentCurrentCourses table (part of the sample data) has several entries for Anne MacDonald, whose StudentID is 777-34-9993. StudentCurrentCourses also has no entries for Bill Jones, StudentID 999-11-0000. Exercise 16.1, which demonstrates the delete action query, deletes all of MacDonald's records and Exercise 16.2 adds them back, along with some for Jones.

16

Exercise 16.1. The delete query.

1. Launch Access and open the College database if necessary. Click the Queries tab. Click the New button to start a new query. Bypass the wizard by clicking the Design View option and clicking OK. Add the BeforeStudentCurrentCourses table to the query. Close the Show Table list box. Your screen should resemble Figure 16.2.

Figure 16.2.

Adding a table to a new query.

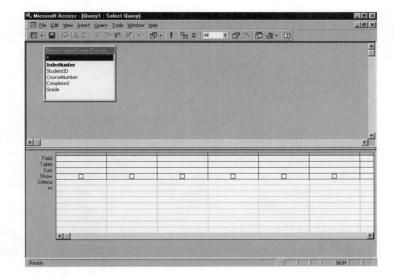

2. Drag the StudentID field from the Field list box to the first column of the query design grid. Add the parameter [Enter StudentID:] to the first criteria row for this query. (See Figure 16.3.)

3. Run the query by clicking the Run button in the toolbar. Enter 777349993 as a query parameter. Your screen should resemble Figure 16.4.

   The point of running this query first as a select query is to make sure it's running right, extracting all the records you want and none that you don't want. This query is working correctly, so it's time to alter it to a delete action query.

Figure 16.3.

Entering a criteria parameter.

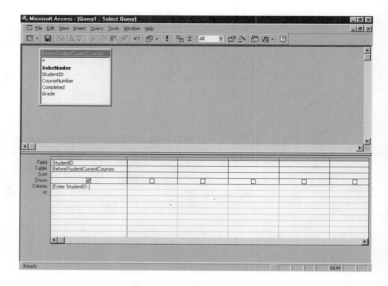

Figure 16.4.

The trial run for the delete action query is a select query.

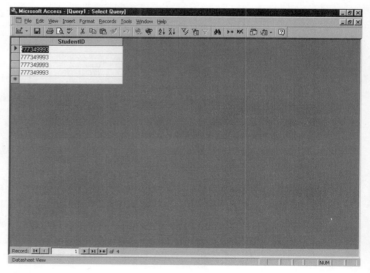

4. Return to Design View. Click the Query menu and click Delete. (You can also click the Query button in the toolbar and choose the Delete option from that.) After you've told Access to change the query from a select one to a delete one, your title bar will change to reflect the new type of query. Also a Delete line will replace the Sort line in the query design grid. (See Figure 16.5.)

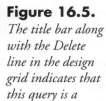

Figure 16.5.

The title bar along with the Delete line in the design grid indicates that this query is a delete one.

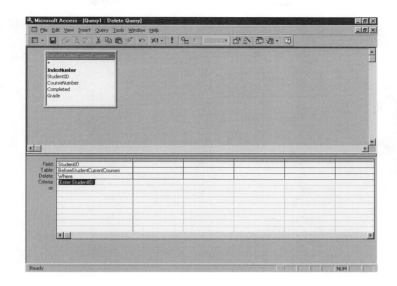

16

5. Click the Run button in the toolbar. Access again prompts you for a parameter, just as it did when this was a select query. Enter 777349993 to choose MacDonald's StudentID. Click OK. (See Figure 16.6.)

Figure 16.6.

By default, Access gives you a warning message box when you run a delete action query.

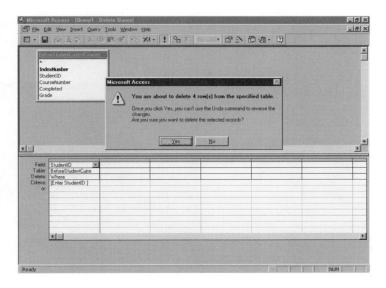

Click OK. Note that even though the query returns only one column of figures, the StudentID column, Access warns you that it will delete four rows or three entire records. The message might vary as to how many rows will be deleted if you've added records to or otherwise manipulated the BeforeStudentCurrentCourses table.

The Access Way

Action queries work on entire rows or records even if the same query running as a select query returns only part of a row or record. Here is the SQL code behind this query.

```
DELETE DISTINCTROW StudentCurrentCourses.StudentID
FROM StudentCurrentCourses
WHERE (((StudentCurrentCourses.StudentID)=[Enter StudentID:]));
```

Note that the keyword Distinctrow (distinct row) clues you that the query will work on an entire row rather than just the single field you saw displayed in the query during the Select stage.

6. Click OK. Change the query back to a select query by clicking the Select choice from the Query button's pull-down menu. If you prefer, click Select Query from the Query menu, as shown in Figure 16.7.

7. Run the query. Enter 777349993 again as a StudentID parameter. This time Access returns no records, as shown in Figure 16.8, indicating that there are no longer any records for MacDonald in the StudentCurrentCourses table.

Figure 16.7.

Changing to a select query from an action query.

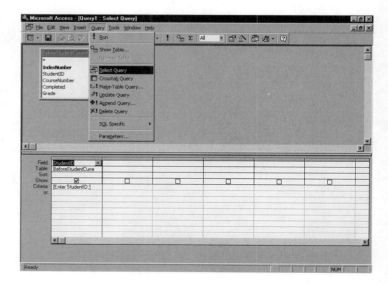

Figure 16.8.

The results of the delete action query are that the deleted records no longer exist in the table.

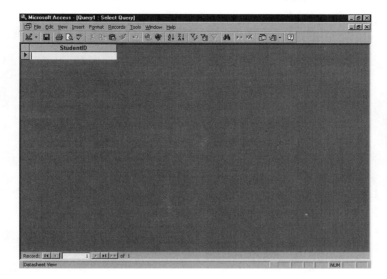

8. Return to Design View and change this query back to a delete action query. Close this query, saving it as Deleter. Figure 16.9 shows the Database window with the new query Deleter as part of the query group. Note the special icon Access assigned to this query, which visually clues you that this is a delete type query.

Figure 16.9.

The new delete action query in the Database window.

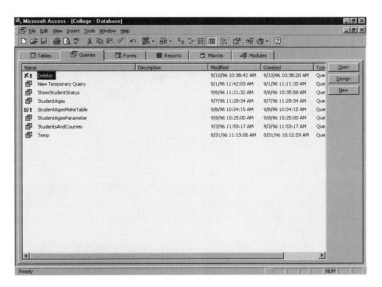

The Access Way

There is no difference between using the menu to switch query types and using the toolbar. How you work is up to you.

You could, for example, manually edit the SQL statement in SQL View to change query types that way.

If you wish to see how flexible Access 97 can be, try this. With the query from the last exercise still as a select type, pull down the leftmost toolbar button. Choose SQL View from the list of three. Access will respond by showing you a screen with the following SQL code:

```
SELECT DISTINCTROW StudentCurrentCourses.StudentID
FROM StudentCurrentCourses
WHERE (((StudentCurrentCourses.StudentID)=[Enter StudentID:]));
```

Edit this to read

```
DELETE DISTINCTROW StudentCurrentCourses.StudentID
FROM StudentCurrentCourses
WHERE (((StudentCurrentCourses.StudentID)=[Enter StudentID:]));
```

by changing the first word, SELECT, to DELETE. Now switch back to Design View by clicking the leftmost button, selecting the drop-down list, and then selecting Design View. Access has reflected the edits you made in SQL to its design grid.

The all caps in the SQL keywords, DELETE, SELECT, and so on, are a convention for SQL keywords. SQL and Access work just fine if you enter mixed case.

Compacting the Database

In many operations, Access leaves "holes" in its databases. For example, when you add a table or query to Access, Access will enlarge the MDB file to accommodate this new object. However, if you later delete these objects, Access won't dynamically shrink the MDB file to its initial size.

After running the action query from Exercise 16.1, Access continues to hold open room for the deleted records, even though they aren't included in the table. Access's wasted space grows worse as you add, then delete, database objects such as forms, reports, and queries.

Compacting a database immediately gets rid of these empty spaces or holes Access leaves in its file structure and only recovers at its leisure. Exercise 16.2 shows how to compact a database and the results of doing so.

Exercise 16.2. Compacting a database.

1. Return to the Database window. Figure 16.10 shows an Explorer View of a file before compaction.

Figure 16.10.

The Saftig database before compacting.

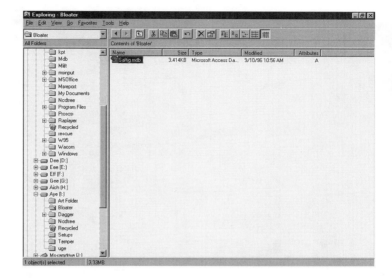

2. The file needing compaction is included in the sample data as `Saftig.mdb`. This is a blown-up version of the Northwind database that's part of Access's sample data. If you are using the sample data, close the College database, then open the `Saftig.mdb` file.

3. Choose Tools|Database Utilities|Compact Database from the menu.

4. Access will grind away a while, open up the compacted file, and then return control of the application to you.

Take a look at Figure 16.11. This is an Explorer look at the Saftig database after compacting. Note that the compacting routine squeezed the database down from approximately 3.4 megabytes to approximately 1.7 megabytes—a substantial improvement. The amount of reduction you see when compacting depends on many factors, such as how often you issue the Compile All and Save All commands that enable Access to recover space without the Compact action.

Figure 16.11.

The Saftig database after compacting.

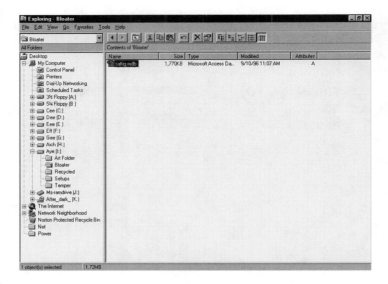

Now look at Figure 16.12. This is the StudentCurrentCourses table after compacting. The empty spaces have been squeezed out with no loss in real data.

NOTE

> The actual before-and-after sizes of your Saftig database might vary from the example shown here. How much your databases grow and shrink depends on the actions you take in them. The example shown in Figure 16.11 is typical, but it can't be identical to similar situations.

The Append Action Query

The append action query extracts data from one table or query and appends, or attaches, it to another table. The target table therefore grows to include all the records it had initially, plus those records extracted by the query. Exercise 16.3 takes the records from the AppendMe table shown in Figure 16.12 (included in the sample data) and appends those records to the StudentCurrentCourses table. Obviously this is a somewhat contrived example, but art does imitate life, doesn't it?

16

Figure 16.12.

The AppendMe table supplied to simplify this exercise.

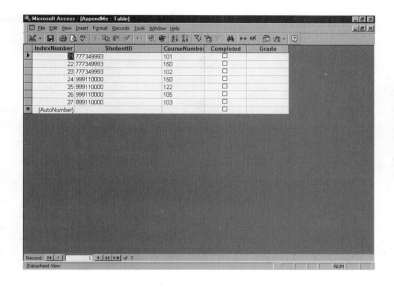

Before doing this query, you need to set the stage. Figure 16.13 shows the StudentsAndCourses query rerun to list the students now signed up for some classes. If you haven't saved this query or don't have the sample data available, look at Figure 16.14, which shows a query in Design View that will help you to follow along with this exercise. If you haven't saved StudentsAndCourses and want to follow along, create the query shown in Figure 16.14.

Figure 16.13.

The StudentsAndCourses query run with current data.

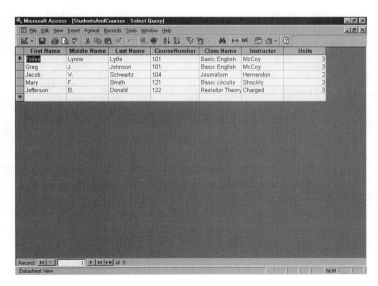

Figure 16.14.

A query designed to illustrate the effect of an append query.

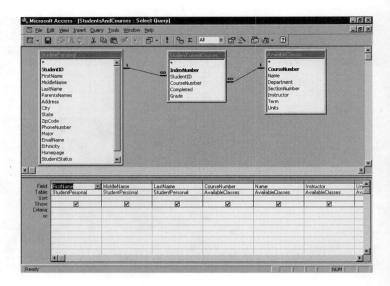

Refer to the StudentsAndCourses query shown running in Figure 16.13 or in Design View in Figure 16.14. Depending on the state of your database and the exercises you've chosen to do, your query might not agree with the return shown in Figure 16.13. If it doesn't and you want to follow along exactly with this exercise, edit the table to exclude any records for MacDonald and Jones.

Note that in the sample data, neither Jones nor MacDonald appears as having taken any courses at this time. Close the StudentsAndCourses query if you have it open. The reason MacDonald is missing is because of the delete action query done in the earlier section of this chapter.

The purpose of the query created in Exercise 16.3 is to extract records from the AppendMe table and append them to the StudentCurrentCourses table. To complete this exercise, you will need the AppendMe table from the sample data. You can enter the table's data now or include this table from the sample set you acquired following the directions in Appendix E, "The Sample Data." Figure 16.15 shows the table in Design View. To see the effect of this exercise, you don't need to have these exact records in AppendMe. Any records that are validated through the StudentPersonal table will work.

16

Figure 16.15.

The AppendMe table in Design View. To simplify this example, this table is the same as StudentCurrentCourses.

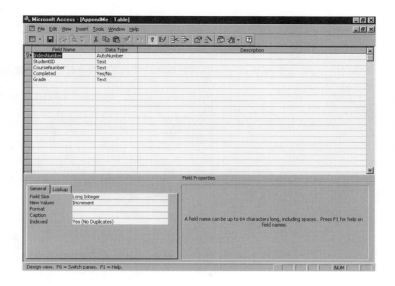

Exercise 16.3. The append query.

1. Close all open tables and queries to clear the work area. Start a new query by moving to the Database window, clicking on the Queries tab, and clicking the New option. Choose the Design View option to bypass the wizards and click OK.

2. Double-click the AppendMe table in the Show Table list box to add this table to the query. Click Close to shut down the Show Table list box. Your screen should resemble Figure 16.16.

Figure 16.16.

Starting the append action query.

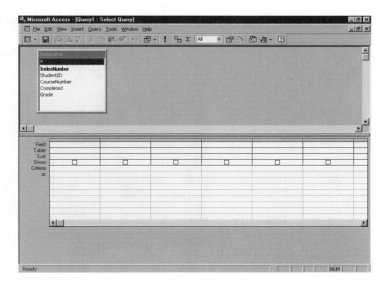

3. Drag the asterisk (*) from the Field list box to the Field row of the first column of the query design grid. (See Figure 16.17.)

Figure 16.17.

Including the asterisk from the Field list box in the query.

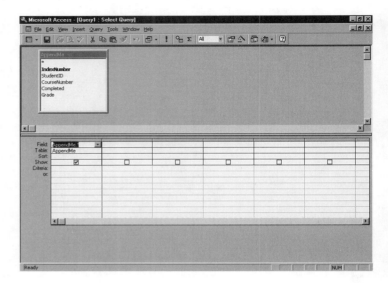

4. Access changes the asterisk to AppendMe.*, which is Access shorthand for "include all the fields from AppendMe in this query." Click the Run button in the toolbar to see how this query runs. Your screen should resemble Figure 16.18.

Figure 16.18.

The effect of the AppendMe. field in a query.*

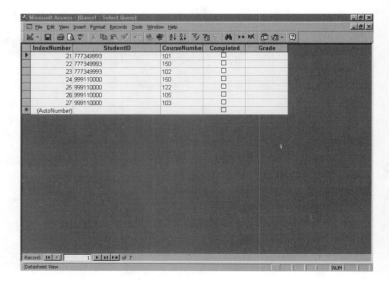

16

The Access Way

When you move the * from a table's Field list box into a query, Access automatically includes all the fields from that table in the query.

This particular query includes all the records from the AppendMe table because you've entered no restricting criteria.

5. Return to Design View. Click the Query Type button in the toolbar and choose Append from the drop-down menu. If you prefer, make these choices from the menu. The Append query button is the one with the green cross in the pull-down. Your screen should resemble Figure 16.19.

Figure 16.19.

The results of changing the select query to an append query.

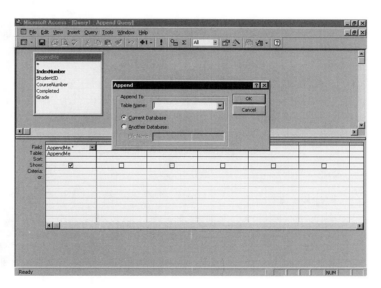

6. Pull down the combo box in the Append dialog and choose the StudentCurrentCourses table to append to. (See Figure 16.20.)

7. Click OK. Access gives you the message box shown in Figure 16.21, warning you that continuing to run this query will append seven rows to the target table, StudentCurrentCourses. Click OK. Note how the query design grid has changed. Not only has the title bar changed to indicate this is an append query, but the design grid itself changed to include rows needed by append queries.

Figure 16.20.

Telling Access which table to append to.

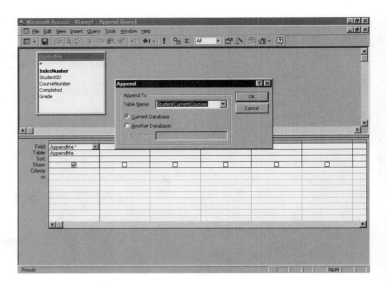

8. As with the delete and make table queries, nothing seems to occur, but it has. Access has added the records in AppendMe to StudentCurrentCourses. Note that Access did what you wanted and not what you told it to. You included the IndexNumber field in the query, yet Access was smart enough to ignore that field without complaint when it added only the relevant parts of the records to the StudentCurrentCourses table.

Figure 16.21.

Access warns you of the consequences of this query.

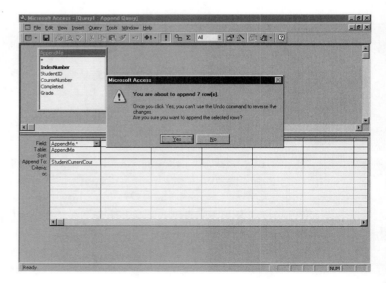

9. Close this query, saving it as Appender. Back at the Database window, note how Access clues you that this is an append action query by using the green cross icon next to the query's name.

10 Now run the StudentsAndCourses query again. This time you'll see new records for MacDonald and Jones. These are the records appended from AppendMe. The results of this query are shown in Figure 16.22.

NOTE

When doing append action queries, keep in mind that the fields' data types must match.

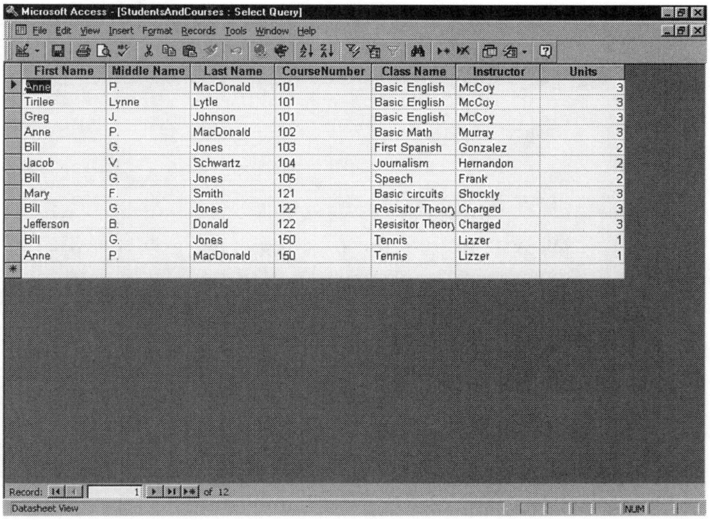

16

Figure 16.22.
The appended records.

First Name	Middle Name	Last Name	CourseNumber	Class Name	Instructor	Units
Anne	P.	MacDonald	101	Basic English	McCoy	3
Tinlee	Lynne	Lytle	101	Basic English	McCoy	3
Greg	J.	Johnson	101	Basic English	McCoy	3
Anne	P.	MacDonald	102	Basic Math	Murray	3
Bill	G.	Jones	103	First Spanish	Gonzalez	2
Jacob	V.	Schwartz	104	Journalism	Hernandon	2
Bill	G.	Jones	105	Speech	Frank	2
Mary	F.	Smith	121	Basic circuits	Shockly	3
Bill	G.	Jones	122	Resisitor Theory	Charged	3
Jefferson	B.	Donald	122	Resisitor Theory	Charged	3
Bill	G.	Jones	150	Tennis	Lizzer	1
Anne	P.	MacDonald	150	Tennis	Lizzer	1

Record: 1 of 12
Datasheet View

The Access Way

Access is a tightly integrated program. The icons shown for the various query types in the Database window are the same as the icons shown in the toolbar for these same queries.

Compare Figure 16.22 with 16.13 to see how the append query added records to the StudentCurrentCourses table. The queries in 16.13 and 16.22 extract records from three tables, one of which is StudentCurrentCourses; therefore, the StudentCurrentCourses table reflects the changes the append performed.

Do	Don't

DO use action queries regularly. An append query combined with a delete query on the same records can act as a powerful archiving tool.

DON'T fail to back up your data. Access will always follow your criteria for action queries perfectly. Sometimes, unless you're very careful, you'll enter defective criteria that will extract and delete the wrong data. The best defense is a solid backup system that's used regularly.

You can see that now records exist for Jones and MacDonald in the StudentCurrentCourses table. Close all queries.

Top Queries

Take a look at Figure 16.23. That's a simple table with two fields and some data. You'll find this table in your sample data with the name PressureData.

This table contains sample labels and the pressure for each sample label. Each label represents a place along a production pipeline. The problem with this table, which is only partially visible, is that you're inundated with numbers. People don't do well looking at long lists of long numbers. It would be a real annoyance to find, say, the top 10 percent of pressures and samples.

Figure 16.23.

Samples and pressures.

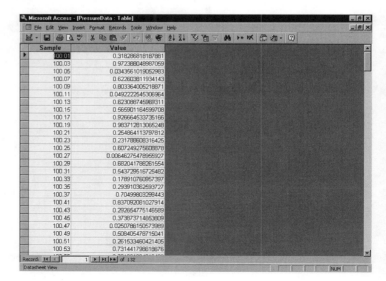

You've probably guessed by now that Access 97 has an easy way to do this. Actually, this capability has been in previous Access versions, but wasn't discovered by many users who don't program in SQL. Microsoft, beginning with Access 97, made things simpler.

To find the top pressures, construct a new query and include the PressureData table. Add both fields from PressureData to the query design grid. Your screen should resemble Figure 16.24.

Run the query. At this point it just returns all records in any order. Figure 16.25 is the running query, and Figure 16.26 is the SQL statement behind the query.

Figure 16.24.

The start of the top query.

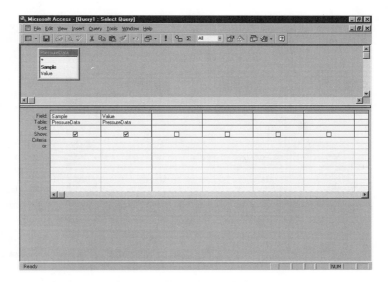

Figure 16.25.

The top query without a top statement.

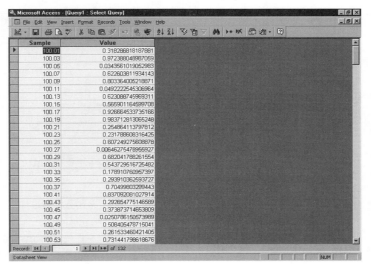

Figure 16.26.

The SQL statement behind Figure 16.25.

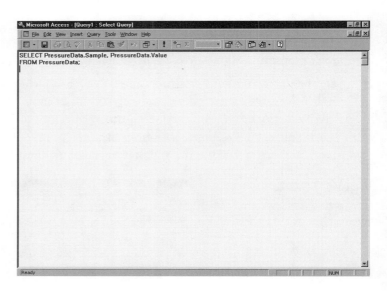

Well, so far this is a big "duh." Here's where things get interesting. Return to the query Design View. Pull down the Sort combo box under the Value column and change it to Descending. Locate the Top Values pull-down combo box as shown in Figure 16.27.

Figure 16.27.

The Top Values box.

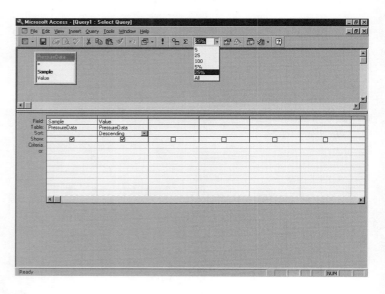

Pull down the box and select 25%. Run the query again. This time Access will return only those values in the top 25 percent, as shown in Figure 16.28. Look at the status bar that shows Access returning only 33 records (the top 25 percent) instead of the original 135 records.

Pretty neat! Except for one thing—the value you were looking for was the top 10 percent, not 25 percent. Access's pull-down Top Value box doesn't have an entry for 10 percent.

Looks like it's time to become an SQL programmer. Click the leftmost button on the toolbar and select SQL View for this query. Your screen should resemble Figure 16.29. (Note that to do this you could also have entered the 10% in the combo box in the query design grid.)

Figure 16.28.

Access returns only the top 25 percent of records in the first part of this query exercise.

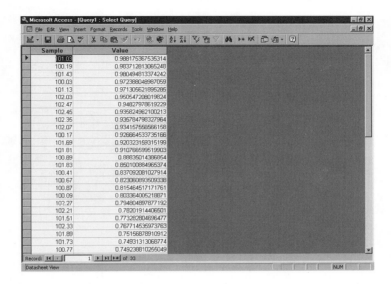

Figure 16.29.

The SQL statement for this query now includes the Top *keyword.*

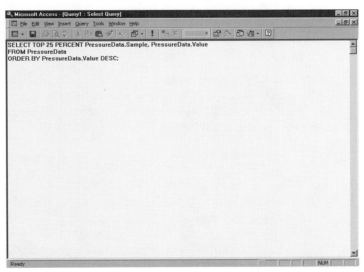

Edit the 25 to read 10. Return to Datasheet View by running the query. Your screen should resemble Figure 16.30. You've found your top 10 percent.

Figure 16.30.

The top 10 percent query.

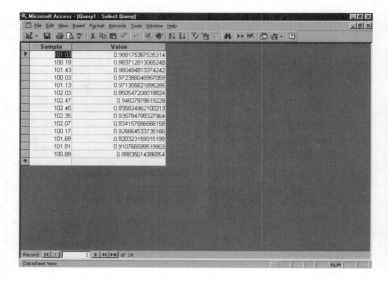

The Secret Behind the Top

The sort order told Access that you wanted the top 10 percent of the values. Had you sorted the query in Ascending order, Access would have returned the bottom 10 percent. Also, Access selects the top from the leftmost column that's sorted. Had you not pulled down the Sort combo box and told Access to sort on Value, Access would have, by default, selected the top values from the Sample field.

Keep in mind that Access works from the left in queries. You don't have to include fields from other queries or tables in the order they are in the table. You could have placed the Value field to the left of the Sample field and then executed the Top statement without a Sort order and your results would have been valid.

> **The Access Way**
>
> Be very careful when executing top queries that you are extracting the top of the field you intend. A good safety measure is to include a dummy record much larger or smaller than any other in the table, then run your top query to see if the record is included. If it is, you have some assurance that your top query is working right.

16

> You can then delete this record from either the underlying table/query or directly from the top query itself.
>
> Remember to rerun the query if you delete records from it.

> **The Access Way**
>
> You can also select top numbers using a method similar to selecting the top percentages. Just change the value of the Top combo box to a number rather than a percentage and run the query.

16

Two Sophisticated Queries

This lesson is a little long, so if you're trying to do this chapter in one sitting, perhaps this is a time to take a break. The following subjects are very important in Access. The importance of the crosstab query varies with the database in question, but the update query is called upon by database users on a regular basis.

Update Queries

An update query is a query that, when run, alters the fields of target records. This is the only action query that acts on fields rather than entire records. For example, if you wanted to delete an entire record or set of records, you could perform a delete action query. If you wanted to delete a field or set of fields in a record (change them to blank), the delete query won't work but the update query will.

Open the Update Demo table in Datasheet View. This table is supplied as part of the sample data. (See Figure 16.31.)

This table is an extract showing the city and ZIP codes from some selected records. The following exercise uses this table rather than the entire dataset so you can more easily see the behavior of the update query.

The fictional college has received word from the U.S. Postal Service that the fictional Skokie ZIP code 38990 will be changed to 38989. Exercise 16.4 shows how to make this change using an update action query in Access.

This exercise creates an update query that looks for any ZIP codes meeting the criteria of 38990 and changes them to 38989.

Figure 16.31.

The table to be updated.

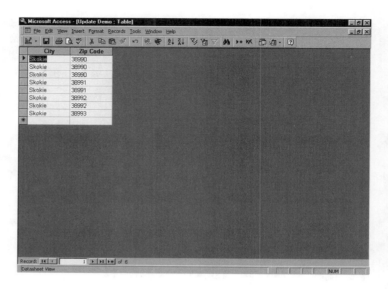

Exercise 16.4. Update queries.

EXERCISE

1. Close the Update Demo table if it's open. Starting from the Database window, click the Queries tab. Click the New button to start a new query. Skip any wizard. Add the Update Demo table to the query design grid from the Show Table list box, then close the list box. Your screen should resemble Figure 16.32.

Figure 16.32.

Starting the update action query.

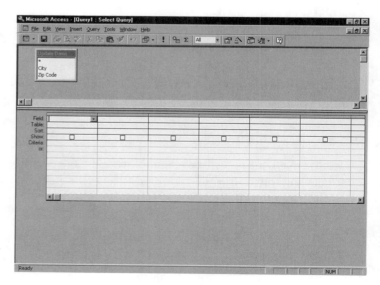

16

2. Click the menu selections File|Save As and save this query as qryUpdater. Add both of the fields from the list box to the query design grid. (See Figure 16.33.)

Figure 16.33.
Adding fields to the query design grid.

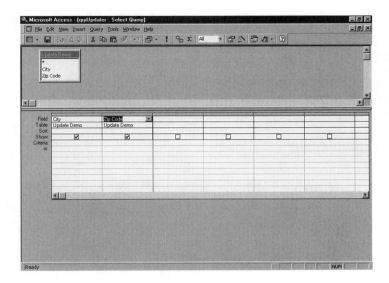

3. Run the query. As expected, Access returns all the records from the Update Demo table because no criteria have been specified. (See Figure 16.34.)

Figure 16.34.
Running the select query.

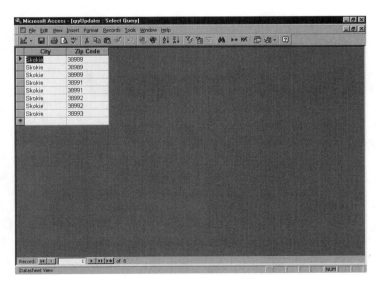

The Access Way

Running this query in Select mode before changing to the action update query might seem overly cautious. In this case it is, as the dataset is so small. However, in most live cases you can't see an overview of your data as you can here and running it as a select query first is important. This example is the right way to run an action query when your live data is at stake, but it's slightly overdoing it for this dataset.

4. Return to Design View. Add the criterion "38990" to the ZipCode field's criteria row. (See Figure 16.35.) When you run the query, Access now extracts only those Skokie addresses with the ZipCode of 38990, as shown in Figure 16.36.

Figure 16.35.

Adding a criterion to the query.

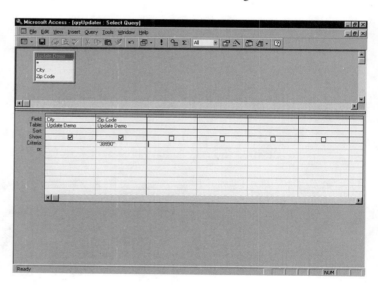

5. Return to Design View. Click the Query type button on the toolbar. (That's the button just to the left of the Run button.) It has an icon of two grids on it. Select Update from the pull-down list. It's the one with the pencil on it. If you prefer, you can change to an update type query by choosing that option from within the Query menu. Either way, Access changes the second row (or third if you have made the menu selections View|Tables) of the query design grid to read "Update To:" and also changes the title bar to indicate this is an Update query. Add "38989" as a criterion in the ZipCode field to update to. Your screen should resemble Figure 16.37.

Figure 16.36.

The results of the criterion.

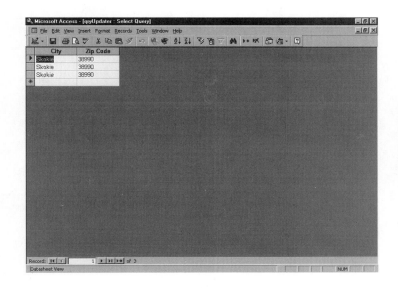

6. Click the Run button on the toolbar. Access gives you the message box shown in Figure 16.38.

7. Click Yes. Access runs the query. Close this query, saving changes.

Figure 16.37.

Updating the criteria.

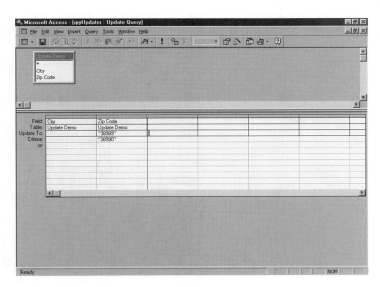

Figure 16.38.

The Update Query message box.

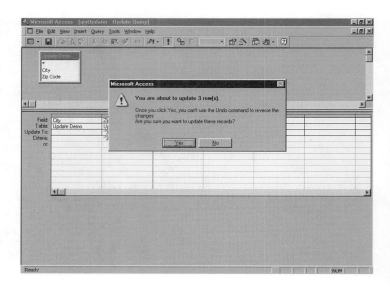

Back at the Database window, notice how the new query qryUpdater has a distinctive icon showing you that not only is it an action query, but an update one.

Click the Tables tab. Open up the Update Demo table in Datasheet View. Your screen should resemble Figure 16.39.

The three records that were formerly "Skokie, 38990" are now "Skokie, 38989." Note that unlike other action queries, nothing in the record was touched except for the specific field you chose to update. Close this table to clear the decks for what comes next.

Figure 16.39.

The update query's results.

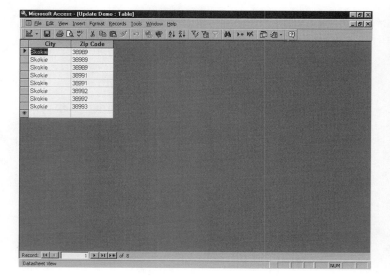

The Crosstab Query

People have a hard time understanding and designing crosstab queries. However, these queries can be quite important when you are analyzing your data. Microsoft has gone to great lengths in both Access 97 and Excel 97 to make the creation of these queries quite simple. The Excel term for a crosstab query is a Pivot Table.

Technically speaking, a crosstab query is a two-dimensional matrix with a mathematical operation performed at each intersection. Once again, a crosstab is much easier to understand in the concrete than in the abstract. Take a look at Figure 16.40. This is the Cross Tab Demo table taken from the sample data. The fictional college has a for-profit subsidiary selling boats of all types from canoes to yachts. This table is a segment of the sales register for this subsidiary.

Figure 16.40.

The Cross Tab Demo table.

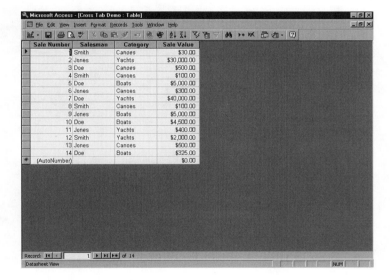

Each record contains the name of the salesman, the classification the sale fits into, and the amount of the sale. The fictional college wants to analyze this data to determine the dollar amount of sales for each salesman in each category and the sales frequency for each salesman in each category. A crosstab query is just the ticket for both of these tasks.

Exercise 16.2 creates two crosstabs—one showing the sum of the dollars and one showing the frequency of sales. If at any time you want to see this query in action, the sample data includes a query called qryCrossTabSample which, when run, will duplicate the results of Exercise 16.5.

Exercise 16.5. The crosstab query.

1. Close the Cross Tab Demo table if it's open. Click the Queries tab. Click the New button. Click the Crosstab Query Wizard option. Your screen should resemble Figure 16.41.

2. Click OK. Click the Cross Tab Demo table in the next list box. (See Figure 16.42.)

3. Click the Next> button. This query should list the salesmen in the rows and the category of sales across the top. Click the field Salesman to highlight it and click the > button to move it to the right list box. Your screen should resemble Figure 16.43.

Figure 16.41.

The beginning of the crosstab query.

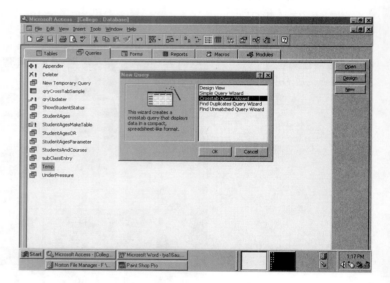

Figure 16.42.

Binding the query to the right table or query.

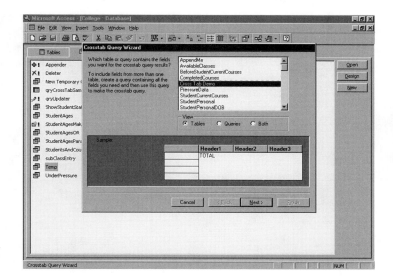

Figure 16.43.

Choosing the rows in a crosstab.

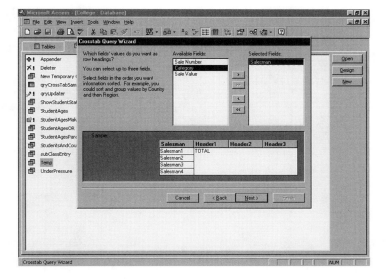

4. Click the Next> button. The column heads are the categories of the sales, so highlight Category in the next list box. (See Figure 16.44.)

Figure 16.44.

Choosing the columns in a crosstab.

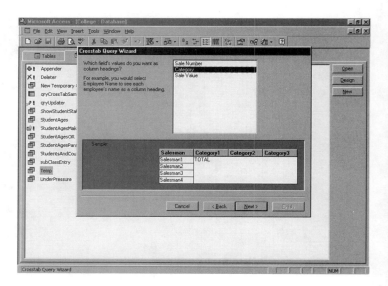

5. Click Next>. The figure to calculate for each salesman in each category is the Sale Value, so highlight that in the left list box and Sum in the right list box (because the first crosstab is a summation one). (See Figure 16.45.)

Figure 16.45.

Choosing a field to sum on.

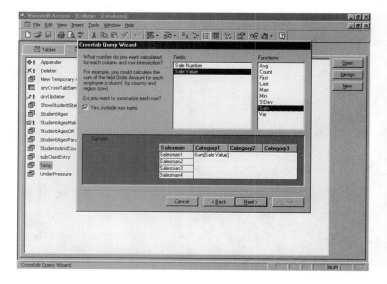

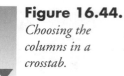

16

6. Click the Next> button. Accept the Access defaults by clicking the Finish button. Access will grind away a while and eventually will finish constructing and running the query. Your screen should look like Figure 16.46.

Figure 16.46.

The finished crosstab query running.

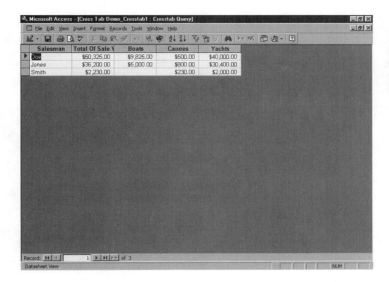

Look how handy the results are. At a glance you can see that Doe outsold everybody else in Boats and Yachts, but Jones was the winner in the Canoes category. The dataset was a little small, so a trained eye could have seen this by examining the raw data in the table, but what happens when sales occurrences are in the thousands or millions? That's what computers are for.

Switch to Design View. Your screen should resemble Figure 16.47.

The underlying design of a crosstab query isn't very obvious. That's why Microsoft went to the trouble of making a special wizard for it. The heart of this query is in the third and fourth columns. Notice that the Total row has the word Sum in it for the third and fourth columns. This tells Access to sum the Sale Values for the crosstab.

Click this row, pull down the combo box for the third column, and click the Count function. (See Figure 16.48.)

Figure 16.47.
The Design View of a crosstab query.

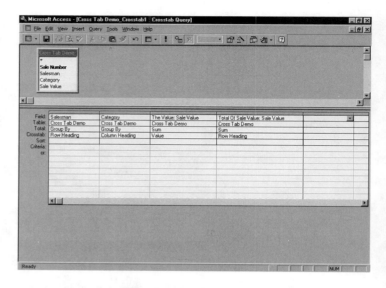

Figure 16.48.
Changing a crosstab's operative.

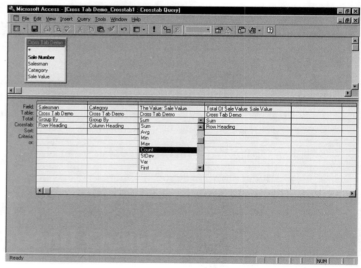

Click the Run button again. Your screen should look like Figure 16.49.

Now you can see at a glance that while Doe and Jones outsold Smith dollarwise, Smith had the greatest number of sales occurrences in the Canoes category. This query demonstrates how useful crosstabs can be. Trying to show this data using most other techniques would have been less clear or more difficult.

Figure 16.49.

The new crosstab.

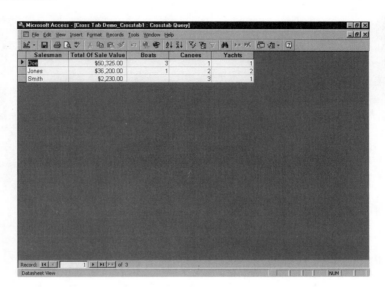

The Access Way

Time-saver: You can make one crosstab and then use many operatives in the same frame by changing the operative (count, sum, avg, and so on) and selecting File|Save As for each operative. This gives you a series of crosstabs that show different aspects of the same data.

Adding Information to the Crosstab

You can add more than one operative to a crosstab. The following is a quick and optional exercise. The final result is part of your sample data for today.

Return to Design View. Click above the fourth column to highlight the entire column just as you would if you wanted to move the column in Datasheet View. (See Figure 16.50.)

Figure 16.50.

Highlighting a column.

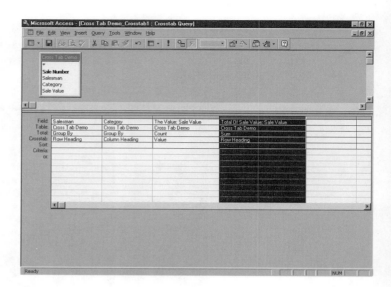

Press Ctrl+C to copy the column to the Clipboard. Now click on the fifth column the same way to highlight it, and press Ctrl+V to duplicate the fourth column in the fifth place. Your screen should resemble Figure 16.51.

Figure 16.51.

Duplicating a column.

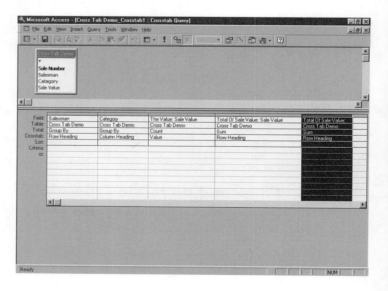

Edit the label for the fifth column to read Number of Sales instead of Total of Sale Value. (See Figure 16.52.)

Figure 16.52.

Editing the duplicate column.

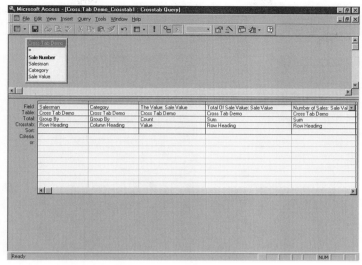

Finally, change the Total row for the fifth column to Count instead of Sum. (See Figure 16.53.)

Figure 16.53.

Changing from Sum to Count.

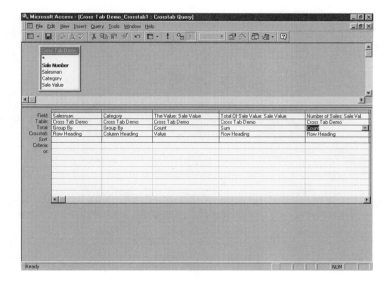

Now click the Run button to see what your changes have wrought. Your screen should resemble Figure 16.54.

Figure 16.54.

The new crosstab with two summary fields.

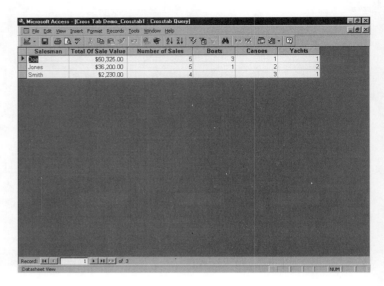

Again, the information in this query is rather obvious from the raw data, but if this table were to contain thousands of fields, it wouldn't be. Access would have no trouble generating a crosstab from thousands of entries.

Close this query, saving changes.

Don't worry if you think you haven't fully grasped crosstabs. This is a difficult topic for just about everybody. Use the wizard to make your crosstabs. After doing a few, you'll catch on to the magic Access performs behind the scenes and if you choose, you can do them yourself manually.

Figure 16.55 illustrates the crosstab in SQL View.

Although the SQL behind this query is more complex (although not the longest) than any other query, you still should get a good sense of how it works from examining it.

Figure 16.55.

The new crosstab in SQL View.

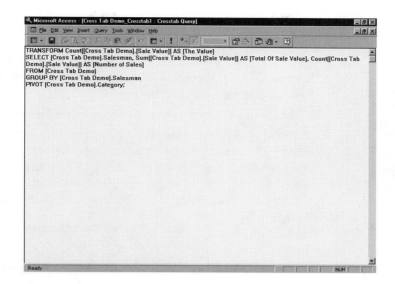

Day Summary

This morning you learned how to construct queries with dynamic criteria—that is, queries that prompt users for input when they're run. These queries "fill in the blanks" and can act the same way queries having standard criteria do. This includes using wildcards as part of the query criteria.

This afternoon you learned how to delete records in groups by using a delete action query. You also learned how to append records from one table to another using an append action query. You saw how Access can leave "holes" or dead space in its files that can be eliminated with the Compact Database utility built into Access. Finally, you learned how to find top or bottom values in numbers or percentages from a query.

Update queries alter data according to your criteria. The updates occur to the queried table or query.

Crosstab queries are complex enough that Access has a specially designed wizard just for them. You need to tell the wizard four essential things: the source of the query, what's to be in the rows, what's to be in the columns, and what operation to perform at the intersections and for a row summary.

Q&A

Q **Can I enter two parameters on the criteria row to create an AND query?**

A Yes. Access will first prompt you for the parameter on the left, but the query will function just like a standard AND query.

Q **What about using parameters to create an OR query?**

A It works the same as the AND query. Just enter the parameters on two different rows. Access will prompt for the parameter on the topmost row first. Figure 16.56 shows the StudentAges query modified to be an OR parameter query. Figure 16.57 is the same query run with MacDonald as the LastName and 22 as the second criterion. This query has been saved as part of the sample data as StudentAgesOR.

Figure 16.56.

Constructing the OR parameter query.

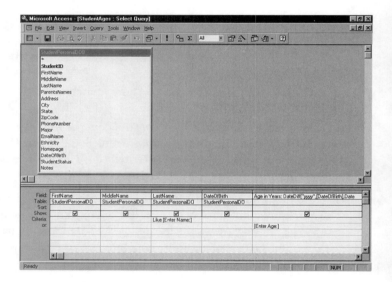

Q **Can I enter a parameter criterion for an artificial field constructed from an expression?**

A No, because Access first applies the parameter, then performs the expression. You can effectively do this by creating a make table query and then running a parameter query based on that table. (See Figure 16.57.)

16

Figure 16.57.

Running the OR
parameter query.

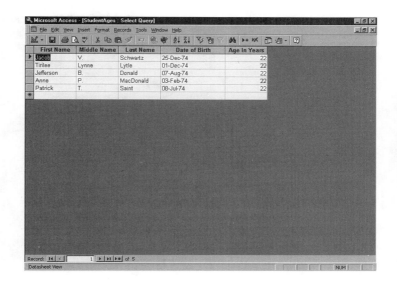

**Q When I update a table to which a crosstab is bound, does the crosstab query
get updated too?**

A Yes, the next time the query is run. If you have both the Cross Tab Demo table
and the Cross Tab Demo_Crosstab1 query open at the same time and you edit the
table, the query won't reflect the edits until it's run again (or queried again).

Q Can I base a form on a crosstab query?

A Sure. Look at Figure 16.58. This is a form based on the crosstab query done in
Exercise 16.5. The advantage of using a form to view crosstab data is that you have
all the form services available to you.

Q How do crosstabs differ from subtotals?

A Crosstabs act on two dimensions, across and down. Subtotals operate on only one,
either across or down.

**Q If I update a field from a table on the one side of a relationship, will Access
update the related fields on the many side(s), or will I lose my link(s)?**

A If you have the Enforce Referential Integrity box and the Cascading Updates box
checked when you establish the link(s), Access will update the many side(s) of the
relationships. If you have only Enforce Referential Integrity checked, Access will
balk at the update. If you have neither box checked, you really don't have a one-
to-many link established.

Figure 16.58.
*A form based on
a crosstab.*

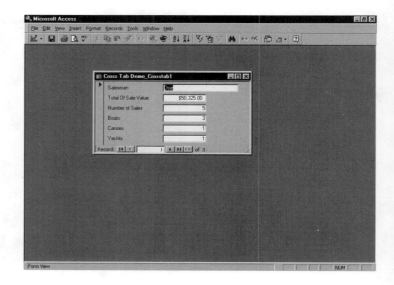

Workshop

Here's where you can test and apply the lessons you learned today.

Quiz

Possible answers to these questions are provided in Appendix A.

1. Can you undo (Ctrl+Z) the action of a delete action query? An append action query?

2. Can you use wildcards in a parameter query?

3. If you have a query selecting the top 25% of a field, how can you change it to show the bottom 25%?

4. Can you use criteria in top queries?

5. Will the parameter Like [Enter a Name:] accept U* as a wildcard criterion?

6. Can you make a crosstab that finds average values?

7. Can the update query act on individual fields in a table, or must it work on entire rows, like the delete query?

16

Put Access into Action

1. Open the StudentAges query in Design View.

2. Delete any criteria for this query.

3. Pull down the Query menu and change this query back to a select one if necessary.

4. Construct a parameter query that will act as an AND query requiring a match on two fields before you can get a return.

5. Modify the query so that both parts of the AND query accept wildcards.

6. Modify the query to keep the same parameters, but make it an OR query.

7. Close the query, discarding changes.

16

Extra Credit

1. Start a new wizard-generated crosstab query based on the Cross Tab Demo table.

2. Place Category in the rows.

3. Place the Salesman fields in the columns.

4. Have the query show the maximum sales in each category for each salesman. Run the query.

5. Look at the SQL code for this query. Which term do you suppose you'd change to make this a summing crosstab?

6. Close the query when you're done with it. This book does not come back to it; however, it is part of the sample data for today.

DAY 9

A.M.

17 Forms with Subforms

P.M.

18 Form Control Properties

Chapter **17**

Forms with Subforms

This morning you'll learn about the following:

- ☐ The need for forms with subforms
- ☐ The steps to create a form with a subform
- ☐ Creating the subform
- ☐ Creating the host or container form
- ☐ Drag-and-drop subforms
- ☐ Embedding the subform in a form
- ☐ Using the form with a subform

Why You Need Forms with Subforms

Access is a relational database system. In any system such as Access, there are relationships between records in various tables; in other words, one record in a table can be related to many other records in other tables. Here are some examples:

> One customer has many orders.
>
> One order has many line items.
>
> One student has many classes.
>
> In a hospital, one doctor has many patients.
>
> In that same hospital, one patient has many medicines required to be given daily.
>
> One person has many CDs.
>
> One CD has many tracks.
>
> One salesperson has many sales.
>
> One company has many salespersons.
>
> One department has many sales items.
>
> One store has many departments.

In each of the preceding examples, and many more you can likely think of, there are one and many sides to a relationship. The link, or common field, in both tables has one occurrence in the one table and potentially an unlimited number of occurrences in the other table.

How do you enter a series of occurrences on the many side of the relationship? For example, you want to enter a series of sales for a particular salesperson. The combo box exercise in Chapter 12, "Intermediate Forms," shows how you can look up a StudentID to make sure the value you added to the StudentID field in StudentCurrentCourses was correct.

The technique shown in Chapter 12 works, but it's slightly cumbersome. It has two drawbacks. First, you can't just enter a series of occurrences for a particular student, but must look up the right StudentID for each record or use Ctrl+'—this key combination, the repeat key for Access, repeats the value from the last record in the current field. Also, you can't see a student's personal information along with his or her current classes at the same time without making a query and a form to host the query.

Forms with subforms are a very convenient and aesthetically pleasing way to show or enter occurrences on the many side of a one-to-many relationship. There's no reason the same form can't be used to create new records on the one side of the relationship, but that's not the most common use of this technique.

You can easily get lost in Exercise 17.1 unless you have a good idea of the goal shown in Figure 17.15. Take a look at Figure 17.15 to see the finished form with a subform. The following list shows how you're going to get there. This list is also a good reference if you need to manually create a form with one or more subforms. Like so much else, the job goes much faster with a wizard.

1. Determine the one and the many sides of the relationship to see if the two tables or queries you wish to include are right for the form with subform technique. If necessary, construct the needed queries or tables.

2. Design the subform. This is where the many table or query will appear. In most cases the subform will be a form using the Datasheet View, but it doesn't have to be.

3. Save the subform, giving it a distinctive name. Access users and developers have adopted a set of naming conventions for objects in their databases. Using these conventions, if a form is to be named ClassEntry, the subform is generally called subClassEntry, but you can make up your own naming convention or not use one at all.

4. Design the (container) form, leaving room for the subform in your design.

5. Drag the subform into the container form.

6. Test the new form with subform with known data to make sure it's working right.

Preparing for the Form

The subform part of this form makes it possible to enter, edit, or display a series of classes for an individual student. The first thing to do is set up a query to bind the subform to. Exercise 17.1 shows you how.

The Access Way

Exercise 17.1 uses a query for this subform with a criterion to return or display only those records for which the completed field is equal to No. The exercise uses a query instead of the original table because if this form were bound to the table, it would show all the classes ever taken by this student, completed or not. This isn't a fatal error, but it would make for an inconveniently long scroll through irrelevant records in the case of students who've enrolled in many classes.

Because this form with subform is only supposed to address current and future classes, we want to restrict it from also displaying completed classes. The best way to do this is to use a query. The way a query can confirm data is another reason to use one for binding to the subform.

Exercise 17.1. Making the subform's query.

1. Launch Access and open the College database if necessary. Click the Queries tab then the New button to start a new query. Click the Design View option, then OK to bypass the wizards. Add the StudentCurrentCourses and AvailableClasses tables to the query design grid. Close the Show Table list box. Your screen should resemble Figure 17.1.

Figure 17.1.

Starting a new query for use on a subform.

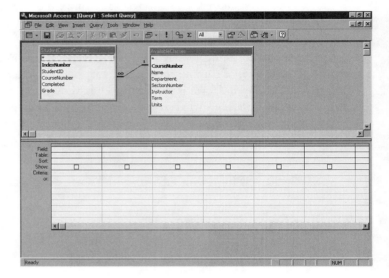

2. Drag the fields StudentID, CourseNumber, and Completed from the StudentCurrentCourses list box to the query design grid's columns 1–3. Uncheck the display check box for Completed and enter No for this field's criteria on the first criteria row. Your screen should resemble Figure 17.2.

3. Drag the Name and SectionNumber fields from the AvailableClasses table to columns 4 and 5 of the query design grid. Your screen should resemble Figure 17.3.

4. Click the Run button in the toolbar. Your screen should resemble Figure 17.4. Remember that the actual return you get when you run this query depends on the data in your database.

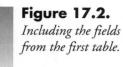

Figure 17.2.

Including the fields from the first table.

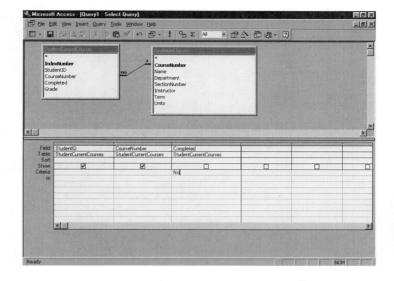

Figure 17.3.

Finishing the query design.

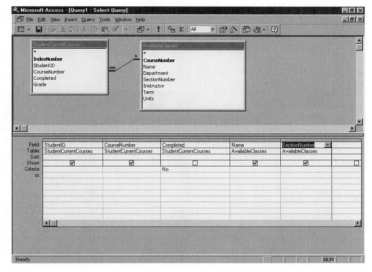

17

Figure 17.4.
Running the new query.

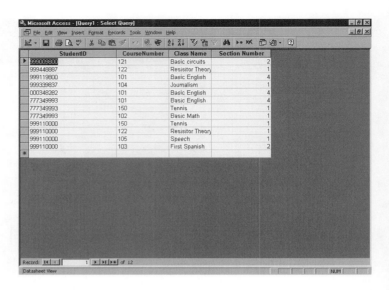

5. Now for something pretty cool. Click in the last row for this query. Press Ctrl+'
   and Access will copy the StudentID data from the record immediately above the
   current record. Press Tab. Enter 101 for the CourseNumber. Your screen should
   resemble Figure 17.5.

Figure 17.5.
Adding a record in a query.

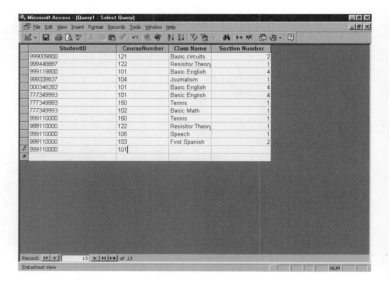

6. Now press Tab. Your screen should resemble Figure 17.6.

Figure 17.6.

*Access automati-
cally looks up and
fills in values.*

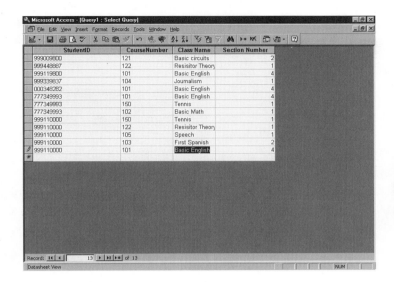

There's a neat trick queries can do that tables can't! Access fills in the information
for you. This happens because the courses at the fictional college are indexed
according to course number, but the fictional registrar demanded a system that
would show the course name and the section number when the data-entry people
entered the index course number. This way they could confirm that a student
wanted to sign up for such and such a course.

7. Close the query, saving it and using the name subClassEntry. This is also the name
it has in the sample data.

The Access Way

Just as Exercise 17.1 shows how you can use a query to look up confirmation
information for classes, you can use this same technique to look up item descriptions from item numbers, employees from employee numbers, customers from
their phone numbers, and so on.

Queries are the heart of any relational database system, including Access. Use them
to make your applications better.

There's only one loose end. The Default Value property for the Completed field of the StudentCurrentCourses should be set to No. From the Database window, click the Tables tab, open the StudentCurrentCourses table in Design View, click the Completed field, and set its Default property to No. Your screen should resemble Figure 17.7.

Close the table, saving changes.

Figure 17.7.
Altering the Default
Value property of a table.

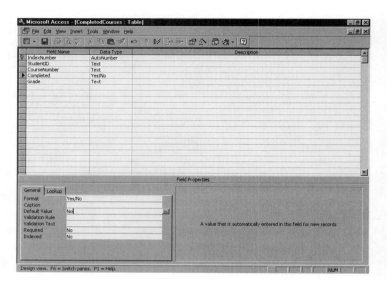

The Form with Subform

You are now ready to create the main form with a contained subform. There are two ways to do this—the easy way and the hard way. You've probably guessed by now that the easy way is to use a wizard, so that's the way to proceed. After creating this form with a subform and seeing it in action, you'll learn the secret of the magic acts the wizard performed so you can manually design the same thing if the need arises. (This comes in the next chapter.) For this morning, just concentrate on making and using the form with subform. Exercise 17.2 uses a wizard to create a form with a subform.

Exercise 17.2. The form with subform.

1. From the Database window, click the Forms tab, then click the New button. Pull down the combo box and choose StudentPersonal for the bound table or query. Click the Form Wizard option to call up a wizard. Your screen should resemble Figure 17.8.

17

Figure 17.8.

Starting the Main/Subform Wizard.

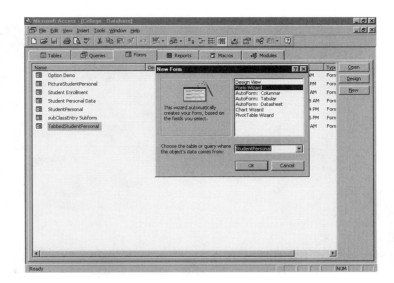

The Access Way

When planning a form with a subform, you must know ahead of time which form will contain the other. The container, or main form, is the form you initially bind to the new form when starting the wizard, as shown in Figure 17.8.

---

2. Click OK to move ahead. Here's the central place where the Access wizard shows its intelligence. Add the StudentID, FirstName, LastName, and Major fields from StudentPersonal to the form by highlighting them, then clicking the > key to move the fields to the selection box.

   Now pull down the combo box labeled Tables/Queries. Locate the subClassEntry query you created in Exercise 17.1. Click it so that it's highlighted. Your screen should resemble Figure 17.9.

3. Add all the fields from this query to the selection box either one at a time or by clicking the >> button. Your screen should resemble Figure 17.10.

Figure 17.9.
*Changing tables or
queries mid-
wizard.*

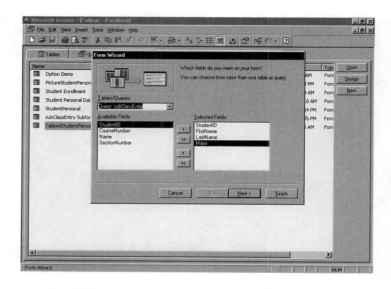

Figure 17.10.
*Adding the fields
that will appear on
the subform.*

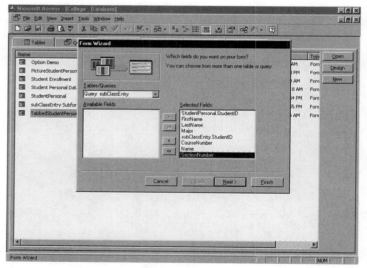

The Access Way

The main, or container, form needs only a few fields from StudentPersonal—the
table it's bound to. These fields—StudentID, FirstName, MiddleName,

LastName, and Major—are all that's required to locate a student from StudentPersonal. The Major field was included at the request of Student Advisement, who also uses this form.

The balance of the fields in StudentPersonal aren't relevant for the purposes of this form. Remember, the fictional college will be using this form only to look up existing records in StudentPersonal, not to create new records. If this form were also going to do double duty as a new record-creating form, it would have to contain all the fields from StudentPersonal.

The Access Way

At this point you have two fields with the same name, StudentID, as part of this form/subform. Access associates these fields with their table or query by using the dot notation that's also used throughout Access. So StudentPersonal.StudentID identifies the StudentID field from StudentPersonal and subClassEntry.StudentID identifies the StudentID field from the subClassEntry query.

4. Click the Next > button to move on. Here you tell the wizard which is the form and which is the subform, but not quite in those words. Access asks the question in plain English: "How do you want to view your data?" Since you want to view the students and their classes, select by StudentPersonal. If you wanted to see the students and classes all mushed up on one form, you'd choose subClassEntry. This part of the wizard is a little tough conceptually. Just follow along for now. If you have the time and inclination after finishing, run the wizard again, but this time view your records by subClassEntry.

   At this point your screen should resemble Figure 17.11. Make sure the Form with subform(s) option button is selected. The other choice is Linked forms. Linked forms are, as you might guess, two forms that share a common field and remain in sync. If you have the time, run this wizard again doing the same steps, but choose Linked forms at this step to see the differences between linked forms and a form/subform.

5. Click the Next> button to move on. Leave Access's default, Datasheet, as the layout for this form. This setting alters the subform. The usual layout for a form/subform is for the form to be in Form View while the subform is in Datasheet View. This isn't a hard and fast rule, however. Your specific needs might

include having a Form View subform. Click Next >. Here is where you can give your form an artistic look. Give this form the Windows 95/97 look by clicking the Standard option. Your screen should resemble Figure 17.12.

Figure 17.11.
Telling Access how you want to view your data within the form/subform.

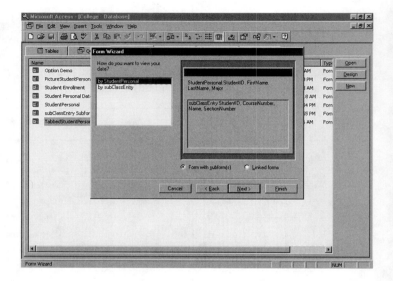

Figure 17.12.
Giving the form the standard Windows 95/97 look.

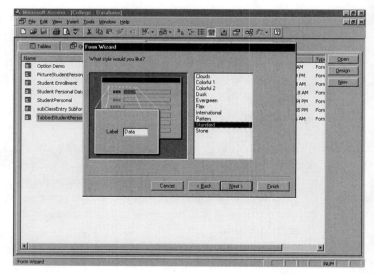

6. Click the Next > button. Give this form the name Class Entry Form and the subform Classes. Your screen should resemble Figure 17.13. The process is now done, so click the Finish button. Click the record advance button (the VCR buttons on the bottom of the screen). As you advance through the students, you'll also see those classes they're signed up to take. (See Figure 17.14.)

Figure 17.13.

Finishing the main/subform.

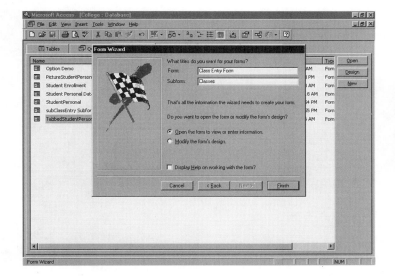

Figure 17.14.

The running form.

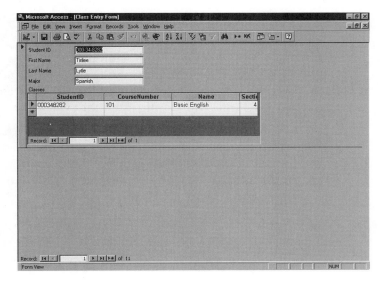

The Main/Subform Wizard creates two forms during its run. The main form is the one you initially bound even before calling on the wizard. The contained, or subform, is the form you told the wizard to bind to the subform in the middle part of the wizard's run. After finishing its run, the wizard called on for Exercise 17.2 should leave you with two forms, Class Entry Form and Classes, as shown in the Database View in Figure 17.15.

Figure 17.15.

The two forms the wizard made in one pass.

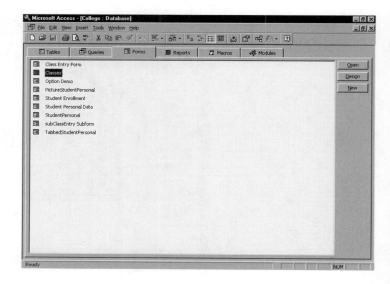

Figure 17.16 shows the wizard-created form from Exercise 17.2 in Design View.

The keys to forms with subforms are the properties Link Child Fields and Link Master Fields. These fields tell Access how to keep the form and subform in synchronization. Access shows only the classes for a particular student by filtering according to the StudentID in the master form. If you are in Design View for the wizard-created form, move back to Form View. The first record, the one for Tirilee Lytle, shows she's taking only one class.

Move to the next record in the Class Entry form, the one for Anne MacDonald, by clicking the right-facing arrow at the bottom of your screen. Your screen should resemble Figure 17.17. If your cursor is just jumping around in the subform section, first click the master form, then click the VCR-style buttons to move to MacDonald.

Figure 17.16.

The Design View of a form/subform created by a wizard.

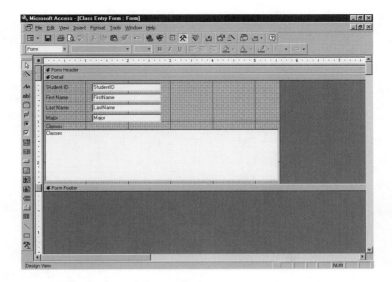

Figure 17.17.

Each form record has a distinct set of records shown in the subform.

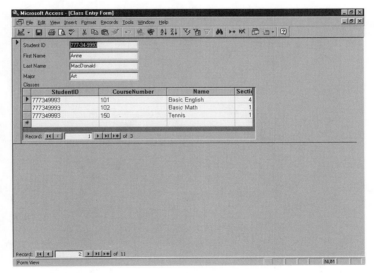

The subform portion of this form shows MacDonald taking Basic Math, Basic English, and Tennis. If you want to check out Access's accuracy, you can open the relevant tables or open the StudentsAndCourses query to view similar data. Although the data in your dataset might be different from the samples shown in the book, your data should agree internally.

The query that the subform is tied to is an Access query. These queries are so powerful that even the inclusion of the StudentID field in this form isn't necessary. Exercise 17.2 included it only so you could see how the StudentID fields remain coordinated in the main and subform.

Try entering a new class for MacDonald. Click in the subform portion of the form in the first empty row of the CourseNumber column. Enter 104. Tab out of the field. As soon as you do, the query bound to the subform supplies the correct student ID in the StudentID field. Your screen should resemble Figure 17.18.

The Access Way

It is impossible to enter uncoordinated data into the subform of a properly constructed main/subform.

Figure 17.18.

Access will not enter uncoordinated data if you construct your forms correctly.

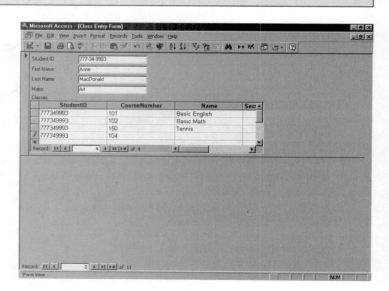

Access isn't done with its magic yet. Press the Tab key to move away from the CourseNumber field. Access knows that course 104 is Journalism, Section 2, so it obligingly fills in the rest of the information for you as shown in Figure 17.19.

17

Figure 17.19.

Access can automatically fill in information for you when told to do so.

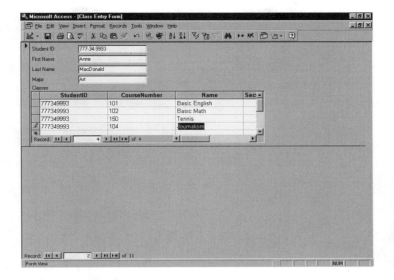

DO generally plan on binding your forms to queries rather than to tables because queries have more flexibility than tables.

DON'T forget that you can't violate table properties by entering data through a query. If your table has a user-supplied primary key field, such as StudentPersonal does, constructing a query without including the primary key field makes data entry impossible.

Close this form. Run the StudentsAndCourses query. You'll see that your entry in MacDonald's form/subform to sign her up for Journalism with the instructor Hernandon is reflected as a change in this database's data. The running query is shown in Figure 17.20.

Close the StudentsAndCourses query if it's open.

The Access Way

Structure is everything. If you structure your database logically, you'll likely have all things go right with your database project. The links in College make it so that data entered in the form/subform is reflected throughout the entire database because tables contain all data and all objects refer to those tables.

The fact that entering data in one place results in its appearing everywhere might, at this point, seem a little baffling to you, but as you go along the advantages will become clear. The *point* of Access is that data entered anywhere by anyone through any means is available anywhere else.

Figure 17.20.
If done right, all data presentations in Access can be of live data.

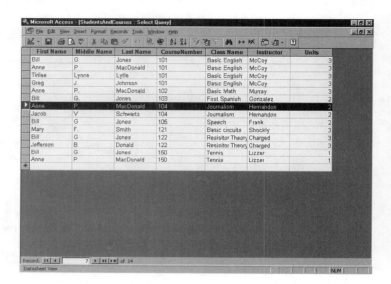

Dragging and Dropping Your Way to Subforms

There is a simple alternative to using the wizard for the design of forms with subforms. This section shows you how to embed a form within another form using the drag-and-drop capacity of Access 97. Although this is not a formal exercise, if you choose to go along you can use the sample data forms DDClass Entry Form and DDClasses. These are the same forms as Class Entry Form and Classes, but they aren't as yet form/subform.

Figure 17.21 shows DDClass Entry Form in Design View. If you wish to follow along, open this form in Design View.

To get the subform DDClasses into the form, drag the subform from the Database window to the design grid of the host form. Figure 17.22 shows the two windows, Database and Form Design, tiled so each shows on the screen. To tile your windows, click the Restore Window buttons for all of the windows you wish to tile. Then make the menu selections Window|Tile Horizontally or Window|Tile Vertically.

Figure 17.21.

A form opened in Design View ready for insertion of a subform.

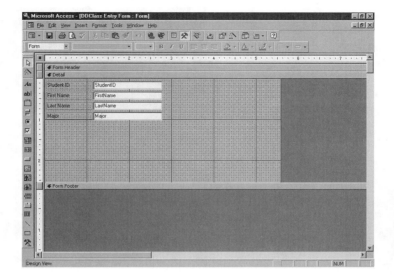

Figure 17.22.

Tiling the windows to make both visible at the same time.

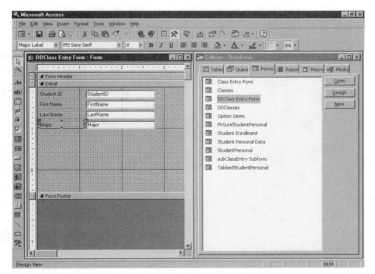

Drag the DDClasses form from the Database window to the Form Design window right below the existing four fields as shown in Figure 17.23.

Figure 17.23.

Dragging the form that will become a subform from window to window.

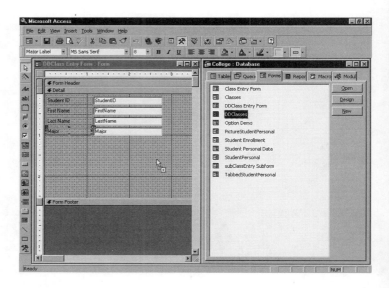

When you drop the DDClasses form into the DDClass Entry Form, your screen should resemble Figure 17.24.

Figure 17.24.

Dropping the dragged form places it into the host form.

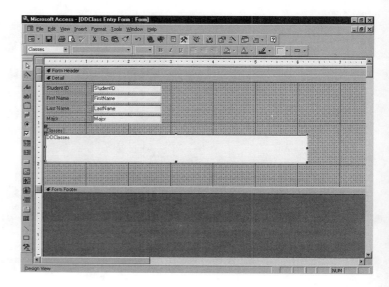

Figure 17.25 shows the form from Figure 17.24 running. If you try this yourself, you'll see that Access has the brains to link the forms so that the records for each student's classes remain in sync with the student's personal records from the host form.

Figure 17.25.

*The finished form/
subform works just like
the form/subform created
by the wizard.*

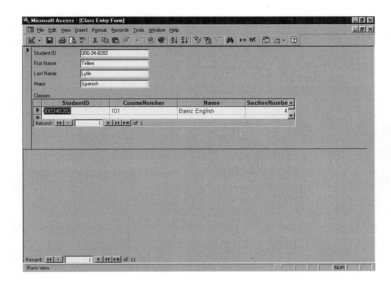

Morning Summary

Forms with subforms, called main and subforms in the terminology of wizards, are forms with other forms embedded in them. Generally speaking, this construction is useful for embedding a form bound to a table or query on the many side of a one-to-many relationship in a form bound to a table or query on the one side. You can construct such a form with subform by starting a new form bound to the table on the one side of the relationship, then invoking the Form Wizard.

You don't have to include the common or link fields for the two tables or queries in a form with a subform to keep the forms in synchronization. Access is smart enough to do this even without the inclusion of these fields on either or both forms. Access will synchronize the form with its subform if you supply a link field in either wizard-created forms/subforms or those made by dragging and dropping.

Chapter 18

Form Control Properties

This afternoon's lesson explains the following:

- ☐ What a form control property is
- ☐ How to synchronize main and subforms with control properties
- ☐ The meaning of enabled and locked controls
- ☐ A better way to find records
- ☐ How to filter records

Control Properties

To a great extent, using Access depends on understanding and setting properties for database objects or controls. You can use the program successfully for minor applications, such as simple list management, even if you know barely anything about properties. But when your needs grow even slightly complex, your time spent learning about this subject will pay off big time.

The Access Way

Much of what applies to form control property settings also applies to reports. Form design and report design are very similar subjects, only diverging where the applications of forms and reports divide. For example, you make no data entry in reports, so there's no reason to have combo boxes there.

Many of the basic property settings can be handled, and should be handled, by wizards. Why reinvent the wheel? Let wizards do what they do so well. However, there's a huge world of ability in Access that the wizards don't even try to address. In some cases, venturing into these worlds will call up other wizards or Access helpers called builders so you don't need to do it all yourself. (See Chapter 14, "Manipulating Dates and Using Expressions in Queries.") There, the Form Wizard wasn't sharp enough to know when a combo box made sense for a form's field (since the lookup properties weren't set properly). As soon as you put a combo box on the form, you called up the Combo Box Wizard, which made the programming job much easier.

Take a look at Figure 18.1. This is a Property list box for a form control (or field, if you prefer). Each of the tabs across the top exposes a different set of properties. The form in the background is the one generated by the exercise at the end of Chapter 17, "Forms with Subforms."

Figure 18.1.

The various types of properties for a control.

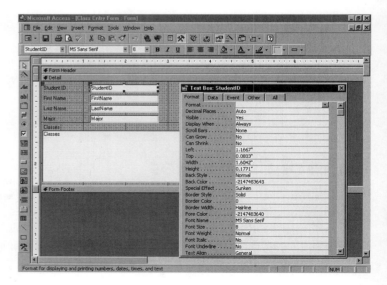

Here are the tabs available in the Property list box, with a short explanation of each set of properties:

☐ **Format**—Format properties control the appearance of the data on the form or report.

☐ **Data**—Data properties determine what can be done and the source for the data that is bound to the control.

☐ **Event**—Event properties determine how a control behaves in response to an event. Examples of events in Access: when the cursor's over the control, when a control's clicked on, when the control gets the focus, and when the control loses the focus.

☐ **Other**—Here you'll find the properties that don't fit in any of the other classifications. Don't think just because these are classed as "other" they are unimportant. Some of the most used and needed properties are in this list.

☐ **All**—All properties from all classifications are listed here.

A Working Example

The ClassSignUp form shown in Figure 18.2 is part of the sample data. Open it now in Form View so your screen looks like Figure 18.2.

Figure 18.2.

The ClassSignUp form.

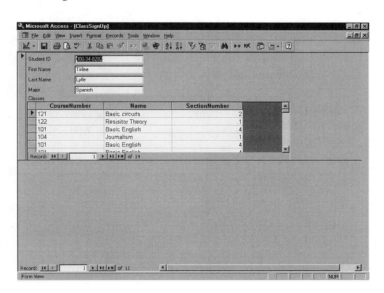

Notice that the subform section of this form isn't particularly useful because it shows more classes than Tirilee Lytle is signed up for. Refer back to the form shown in Figure 17.25 to see how this form should work. For some reason, this form isn't filtering out unrelated records in the subform. Scroll down one record by clicking on the Record selector VCR-style buttons at the bottom of the screen. Your screen should look like Figure 18.3.

Figure 18.3.

Moving through records has no effect on the subform.

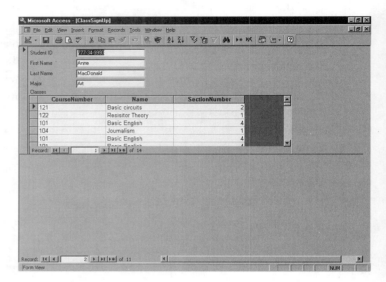

The same wrong information is still shown in the subform. Unlike the form done in Exercise 17.2, this form shows all the records for all the classes everybody's signed up for in its subform section. This form malfunctions because two inconspicuous form control properties are set incorrectly.

Switch to Design View and click on the subform section—that's the large white rectangle with the label Classes—and open the Properties list box.

Click the Data tab to restrict viewing to those properties related to the subform's data. Your screen should resemble Figure 18.4.

Two properties, Link Child Fields and Link Master Fields, are blank. These properties tell the Access form what fields the main and subform have in common. Enter StudentID for both of these properties, as shown in Figure 18.5.

Figure 18.4.

The data properties for a subform control.

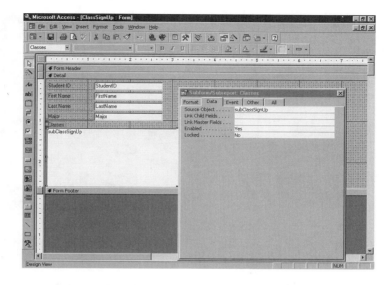

Figure 18.5.

Setting the link between main and subform.

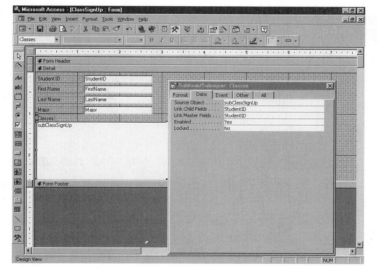

Return to Form View. Now the main and subform are in synchronization. The correctly running ClassSignUp form is shown in Figure 18.6.

Figure 18.6.

The once unsynchronized form running correctly.

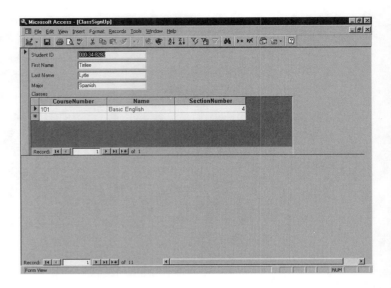

Close the ClassSignUp form, saving changes.

Exercise 18.1 reviews the Link field control properties.

Exercise 18.1. Field control properties.

EXERCISE

1. Launch Access and open the College database if necessary. Open the Class Entry Form object, done in Exercise 17.2, in Design View. Your screen should look like Figure 18.7.

Figure 18.7.

Preparing to alter control properties.

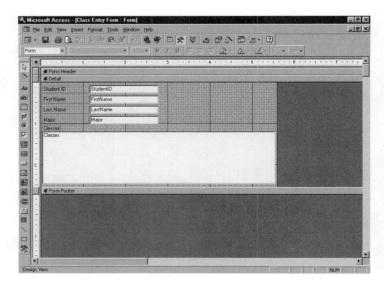

18

2. Open the Properties list box by clicking on its button in the toolbar. Click anywhere in the subform Classes section to highlight it. Click the Data tab. Your screen should look like Figure 18.8.

Figure 18.8.

Restricting the number and type of properties shown.

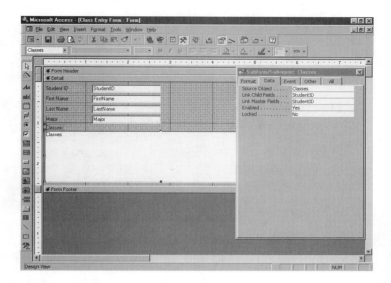

18

3. Delete the entries for Link Child Fields and Link Master Fields by highlighting them with the mouse cursor, then pressing the Delete key on your keyboard. Alternatively, you can press Ctrl+X or choose Edit|Cut to cut the last selection to the Clipboard. Switch to Form View. Your screen should look like Figure 18.9.

Figure 18.9

The effect of breaking the link.

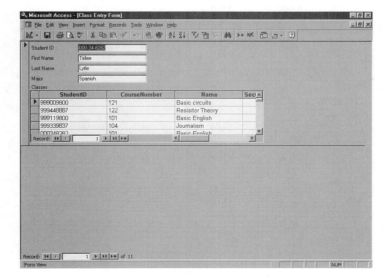

The effect of the link breakage is as apparent in this form as in the ClassSignUp form shown earlier. Look at Figure 18.9's subform section. You can see that all the classes for all the students are dumped here rather than just the ones that are associated with the record in the master, or main, form.

4. Return to Design View and restore StudentID as the entry for the Link Child Fields and Link Master Fields properties. If you cut the entry to the Clipboard, click in a field, then press Ctrl+V to paste from the Clipboard. Do this for both fields. Switch back to Form View. Your screen should resemble Figure 18.10.

Figure 18.10.

The link restored.

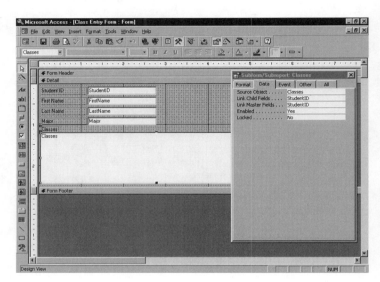

Gah! I'm Sick of This!

If you're the counting type, you know you've now hit three sections in a row dealing with the one topic of linking fields between forms and subforms.

It's not that this itself is a terribly difficult topic, but rather the entire concept of links is quite important in the relational model. I've been pounding on this topic almost ad nauseam to communicate the idea that using Access properly means dividing data into pieces and then reassembling them using links.

The links in this and the previous chapter have been form field links, but the same general principles apply to links in queries, or for that matter, reports.

18

Enabled and Locked

In many situations you'll want to protect your data from being altered. The people doing the class entry at the Registrar's and Student Advisement offices not only need to enter data in the subform, but they also need to be able to view data in the main form. Exercise 18.2, which demonstrates the use and limitations of the Locked and Enabled properties, addresses this need.

Exercise 18.2. Locked and Enabled properties.

1. Starting where you left off in Exercise 18.1, return to Design View. Using the marquee or the Shift+click method, select all the fields in the main form. If your Properties list box isn't on Data, change that to make it so. Locate the Enabled property in the list box. Click in the Enabled field. Pull down the combo box and choose No or double-click on this field to toggle it from Yes to No. Your screen should resemble Figure 18.11.

Figure 18.11.

Changing the Enabled property to No.

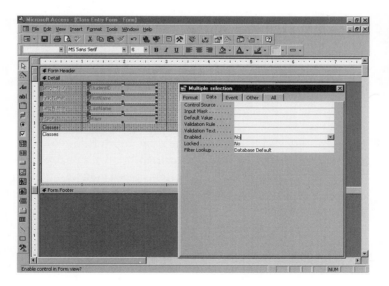

Did you catch Access changing the color scheme of the fields in the main form when you switched the property to No? This is Access's visual clue that these fields aren't enabled. Return to Form View. Your screen should resemble Figure 18.12.

Figure 18.12.
*All fields in the
main form disabled.*

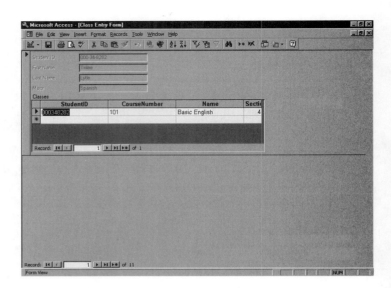

The Access Way

Access enables you to set the common properties for many controls at the same
time. Just select as many controls as you want to set the same property to, change
the common property in the list box, and let Access do the rest.

Try clicking in any of the main form's fields. You can't get your cursor in them at
all. In fact, with all the main form's fields disabled this way, you can't leave the
subform. In some applications this would be quite efficient. Setting the Enabled
property for a control or group of controls to No prevents not only data entry into
the field(s), but any entry.

The Access Way

Well, that's ugly and hard to read. If you're like many people, you don't like the
way the Enabled set to No makes the form look. If you don't want people to change
the values in a form, you can prevent them by either setting the Enabled property
to No or the Locked property to Yes, as you'll see later on in this exercise. Locked-
Yes has several advantages over Enabled-No, including the way controls look.

However, there's a drawback to using this form with all the main form's controls disabled. How do you find the record for a particular student? The only way is to scroll through the records until you hit the one you want. You could click in the Record selector section and enter the particular record you want, but that won't work unless you know the record number for a particular student in the StudentPersonal table. If you supplied the Registrar and Student Advisement with such a list, they could look up the student numbers, but this would slow each office down considerably.

Setting the Enabled property to No did safeguard the data, but at too great a cost. It would be better to let people enter the main form's fields so they can use Access's search capacity, but prevent them from altering data. The answer is the Locked property.

2. Return to Design mode. Again, select all the fields on the main form either by using a marquee or by the Shift+click method if necessary (it shouldn't be). Change the Enabled property back to Yes. Locate the Locked property, right below Enabled. Set that property to Yes. Your screen should resemble Figure 18.13.

Figure 18.13.

Setting the Locked property.

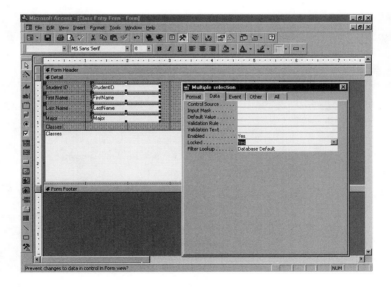

DO use the marquee or Shift+click method to set the properties all for the form's fields.

DON'T choose the Edit|Select All menu selections. That chooses not only the field, but all the controls (including the subform's) associated with this form.

3. Return to Form View. Try editing any field in the main form part. You can't edit the fields, but you can enter them (give them the focus). You can also copy from, but not paste to, locked fields. You can't do anything with fields for which Enabled is set to No.

Searching About

Keep the form from Exercise 18.2 open. Move to the first record, the one for Tirilee Lytle, if it's not already current. Click in the LastName field, then click on the Find button in the toolbar. This is the button with the binocular icon. Access will bring up the Find in field dialog box. Your screen should resemble Figure 18.14.

Figure 18.14.

Finding records in a form.

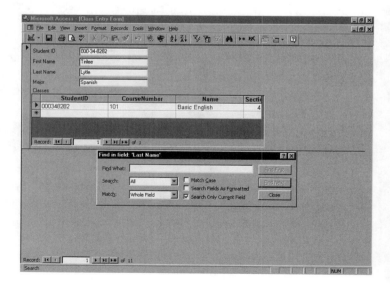

Enter *Jones* as a Last Name to search for. Click the Find First button. Access will move to the first record that matches the criterion of Last Name being Jones. Look carefully at the bottom of your screen toward the left of the status bar. Access quietly tells you that your search was successful. (See Figure 18.15.)

Figure 18.15.

A successful search for a particular record.

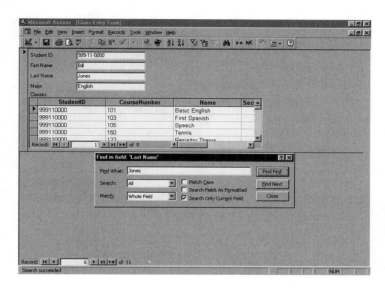

That worked, but because Access obscured part of the view of the main part of the form, it was a pretty subtle success. Try this as a better way to search. Close the Find in field dialog box and again move to the first record by clicking on the Record button at the bottom of the screen. If you prefer, you can choose Edit|Go To|First from the menus.

This last step isn't really necessary, but included to set things up identically to the last time. Click the menu choices Records|Filter|Filter By Form. Access brings up a blank form with two new tabs on it (toward the bottom). Here is where you can enter criteria to restrict which records Access displays. Your screen should look like Figure 18.16.

Figure 18.16.

Filter by Form blank.

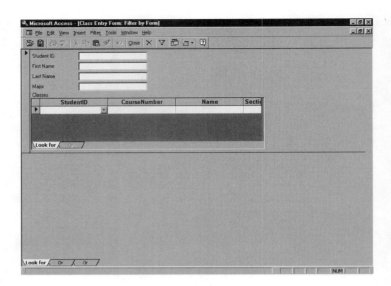

Move down to the LastName field (captioned Last Name) and enter *Jones*. As you enter the name, Access tries to help you by Auto Expanding your entry to match the data already entered in the bound table or query. If you wanted to add more than one criterion to the filter, you'd click on the Or tab, which would bring up another blank-looking form. Click the Or tab. (Make sure you click on the tab in the form, not in the subform.) Refer to Figure 18.17 to be sure. After clicking on the Or tab, enter *Smith* as another criterion.

Figure 18.17.

An Or criterion added to the filter.

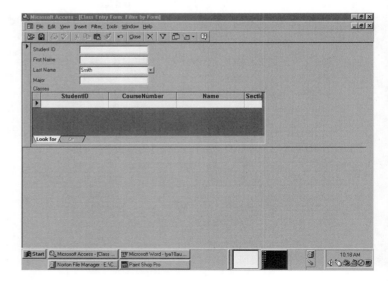

18

To apply the filter, that is, to restrict the display of records to only those in which the LastName field is Smith or Jones, click on the toolbar button with a funnel on it. (See Figure 18.18.)

After applying the filter, you'll find you have only two records to choose from, Smith and Jones. Access hints that this is the case, and that you are applying a filter, by adding the word Filtered to the record number enunciator at the bottom of the screen. Your screen should look like Figure 18.19.

Figure 18.18.
Applying, or activating, the filter.

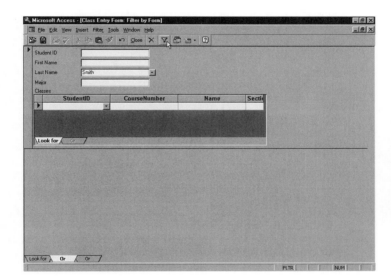

Figure 18.19.
Records displayed limited by the filter.

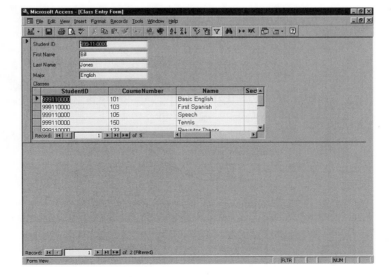

If you have many Joneses, or want to be sure you go to the right Jones, add in as many additional criteria as you need to in the Filter by Form design screen. For example, this college does advising by phone. When a student calls in, the advisor asks the student for his or her ID number. If the student is unsure of this, filtering by first, last, and middle names should bring up the right student.

Remove the filter by clicking on the toolbar button that looks pressed in—the one with the funnel on it. (See Figure 18.20.)

Figure 18.20.

Removing the filter.

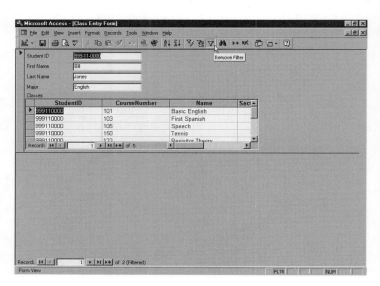

> **The Access Way**
>
> If your users will have to locate records by querying or filtering, make sure when you design your forms that you include sufficient fields to cover all possible eventualities. This form doesn't do the job. It should have address and phone number fields, too, to cover the possibility of two students with the same first and last names and the same middle initial.
>
> The advantage of using a phone number for a find or filter criterion is that people usually remember their own phone numbers.

Filtering Records by Selection

Sometimes you'll only want to see a subset of your data based on the data displayed in the form. Suppose you have a record on screen showing a student who's an English major, and you wish to see only those students who have the same major. Access contains a shortcut to get you there on the express track.

Exercise 18.3. Filter by selection.

1. If the Class Entry Form object isn't running in Form View, make it so. Click in the Record number box at the lower-left portion of your screen. Access will prompt you to enter a new number. Enter 7. You will jump to Mack's record, as shown in Figure 18.21. The cursor in Figure 18.21 is pointing to the box where you enter a record number. If you've added or changed the data in StudentPersonal, you might not have Mack as the current record. It makes no difference for the purposes of this exercise.

Figure 18.21.

Jump to a record number.

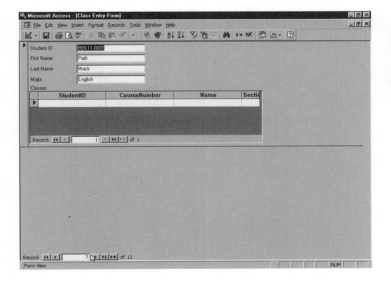

2. Click in the Major field. Now locate the toolbar button with the funnel and lightning on it. Click it, as shown in Figure 18.22. Access will restrict the records to those students who have declared English as a major.

3. That's it! Remove the filter by clicking the pressed-in toolbar button with the funnel on it, just as you did when you filtered by entered criteria (Filter by Form). Access will save this filter for quick use next time.

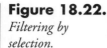

Figure 18.22.
*Filtering by
selection.*

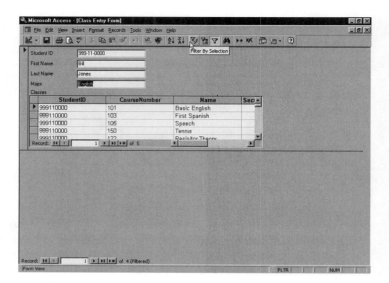

The Access Way

Oops—there were four English majors, I thought! Take a look at Figure 18.23. This is the Datasheet View of the form used in the preceding examples. At first glance, you might think there are only three English majors, right?

Why did the filter by selection miss Jones? The reason is because the major entered for Jones is Engish, not English. It's detritus like this that make for such grief in a computer system.

Had either a lookup table (link) with referential integrity or a simple validation rule been in force when Jones's record was entered, the data-entry error Engish could not have been made when the data-entry person really meant English.

Having Jones misidentified in such a way is what gives computers a bad name. What if Student Advisement had been going through all English majors to make sure they had all the required courses before graduation? S.A. surely would have missed Jones and his graduation might have been delayed. At the very least, such an oversight would have raised some hackles.

Although the failure to pick Jones up as an English major is usually identified as a computer error, it's really a computer programmer error. There is no excuse for allowing such bogus data to enter a system you've designed. Take great pains to not only structure your data correctly, but to make sure that the users entering the data won't make such errors.

18

Figure 18.23.

Three English majors, right?

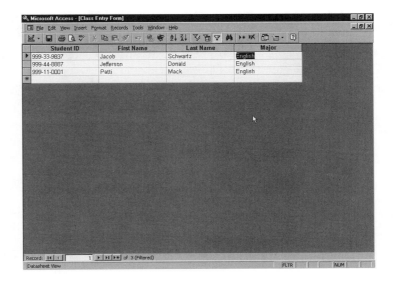

The only other thing to note in this area are those two buttons to the left of the filter buttons. They have arrows pointing up or down with the letters *Z A* or *A Z* on them. Figure 18.24 shows the cursor on the leftmost one of them.

Figure 18.24.

Sorting by first name using the toolbar button.

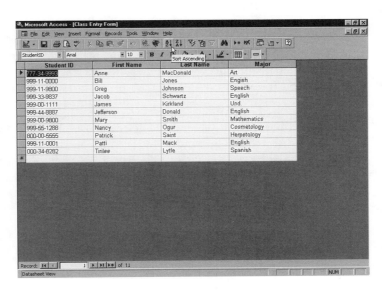

These two buttons will sort the records underlying the form by any field that currently has the focus. After clicking in the First Name (FirstName) field, click the leftmost button, Sort Ascending, and you'll sort the StudentPersonal table by FirstName, as shown in Figure 18.24. Figure 18.24 is shown in Datasheet View for clarity. The sort order applies to Form View as well.

The Access Way

Sorting the records using Form View's sort buttons does not change the order of the records in the underlying query or table.

Day Summary

Access controls have many different classes of properties. These properties can be set during the design phase, and in many cases during runtime. These properties affect how a control behaves, reacts, or looks, and where a control gets its data from or outputs it to. It's fair to say a control is the sum of its properties.

Four important properties are Link Child Fields, Link Master Fields, Enabled, and Locked. The first two properties determine which fields in the main form and subform are in common, or linked. The last two properties control entry and editing of the fields and data. The more you know about properties, the better off you are. Feel free to click on various properties, keeping an eye out for the status bar text changes to see what they do. If you wish to explore further, use online help. More properties are discussed in Chapter 19, "Instantly Smarter Forms."

You can filter or sort the underlying data shown in a form (or report) by clicking on the appropriate toolbar buttons or by making menu selections. You can filter by criteria, complete with a series of ORs if necessary; you can filter by more than one field and more than one OR if you want to. You can filter by selection and sort the filtered or unfiltered records in ascending or descending order.

Forms with subforms or linked forms make a handy way to show related data. The easiest way to create a form with a subform is to use the wizard, but you can drag a subform from the Database window onto a form when that form is in Design View.

Q&A

Q **Why not just use a form based on a query to do what a form with a subform does?**

A Subforms are much more efficient in situations such as those outlined for Exercise 17.2. If you want to enter classes for a student using the form/subform, you simply enter many classes while the main part of the form remains static.

If you used a *unitary* form (a form without a subform) based on the query, you'd have to navigate through all the fields on the form to make each new record. There are shortcuts making that last statement not precisely true, but that doesn't alter the fact that forms and subforms are much more efficient for entering records to the many side of the one-to-many relationship than any unitary form.

Q **I didn't understand how Access knows what records in the subform belong to the main form.**

A The properties that link form with subform data are the Link Master Field and Link Child Field located in the Data tab of the subform's Property list box. Access's wizard is good at making guesses as to which fields are link fields when you include these fields in the wizard process.

Q **Can I customize a form with a subform or must I accept what the wizard created?**

A You can customize forms with subforms just as you can any other forms then drag and drop that subform onto the form, as shown in Chapter 17.

Q **Can I use greater- or lesser-than operatives as filter criteria?**

A Yes. The < and > operators, just like all the rest, work the same in filters as in queries. For example, Not "IL" returns all those records that don't have IL as part of their data.

Q **How do I apply a sort without a filter to records shown in a form?**

A Click in the field you want to sort on, then click the Sort Ascending or Sort Descending toolbar button.

18

Workshop

Here's where you can test and apply the lessons you learned today.

Quiz

Possible answers to these questions are provided in Appendix A.

1. Generally speaking, which would you say are more flexible, queries or tables?
2. Can you bypass table property settings such as primary key entry by entering data through a query?
3. After append queries select data, do they then append it to the table they extracted it from or to a different table?
4. Do delete queries act on the table or tables they select from, or on different tables?
5. How do you display only Data properties from the Properties list box?
6. You have a main and subform with a link field SSN. How does Access know how to synchronize the main and subform using the SSN field?
7. How can you confirm that the delete or append queries are going to select records according to your intentions?

Put Access into Action

1. Create a simple form (hint: use the AutoForm Wizard) for the StudentsAndCourses query.
2. Using Filter by Form, filter out all records other than those for FirstName Tirilee and Anne.
3. Remove the filter.
4. Filter all the records using Filter by Selection to limit the records shown to Course 101. Can you easily see how many people are signed up for 101?
5. Close the form, saving it if you choose to. This book does not come back to it.

DAY 10

A.M.

19 Instantly Smarter Forms

P.M.

20 Fancy Form Layout

Chapter 19

Instantly Smarter Forms

This morning you'll learn

- [ ] What an event is
- [ ] How to place event-only controls on a form
- [ ] How to have a picture-perfect command button
- [ ] How to use a wizard to program controls to respond to certain events

You might have heard that programming computers is a job for brilliant social misfits. For some programming tasks, that's still true, but you can do quite a bit of programming in Access with little effort and without losing your social skills. This morning's lesson shows you how. If you're a user-designer, much of what you need to do in Access is simplicity itself. If you plan to use Access as a professional development tool, the program has the power. Thousands of professional applications demonstrate this to anybody's satisfaction. However, using the more esoteric Access functions does take at least a little work. You can still learn all of it while retaining your knowledge of which fork to use for a salad.

The First Programmed Command Button

So far you've made use of Access's excellent design to create static forms and reports. You can open and display data using supplied controls, and you can edit data when you are using forms. Your needs at this point probably don't go beyond using Access's supplied tools. However, this chapter starts you on the path of being able to design your own tools.

Exercise 19.1 shows you how to make controls that scroll through records.

Exercise 19.1. Record manipulation.

1. Launch Access and open the College database if necessary. Open the Class Entry form in Design View. If you're picking up where Chapter 18, "Form Control Properties," left off, clear any filters and return to Design View for the Class Entry form. (See Figure 19.1.)

2. Rearrange and resize the controls on your form to resemble Figure 19.2. The point of the rearrangement is to create some room at the form's bottom for some new controls and keep the form at a reasonable size. Your screen doesn't have to look like Figure 19.2. Just allow for some room for two new controls. If you prefer, you can just open up a little space at the bottom of the form by enlarging the form itself and leaving the controls where they are.

Refer to Figure 19.2 and note that the Control Wizard toggle button is selected in the toolbox. Make sure your Control Wizard button is similarly selected, or the following steps in this exercise won't work the same for you as they do in this example.

Figure 19.1.

Getting ready to add event-only controls to the form.

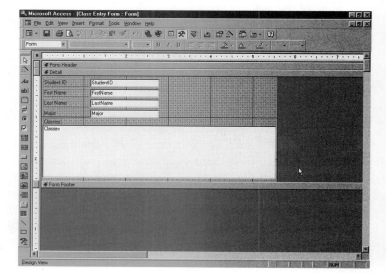

3. Click the Command Button control in the toolbox. It's the one right in the middle of the toolbox toolbar in Figure 19.2. Move your cursor on the form and click just below and toward the left of the subform section. Your screen should resemble Figure 19.3, except the number on your Command button is probably different from the one you see in the figure.

Figure 19.2.

The rearranged form.

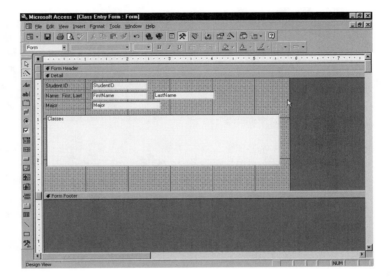

Figure 19.3.

Starting the Command Button Wizard by placing a command button on the form.

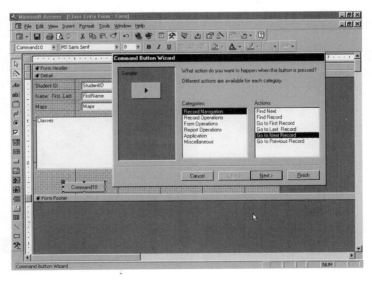

19

4. Select Record Navigation from the Categories list and Go to Next Record from the Actions list. (See Figure 19.3.) Click the Next> button. Your screen should look like Figure 19.4.

The Access Way

As you'll see later in this chapter, you can manually program command buttons, but it makes little sense to do so if what you want is available from this wizard. Look over the lists to get a feel for what's available. When you need a service available from these lists, invoke the wizard. Unlike some things, the way the wizard handles programming command buttons is at least as good at most programmers' methods.

5. The standard left- and right-facing VCR-style controls Access uses for record navigation make sense as analogs for tape operation when the movement is horizontal, but most people think of moving up and down in a record set for navigating records. To give these people an icon on this button that fits their conceptions, click the first entry in the Picture list box—the down-facing arrow with the entry Go To Next. You can show a huge variety of icons for your command buttons by selecting the Show All Pictures check box. You'll probably consider many of these icons to be unrelated to your application. (See Figure 19.5.)

Figure 19.4.

The layout section of the Command Button Wizard.

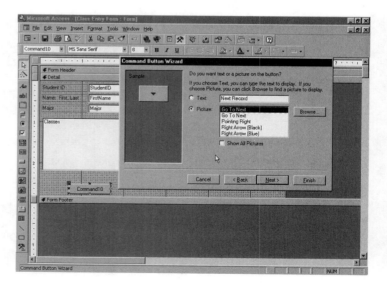

Figure 19.5.

Selecting the Show All Pictures check box will bring up a larger variety of icons for use on your command buttons. Some of the expanded icon selections are more whimsical than practical.

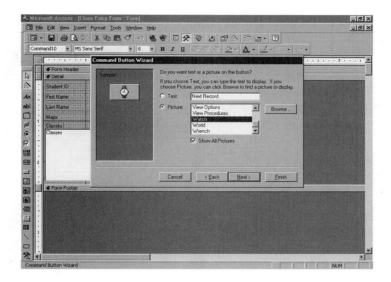

6. Click the Next> button. You can name this command button just about anything you want, but as I have preached in past chapters, it's best to use descriptive labels. A common naming convention for command buttons is to prefix them with the three-letter mnemonic *cmd*. Further, you should include a descriptive part of the control name so you or anybody else can tell at a glance what this control is supposed to do. Name this button cmdNextRecord. This name tells the world that this is a command button (cmd) that moves to the next record (NextRecord). (See Figure 19.6.)

Figure 19.6.

Using standard naming conventions for this command button.

19

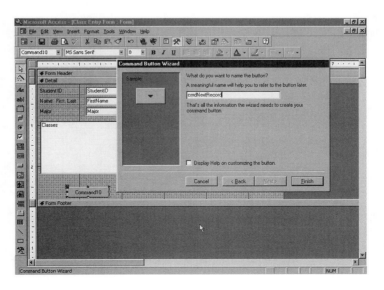

7. Click the Finish button. Your screen should look like Figure 19.7.

Figure 19.7.
The finished command button.

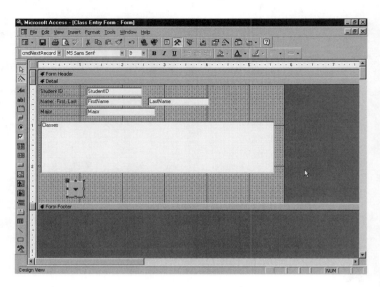

Switch to Form View to try out the new command button. (See Figure 19.8.)

Figure 19.8.
The new command button awaiting a command.

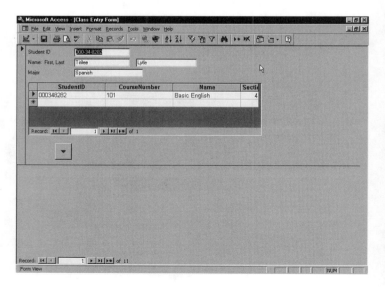

Click the new button twice. Access scrolls down through the records until record 3 shows up. (See Figure 19.9.) Your button works to navigate through the records. Although this button duplicates the Record Navigation button down at the record selector's area of the screen, the size and icon on the button make it much easier for people to understand and use.

Figure 19.9.

The new command button in use.

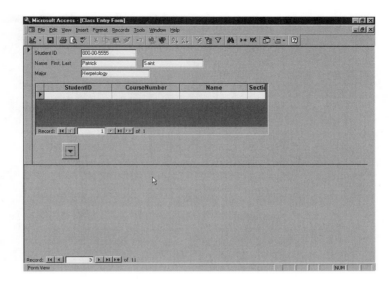

A Complementary Command Button

Exercise 19.2 creates a command button that is similar to the one Exercise 19.1 creates. This second button complements the first one.

Exercise 19.2. Another command button.

1. Return to Design View.
2. Click the Command Button control in the toolbox. Click the form next to the cmdNextRecord button.
3. Choose Record Navigation and Go to Previous Record from the wizard's list boxes. Click the Next> button.
4. Select the up-facing arrow from the layout section of the wizard. Click Next>.
5. Give the button the name cmdPreviousRecord.
6. Click Finish. Your screen should look like Figure 19.10.
7. Open the Properties list box. Locate the ControlTip Text property on the Other tab. Edit the entry to read Previous Student for the command button cmdPreviousRecord and Next Student for the command button cmdNextRecord.

EXERCISE

19

Figure 19.10.

The do-it-yourself command button.

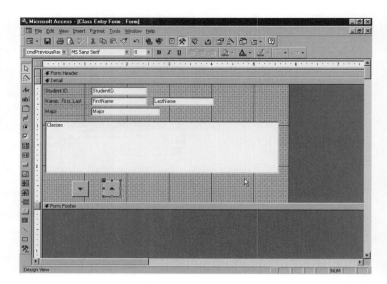

Return to Form View. (See Figure 19.11.) Try using your new command buttons to navigate around your records. They work just fine. Congratulations—you're a computer programmer!

Figure 19.11.

The two command buttons work in conjunction with each other.

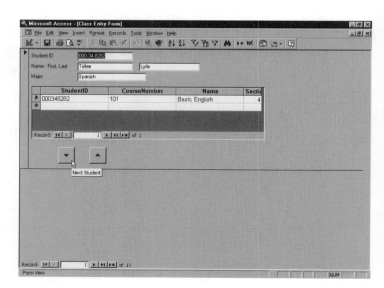

Event Properties

The Command Button Wizard from Exercises 19.1 and 19.2 actually wrote Visual Basic code. This section takes a look at what that code is.

Return to Design View and open the Properties list box if it's not already open. Click the Event tab. Click the first command button you made, the one that moves down one record at a time. (See Figure 19.12.)

Figure 19.12.

The Properties list box with an event procedure for an On Click event.

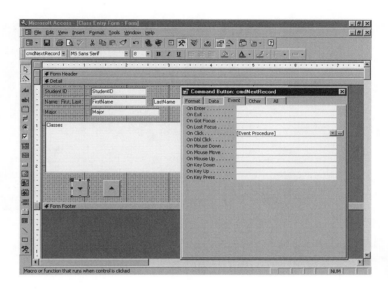

The On Click property has been set to [Event Procedure] by the wizard. It means that the wizard has created some Visual Basic code that will be called into action whenever the control is clicked.

Examine the other event properties for on this tab. Command buttons can react to such events as Got Focus, On Mouse Move, On Enter, and other such odd-sounding events, but the vast majority of things you program a command button to do are in response to the On Click event. On Click is programming-speak for clicking the left mouse button when the cursor is over the object in question. The wizard you used in Exercises 19.1 and 19.2 programmed the On Click event for this command button based on what you told it to do during the wizard process.

Take a look at Figure 19.13. This shows the events a form (not a command button) can react to. This is only a partial list. The screen isn't large enough to hold them all.

Keep in mind that Figure 19.13 only shows the event properties associated with a form. There are also Format, Data, and Other properties. Don't be concerned if some of these properties' behaviors aren't obvious to you by their names. And don't worry about memorizing all of these properties. The online help system in Access has all of them memorized for you.

Figure 19.13.

A partial list of Event properties for a form.

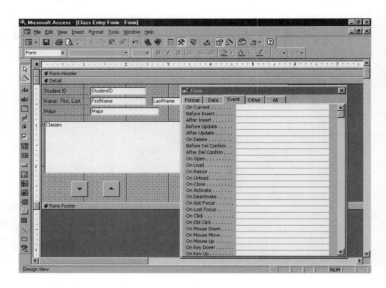

Context-Sensitive Help to the Rescue

Here's an example of how to get help about any property. Click the Format tab and then click in the entry area next to the Caption property. You should have a good idea of what the Caption property does—it's the label for a control. In the case of the command buttons you just did, the caption is invisible because that space is occupied by a picture. If you look right below the Caption property in the list box, you'll see the property Picture. An entry in the Picture property will override the Caption text.

You have some idea of what this or any property means because Access gives you a limited explanation in the status bar at the bottom of the screen. But these status bar hints really only refresh your memory; they aren't comprehensive enough to teach you how to use an event in your application.

To get more information, press F1 with your cursor in the Caption property field to call up context-sensitive help. Access responds with the help screen shown in Figure 19.14.

This section provides comprehensive information about the Caption property. It tells you what objects have the property and how Access will act if you don't supply a Caption. Across the top of the screen you'll see entries for See Also, Example, and Applies to. These entries vary depending on the help topic and help's contents. Down toward the bottom of the screen note the underlined words "access key." The broken underline means that when these words are clicked, Windows help will bring up a pop-up explanation box. Move to these words with your cursor. Your cursor will change to look like a hand. Click once. Help pops up an explanation of what an access key is, as shown in Figure 19.15.

Figure 19.14.

A context-sensitive help screen about one property, the Caption property.

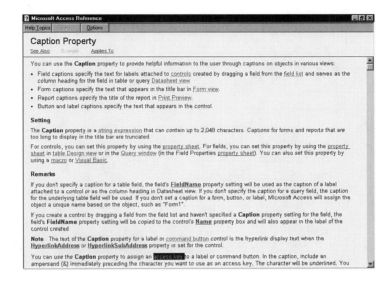

Here, in plain English, is the explanation you needed. For example, the Mouse Down event (a property just like Caption is a property) applies when a person clicks the mouse button. The help system also explains how this event differs from the On Click event that it superficially resembles.

Figure 19.15.

A help system pop-up.

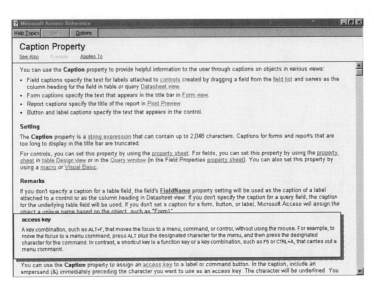

19

This is as good a time as any to pull down the three underlined topics at the top of Figure 19.15. Pay special attention to the See Also entry. This is an effective cross-reference to other related Access or Windows topics. As you use Access, you'll find online help—and especially the cross-reference—invaluable.

> **The Access Way**
>
> Microsoft took an informal poll of about 40 well-known and high-profile professional Access programmers to learn how often and in what manner they used the Access help system.
>
> The response Microsoft got was overwhelming. This group of dyed-in-the-wool professional programmers used help regularly (every day) and especially praised the cross-reference. So if you think that only wimps use help and real programmers memorize, think again.

Back to the Event Procedure

Close the help system for now, and see what an event procedure is like. With your screen like Figure 19.12, click in the entry area that now contains [Event Procedure], next to the On Click property. Access responds by showing two icons at the right side of the line: a combo box down arrow and an ellipsis (...). Click the ellipsis. This action calls up the Visual Basic code that runs when you click this button. Your screen should resemble Figure 19.16.

Figure 19.16.

The code attached to the On Click event of a command button. Depending on how you have your global options for Access set, your screen may or may not resemble the screen shown here. The screen shown here is the default view as supplied by Microsoft.

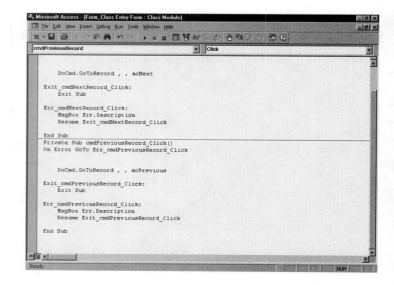

The Access Way

Clicking the ellipsis in this context brings up the code builder, where you can enter your own code or edit code already associated with the Event property. Access also has an expression builder that helps you build complex expressions.

At first blush this looks like some arcane and imposing foreign language. Like so many things that look complex at first, however, it's really quite simple when it's taken apart. Although you obviously didn't need to know what this code does to create it, here is the same code, taken line by line with a short, nontechnical explanation for each line.

1. `Private Sub cmdNextRecord_Click ()`

   This line declares the start of a new sub or routine that's going to run when the `cmdNextRecord` control (the command button) is clicked. Remember that you named your control `cmdNextRecord` at the end of the wizard process. Had you named your control `cmdHelloThere`, this line would read `Private Sub cmdHelloThere_Click ()`. The `Private` keyword states to Access that this sub or procedure is only available (visible really) from within this module. All the subs within this exercise are part of a module that's bound to this form. Declaring this sub as `Private` keeps it private to the code within the module for this form and this form only.

2. `On Error GoTo Err_cmdNextRecord_Click`

   This instructs the computer in the case of an error condition—which means something unforeseen has occurred—to jump down to the line `Err_cmdNextRecord_Click:` (line 6) and continue execution from there.

3. `DoCmd GoToRecord , , acNext`

   `DoCmd` is the Visual Basic code that essentially calls on a macro action. There are many actions, such as changing cursors, moving through records, opening and closing forms, and dozens of others. The two commas are placeholders for options unneeded by this On Click sub. The `acNext` tells the `GoToRecord` command to go to the next record.

4. `Exit_cmdNextRecord_Click:`

   This is a label used as a location for code to jump to in case the routine that handles a trapped error gets called. You can tell at a glance that it's a label since it ends with a colon (:). In this code fragment, line 8 will jump here if it does run.

5. `Exit Sub`

   Exit this routine.

19

6. `Err_cmdNextRecord_Click:`

   Another label. This is the place line 2 jumps to if something goes awry. This entire section of code runs only in the case of an error condition.

7. `MsgBox Err.Description`

   Display a message box telling the user the specific description of the type of error that occurred.

8. `Resume Exit_cmdNextRecord_Click`

   After the message box closes (the user clicks a button), jump to line 4.

9. `End Sub`

   This signals Access that this code segment ends here.

Don't Worry

Don't be concerned if even with an explanation you don't feel confident about your understanding of this code. Remember, you programmed the cmdNextRecord command button without knowing a line of code. You did it once, you can do it again.

Do	Don't
DO feel free to experiment with this code to see what changes you can make. **DON'T** worry if what you do results in obscure complaints from Access. Just remember what you did so you can undo it. If things get totally out of hand, delete the entire code section and delete the offending control from the form; then use the wizard to re-create it. That will put all things right again.	

For now, close the code window if it's open, and close the Class Entry form, saving changes. The sample data saves the form at this point, using the name Class Entry Form1.

Pretty Pictures on Buttons

Some people like pictures; other prefer icons; others still like text. You can tailor your command buttons as well as other Access objects to appear as you like them to. Microsoft supplies a variety of icons for use on objects. To see a list of these objects, open a form or report in Design View, click any object like a command button that has a Picture property, then click the Picture property. Click the Build button—the one with the ellipsis on it. Figure 19.17 shows the list box the ellipsis will bring up.

19

Figure 19.17.

Microsoft supplies a large variety of icons to use on your objects.

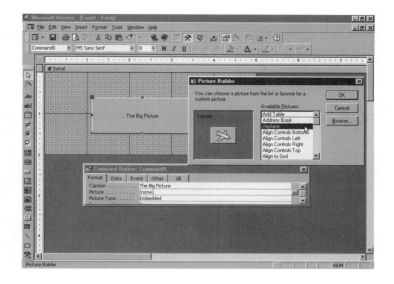

You can go further than this, however. By clicking the Browse button in the Picture Builder list box, you can browse for and include bitmap images beyond what Microsoft supplies.

Take a look at Figure 19.18. This is an unbound form with four unbound command buttons inserted. As you can see, you can add a great deal of variety to your command buttons by changing the Picture property and adding a few bitmaps. The bitmap files used to make these buttons are part of the sample data, but the form isn't.

Figure 19.18.

Adding a few bitmaps to your objects can make them look more than lively.

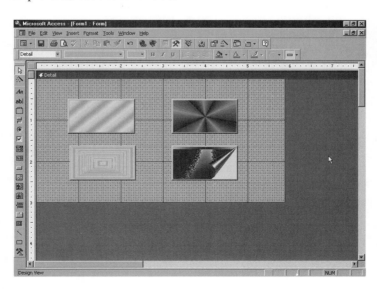

If that's not enough, you can change the Picture property for the form itself. This gives the form a background similar to what the Access Form wizard itself does. Figure 19.19 shows how adding a picture to the Picture property of a form can change the form's look quite a bit. This form is the StudentPersonalDOB table run through the AutoForm with a picture added.

Figure 19.19.

Adding a picture to a form can help or hurt the look of the form.

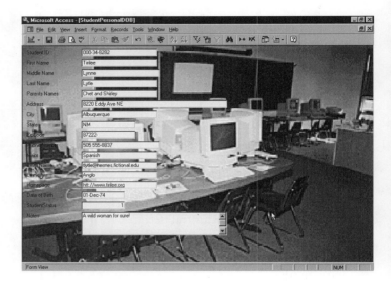

Take it easy using graphics in your forms and reports. A little decoration goes a long way.

Morning Summary

Access controls have many different properties. Each item in Access has its own set of control properties. For example, the form itself has an On Resize property that makes sense for it, but doesn't apply or appear for the command button control.

Event properties describe how controls respond to certain events, such as being clicked or double-clicked over. One class of Event properties is the Event procedure. Event procedures are Visual Basic code that activates when the Event property it's attached to fires.

19

Visual Basic? I Thought This Was Access

Both *Teach Yourself Access 97 in 14 Days* and the Microsoft documentation make liberal mention of Visual Basic.

This is both a Microsoft product and one of the languages used by Access, the other one being Structured Query Language (SQL). The "real" name for the Basic language in Access is Visual Basic for Applications (VBA), and the independent product is Microsoft Visual Basic. Both seem to be called just Visual Basic, so this book follows that convention.

Control wizards can save you a lot of programming headaches and, equally important, won't make any typographic errors when writing Access Basic code. To save a lot of time and possible grief, use the wizard if one exists for your purposes.

You can add either an icon or a picture to objects. Just be careful not to get overly enthusiastic when doing so. A little bit of a bitmap goes a long way.

19

Chapter 20

Fancy Form Layout

This afternoon you'll learn the following:

- [ ] How to clean up a form's look
- [ ] What tab order is and how to change it
- [ ] How to alter the design of a subform
- [ ] How to use graphic elements in form design
- [ ] About form page layout considerations

Your Own Tools

Having record navigation tools both on the form and below it uses up extra space and is redundant because the form already has navigation buttons at the bottom. The first exercise this afternoon extends the subject of control properties to eliminate this duplication.

This chapter starts out with the form saved as Class Entry Form1. This is part of the sample data. If you want your screens to closely resemble those shown here, you should use either this form from the sample data or your Class Entry Form as modified in Chapter 19.

Exercise 20.1 demonstrates the placement of record selectors and navigation buttons in forms.

Exercise 20.1. Record selectors and navigation buttons.

1. Launch Access and open the College database if necessary. Click the Forms tab and open the Class Entry form (or Class Entry Form1 if you are using the sample data) in Design View. Your screen should resemble Figure 20.1.

    Open the Property list box. Click the Format tab. The default view for this form is Single Form. This means that by default Access will only show one record at a time. This makes sense for this form because it includes a subform. There's no practical way to show many records bound to the main form and also show the records bound to the subform.

2. Pull down the leftmost button in the toolbar and click the Datasheet View option. (See Figure 20.2.)

Figure 20.1.

A form ready for modification.

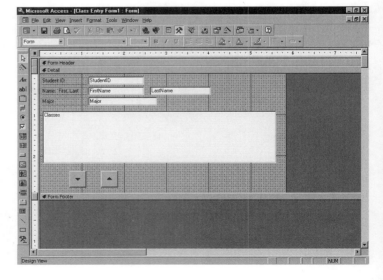

20

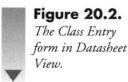

Figure 20.2.

The Class Entry form in Datasheet View.

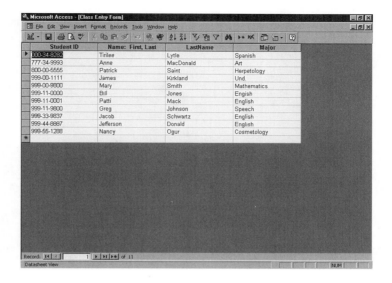

As you can see, it is possible to view the Class Entry form in Datasheet View, but because all the class information is lost in this view, it isn't useful in a form containing subform data. The Datasheet View is useful for quickly scanning through the records in the master form, however. After locating a record, switch to Form View again. The found record is in the master form and the related data is in the subform. Additionally, it makes little sense to have record selectors (the gray bars at the far left in Form View) for this form, as only one record is ever going to show at one time.

3. Return to Design View. Change both the Record Selectors and Navigation Buttons properties to No. Record selectors do nothing but litter the screen in Form View. Your screen should resemble Figure 20.3.

4. Switch to Form View. (See Figure 20.4.) Notice how much cleaner your screen looks without record selectors or navigation buttons in the main part of the form/subform. Since you've made no changes to the subform, the record selectors and navigation buttons remain there. There's no loss in function as long as you want to move through the records one by one because the buttons added through the wizard this morning replace the navigation buttons. If you wanted to come close to the functionality of the standard Access navigation buttons, you'd have to add some more command buttons to jump to first and last records.

20

Figure 20.3.
Eliminating the record selectors and navigation buttons from a form.

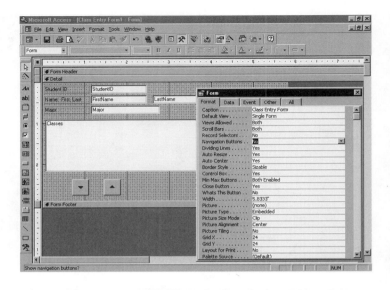

Figure 20.4.
The new, cleaner look for this form.

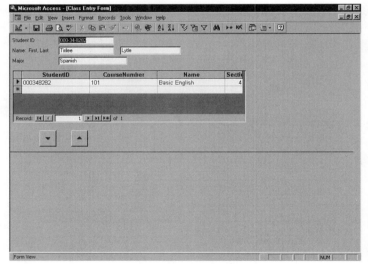

Tab Order

Click in the StudentID control and press Tab three times. When you tab through a form, you expect to move from left to right and then back to the far left and down. This is the way we read, and users expect forms to behave the same way. However, in this case, the tab moves from the StudentID control to the FirstName, then to Major, then MiddleName, and finally to LastName. Tab action such as this is sure to annoy users, so get ready to change it to a more intuitive pattern. The tab order for Class Entry Form1 has been altered in the sample data for the sake of this exercise. If you don't have the sample data, your tab order is currently as it will be at the end of this exercise.

Exercise 20.2 shows how to alter the tab order in a form and eliminate controls from the tab order.

Exercise 20.2. Changing the tab order.

1. Starting where Exercise 20.1 ended, return to Design View. Choose Tab Order from the View menu. (See Figure 20.5.)

Figure 20.5.

The Tab Order list box.

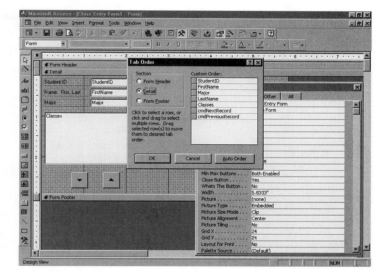

Figure 20.5 shows the Tab Order list box. This list box shows the order in which controls receive the focus when you tab through a form. By default, Access places the first inserted control at the top of the Tab Order list box. The wizard that made this form placed the StudentID field first and the subform last. This morning you added three button controls to the end of the tab order. The only change needed at this point is to move the Major field from third to fourth in the tab order.

2. Click just to the left of the Major entry in the list box, on the gray area that looks like a record selector. (See Figure 20.6.)

3. Click again on the now-pressed gray square. Your cursor should change to gain a box at its end, indicating that the cursor is in Move mode. Continue to press your mouse button and drag the Major field until it's just below the LastName field. Release the mouse button. Your screen should resemble Figure 20.7. Click OK to close the Tab Order list box and save your changes.

20

The Access Way

The technique for changing the order of controls in the Tab Order list box is the same as changing the order of almost anything in Access. It is a bit tricky at first, but once you get the hang of it for any function (such as changing column order in a query), you have it made for them all.

Figure 20.6.

Indicating which control's tab order to change.

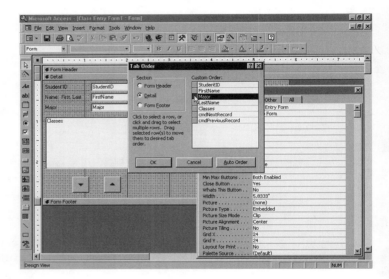

Figure 20.7.

Moving a field to change the tab order.

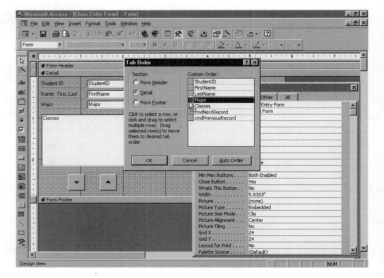

4. Return to Form View and again click in the StudentID field. Again press Tab three times. Due to your efforts, the cursor now behaves as people expect it should.

   There's another important tab characteristic called Tab Stop. This property determines if a control ever receives the focus when a form is tabbed through. The two command buttons should only need to be clicked using the mouse, rather than tabbing to them and pressing Enter—the alternate way to activate the On Click property of a command button. Also, having these buttons in the tab order is inconvenient because they must be passed through when someone is tabbing. You don't want your users accidentally tabbing to and pressing an Exit button, either.

5. Return to Design View. Select both of the command buttons either through a marquee selection or by using the Shift+Click method. Open the Properties list box if necessary and select Other. Change the Tab Stop property to No. Your screen should resemble Figure 20.8.

Figure 20.8.

Removing controls from the tab order.

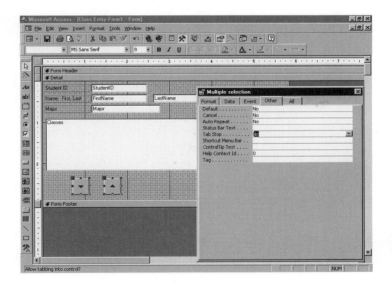

6. Return to Form View. Locate a record without many class entries, as shown in Figure 20.9.

   Start tabbing anywhere on the form. As soon as your cursor reaches the end of the records in the subform, further tabbing doesn't move it at all. There's no way to tab to the command buttons.

20

Figure 20.9.

The effect of the Tab Stop property.

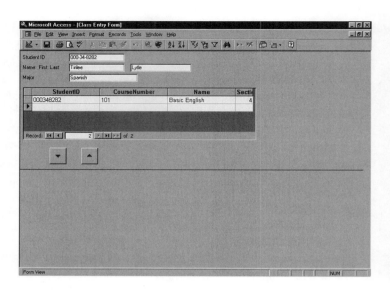

Take a look at how the Tab Stop property acts when set to No. Click the cmdNextRecord button and press Tab. Instead of jumping to the cmdPreviousRecord button, Access jumps to the StudentID field in the next record. Access will not tab to any control with the Tab Stop property set to No. At the last record Access will, by default, move to the next record when you hit Tab. If you want the Tab to cycle from the last field to the first, change the Cycle property of the form from All Records to Current Record.

7. Close this form, saving changes. The form at this point is saved as part of the sample data under the name Class Entry Form2.

Modifying Subforms

While the main form is open in Design View, the subform is available only as a white rectangle. You can click it to highlight it, but there's no way to alter the subform's properties except those that relate to its functioning as a control in the main form. Additionally, there's no way to get to the subform's separate controls.

Exercise 20.3 shows how to alter the internal characteristics of a subform.

Exercise 20.3. Altering a subform.

1. From the Database window, locate the form Classes. The Classes form serves as the subform for the Class Entry form and its derivatives. Open it in Design View. Your screen should look like Figure 20.10.

Figure 20.10.

The subform opened in Design View.

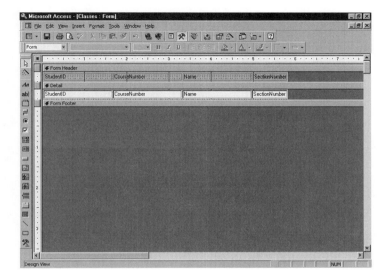

This wizard-generated form probably appears just about as you thought it would. Open the Properties list box. Click the Format tab and look at the Default View property. This property sets how the form appears when its host or main form is in Form View. Access assigned the default view of this form to Datasheet. It's now set to Datasheet, which is a logical choice because the records bound to this form are on the many side of the one-to-many relationship.

2. Staying within the Format tab, change the Navigation Buttons property to No and the Border Style property to Thin. Click in the form detail section on the StudentID field to give this control the highlight. This field doesn't need to be displayed, so press the Del or Delete key to eliminate it from the subform. Click its label in the form header section and likewise delete that.

3. Use a marquee or the Shift+Click method to highlight all the remaining controls in the detail section of the form. Center them vertically and left-justify them within the detail section of the form. Move their labels to correspond with their new locations. Move your cursor to just above the Form Footer bar until it changes to a bar with up- and down-facing arrows. Click and drag the detail section of the form until it's just large enough to accommodate the remaining fields. Move the right border of the form to the left to take up the slack left from the deleted StudentID field. Your screen should resemble Figure 20.11.

4. Close this form, saving changes. You'll find the subform as modified by this exercise in the sample data with the name Classes2. The modified subform is part of the Class Entry Form2 form.

Figure 20.11.

Finishing up the changes to the subform.

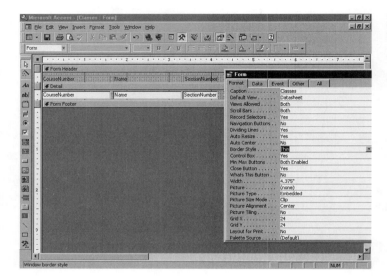

Your form now has a cleaner look after the elimination of the unnecessary controls. From the Database window, open the Class Entry form. If you are viewing the sample data rather than working along, open Class Entry Form2. Your screen should resemble Figure 20.12.

Figure 20.12.

The main form reflects the changes made in the subform.

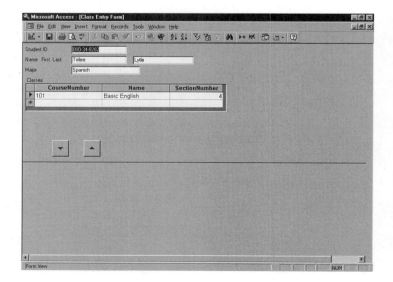

Right now there's too much unneeded real estate surrounding the subform. This is the result of having shrunk the effective area of the subform by deleting the StudentID control. The main form has a container that was sized correctly for the subform when it included the StudentID control. This container wasn't automatically sized to fit the new needs of the subform.

Change to Design View and resize the subform's container. This operation is shown in Figure 20.13.

Figure 20.13.

Resizing the subform's container.

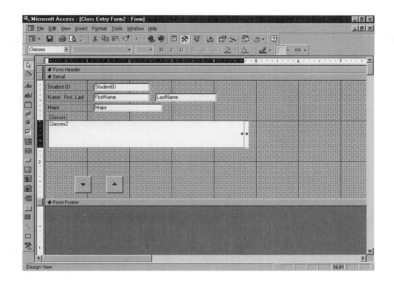

Size the subform's container and, if necessary move and resize the main form's controls around until they look right given the new proportion of the subform. (See Figure 20.14.)

The Access Way

One way to size a main form's subform container is to switch Snap to Grid off in the Layout menu, then alternate small changes with many switches back and forth between Form and Design views until you have the look you want. Another way is to monitor the rulers across the top and sides of the form as you size the controls.

You can also edit a subform by opening a form/subform in Design View and double-clicking on the subform. This saves you from having to locate the subform in the Database window.

20

Figure 20.14.

The form reorganized for the new subform's size.

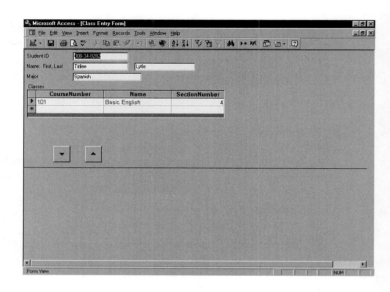

The Access Way

If you size a subform to fit exactly inside its container within a main form, you might hit a problem when the data within the subform exceeds the vertical space you allotted for the subform. Access will automatically add a scrollbar to the side of the subform when this occurs. The scrollbar will take up real estate you need to display the data.

To eliminate this problem, you can either set the Scroll Bars property for the subform to None or Horizontal, or you can allow sufficient room for the scrollbars when you design the subform container.

Graphic Elements in Forms

Access gives you two graphic elements you can use to spruce up your forms: lines and rectangles. By changing the properties of these elements, you can radically alter your forms' looks. Use these elements to isolate form controls into logical groupings, to enhance the aesthetic appeal of your forms, and to break your forms into sections.

The following exercise takes the rather barren-looking Class Entry form and gives it some fancy elements. It's up to you how ornate to make your forms. Remember, because you can embed any graphic in your form, you have no effective limit as to how elaborate you can be.

20

The problem with forms containing too much fru-fru is that they might appear frivolous. Also, keep in mind your target audience. What's overly baroque for financial analysts might be overly stark for children.

Exercise 20.4 shows some uses for graphic elements in forms and illustrates how these elements' properties affect their appearance.

Exercise 20.4. Graphics elements in forms.

EXERCISE

1. Open the Class Entry form in Design View, or if it's already open, switch to Design View. If you are using the sample data, open the Class Entry Form2 in Design View. Your screen should resemble Figure 20.15. Locate the Rectangle tool in the toolbox. (Refer to Figure 20.15 for help finding this tool.)

Figure 20.15.

Getting ready to add graphic elements to a form.

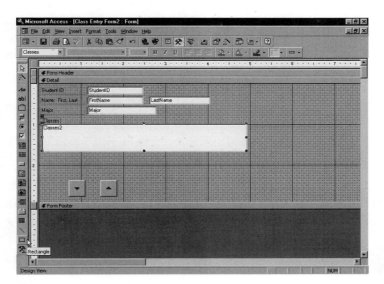

20

2. Click the Rectangle tool, then move your cursor to slightly above and to the left of the StudentID field label. Depending on the exact layout of your form, you might need to move all the controls away from the form design grid's border to complete this action. Figure 20.16 shows the Class Entry Form2 with its controls moved to allow for easy rectangle making. After you've made some room, click and drag a rectangle starting above and to the left of the StudentID field including its label and ending below and to the right of the Major field. Your screen should look like Figure 20.16. Keep an eye on the rulers to monitor the progress of your rectangle as you drag.

Figure 20.16.
Adding a rectangle to a form.

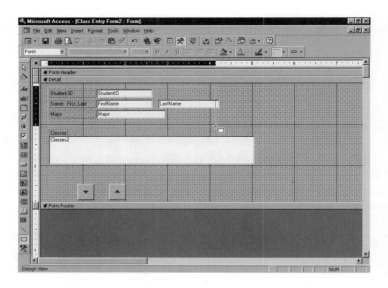

If the rectangle Access adds is a solid one obscuring the fields and labels, locate the Back Color button on the Formatting toolbar. Click on the button to activate the pull down list, then click the Transparent choice.

3. Click the Border Width button in the Formatting toolbar and change the width to 1. Click the Special Effect button and choose Shadowed from the pull-down list. (See Figure 20.17.)

Figure 20.17.
Applying some special effects.

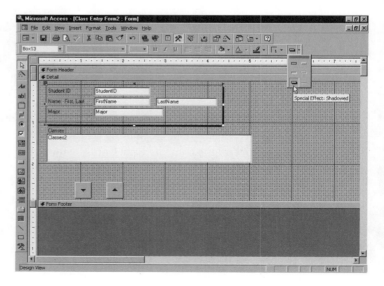

20

4. Click the Border Color button to activate the pull-down list and change the color from black to deep blue. Your screen should resemble Figure 20.18.

NOTE

Because *Teach Yourself Access 97 in 14 Days'* figures are grayscale, Figures 20.18, 20.19, and 20.20 only approximate the look of the form with its added color.

5. The command button section of this form is separate in function from either of the other two sections, so let's set it apart visually. Click the Line tool just to the right of the Rectangle tool in the toolbox. Move to the form's detail area and draw a horizontal line between the subform and the buttons, spanning the entire width of the form. Widen the form and extend the line so that the line extends the entire horizontal length of the screen when in Form View. Getting this right might take some trial and error.

Figure 20.18.

Adding some color changes to the rectangle.

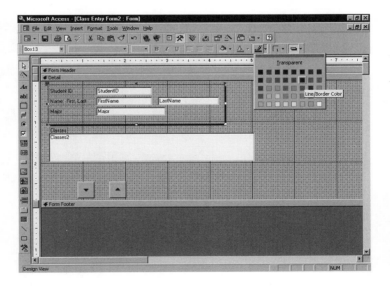

6. In the Formatting toolbar, click deep blue as this line's color and 3 as its border width. Shrink the form if necessary to be appropriate to the number and location of the controls. Your screen should resemble Figure 20.19.

7. Switch to Form View. Your screen should look like Figure 20.20 if you have your form in a window rather than maximized.

Figure 20.19.
*Adding a line to
a form.*

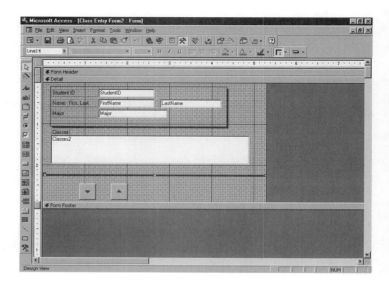

Figure 20.20.
The finished form.

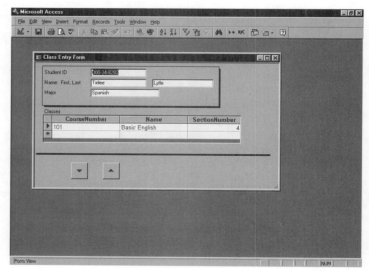

While hardly a work of art, this form does succeed at many design goals. It contains all the information needed by the registrar and Student Advisement, with nothing extra. People using the form won't be confused by excessive design elements, yet will clearly be able to determine the three separate form areas. Close this form, saving changes. You'll find the form as modified by this exercise in the sample data as Class Entry Form3.

All Windows 95/97 native applications such as Access 97 have inherently good-looking designs. You have to make an effort to produce a lousy-looking form. You might think that the final exercises today have taken a nice, clean, grayscale form and dolled it up to the point of being grotesque. Or you might think the design still is too conservative for your tastes.

The beauty of personal computers is that they are, well, personal. It's your copy of Access, it's your computer, and it should be your design decisions.

Page Layout Considerations

This form's only view is Single Form, so it doesn't make any difference where the command buttons appear. If this form could be displayed as a series of continuous forms, each detail section would have its own command buttons, which just take up room with no added function. Figure 20.21 is the form from Figure 20.20, with the subform deleted and the view changed to Continuous Forms. This figure shows the command button duplication that would occur in Continuous Forms View.

The safe way to handle controls you want to see only once on a form is to locate them in the form header or footer sections. Figure 20.22 is the form from Figure 20.21, with the command buttons located in the form footer.

Figure 20.21.

Command buttons in the detail section don't work right in continuous forms.

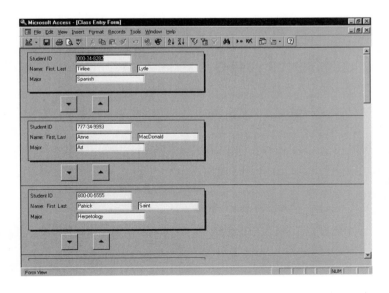

20

Figure 20.22.

Moving the command buttons to the form's footer solves the problem.

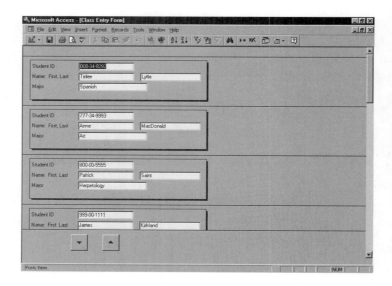

Locating the command buttons in the form's footer recovers lost room and makes for a better form overall than locating them in the detail section. If you'd like to examine the form shown in Figure 20.22, it's saved as Continuous Class Entry as part of today's sample data. The buttons aren't attached to any Event Procedure in this form.

Further Fancy Forms

This short section sprints through some form creation options. By this time you should have a good idea of how to use menus and toolbars, so the steps will come faster than in previous sections.

Take a look at Figure 20.23. This is an unbound form containing an unbound text box.

If you want to play along, create the unbound form by clicking on the Form tab at the Database window, then clicking on New. Choose Design View with no table or query showing in the combo box.

Add an unbound text control to the form, as in Figure 20.23. Using the Formatting toolbar's appropriate buttons, change the text box to a raised look with blue text and a light gray background. Now pull down the Format menu and choose Set Control Defaults. (See Figure 20.24.) This sets the default control style to the selected control. Add another unbound text box and note that this one has the same formats as the first one.

Try adding a label control. Note the new default only applies to text boxes.

20

Figure 20.23.

A form for experimentation with formatting options.

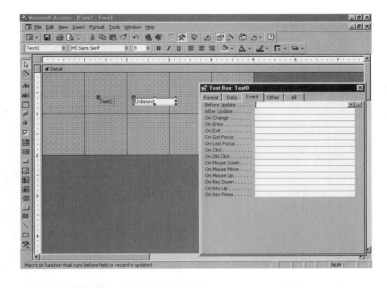

Figure 20.24.

Creating a new default for one control type.

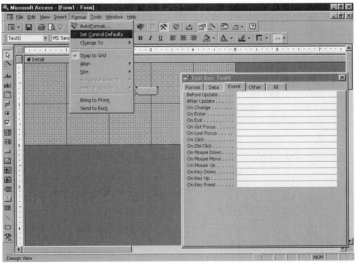

Now click either one of the text box controls and then on the toolbar button with the paintbrush. Move back to the form design area and note that your cursor changes to look like a paintbrush in a circle. Click the label control to "paint" it like the text boxes.

Sinking and Rising

You can combine several sunken or raised looks to yield interesting results. Add three rectangles to the form, as shown in Figure 20.25.

Figure 20.25.

Setting up for a deep sunken look.

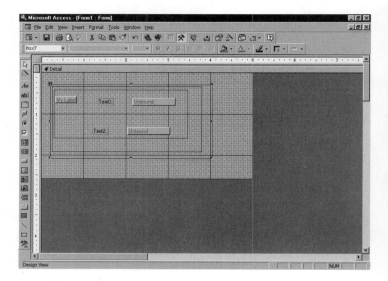

Now highlight all the rectangles either by a marquee selection or by the Shift+Click method. Pull down the Special Effect button and choose the Sunken look. Figure 20.26 shows the results of this in Form View.

Figure 20.26.

Applying a special effect to layered form elements.

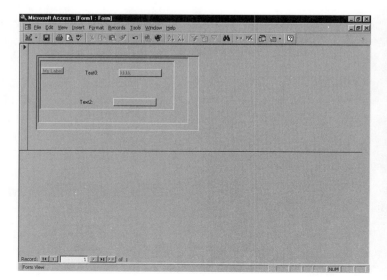

Figure 20.27 is the same form in Form View but with the rectangles given a raised look.

Figure 20.27.

Applying a different special effect to concentric form elements.

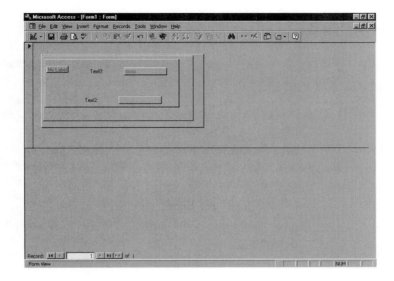

Add the date and time to the form by clicking in the detail section while in Design View. Make the menu selections Insert|Date and Time. Access cooks up an expression in a label control that will display the current system date and time, as shown in Figure 20.28. Since the date and time are part of a text box, Access uses your newly created default style for this control.

Figure 20.28.

Adding the date and time is a menu choice away.

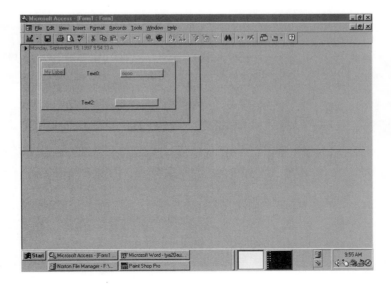

20

In a similar way you can add pictures or other OLE objects to the form by choosing the appropriate Insert menu choice or by altering the relevant properties in the Properties list box. Figure 20.29 is the form with chain.bmp (part of the sample data) added. The reason the picture is repeated in this figure is because the property Tiled has been set to Yes.

Figure 20.29.

Adding a picture to a form and setting the Tiled property to Yes.

You can save or discard your forms at this point. The book does come back to them.

AutoFormatting

One final thing before leaving the section on formatting fancy forms. Pull down the Format menu with any form open in Design View. Click the AutoFormat entry. This will enable you to add those fancy formats and backgrounds you saw in the wizard-generated forms to your own.

Some people think the fancy formatting distracts from the utility of a form. Others think formats such as these make a good form great. Just remember not to get carried away with frivolity and always keep your target market in mind when playing with these fancy options, and you won't go wrong.

Day Summary

This morning you saw how you can use the wizard to create command buttons that will react as you choose to various events such as a mouse click.

By default, Access equips forms with a complete set of selectors, scrollbars, and navigation tools. In many cases you can delete one or all of these items. In doing so, you can simplify your forms, making more room for data display (if you're careful) without decreasing your form's functionality.

The tab order is the order in which controls get focus as you tab around your form. Access assigns tab order in the same order in which controls are placed on a form. You can change the tab order to one of your choosing. Additionally, you can leave a control out of the tab order by setting its Tab Stop property to No.

Creative use of lines and rectangles can highlight or separate sections of forms. Remember, you can assign lines and rectangles to be in the foreground or background, according to your needs.

The final part of the chapter was a fast sprint through several options and combinations you can apply to your forms to give them a custom look. Use these options sparingly and keeping your target audience in mind.

Q&A

Q Can I attach more than one `DoCmd` action to an event?

A Yes. You can attach as many as you like.

Q I have many forms with the same look, only differing in details. Is there some way I can define a generic form as a template for others?

A Yes. You can do this two ways. The first is to just create the template form, then use Copy/Paste in the Database window to create other identical copes of the form. You can then modify the copies to fit your needs. Alternatively, you can define your template form as the standard form by selecting Tools|Options from the menu. Once there, click on the Forms/Reports tab, then change the Form Template option from "Normal" to the name of your form.

Q Is there a list of all the actions I can do with the `DoCmd` I found in the wizard-generated code for command buttons?

A Access's online help has all these actions grouped both by name and by function. Search on `DoCmd`.

20

Q Can I vector graphics files for form backgrounds?

A A shortcut to bitmap conversion is to copy them to the Windows You'll have to convert them to a bitmap before you do so. A clipboard then pastes them either into your form or into a program such as Windows Paint.

Q Can I use my own pictures on button faces?

A Yes. You can use any program that can create a bitmap file that Access can understand. Create your artwork, save it, then use the Browse button in the wizard to set the button's face with your creation. You can also set the button face by directly entering your filename in the Picture property of the button's layout properties.

Workshop

Here's where you can test and apply the lessons you learned today.

Quiz

Possible answers to these questions are provided in Appendix A.

1. Are the types of control properties the same no matter what type the control?

2. If you want to repeat a small picture throughout your form, which property must be set to Yes in the form's Properties list box? Hint: This property is on the Format tab.

3. How would the code line Sub cmdNextRecord_Click() change if the event you wanted the sub for was called Clack?

4. Will the filter Like "Ka" let the name Kaplan through? What about Kramer? Will the filter Like "Ka*" let the name Kaplan through? What about Kramer?

Put Access into Action

1. Open the Class Entry form (or Class Entry Form3, if you're using the sample data) in Design View.

2. Make sure the Wizard button is selected in the toolbox.

3. Place a command button on the form at the right side, under the subform section.

4. Use the wizard to set this button's On Click property to an event procedure that will, when clicked, close the form. Hint: Look under Form Operations in the wizard.

5. Give the button a stop sign icon and name it cmdExit. Switch to Form View. Your screen should resemble Figure 20.30.

20

Figure 20.30.

The form with an Exit button added.

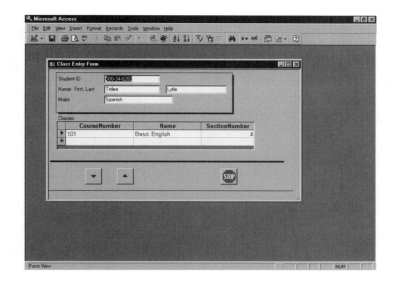

6. Save the form by selecting File|Save Form from the menu. Click the button to see if it works. In the sample data, this form is saved as Class Entry Form4.

DAY 11

A.M.

21 **Expressions in Reports and Queries**

P.M.

22 **Complex Reports**

Chapter **21**

Expressions in Reports and Queries

This morning, you'll learn the following:

- ☐ How to create a complex query with an expression
- ☐ What joins are
- ☐ How to add a table to a query
- ☐ How to manually design a report
- ☐ How to group records in a report
- ☐ How to use expressions in reports

The Situation

You might have feared report cards when in school—or perhaps you're still in school and living in fear of report cards. However, this morning you get to design report cards for others.

At the end of each term, the instructors at the fictional college sit down at computers and call up a query that lists all the students who were in their classes the past semester. The instructors check a box indicating whether the course was completed and, if so, enter a grade for the student. This information is entered in the StudentCurrentCourses table.

After the instructors have done their entry chores, the computer folk run a query that extracts those records from the StudentCurrentCourses table and puts the course information with the grades into a new table, CompletedCourses. Figure 21.1 shows the CompletedCourses table for the students at the fictional college.

The college tracks students' performances with a numerical scale; the highest grade one can get is 4.5 for an a+. This, times the number of units a course is worth, equals the entire weighted grade value for having taken that course. Figure 21.2 shows the linked table, GradeValues, which, when used in a query, assigns a numerical value to the letter grade the instructors assign a student. Both CompletedCourses and GradeValues are part of the sample data.

Figure 21.1.

The CompletedCourses table.

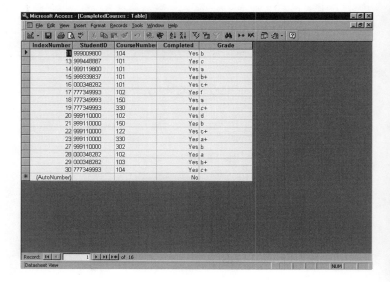

21

Figure 21.2.

The linked table for calculating grade values.

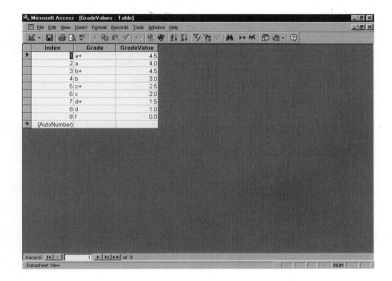

The Access Way

Efficiency is the mark of good database design, but neither of these tables is optimally efficient. Take a look at the CompletedCourses table first. There's a field for course completion containing a Yes entry for each record. Since this table is the result of a make table action query—in which the criteria is that the Completed field is Yes—all records in this table, by definition, have a Yes entry in the Completed field; therefore, including this field in CompletedCourses doesn't add any informational value.

Can you guess what's wrong with the GradeValues table? This is less obvious, so don't feel bad if you missed it. GradeValues uses an AutoNumber-Increment field as the primary key for this table. Since there aren't any repeating grades (or GradeValues, for that matter), this field likewise adds nothing to the table and just eats up space. You could use the Grade or GradeValue field for a primary key. Little things like this demonstrate an in-depth knowledge of proper database design. However, Access is powerful enough so that minor design errors like these won't materially affect your application's performance.

Before designing the report, you need a table or query to bind it to—that is, to base it on. No single table now holds all the information you need, which is the following:

- ☐ Student name
- ☐ Student ID

21

☐ Student address

☐ Classes completed

☐ Grades given

☐ Unit values for the classes completed

☐ Weighted values of grades

The first exercise this morning constructs a moderately complex query containing all this data and a mathematical expression. This is a long exercise, but one that goes over some familiar ground. Before starting this exercise, establish a one-to-many relationship between the StudentPersonal and CompletedCourses tables, if you haven't already done so. The sample data for today has done this for you.

If you need to do this on your own data, start from the Database window and click on the Table tab, then Tools|Relationships from the menu. Click the Show Table button on the toolbar and add the CompletedCourses table to the Relationships grid. Drag your mouse from the StudentID field in StudentPersonal to the StudentID field in CompletedCourses. Now you're ready for Exercise 21.1.

Exercise 21.1. Calculation Expressions in queries.

1. Launch Access and open the College database, if necessary. Click on the Queries tab, then click the New button to start a new query. Click on the Design View selection and click OK to bypass the wizards. Add the StudentPersonal, CompletedCourses, and AvailableClasses tables to the query, then click Close. Your screen should look like Figure 21.3.

   Access knows there's a link between the CompletedCourses and StudentPersonal because a one-to-many relationship has been established for these tables, with StudentPersonal on the one side. So far, no relationship has been created that tells Access whether any link exists between CompletedCourses and AvailableClasses.

   The common, or link, fields are CourseNumber in CompletedCourses and CourseNumber in AvailableClasses. Access should be smart enough to know the two CourseNumber fields are related and show that by a link line. If it fails to do so, it's up to you to tell Access about this link so it can synchronize records from both tables in this query.

2. Sometimes Access misses. If you don't show a link line between the two CourseNumber fields as shown in Figure 21.3, then do step 3. If you already have that link, skip to step 4.

Figure 21.3.

The new query just starting. Access is smart enough to link to fields from the two tables without being told.

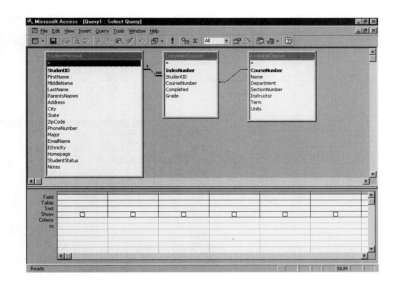

3. Click on the CourseNumber field in CompletedCourses, as shown in Figure 21.4. Click and hold your mouse over the highlighted field. Without letting go of the mouse button, drag your cursor until it's over the CourseNumber field in the AvailableClasses list box, then release the mouse button. Your screen should resemble Figure 21.5.

Figure 21.4.

Showing Access the link field.

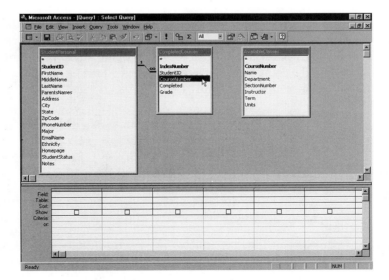

21

Figure 21.5.

Manually establishing a link.

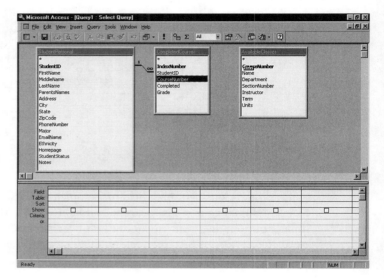

4. There's something missing. The CompletedCourses table has the grades themselves, but not the numerical value for the grades, located in the GradeValues table. Click the Show Table button (with the yellow plus sign) in the toolbar to bring up the Show Table list box, then click on the GradeValues table. Your screen should now look like Figure 21.6.

5. Click the Add button to add it to the query and close the Show Table list box. Figuring out the Grade fields in these two tables is too much for Access, so click on the Grade field in the CompletedCourses list box and drag a link to the Grade field in GradeValues, just as you did in step 3. To make better sense of this query, rearrange your screen to resemble Figure 21.7.

Figure 21.6.
Adding a table to a query.

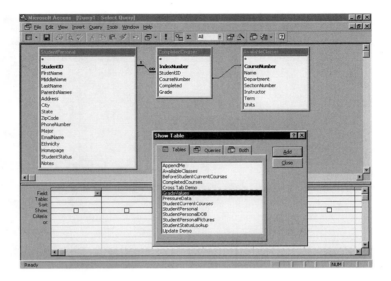

Figure 21.7.
Linking the new table to the query.

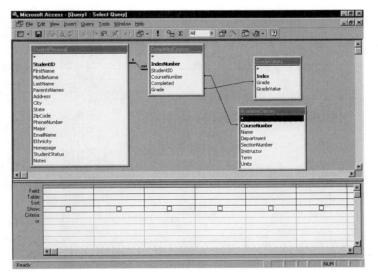

6. Drag the StudentID, FirstName, MiddleName, LastName, Address, City, State, and ZipCode fields from StudentPersonal to the query design grid. Your screen should look like Figure 21.8.

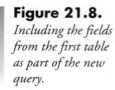

Figure 21.8.
Including the fields from the first table as part of the new query.

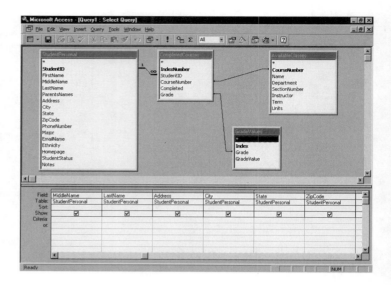

7. Drag the CourseNumber, Name, and Units fields from the AvailableClasses table to the next columns in the query design grid. (See Figure 21.9.)

Figure 21.9.
Adding fields from the second table.

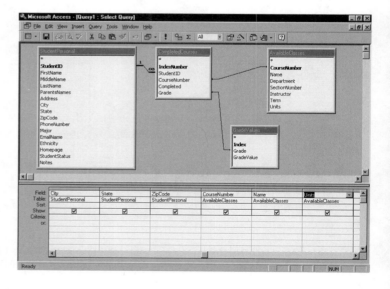

8. Add the Grade field from the CompletedCourses table and the GradeValue field from the GradeValues table to the query design grid. (See Figure 21.10.)

Figure 21.10.
Adding fields from the last two tables into the query.

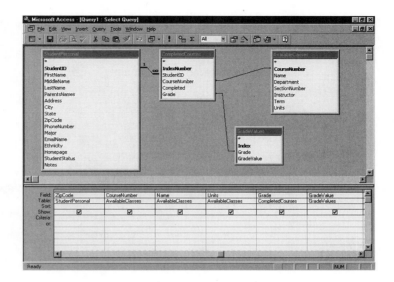

9. Scroll back to the StudentID field, click in the sort row for this field, and choose Ascending for a sort order. Run your query now to make sure it's working properly. Figure 21.11, which shows this query running, has been scrolled to show the query's last columns.

Figure 21.11.
The raw query in operation, scrolled to show linked-in values.

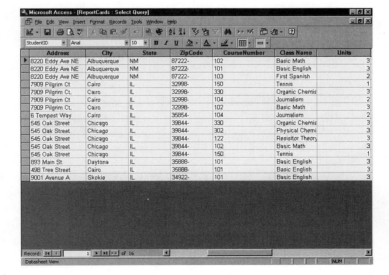

There's one more thing to do. This query shows the unit values for each completed class, the grade, and the grade value, but not the weighted value the student gets credit for. That value is called the Weighted Value and is the Units times the Grade Value. You need to calculate that also.

10. Return to Design View and scroll until you see an empty column to the right of the GradeValue field. Click in that field and press Shift+F2 to enter Zoom. Enter `Weighted Value: [Units]*[GradeValue]` in the Zoom box, which tells Access to create a column called "Weighted Value" and insert the product of the Units field times the GradeValue field in that column. (See Figure 21.12.)

Figure 21.12.

An expression to do calculations in a query.

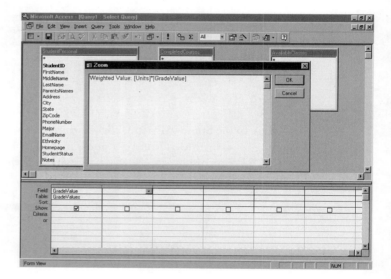

11. Click OK to close Zoom. Run the query again to make sure all's right with it. Check the rightmost field, Weighted Value, to make sure it's calculating correctly. If it's not, check to make sure you entered the expression correctly. Close and save this query as ReportCards.

After finishing Exercise 21.1, you have a query that report cards can be based on. This is the first step needed for the finished report cards report. Exercise 21.2 picks up where 21.1 left off. Designing the actual report cards report would be easier with a wizard to do some of the work, but Exercise 21.2 doesn't use one so that you can learn some important details about report design. This exercise manually creates a grouped report with several expressions and a secondary sort order.

Exercise 21.2. Grouping and sorting in reports.

1. Click on the Reports tab to move to the Reports section of your database, then click the New button to start a new report. Choose ReportCards as the query to bind to this report. Your screen should look like Figure 21.13.

Figure 21.13.

Starting the new report.

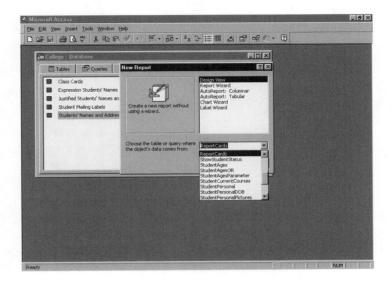

2. Click the Design View option, then click OK. If necessary, click the Field List button in the Report Design toolbar (the standard one for this view). Access moves you into the report design grid. Increase the vertical width of the page header area to about 1.5 inches to give you some working room. Click on and drag the StudentID field from the Field list box to the page header area. Your screen should look like Figure 21.14.

This report will have a student's ID, name, and address in the page header area, details about courses completed and grades given in the detail area, and, when finished this afternoon, summary information in the group footer area. The page header will also act as an address for windowed envelopes.

21

Figure 21.14.
Starting to place fields in a report.

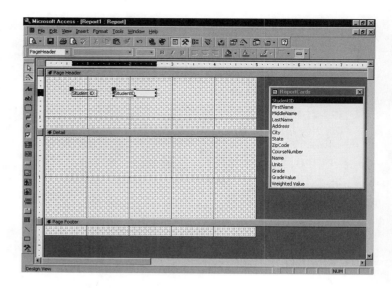

The Access Way

Remember, Access can appear many different ways in any view. Your screen might look quite different from the book's, as shown in Figure 21.14. For example, you might not have the toolbox in view, or it might be floating instead of docked at the left side of the screen. You might not have the Grid checked in the View menu. If you don't, you won't see the dots shown in this exercise. Even if you do, your dots might be finer or coarser than the book's.

If you want to come as close to the book as possible, arrange the screen as shown in Figure 21.14, then open up the Properties list box. Locate the Grid X and Grid Y properties on the Format tab and change each to 12. Then pull down the View menu and select Grid if it doesn't have a check mark next to it.

---

3. Create an expression for the student's name by inserting an unbound text box right below the StudentID field. Delete the label for this field and enter the following expression:

```
=Trim([FirstName] & " " & [MiddleName] & " " & [LastName])
```

This expression is shown in Figure 21.15 for a Control Source for this unbound field. Figure 21.15 shows the Control Source property line in Zoom mode. If you prefer, you can add this line directly into the unbound text field itself, which inserts it into the Control Source line of the Properties list box as well.

Figure 21.15.

Inserting an expression in a text box.

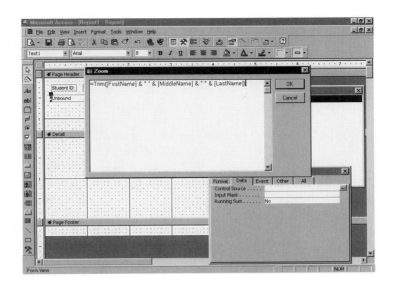

4. Add the Address field right below the unbound text field containing the student's name, then delete this field's label. Add another unbound text field below the address and enter the expression =Trim([City] & ", " & [State] & "   " & [ZipCode]), as shown in Figure 21.16, as a control source. Delete this field's label, too, then delete the label for the StudentID field.

Figure 21.16.

Making the third line of the address.

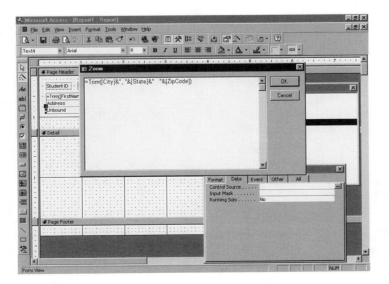

21

> **NOTE**
>
> Report designing is a skill acquired over time. Rather than finish your report only to find that something at the start has gone awry, switch back and forth between Design and Layout or Print Preview Views to see your progress and to catch any misdirection early.

5. These next two steps are a little tricky. You want the course information for each student in the detail section of the form, but the labels for the course information in the page header. This prevents repeating these labels for each course the student has completed. Drag the fields CourseNumber, Name, and Grade onto the Detail section of the form. Using either a marquee or Shift+mouse click, highlight only the labels for these fields. (See Figure 21.17.)

Figure 21.17.

Moving the field labels to the page header starts by highlighting them.

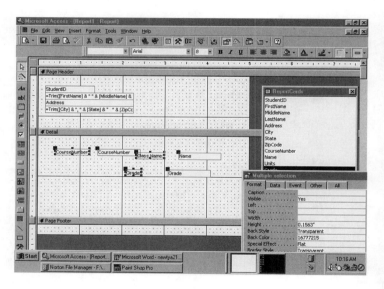

6. Press Ctrl+X to cut these fields to the Clipboard. Click in the Page Header section of the report design grid, then press Ctrl+V to paste the label fields into this section of the report. Arrange all the fields so they resemble Figure 21.18.

7. You need to tell Access to group the details of the completed courses and grades according to StudentID. Click the Sorting and Grouping button in the toolbar. Next, click in the first column of the list box that pops up and enter or scroll to StudentID as a field to group on. Access will, by default, add the Ascending value to the Sort Order column. Make sure the Group On and Keep Together properties are set to Each Value and Whole Group respectively, as shown in Figure 21.19. The

Keep Together setting tells Access to keep the group on a single page, if at all possible. Click the Sorting and Grouping button in the toolbar again to close the list box.

Figure 21.18.

Placing proper elements in the Header and Detail sections.

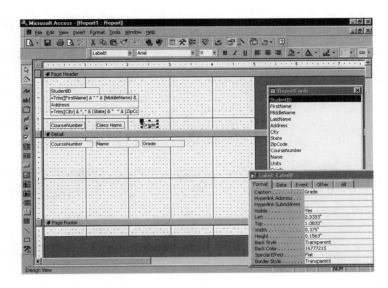

Figure 21.19.

Creating a sorted grouping for the report.

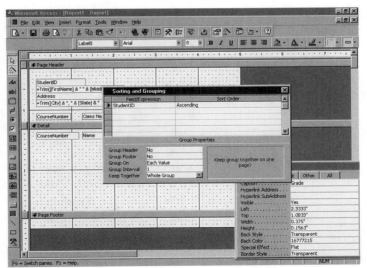

Do **Don't**

DO make sure you group on unique values from your dataset.

DON'T make the mistake of assuming values are unique when they're not. For example, grouping on LastName might seem all right for this dataset, but there can be any number of identical last names in any dataset.

At this point, it's a good idea to check the progress of your report. Shrink the Details section of your report to be just large enough to accommodate one line of fields. Click on the Sample Preview button to see how the report's coming along. Your screen should look like Figure 21.20.

Figure 21.20.

The report still needs some work.

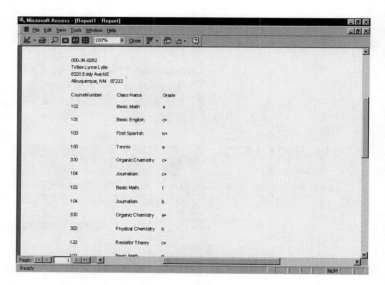

Well, that's not exactly what you had planned. This report seems to attach all the completed courses to one student, Tirilee Lytle. Actually, this report does have the courses grouped by student, but it lacks the breaks needed to make that obvious.

8. Return to Design View. If you have the Sorting and Grouping list box closed, open it by clicking the Sorting and Grouping button in the toolbar. Add a group header and footer section for StudentID by selecting that criterion and changing the Group Header and Group Footer properties for it to Yes. Then add CourseNumber as the second criterion on the second row of the list box. (See Figure 21.21.)

Figure 21.21.

Creating a secondary sort order and adding group headers and footers.

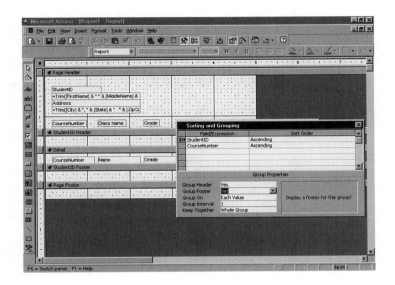

Try switching to Print Preview View again. Your screen should resemble Figure 21.22.

Figure 21.22.

The groups are now visible.

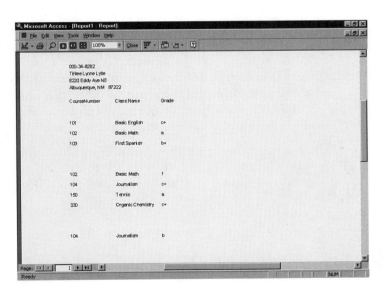

The only thing needed to finish this report's basic structure is to break the report's page on each group and add the right header to the groups.

9. Return to Design View. Click in the StudentID Header section to make it current. Open the Properties list box and locate the Force New Page property under Format Properties. Change this property from None to Before Section. (See Figure 21.23.)

Figure 21.23.

Forcing the report to page break on groups.

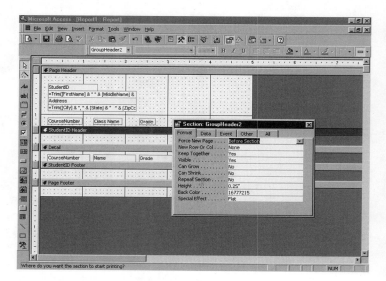

Click the Print Preview button in the toolbar and scroll through several report cards. Access finally has it right, thanks to your efforts. The courses completed by each student are grouped with the student's personal information, the courses are sorted according to course number, and each student's personal and course information is contained on a single page. Figures 21.24 and 21.25 show the results of placing a group on each page. As you scroll through the report at this time you'll see one student on each page.

Close this report, saving it with the name ReportCards. The report's still not quite ready for prime time because it lacks grade point calculations and is a little confusing to read. These problems are addressed in an exercise in Chapter 22, ""Complex Reports."

21

Figure 21.24.
The first record of the grouped report.

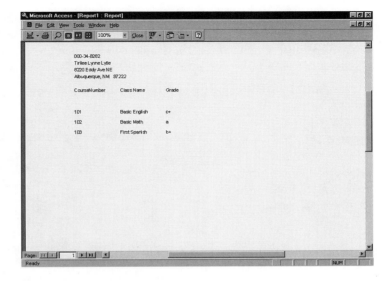

Figure 21.25.
The second record of the grouped report.

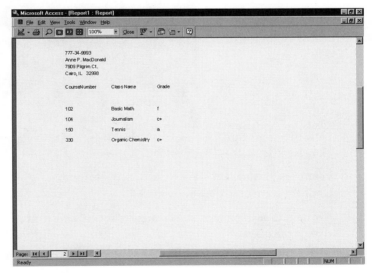

Joins

So far, all the queries you've seen have been *inner joins*, joins in which records in the righthand table must match those in the lefthand table to show up in the query selection. In other words, there are no blank linked fields in any part of the query.

21

Access can also do *outer joins*, which will return all the records from tables, not just matching ones. To demonstrate this, the sample data has two tables, Names and Fruits, along with a query called Fruit Choices. These tables and the query are small with simple contents so that you can easily get a good idea of how the differing joins work.

Figure 21.26 shows both the tables used in the query side by side so you can see their contents.

Figure 21.26.

The two tables used to demonstrate the different kinds of joins Access can do at a mouse click.

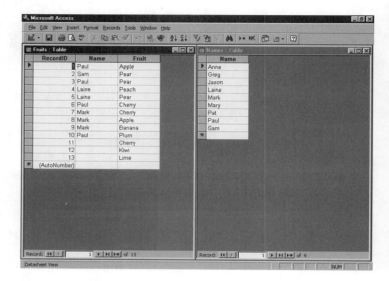

Note that some fruits, such as kiwi, aren't attached to any name, and there are names in the Names table, such as Pat, that don't appear in the Fruits table.

Figure 21.27 shows the Fruit Choices query running after having been created with the familiar procedures you've seen before.

As you'd expect, each name is matched up with the fruit or fruits of his or her choice. To change the query to an outer join of the first type, return to Design View, then right-click on the join line. You'll get a menu with a Join Properties choice, as shown in Figure 21.28.

Figure 21.27.

A common query showing the results of an inner join.

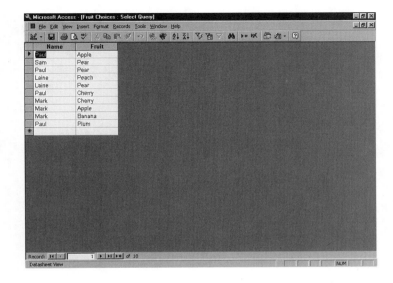

Figure 21.28.

A right-click on the join line calls up a menu with a Join Properties choice.

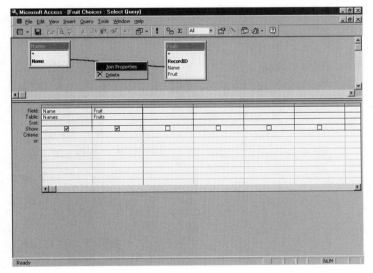

Choosing the Join Properties selection takes you to a dialog box, as shown in Figure 21.29.

21

Figure 21.29.

The Join Properties dialog box gives you three options.

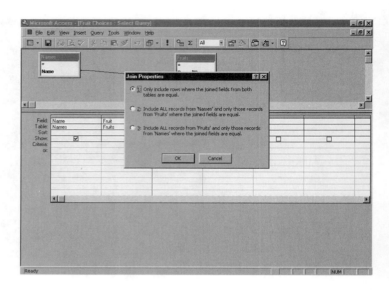

Changing the join type to the first kind of outer join, choice number 2, results in Figure 21.30 when run.

Figure 21.30.

The first type of outer join returns all records from the righthand side of the joined tables.

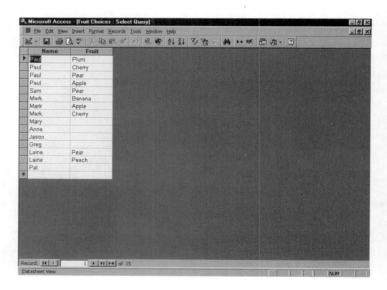

Choosing the third option results in the return shown in Figure 21.31.

Figure 21.31.

The second type of outer join returns all records from the lefthand side of the joined tables.

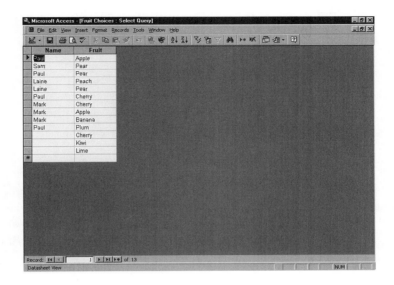

People typically use outer joins to show all records in the righthand, or many, side of a join. Say you're assigning rooms to certain committees. An inner join between the committee and a rooms table will show you all committees that have assigned rooms, but you might want to show vacant rooms, too. An outer join works well for this task. You can also include two or more tables or queries in a query with no joins. This will enable you to choose, through criteria, any or all records from all objects selected in a query.

Morning Summary

Access has no trouble creating a query from many tables. The report card query needed four to work correctly and also needed an Expression field. You create Expression fields in a query by adding Field Name:[Expression] to an otherwise empty column in the query design grid. Field Name is the name you want to appear at the top of the column and the expression is any valid Access expression. Be sure to end your field name with a colon (:) as this tells Access the string to the left of the colon is the column label.

The first field placed in the Grouping and Sorting box while in the report's Design View is the field Access will group on. Subsequent fields placed in this box are fields to sort on within a group. Access's grouping isn't particularly obvious unless you break the groups with a group header, group footer, or both. If you want your groups one to a page, you have to set the group's Force Page Break property to anything other than None, the default.

Access, by default, gives you an inner join, but you can also choose an outer join, either righthanded or lefthanded. Outer joins add to the flexibility of Access's queries as they will return both matched and unmatched rows.

21

Chapter 22

Complex Reports

This afternoon, you'll learn the following:

- ☐ How to enter calculation expressions in reports
- ☐ How Access evaluates expressions
- ☐ How to create better report layouts
- ☐ How to create dynamic report controls

Calculations in Reports

This morning's report, saved as ReportCards, does several things needed for the fictional college. Refer to Figure 22.1, which shows the ReportCards report in Print Preview. This report does the following:

☐ Groups the completed classes with the right student

☐ Puts students' personal information and completed courses on separate pages

☐ Reports the completed courses by name and letter grade

Figure 22.1.

The ReportCards report.

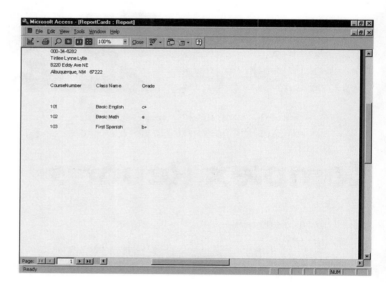

This is fine, but the college needs more information from this report, such as a student's completed course load, unadjusted grade point average (GPA) for the current term, and the weighted value GPA for the courses taken. You can do this by placing an unbound text field where you want these figures to print (or appear), then entering an expression to calculate these values.

The Access Way

The exercises in this chapter might seem a bit irrelevant to business users of Access, but the principles shown this afternoon can be applied to calculating order totals, salesperson average sales, or any other calculation not done in a bound table or query.

22

The Access Way

Many calculations can be performed at either the query or report level. In some cases, it's a toss-up as to where you choose to place your expressions. Keep in mind that you can query queries, so you can create several in-query expressions or totals-type queries (that yield sums, counts, and other math or statistical functions from query contents), then create a "master" query that queries the queries and base your report on that.

Generally speaking, the shorter the chain of queries behind your reports, the faster the reports will run. So if performance is your goal, try to use as many expressions in reports as you can instead of having multiple queries. However, if you want your calculations to be viewed from the Datasheet View of queries themselves, you'll have to include the expressions there.

Exercise 22.1 demonstrates how to create calculations in reports. The technique shown is identical to the technique used for forms. All the material in this exercise applies to forms also.

Exercise 22.1. Calculation expressions in reports.

1. Launch Access and open the College database, if necessary. Open the ReportCards report in Design View. Your screen should look like Figure 22.2.

Figure 22.2.

The ReportCards report in Design View.

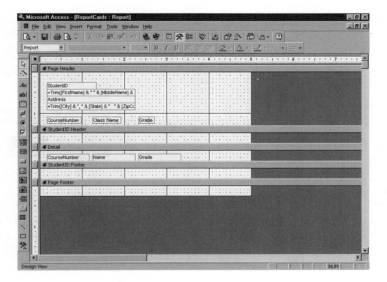

The first thing to do with this report is calculate the entire completed course load, which is simply the sum of the units from the ReportCard query. This and other calculations will appear in the Group Footer band because you want the total to be for each student. Remember, this report groups on StudentID. If you need a refresher, click the Sorting and Grouping button in the toolbar and note that the group icon is to the immediate left of the StudentID field in the list box.

2. If you don't have a band called StudentID Footer in your report from this morning's exercise, you'll need to reveal one now. If you have such a band, open it slightly to give you some working room and skip to Step 3. Open the Sorting and Grouping list box and click in the StudentID field. Locate the Group Footer property and change it to Yes to open up a narrow group footer band in your report. Now that you have the band opened, widen it to give yourself some working room.

3. Refer to Figure 22.3. Add an unbound text box control to the StudentID group footer band. Edit the label for this unbound text control to read Units Completed. (See Figure 22.3.)

Figure 22.3.

Adding the unbound control, which will soon contain an expression that calculates data from the Details section of the report.

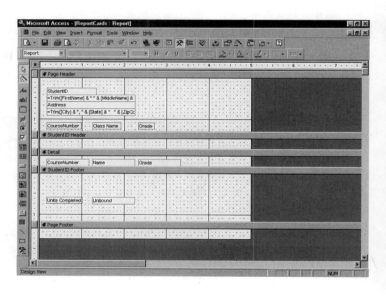

Access can do calculations using any field in the bound query or table, not just those showing in the report. In this way, reports are similar to queries because queries can filter, sort, or use criteria based on fields not included or showing in the query. The following step uses the Access built-in function Sum() to calculate the sum of units taken. Access knows you want the sum of units for a group based on StudentID, and not the entire mass of students, because the Sum() expression is in the StudentID group footer band, rather than the report footer band.

The Access Way

If, for example, you wanted to calculate the sum of all credits taken for all the students in this report, you'd locate the Sum() statement in the Report Footer band. If you wanted to calculate the sum of anything on a page, you'd locate the Sum() function in the Page Footer band. You can include multiple Sum()Sum() (or other) functions in a report, so you could calculate the sum of credits for each student and also for the entire student body.

4. If necessary, click on the unbound text box to highlight it and open the Properties list box. Click on the Data properties tab and edit the Control Source property for the unbound text box to read =sum([Units]).Sum() Remember, you can also add this expression directly into the control, or you can use the Zoom view (Shift+F2) to do the entry. Your screen should look like Figure 22.4.

Figure 22.4.

Inserting the built-in function Sum().

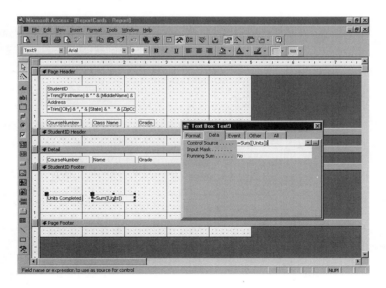

5. Click on the Other tab and edit the Name property for this unbound control to read txtTotal. Switch to Print Preview View; your screen should resemble Figure 22.5. The Name property is how you can refer to controls from other expressions. You'll see the need for this soon.

Figure 22.5.

The report now calculates totals.

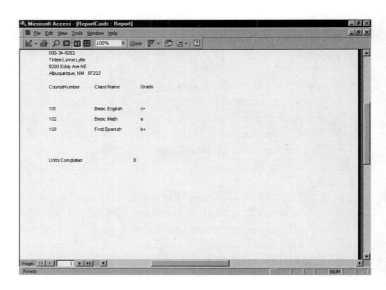

Refer to Figure 22.6, which is the ReportCard query running with the Units column moved next to the LastName column. Check a few students both in the query and the reports to make sure Access is calculating the correct number of units for each student. In this case, it is.

NOTE

The exact calculations of your report and query might differ from the book's examples if you've added or removed records during your learning process. What's important isn't that your data matches the book's, but that your data is internally consistent.

The Access Way

Remember, you can press the F11 key to bring up the Database window and from there click on the Queries tab and run the ReportCards query. You don't need to shut down the ReportCards report to run the query to check your results.

Figure 22.6.

Double-checking for accuracy.

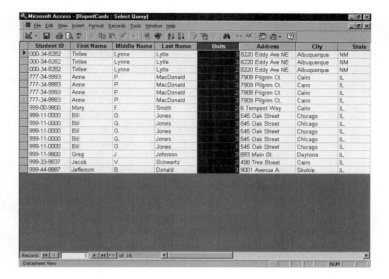

NOTE

Access is a computer program. As such, it's incapable of making math errors, but you can enter the wrong expression, which Access will correctly calculate to yield the wrong answer. Always check Access's output against known data before committing critical applications to the computer. This applies to any computer program, not just to Access.

The next step is to calculate the raw GPA for this term, which is simply the non-weighted average of the grade values for courses taken.

6. Switch back to Design View and enter a new unbound text box right below the txtTotal one. Edit its Name property (from the Other tab) to read txtRawGPA and its label to read Raw Term GPA. Enter =Avg([GradeValue]) as the Control Source property for this control. (See Figure 22.7.)

Again switch back to Print Preview mode to check whether the report's doing the calculations correctly. Refer to Figure 22.8.

Figure 22.7.

Calculating an average value for a group.

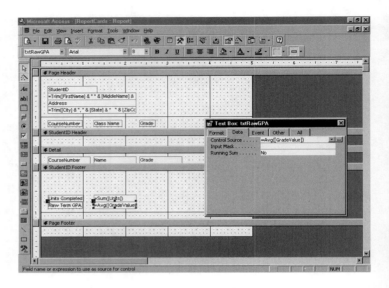

Figure 22.8.

It's a good idea to check your report's progress to prevent you from wasting time on a wrong direction.

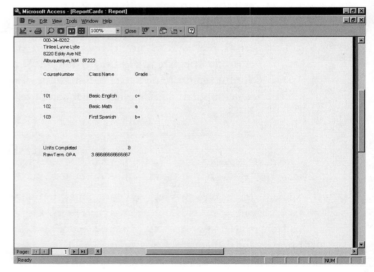

Things look all right at first glance. However, closer examination reveals a problem. In this example, Tirilee has a *c+*, an *a*, and a *b+*. This means Access should be calculating the average of 2.5, 4.0, and 3.5. The correct answer is 3.33, but Access has 3.66! Something's awry, for sure.

7. Take a look at Figure 22.9. This is the GradeValue table, which serves as a lookup to match the letter grade with the grade value.

Figure 22.9.

The lookup table for grade values has an error that's currently adversely affecting many parts of the entire database.

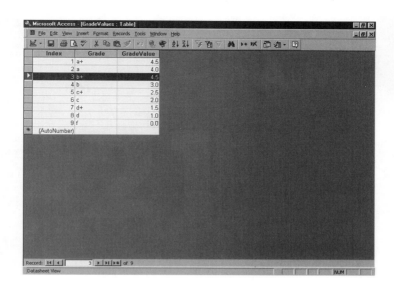

Examine the entry for *b+*. This should be 3.5, but a data entry error shows it as 4.5—this is what's causing the error in the report.

> **The Access Way**
>
> An error in a foundation table such as this lookup for grade values can have severe repercussions throughout your database. Access has no way of knowing that 4.5 was the wrong entry for a *b+* grade when this value was entered. Access would merrily use this wrong value throughout the entire database if left unchecked.

8. Open your GradeValues table by pressing F11 to enter the Database window, clicking on the Tables tab, and opening the GradeValues table in Datasheet mode. Edit the *b+* entry to the correct value of 3.5 and close the table. Return to the ReportCards report, still in Print Preview View.

   Access updates the queries when they're run or when a form or report bound to them calls them by switching into Print, Sample, or Print Preview mode. To trigger the re-query, close this report, saving changes if prompted to do so. Open it again in Print Preview mode. Access reruns the query and now the correct value is reported in your report. You can also switch into Design View and then back to Print Preview. In either case, your screen should look like Figure 22.10.

Figure 22.10.

Opening a report updates the bound query.

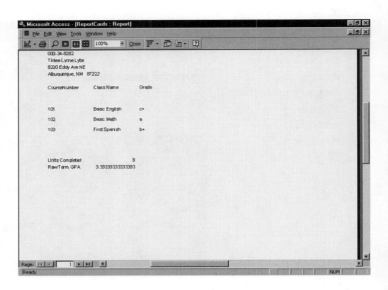

The correct value's now in the Raw Term GPA field, but it looks a little long and overly precise for this field.

9. Return to Design View. Click on the Format tab in the list box, making sure the text box, txtRawGPA, has the highlight. The first property is called Format (to help in the confusion). Pull down the combo box for the Format property on the Format tab. Locate the Fixed property and click on it. Your screen should resemble Figure 22.11.

10. Return to Print Preview mode to see the effect of altering the Format property. (See Figure 22.12.)

That's more like it. The final thing to add as a calculation is the weighted value GPA. The weighted value GPA is the sum of the grades' weighted values, divided by the total units completed.

11. Return to Design View. Add a new unbound text box to the StudentID group footer band. Edit its label to read `Weighted Value GPA`. Enter `=(Sum([Weighted Value]))/(Sum([Units]))` as the Control Source property for this control. Remember the weighted value for a grade is the grade value times the number of credit hours. You might want to enter Zoom by pressing Shift+F2 to enter this long expression. Edit the Name to read `txtWeightedGPA` and change the Format property to `Fixed`. Arrange your fields to resemble Figure 22.13.

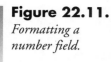

Figure 22.11.
Formatting a number field.

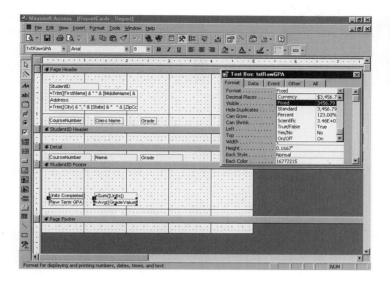

22

Figure 22.12.
The effect of setting the Format property.

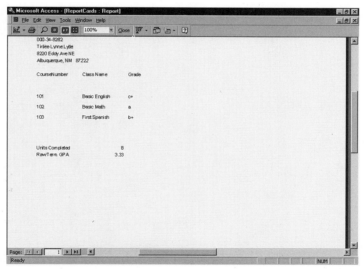

Switch to Print Preview mode. Figure 22.14 shows the ReportCards report with the modifications done in this exercise and with the fields slightly adjusted for alignment.

Figure 22.13.
Entering a complex expression.

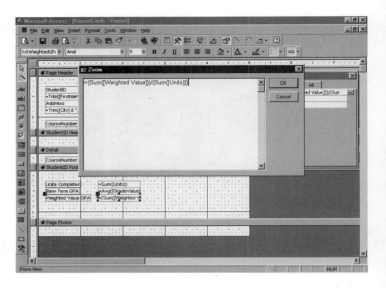

Figure 22.14.
The fully functional report.

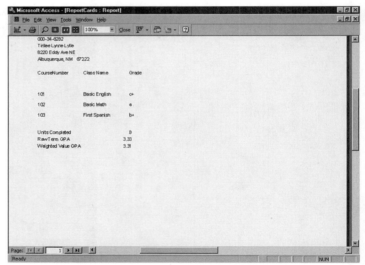

The Access Way

Avoid using circular expressions, which happen when you have the input of expression B set to the output of expression A, and the input of expression A set to the output of expression B. Setting up such references results in infinite regression—something worth avoiding because Access can't resolve the loop.

A Few Handy Expressions

Access is loaded with built-in functions (such as Sum()) and expressions. Here are some of the more handy ones:

Function	What It Does
IsNull()	Tests to see whether a field is blank. Null is *not the same* as a zero value. Access will treat an expression as null if it finds any null values as part of that expression.
IIF()	Immediate if. Tests a value and evaluates to one of two possible returns, depending on what if finds. A very simple If...Then...Else construct you can use in an expression.
DateDiff()	Determines the interval between two dates or times.
Left()	Returns the left part of a string. How much is returned depends on the entered parameter. For example, Left([MyField],2) returns the two leftmost characters in the MyField field. Similar functions are Right() and Mid().
Count()	Returns the count (number of entries) in a set.
Avg()	Returns the average of a set of numbers.
Now()	Returns the date and time of the system.
DateAdd()	Returns a future date.
NZ()	Converts any nulls it finds to the value zero.

How Access Evaluates Arithmetic Expressions

Access uses the standard algebraic hierarchy to evaluate expressions. Take the following expression:

```
6 + 3 * 4 = ?
```

If you add 6 + 3 and then multiply by 4, the answer is 36. If you multiply 3 * 4 and then add the 6, the answer is 18. Which is right? Well, there's no right answer unless you tell Access what you want. In this case, Access does the multiplication first and then the addition because it adheres to the standard algebraic hierarchy, which says do calculations in the following order:

1. Exponential
2. Multiplication
3. Division
4. Addition
5. Subtraction

These words form the acronym EMDAS. The mnemonic for remembering this is "Eeks—My Dear Aunt Sally!" If you want Access to evaluate expressions out of the standard hierarchy, enclose your expressions in parentheses, as in the following example. Contrast

```
(6 + 3) * 4 = 36
```

with

```
6 + 3 * 4 = 18
```

Expressions within parentheses are always evaluated first and separately. The expression from Exercise 22.1, `=(Sum([Weighted Value]))/(Sum([Units]))`, uses parentheses to make sure each sum is evaluated first; only then does Access perform the division. This is, strictly speaking, unnecessary here because these particular expressions aren't sensitive to order. The placing of the parentheses is just a good habit, like enclosing all control names in square brackets.

Do	**Don't**

DO create expressions in queries for values needed in the queries.

DON'T create expressions in queries for values needed only in the bound forms or reports. The ReportCards report violates this rule by including the Weighted Value expression in a query. The reason for the violation was to demonstrate technique, not to show the right way to create a report.

Layouts for Reports

At the end of Exercise 22.1, the ReportCards report is functionally all right, but not very attractive. The method for adding layout elements to a report is identical to that for forms. Reports can have more bands, which adds slightly to possible complexity, but it's hardly overwhelming.

Exercise 22.2 adds some graphics to the ReportCards report.

Exercise 22.2. Graphics elements in reports.

1. Starting where Exercise 22.1 leaves off, return to Design View. Rearrange your report controls to resemble Figure 22.15. If you followed Exercise 22.1 literally, you shouldn't need to do much rearranging.

Figure 22.15.

Getting ready to add graphics to a report.

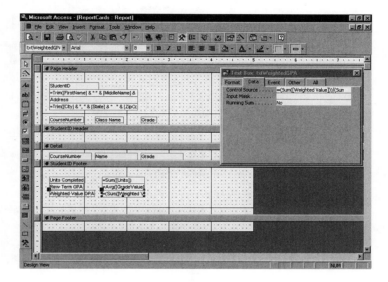

2. Add a rectangle over the controls in the StudentID group footer area. Send it to the back by choosing Format|Send to Back from the menu. Your screen should look like Figure 22.16.

3. Add underlines to the column titles in the Page Header area. Open the Formatting toolbar and increase these lines to width 2. (See Figure 22.17.)

4. Change the alignment for the CourseNumber and Grade text boxes to Center. Switch to Print Preview. Your screen should look like Figure 22.18.

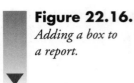

Figure 22.16.
*Adding a box to
a report.*

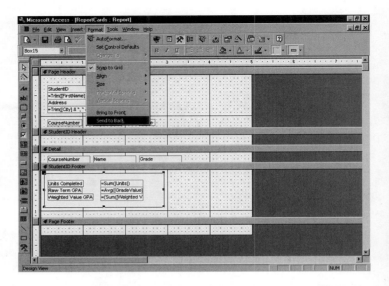

Figure 22.17.
*Adding lines to
column heads in
a report.*

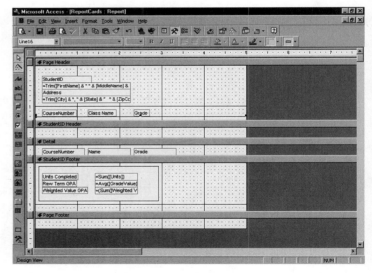

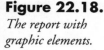

Figure 22.18.

The report with graphic elements.

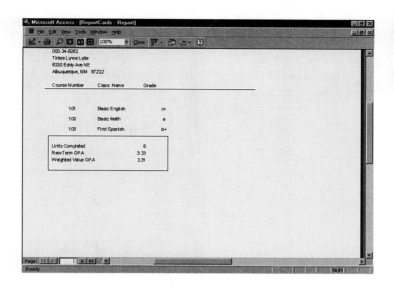

22

This report is a bit easier to read now. It's still not anyone's idea of a work of art, but its sections are at least set off from each other.

Dynamic Controls on Reports

The fictional college awards dean's list recognition to any student with a weighted grade point average over 3.1 for a semester, so the registrar wants to have a visible indication of this award on the report card.

Exercise 22.3 places an option button on the report card that evaluates students' weighted GPAs and visibly indicates whether they merit being included on the dean's list.

Exercise 22.3. A dynamic control.

1. Picking up where Exercise 22.2 leaves off, return to Design View. Your screen should resemble Figure 22.19.

2. Enlarge the rectangle surrounding the calculated fields to accommodate an option button. Place an unbound option button control in the StudentID footer rectangle just to the right of the previously placed fields. Edit the label for the new option button to read `Dean's List`. Orient the control and its label to resemble Figure 22.20.

Figure 22.19.

Getting ready to place a dynamic control on the form.

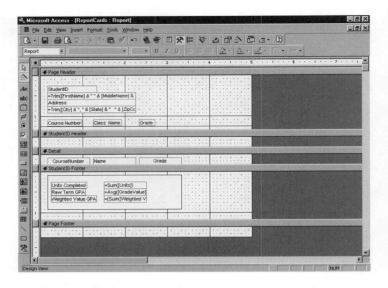

Figure 22.20.

Adding the dynamic control.

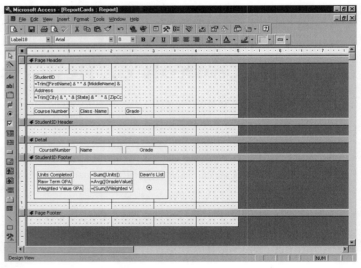

3. Click on the control portion (rather than the label) of the new control. Locate the Name field in the Properties list box and name this control optDeansList. Locate the Control Source property and enter the expression =[txtWeightedGPA]>3.1. (See Figure 22.21.)

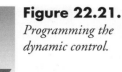

Figure 22.21.
Programming the dynamic control.

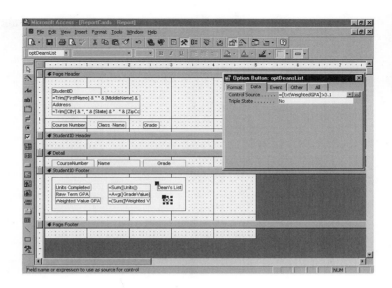

This expression tells Access to examine the txtWeightedGPA field, and if the value of that field exceeds 3.1, to change the value of the option button to True. Otherwise, the option button's value is False.

Switch to Print Preview. Take a look at Tirilee's report card, shown in Figure 22.22. Because her weighted GPA is 3.31, it's above 3.1 and the Dean's List option button is set to True.

Scroll to the next record, the one for Anne MacDonald. Anne didn't do too well this term, as shown in Figure 22.23. Because her weighted GPA is less than 3.1, her Dean's List option button is set to False.

Close this report, saving the changes. The report at this stage is included in the sample data as ReportCards1.

Figure 22.22.
A report card rating dean's list status.

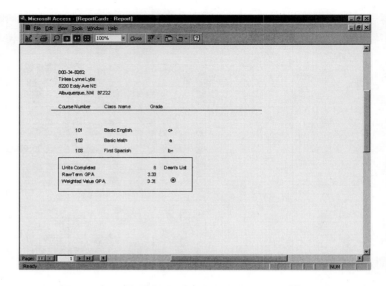

Figure 22.23.
A report card failing to meet dean's list status.

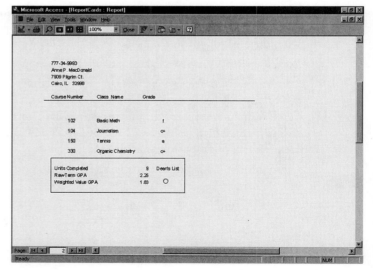

The Access Way

Using an option button to visibly show whether a student made the dean's list probably isn't the best idea since it's not as noticeable as other strategies. You'd probably be better off using a label and altering its Visible property from No to Yes, depending on the value in the group's txtWeightedGPA text box.

However, you need familiarity with either Visual Basic code or macros to do this, and this book hasn't covered those topics yet. To preserve the book's flow, I've used only those tools already covered in past days.

Day Summary

Access can use either inner or outer joins in queries. An inner join returns only matching records; an outer join returns all records from one table or query along with matching records from the other table or query included in the join.

Adding expressions to reports is as simple as entering them in unbound text boxes. It's vital to check with known data to determine that these expressions are working as you think they should. Access can neither make a mathematical mistake nor read your mind to determine what you mean. An expression in Access is only as accurate as the person who designed it.

You can format the appearance of a text box's data by altering the Format property in the Properties list box. Access gives you almost unlimited ways to format fields. You can make your fields look just about any way you choose.

Adding boxes and lines to a report works exactly as it does in forms. Because most printers are grayscale, using color in a report generally makes little sense.

You create a simple dynamic control in a report or form by entering an unbound control to the report—usually a check box or option button—and then entering an evaluating expression as that control's Control Source.

Q&A

Q How can I set the page size for my reports?

A Use the Print Setup dialog boxes in the File menu to change the defaults. Remember, Access's wizards use these defaults when making a report. If your wizard made reports that seem to be aimed at bizarre paper sizes, the fault's in the Print Setup settings under the File menu selection.

Q **Can I calculate on a calculated field in a query?**

A Yes. Look at Figure 22.24. This shows a field called Demo added to the ReportCards query that performs a calculation on a calculated field: Weighted Value.

Figure 22.24.

A calculation on another calculation.

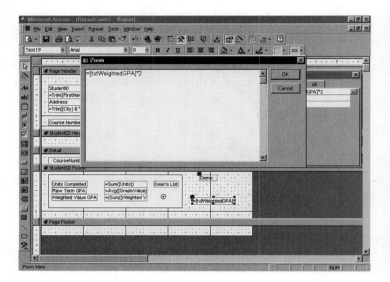

When run, the Demo field calculates and returns 200 percent of the value calculated in the Weighted Value field. Refer to Figure 21.25 to see the results of running the ReportCards report with the Demo field.

Q **Could I have put the labels for Course Number, Name, and Grade in the Group Header band?**

A Yes, and your results would have been effectively identical to those in Exercise 21.2. Your method is actually better, but because of the exercise's flow, the headers for the detail band were placed in the Page Header band.

Q **Could I have created a report with a subreport as I did in forms?**

A Yes, and the method is almost identical. Access gives you many ways to get to the same place. For example, the calculation done in the ReportCards query could have been done in the report itself.

Figure 22.25.

Running the modified report with the Demo field. Note the slight differences due to rounding.

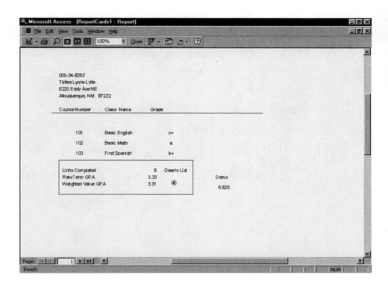

Workshop

Here's where you can test and apply the lessons you learned today.

Quiz

Possible answers to these questions are given in Appendix A.

1. What's the significance of the colon in the query column label `Weighted Value:`?

2. Does a report with a subreport use the Link Master Fields and Link Child Fields properties like forms with subforms do?

3. Refer to the ReportCards query. If the expression `Name:[FirstName]&" "&[LastName]` were entered in a column's Field row, would it be valid?

4. Does the StudentID field need to appear on a report for the report to group on it?

5. Name two ways to change the width of a line or box in reports or forms.

6. Refer to Figure 21.21. What icon does Access use to distinguish the group field from a sort within the group field?

Put Access into Action

1. Use a wizard to create a report that groups on courses and includes all the students signed up for those courses.

2. Add the names of the students' parents to the report.

3. Sort on the parents' names within each group.

4. Alter the report to make each class print out on a separate piece of paper.

5. Save this report, if you want to; however, *Teach Yourself Access 97 in 14 Days* doesn't refer to it again.

DAY
12

A.M.

23 Introduction to Macros

P.M.

24 More Macro Magic

Chapter **23**

Introduction to Macros

This morning, you'll learn the following:

- ☐ What a macro is
- ☐ What three programming languages Access supports
- ☐ More about Structured Query Language (SQL)
- ☐ How to use the macro design grid
- ☐ How to make simple macros
- ☐ How to make a switchboard form

Macros

A *macro*, as far as Access is concerned, is a simple programming language that enables you to automate certain tasks. Fundamentally, a macro is a series of actions executed either linearly in response to an event or upon certain conditions being met after an event. Like so many computer topics, macros are easier to understand after you've seen one or two in action than from abstract text.

You can use macros for many tasks; here are some of the more common uses:

- [ ] Programming buttons to do a series of actions, such as opening or closing forms
- [ ] Setting or removing filters or sort orders in forms and reports
- [ ] Changing the properties or values of controls during runtime
- [ ] Helping ensure accurate data entry by watching the data entered and advising data-entry people of any errors they're making
- [ ] Automating tasks that you do often

Access's Three Programming Languages

Access supports three programming languages: Visual Basic, macros, and Structured Query Language. Structured Query Language, used mostly in queries, is often abbreviated SQL—pronounced "seekel" or "sequel." If you care to split hairs, you can add a fourth language, expressions, to the list, but few people do.

Keep in mind that every query you construct "by example" using the query design grid is "backed up" by SQL. Take a look at Figure 23.1, the ReportCards query's SQL code.

To see the SQL code that makes up a query, enter Design View for a query, pull down the leftmost button on the toolbar, and click on the SQL view option. If you chose to, you could construct an Access query by using native SQL rather than the query design grid, which uses a technique called QBE (Query By Example). Few people use native SQL exclusively in Access queries because QBE is much easier.

Take a look at the simple query shown in Design View in Figure 23.2. This query contains the two fields StudentID and FirstName from StudentPersonal table and returns only the FirstName because the box under StudentID is unchecked. Figure 23.3 shows the query running, and Figure 23.4 illustrates the SQL that makes up this query.

23

Figure 23.1.

The SQL code from a moderately complex query.

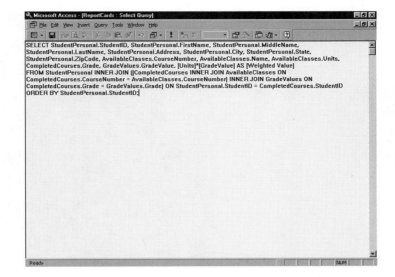

Figure 23.2.

A simple query to demonstrate SQL.

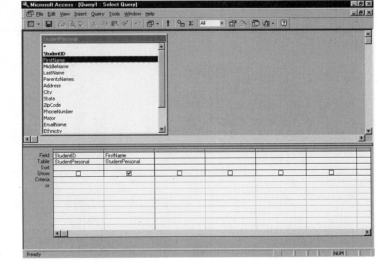

Figure 23.3.

*The simple query
in action.*

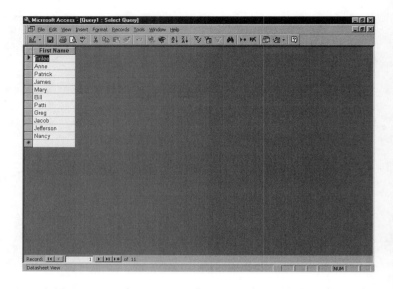

Figure 23.4.

*The SQL code behind the
simple query.*

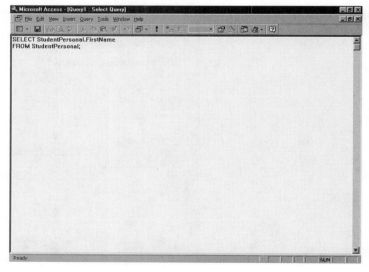

The SQL code should seem fairly obvious—it's English with some operators or keywords to provide the action. The SELECT statement means, well, "select" or "choose from," so this query states to choose (or display) the FirstName field within the StudentPersonal table from the set that includes the StudentPersonal table. Yes, it's slightly redundant, but the duplication of StudentPersonal is necessary for clarity when more than one table comes into play in a query.

Criteria in SQL comes from the WHERE statement. Look at Figure 23.5, the query design grid with a criterion added. Now look at Figure 23.6, the same query's SQL, and note the change from Figure 23.4.

Figure 23.5.

Adding a criterion to Access's QBE.

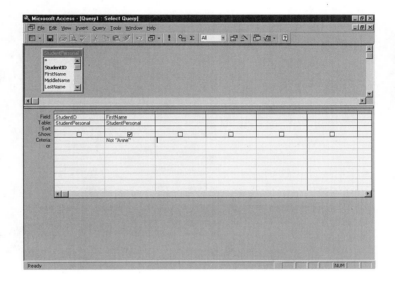

Figure 23.6.

The effect of adding a criterion as seen in SQL.

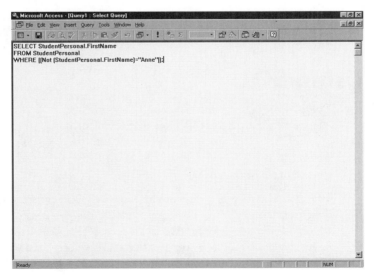

Access has added the line WHERE ((Not (StudentPersonal.FirstName)="Anne")); to the query in SQL. When run, the query's return is shown in Figure 23.7.

Figure 23.7.

The results of a WHERE *statement in SQL.*

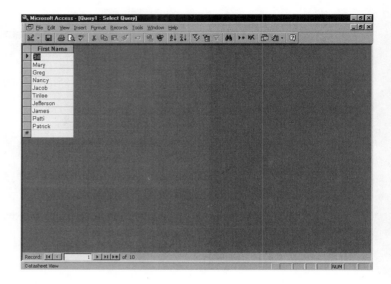

SQL is a topic that's simple in details yet huge in scope. It has very few operatives, or keywords, but by combining these few operatives you can query SQL-compliant databases in almost any way imaginable.

Using SQL

There's little reason for most people to write SQL in Access queries. A hand-entered SQL query isn't superior to a QBE one done by using the query design grid. The SQL capability of Access isn't even known to most users. Some database systems require SQL to query them, and Access acts as a good front-end for those systems. It's also a great training ground for those who want to learn SQL.

One area where some people use SQL natively is in constructing code in Visual Basic to be used for querying Access databases. Because this topic is both complex and more suited to a Visual Basic text than an Access one, *Teach Yourself Access 97 in 14 Days* ends the SQL discussion here. However, this is a rich topic well-covered in other texts. If you're planning on using Access as a professional developer, it's also a topic with which you need at least basic familiarity.

Also keep in mind that you use SQL in places other than the query design process. Forms and reports can use SQL as their control source properties to control displayed data. If you use the database wizards to create frameworks for your own applications, you'll find that Microsoft uses SQL for control sources on forms extensively. You'll see this technique also used in the sample files, such as Northwind, that Microsoft supplies with Access. Studying these control sources is a good way to learn practical SQL.

If you want to see SQL in action, construct the simple query from Figure 23.6, then edit it in SQL view to read:

```
SELECT StudentPersonal.*
FROM StudentPersonal
WHERE ((Not (StudentPersonal.FirstName)="Anne"));
```

What do you suppose the change from `StudentPersonal.FirstName` to `StudentPersonal.*` will bring?

Looking at Macros

Chapter 19, "Instantly Smarter Forms," introduces Visual Basic with an exercise that programs a command button to respond to an event. The earlier part of this chapter gives you a brief introduction to SQL, so now is the time for the third Access language, macros—what they look like and how they work.

You construct macros in a macro design grid, just like many other Access objects. Also, like many other Access parts, making macros consists mainly of pulling down lists and choosing options. Take a look at macros yourself now by following along with Exercise 23.1, which shows the macro design grid and constructs a simple macro.

Exercise 23.1. The macro design grid.

1. From the Database window, click on the Macros tab, then click the New button to start a new macro. Your screen should look like Figure 23.8.

2. Click on the down arrow for the combo box in the Action column. (See Figure 23.9.)

   Macro actions are the heart of the macro. In some cases, macro actions take no arguments or parameters; in others, macro actions require rather elaborate and specific parameters or arguments. To start, make a simple macro that just causes your computer to beep.

Figure 23.8.
The macro design grid.

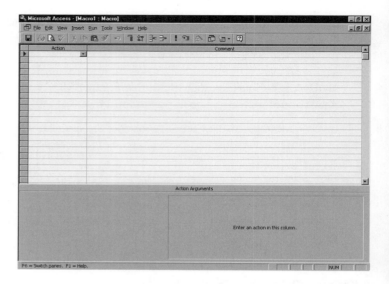

Figure 23.9.
The list of macro actions.

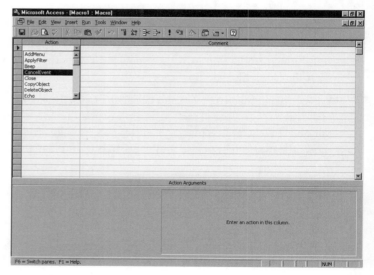

3. Pull down the Action combo box and click Beep, then click the Run button in the toolbar, the one with the exclamation point, just as in the query section of Access.

4. Access beeps and gives you a message box like the one shown in Figure 23.10. Click OK and save the macro, naming it macBeeper. After you save it, the macro runs, beeping your system once. Try clicking the Run button several times to cause

Access to beep your computer several times. If you have a special sound assigned to beep in Windows, you'll hear your assigned sound. Congratulations! You've just programmed your first macro.

Figure 23.10.

Access prompts you with a message box that insists you save your macros before you can run them.

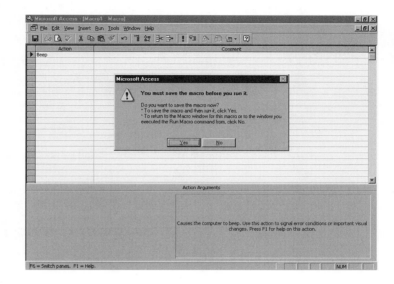

That was awfully easy and so are most macro tasks. There's no real way to run a macro with an error trap like the Event Procedure in Chapter 19. For this reason, some professional programmers frown on using a lot of (or even any) macros in Access applications. If there's no error trap, Access doesn't know what to do in case of an error condition and generally exits rather ungracefully.

The lack of an error trap in macros is a disadvantage. However, error traps are mostly a concern for those distributing applications to others, especially outside the developer's organization. Most internal or for-your-own-use Access applications seem to survive without error traps. The ease of programming macros counteracts the lack of traps in macros for the vast majority of Access users. However, any system lacking these traps, or ways to handle things when something unexpected happens, is significantly more prone to crashing, data losses, and other woes than one that's programmed to anticipate that something will go wrong. Worse, the unexpected and uncontrolled behavior of untrapped errors will cause you, the developer's, phone to ring with irate users on the other end. Of all problems with unexpected errors, this is the worst.

There are too many Access applications merrily running along on macros alone to condemn the practice of using macros extensively, but keep in mind that you're safer using properly constructed Visual Basic code than you are using just macros.

Do   **Don't**

DO use a wizard to program your command buttons when you have the right wizard. This will give you the best of both worlds: easy button programming and error trapping through Visual Basic. Also remember that you can modify the "canned" error traps the wizard produces.

DON'T get overly worried if you find programming in Visual Basic to be overwhelming and you choose to use macros for actions where no wizard exists. Most noncommercial Access applications do just fine while lacking a few error traps, even though this practice is roundly condemned by the Access elite corps.

Bah! That's enough verbiage for now. Time to give this macro and you a little more to do.

5. Pull down the combo box in the second row of the Action column. Scroll to and select OpenForm. Access automatically brings up the Action Arguments section at the bottom of the screen. Click next to the Form Name argument section and pull down the combo box. Click on Class Entry Form as the form to open. Your screen should resemble Figure 23.11, depending on the state of your Class Entry Form.

Figure 23.11.

The OpenForm macro.

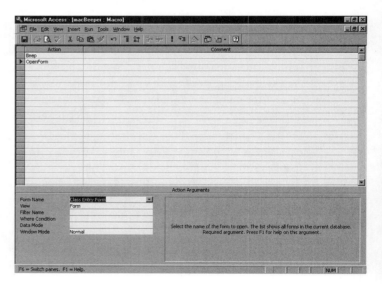

6. Again, click the Run button in the toolbar. Access again reminds you that you must save the macro, so click OK. Access lets fly with another beep in response to your programmed Beep line as the first action in this macro, then opens the form, Class Entry Form, responding to the second. Your screen should look like Figure 23.12.

Figure 23.12.

*Running an
OpenForm macro.*

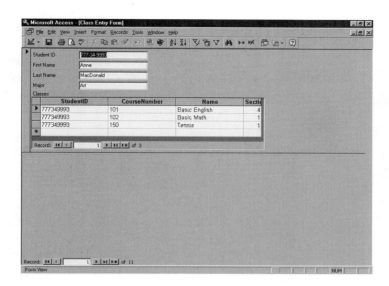

7. Click the cmdExit button to exit this form—that's the one with the stop sign on it.
   If you don't have a cmdExit button on your form, exit the form by clicking its
   close (×) icon or choose File|Close from the menu. Access returns you to the macro
   design grid. (See Figure 23.13.)

8. Close the Beeper macro. Back at the Database window, you can delete it by
   clicking on it, then pressing the Del or Delete key and confirming to Access that
   you want to delete this macro. *Teach Yourself Access 97 in 14 Days* won't come back
   to macBeeper, but you might want to keep it around for experimentation.

Figure 23.13.

*Access closes the
form and returns
to the design grid.*

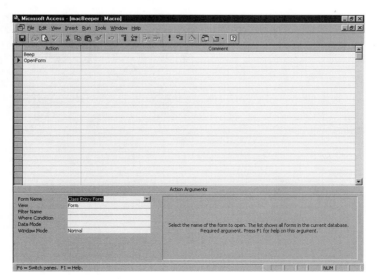

A Switchboard Form

You saw how easy it was to create a macro that, when run, opens a form. Doing many other things with macros is equally easy. Exercise 23.2 shows you how to make a switchboard form. This specialized unbound form has command buttons that act as a menu system for your applications.

Exercise 23.2. The switchboard or menu form.

1. With Access launched and the College database open, click on the Forms tab, then click the New button to start a new form.

2. Click on the Design View option without binding any table or query to the new form, then click OK to launch the form in Design View. Your screen should look like Figure 23.14. Move your mouse cursor to the lower-right corner of the form design area. When you hit the corner, the cursor will change to a box with four arrows sticking out from it. Click your mouse button and drag the form until it fits the screen. This operation is shown completed in Figure 23.15.

Figure 23.14.

Starting a switch-board form.

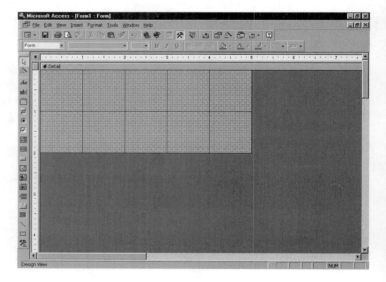

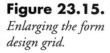

Figure 23.15.

Enlarging the form design grid.

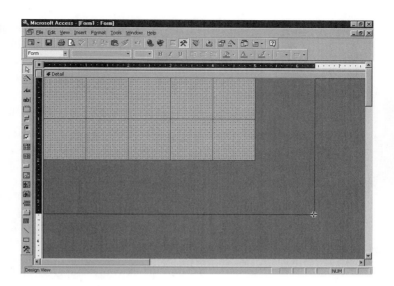

These next steps give the form its basic design elements.

3. Click on the Label control in the toolbox and click again in the upper-left corner of the form design grid. Enter Fictional College as a label. Next, change the font size to 18 and the style to bold, as shown in Figure 23.16. You will have to resize your label to make the new font fit.

Figure 23.16.

Inserting a Label control.

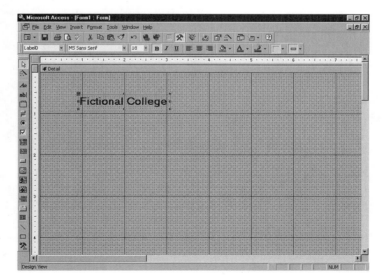

4. Make sure the Wizard button in the toolbox is deselected, then double-click on the Command Button control in the toolbox. This locks the Command Button control choice, allowing you to place more than one control without reselecting it. Unlock a control selection by pressing Esc. Place three command buttons on the form; you can place them as shown in Figure 23.17 or wherever you think they look good.

The next step is to name and caption the Command Button controls.

5. Press Esc to remove the control lock. Click on the Select Objects tool in the toolbox to deselect the Command Button tool. Open the Properties list box if necessary. Highlight each button in turn and change its Name property (on the Other tab) to cmdOpenClassEntry, cmdOpenReportCards, and cmdExit, respectively. While in the Properties list box, change the buttons' Caption property (on the Format tab) to Class Entry Form, Report Cards, and E&xit, respectively. Figure 23.18 shows what your screen should look like after changing the last button's Name and Caption properties.

Figure 23.17.

Placing command buttons in the form.

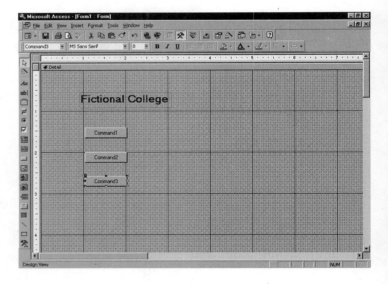

Figure 23.18.
Altering the command button's properties.

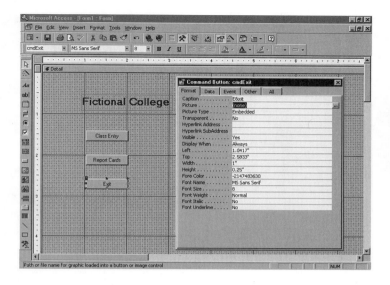

6. Choose File|Save As|Export from the menu and name this form Switchboard.

The Macros

Exercise 23.3 creates a macro for the Switchboard form you made in Exercise 23.2.

Exercise 23.3. The compound macro.

1. If the form from Exercise 23.2 is still open, press the F11 key to bring the Database window forward. If you're looking at the Database window already, you don't need to press F11 (naturally). Click on the Macros tab, then click on New. Locate the Macro Names button in the toolbar and click on it. (See Figure 23.19.)

   Macros have one overall name that appears in the Database window, but they can also have subnames that appear in the Macro Names column. When you attach this macro to the Switchboard form, you'll see how it works.

2. Click in the first row of the Macro Names column and enter OpenClassEntry for a name. Move to the Actions column, pull down the combo box, and click on OpenForm. In the Action Arguments section, specify the Class Entry Form as the one to be opened. Your screen should look like Figure 23.20.

Figure 23.19.
Starting the compound macro.

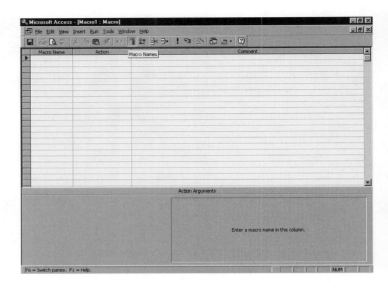

Figure 23.20.
The OpenForm macro.

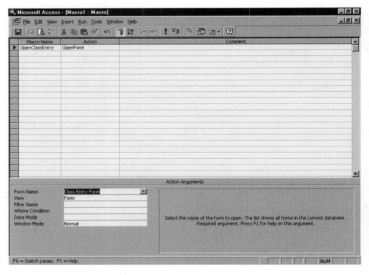

3. Click in the second row of the Macro Names column. Enter OpenReportCards. Move to the Action column and enter OpenReport. Specify ReportCards as the Report Name and make sure the view is Print Preview. Your screen should look like Figure 23.21.

Figure 23.21.

The OpenReport macro.

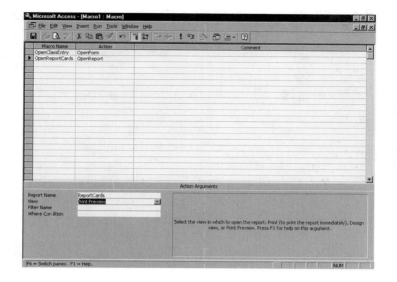

4. Click in the third row of the Macro Names column. Enter Exit as a name and move to the Action column, then enter Quit as an action. (See Figure 23.22.)

Figure 23.22.

The Exit macro.

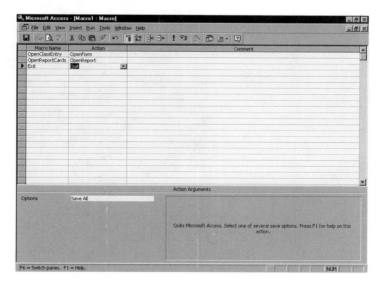

5. Close and save this macro, giving it the name macSwitchboard. The *mac* prefix is a popular naming convention for macros. Using it here is an example of using naming conventions for Access objects.

Putting It All Together

All's ready now to attach the macro from Exercise 23.3 to the form from Exercise 23.2.

Exercise 23.4. Activating the form.

1. Open up the Switchboard form in Design View, either by switching to it (Ctrl+F6) or clicking on the Forms tab, then clicking on Design after highlighting the Switchboard form. Your screen should look like Figure 23.23.

2. Click on the cmdOpenClassEntry command button and open the Properties list box if necessary. Click on the Event tab to show only Event Properties. Locate the On Click event in the list box and pull down the combo box, then find and click the Switchboard.OpenClassEntry entry. (See Figure 23.24.)

Figure 23.23.

The Switchboard form in Design View.

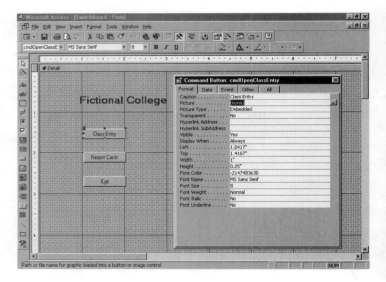

Figure 23.24.

Attaching the macro to the command button.

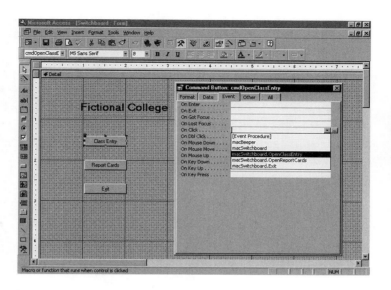

3. Click on the cmdOpenReportCards control, and assign the Switchboard. OpenReportCards macro to its On Click property. Your screen should resemble Figure 23.25.

Figure 23.25.

Attaching the next macro to the next command button.

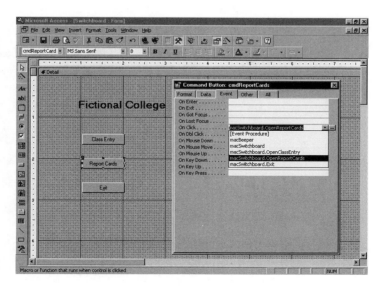

4. Using the same technique, attach the Switchboard.Exit macro to the cmdExit button. (See Figure 23.26.)

Figure 23.26.

Attaching the last macro.

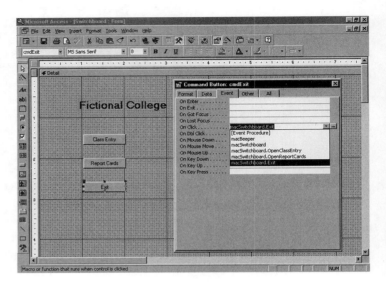

5. Choose File|Save from the menu to save the form's changes, then switch to Form View. Your screen should look like Figure 23.27.

Figure 23.27.

The new Switchboard form up and running.

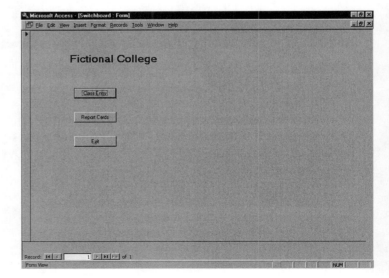

Try clicking on the button labeled Class Entry Form. You'll switch to the Class Entry Form. Click the button with the stop sign on it within the Class Entry Form or exit this form in some other way. You'll return to the Switchboard form.

Experiment with these buttons, starting and ending the Class Entry Form and the ReportCards report. One caution: The button labeled Exit exits you from Access. Try pressing Alt+X to use this button.

Morning Summary

Access has three native languages: Visual Basic, SQL, and macros. You can design queries with SQL if you're so inclined, but most people prefer to use the query design grid (QBE) and let Access do the SQL dirty work.

Macros have two parts: Actions and Action Arguments. Simple macro actions, such as the Beep, take no arguments, but most others do. Programming Access macros can be as simple as clicking on the macro action, then clicking on the right arguments. Macros can get more complex, as you'll see later, but much can be done by point and click.

23

Chapter 24

More Macro Magic

This afternoon's lesson covers these topics:

- ☐ The concept of conditional branching
- ☐ How to program branching or conditional macros
- ☐ Practical uses for conditional macros
- ☐ Macros that change control values
- ☐ Access identifiers

Conditional Branching in Macros

All but the simplest computer programs rely at times on evaluating a condition, then taking action based on the results of that evaluation. You created a program that evaluated a condition and reacted accordingly yesterday afternoon (Chapter 22, "Complex Reports") when you added a dynamic control to the ReportCards report. The optDeansList option button had as a control source an expression that examined the value for the weighted GPA and set itself to True if it was above 3.1; otherwise, it set itself to False. This is a simple example of an evaluate-then-branch computer routine. Although simple, it was useful, too.

The optDeansList option button set itself according to a value for another control. On their own, controls can do only limited things, but team them up with macros and the field widens quite a bit. The problem is how to get the macro, rather than the control, to evaluate a condition and act on what it finds. As you've probably guessed by now, Access gives you a simple way to do this evaluation. The second problem to address is how to decide when the macro should do the evaluation.

Figure 24.1 shows the macro design grid with two columns, as it appears by default. Figure 24.2 is the macro design grid with all the possible columns showing. Note that in addition to the Macro Name column, there's also a Condition column. By default, macros execute under any condition when called. If you make an entry in the Condition column, the macro starts, does the evaluation, and executes, depending on the results of the evaluation. In other words, it *branches*.

One handy thing a macro can do is flash a message box informing data-entry people of just about anything, from a credit overrun to an error condition to a sales suggestion. Exercise 24.1 creates a macro that brings up a message box if certain conditions are met. It evaluates the contents of the Ethnicity field when a new student is registered and then responds accordingly.

Exercise 24.1. Conditional message box macro.

1. Launch Access and open the College database, if necessary. Click on the Macros tab, and click on New. Click both the Macro Names and the Condition buttons in the toolbar to open both these columns. If you're a menu enthusiast, you can choose both columns from the View menu. Your screen should resemble Figure 24.2. Figure 24.2 shows the cursor at the Conditions button, in case you have difficulty locating it; the Macro Names button is just to the left of the Conditions button.

   Generally speaking, the first thing to do with a macro is to give it a name, unless the macro will have only one routine. It's good practice to group macros according to usage. Since this macro will work on the StudentPersonalData form, it could be made part of the macro done for that form as part of this morning's chapter. This macro will have the overall name macStudentPersonalData because all the macros (or macro names) in it are called from this form. In this specific case, including the macro in a group is another example of good practice—it isn't absolutely necessary.

Figure 24.1.

By default, the macro design grid has a total of two columns.

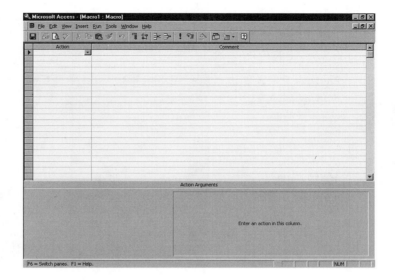

Figure 24.2.

Adding the Condition and Macro Name columns.

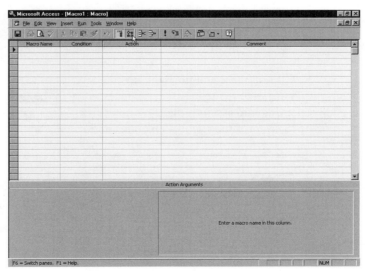

2. Click in the Macro Name field in the first row and enter the name `Exit` for the first macro action. Select the Close action for the Action column, then edit the Action Arguments to read `Form` for the Object to close and `StudentPersonalData` for the particular form to close. Set the Save action to `No`. This last setting is unnecessary, as the form will be opened only in Form View. Choose File|Save As|Export from the menu and name the macro `macStudentPersonalData`. Click in the second row of the Macro Names column and add the name `Scholarship`. Your screen should now look like Figure 24.3.

Figure 24.3.

Starting the multifunction macro by adding the first and second macro names to the Macro Name column.

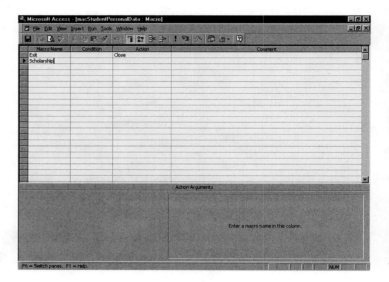

3. Click in the Condition column and enter `[Ethnicity]="Black"`. This means you want to have the macro evaluate the entry in the Ethnicity field (or control) and spring into action if the condition's met. In this case, the condition the macro looks for is the text in a text box control. Your screen should look like Figure 24.4.

The Access Way

Remember, you can expand or contract macro columns just as you can other columns (such as in a table or query). You can also Zoom by pressing Shift+F2 to enter criteria or data within the macro design grid.

Figure 24.4.

Entering a condition for the macro to evaluate.

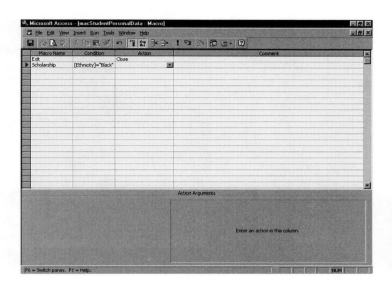

Now you need to enter the action to be taken in case the condition is met. The fictional college has an equally fictional Roy Wilkens Scholarship for students of African heritage. This macro reminds the data-entry person to tell the student about this scholarship.

4. Click in the Action column of the second row, pull down the action combo box list, and click on MsgBox. (See Figure 24.5.)

5. Edit the Title argument to be `Scholarship Alert!` and the message box type to be `Information`, then enter the text `Is this student aware of the Roy Wilkens scholarship?` as the Message argument. Figure 24.6 shows what your screen will look like when you're done. In Figure 24.6, the Message argument is being entered in Zoom mode.

6. Close this macro, saving the changes.

24

Figure 24.5.
Specifying that the macro action is to show a message box.

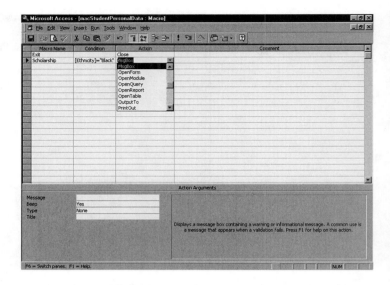

Figure 24.6.
Entering arguments for a message box.

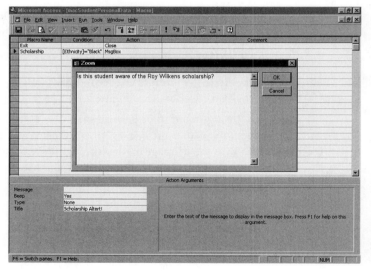

Prepare to Use the Macro

Two more things need to be done at this point. First, you need to add a command button for the macStudentPersonalData.Exit macro. Second, you must attach the macStudentPersonalData.Scholarship macro to the form in just the right way so it will spring into action at an appropriate time.

In Exercise 24.2, you add a command button to the form with a slightly different technique than before. If you've been doing the optional exercises at the end of the chapters, you've seen this already.

Exercise 24.2. Attaching macros.

EXERCISE

1. Back in the Database window, click on the Forms tab, highlight the StudentPersonalData form, and click the Design button to open this form in Design View. Open the form footer, if necessary, by clicking on the View-Form Header/Footer. You may need to drag and expand your form footer area to have it show. (See Figure 24.7.)

Figure 24.7.

Ready to add macros to a form.

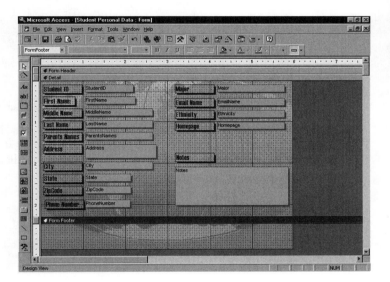

2. If necessary, scroll down to see the form's footer. Open the Properties list box, if necessary, by clicking its button in the toolbar or choosing View|Properties from the menu. Make sure the Wizard button in the toolbox isn't selected. Place a command button in the form footer and give it the caption &Close Form and the name cmdExit. Click on the Event tab. Pull down the On Click combo box, locate the macStudentPersonalData.Exit macro, and click on it. (See Figure 24.8.)

Figure 24.8.

Editing the On Click property.

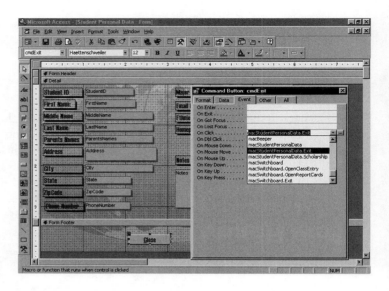

Well, that's done. Now move on to assign the other macro name to the appropriate event.

3. If necessary, scroll back up so the detail portion of the form is showing again. Click on the Ethnicity field to highlight it. Make sure you click on the field itself, not the label for the field. After finding the After Update property in the Properties list box, click on it and pull down its combo box. Next, locate the macStudentPersonalData.Scholarship macro and click on it. Your screen should look like Figure 24.9.

Do	Don't

DO make sure to have the field itself highlighted when trying to enter event-driven macros.

DON'T highlight the field's label or you won't see the events for the control shown in the list box. No events can happen to a label.

Figure 24.9.

Adding a macro to the After Update property of a text box. This macro will "fire" after the data in the text box has been edited.

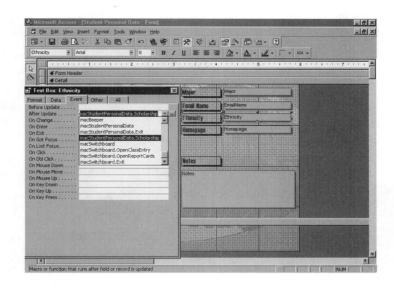

Macros in Action

Now take a look at how this new macro works. Switch to Form View for the StudentPersonalData form. Click the New button in the toolbar and enter the information for a new student shown in Figure 24.10. You can use data of your own choosing, as long as you make sure you set the Ethnicity field to anything but Black.

NOTE

When entering data for this and the next student, you might find your tab order to be wrong for the natural order of this form. If you prefer a different tab order, switch back to Design View and adjust it.

Now enter the data for the next student, as shown in Figure 24.11, just to the point of exiting the Ethnicity field after entering Black as this student's Ethnicity. Again, you can enter data of your own choosing as long as you set the Ethnicity field to Black this time.

Figure 24.10.

A new non-Black student.

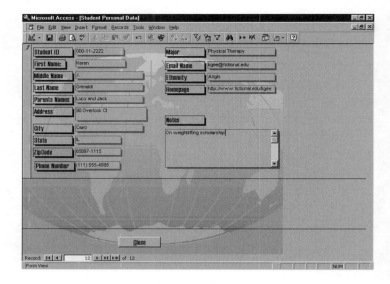

Figure 24.11.

Another record set to call the macro.

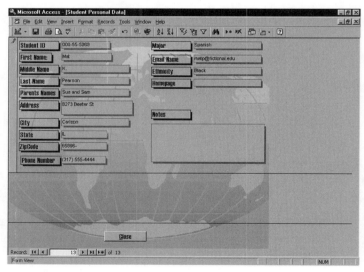

Press Enter or tab out of this field. Access looks at the entry, finds it's `Black`, and executes the macro, now that the condition's met. Your screen should look like Figure 24.12.

Figure 24.12.

The macro executing.

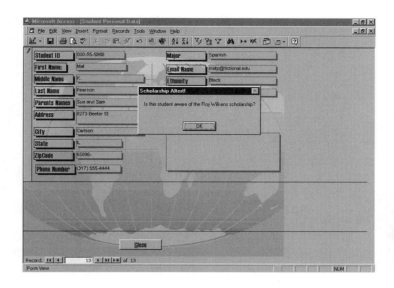

It works just as it should, so click OK to close the message box. Return to the Ethnicity field by clicking on it, and again tab out. The message box doesn't appear because the macro executes only when the field's been updated. That's the meaning of the After Update event property. Click the Close button to end the session with this form, and save the changes when prompted by Access.

The Access Way

This macro could have been successfully added to the On Exit property of this control. However, the fictional college wanted this macro to be executed only when a new student is registered. If the macro executed each time the field was exited, it would execute every time someone tabbed through this field. This macro will also "kick" when the Ethnicity field is edited or updated. Try that yourself. Enter the field, edit it by pressing the spacebar, then Delete to eliminate the added space, and exit the field. You'll see the message box again.

Macros That Alter Properties

A macro can have an action that alters control properties. The next two exercises show how this works. The form and the controls that have their properties altered aren't terribly useful, but the technique is. The reasons for the rather "hokey" example are simplicity and a desire to focus only on the issues, rather than on irrelevant details.

Exercise 24.3 creates a simple form with four controls. Two of the controls respond to events by altering the other two controls' properties with a macro. Each macro in this exercise is a multiline one and represents an increase in complexity in several areas.

Exercise 24.3. The form.

1. If you have any Access objects open, close them, saving the changes if you want. From the Database window, click on the Forms tab, then click the New button. Click on the Design View option without binding the form to any table or query and click OK. Increase the size of the form design grid to give yourself some working room. (See Figure 24.13.)

Figure 24.13.
An unbound form in Design View.

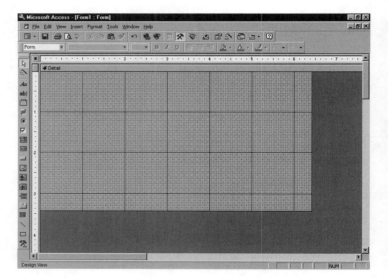

2. Place a Label control on the form with the caption I'm Green in 18-point font. Open the Formatting toolbar and select green as the background color of this label. Your screen should look like Figure 24.14.

3. Open the Properties list box, click on the Format tab, and set the Visible property to No. (See Figure 24.15.)

Figure 24.14.

The Green label control.

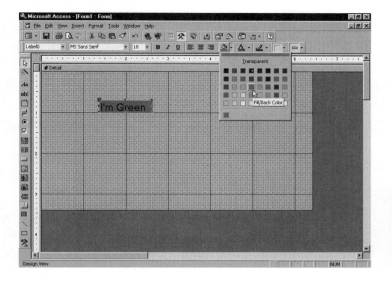

Figure 24.15.

Making the control invisible.

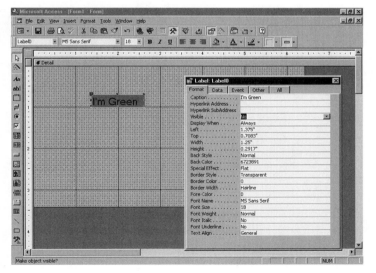

4. Create another Label control exactly the same size and location as the one in step 2. You can right-click on the existing label then choose Copy|Paste to duplicate this control. You'll need to move the two controls over each other if you use this technique. Give this label the caption I'm Red in 18-point font. Select red as the background color and set the Visible property to No. (See Figure 24.16.)

The Access Way

Another shortcut to step 4 is to choose Edit|Duplicate from the menu, then edit the caption and the background color of the new control.

Figure 24.16.

The Red label control.

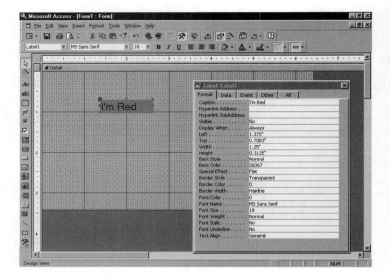

The Access Way

If you were making this form for your use, you'd probably also change the Name properties for this and other controls on this form to conform to a naming convention. This exercise skips these steps to remain focused on the goal: the macro that alters control properties.

5. Switch to Form View. Since both label controls have their Visible properties set to No, the screen looks blank, as shown in Figure 24.17.

6. Return to Design View and add two command buttons. Edit the caption of one to read Green and the other Red. (See Figure 24.18.)

Figure 24.17.

The running form with invisible controls.

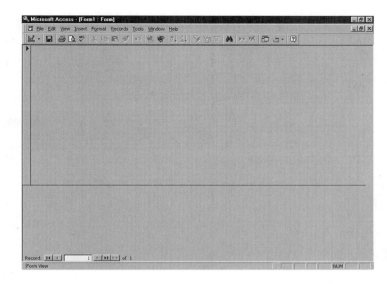

Figure 24.18.

Adding two command buttons to the form.

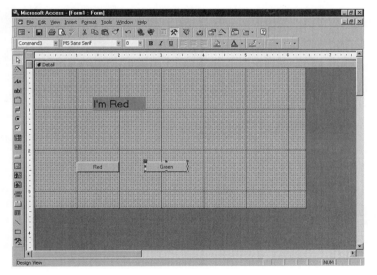

   7. Close this form, saving it as RedGreen.

Exercise 24.4 creates a macro that changes the control properties when called by the command buttons. It creates one macro that has two macro names. When called by its command button, this macro changes the labels' Visible properties.

Exercise 24.4. Control property macros.

1. From the Database window, click on the Macros tab, then click New to start a new macro. Open the Macro Names column. This macro doesn't evaluate conditions, so you can have that column open or shut. Choose File|Save As from the menu and name this macro macRedGreen. (See Figure 24.19.)

Figure 24.19.

Starting the RedGreen macro.

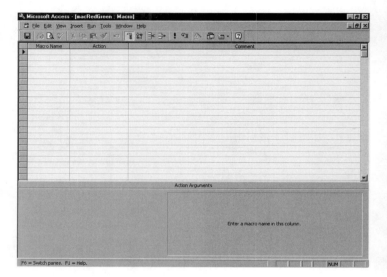

2. The first part of this macro makes the Red label visible. Enter the macro name ShowRed in the Macro Names column, then tab to the Action column and select SetValue as an action. Click in the Item line of the Action Arguments section to bring up the three-dot ellipsis (…) builder button. Click it to bring up the Expression Builder. (See Figure 24.20.)

   These macros do the same thing, but work in opposition. One positively sets the Green label's Visible property to No and the Red label's Visible property to Yes; the other sets the Red label's Visible property to No and the Green label's Visible property to Yes.

3. In the Expression Builder dialog box, double-click on Forms and All Forms, then click on RedGreen to tell the Expression Builder you're interested in this form. Locate the Label0 field in the second column and click on that. If you've renamed the Green label to something else, find that name and click on it. Next, click on the Visible property in column three, then click the Paste button to paste this argument into the Expression Builder. (See Figure 24.21.)

Figure 24.20.

Getting ready to use the Expression Builder.

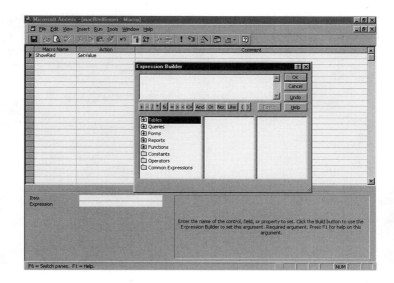

The Access Way

Access, in this context, might not construct the entire expression shown in Figure 24.21 when you click the Paste button. If it doesn't, edit the expression to be the same as the one shown in the figure. You can freely edit expressions pasted into the Expression Builder's text box.

4. Click OK to place your expression in the Item line of the Action Arguments. Because Label0 is the Green label, the ShowRed macro should have its Visible property set to No. Click on the second line of the Action Arguments section and set the expression to No.

5. Click in the second line of the Action column and again choose SetValue as an action. Click in the Item section and again bring up the Expression Builder. This time, choose Forms![RedGreen]![Label1].Visible by clicking those items as they appear in the columns, then paste them to the Expression Builder area. (See Figure 24.22.)

Figure 24.21.

Using the Expression Builder.

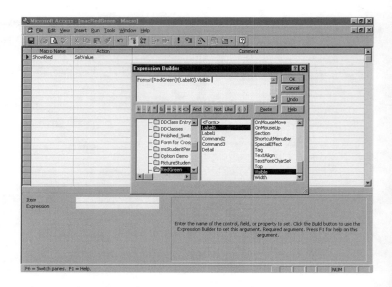

Figure 24.22.

Setting the second `SetValue` *argument.*

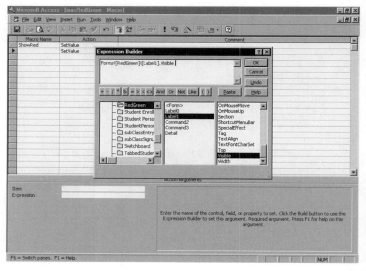

6. Click OK, then click on the Expression line of the Action Arguments section and enter Yes. (See Figure 24.23.)

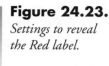

Figure 24.23.

Settings to reveal the Red label.

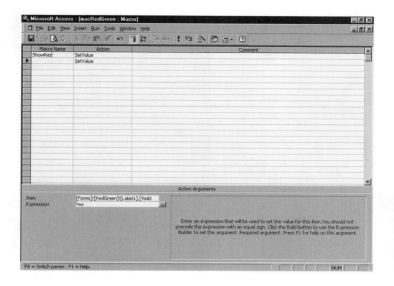

7. Create a new macro name, ShowGreen, on the next line of the Macro Names column. Enter two SetValue actions for this macro, too. This time set them to just the opposite of the ShowRed macro.

The Access Way

A shortcut to doing step 7 is to click in the Item line for the first SetValue, press Shift+F2 to enter Zoom, copy the expression to the Clipboard, close Zoom, click on the new SetValue, and paste the expression into the new Item line. Do this for both SetValues in the ShowGreen macro, then set the expressions for each SetValue to the opposite of those for ShowRed.

Have the Label0 Visible property set to Yes and the Label1 Visible property set to No. After you enter these two values, your screen should look like Figure 24.24.

8. Close this macro, saving the changes.

Figure 24.24.

Settings to reveal the Green label.

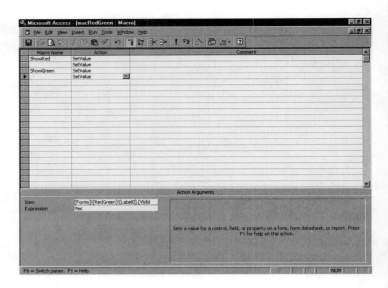

Placing the Macros on the Form

You now have a demonstration form and the macros that will, when called, change the label control's Visible property—or so you hope. Although this set of exercises focuses on the Visible property, you can change many other properties while a form is running.

Exercise 24.5 attaches the macros done in Exercise 24.4 to controls in the RedGreen form.

Exercise 24.5. Putting it all together.

1. From the Database window, click on the Forms tab and open the RedGreen form in Design View. (See Figure 24.25.)

2. Open the Properties list box, if necessary, and click the Event tab to display only the Event Properties. Click the Green button to highlight it. In the Properties list box, click on the combo box pull-down arrow for the On Click property to show a list of macros available in this database. Select the macRedGreen.ShowGreen macro. (See Figure 24.26.)

24

Figure 24.25.

The RedGreen form open in Design View.

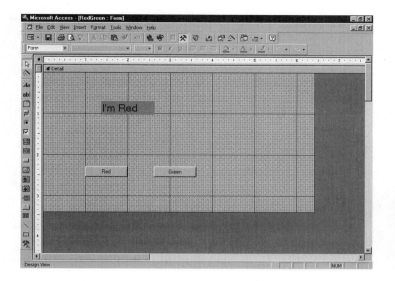

Figure 24.26.

Programming the Green button.

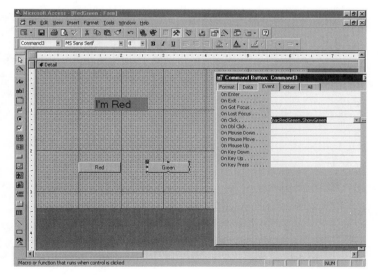

3. Similarly, click the Red button to highlight it and set its On Click property to
   `macRedGreen.ShowRed`. (See Figure 24.27.)

Figure 24.27.

Programming the Red button.

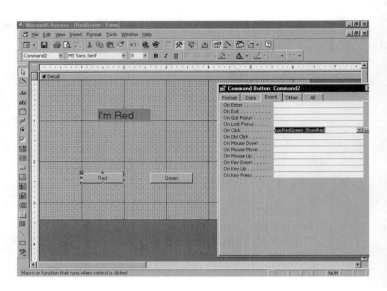

Switch to Form View. When launched, each label control has its Visible property set to No, so you see a screen like the one in Figure 24.28.

Figure 24.28.

The RedGreen form at launch time.

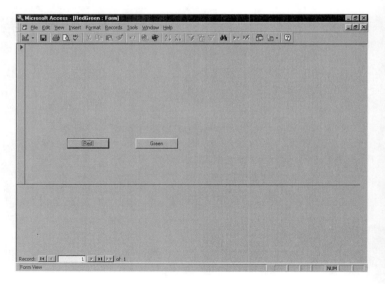

Click the Green button. This sets the I'm Red label's (Label1) Visible property to No and the I'm Green (Label0) to Yes. Setting a Visible property to No when it's already at No, as with the I'm Red label, has no effect, but it's important, as you'll see later. After clicking the Green button, your screen should look like Figure 24.29.

Figure 24.29.

The effect of clicking the Green button.

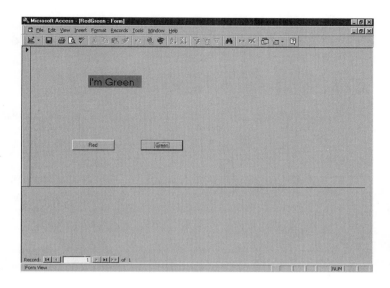

Click the Red button; your screen should look like Figure 24.30.

Figure 24.30.

The effect of clicking the Red button.

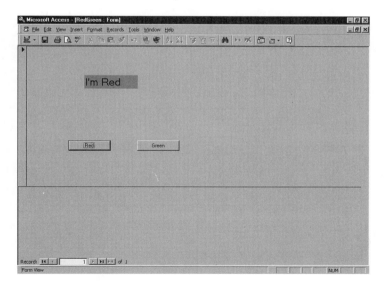

The Red button's ShowRed macro sets the Visible property for the Red label to Yes and the Visible property for the Green label to No. Try clicking each button. The colors and labels switch, just as you would expect them to. If the macros left out switching the "off" label's Visible property to No, both labels would be visible after clicking both buttons, and only the one to the front would actually show up in the form. Close this form, saving the changes. Both this form and the accompanying macro are part of the book's sample data.

Access Identifiers

The Expression Builder (or your edits) placed constructions such as the following in the macros:

```
[Forms]![RedGreen]![Label0].[Visible]
```

The exclamation points and periods are Access identifiers that help find the controls and properties you want to address. In the preceding expression, you're telling Access that the control you want to address is named Label0, it's located in (or on) an object called Red-Green, and that object is one of Access's forms.

You must be explicit when telling Access where to find the control you're interested in because controls can have the same names on different forms or reports; for that matter, forms and reports (for example) can have the same names. Therefore, the field Label0 might appear on two or more forms and two or more reports. Look at the following expressions:

```
Reports![CaseStudy]![Label0].Visible
Forms![CaseStudy]![Label0].Visible
```

Both expressions refer to discrete controls that have the same name and are on a same-named report and form. Access will have no trouble finding the correct control because you've told it to look for one Label0 in the reports and one in the forms.

> **The Access Way**
>
> Access uses the Me expression to refer to the current object. So the expression Me![MyControl].Visible refers to the Visible property of the control, MyControl, located on the currently active form, report, subform, or subreport.

Dots and Bangs

Generally speaking, the exclamation point is followed by a user-named Access object, and the period is followed by an Access-named object or property. For example, in the following expression, [RedGreen] and [Label0] are user-named objects (or can be), but [Visible] is Access-named:

```
[Forms]![RedGreen]![Label0].[Visible]
```

Also (generally speaking), you don't need to use full identifiers in macros. Access automatically looks on the current form or report for the named controls. This exercise forced the use of full identifiers to introduce you to them. When using Visual Basic, you must use fully qualified and syntactically correct identifiers, with the exception of the Me identifier discussed in the preceding sidebar.

Access is intentionally programmed not to need full identifiers in macros, so you can construct more macros for very generalized use. For example, the same macro works on [Label0]-named fields on both the report CaseStudy and the form CaseStudy when called from within those objects.

Day Summary

Access has three programming languages—Visual Basic, macros, and SQL. SQL is the basis of all Access queries, and you can use SQL statements for control sources in forms and reports. Macros are a simple point-and-shoot method to program Access, with the disadvantage of not having any error-trapping capacity. However, many of the macro actions are fairly simple and don't suffer too much from operating without an error trap. Even so, many professional Access developers prefer to avoid macros for Visual Basic whenever possible.

Macros can evaluate a situation, such as a text entry or numeric value, and take action accordingly. This afternoon's exercise evaluates a text box field when it's updated and responds with a message box if it finds the entry to be "Black".

Macros can also change control properties. This afternoon you saw how to create a macro that set two controls' properties from Visible = True to Visible = False when called.

You can combine the abilities of macros. For example, you could create a macro that evaluates a condition and alters properties, rather than one that flashes a message box.

Access uses the exclamation point and period as identifiers. Exclamation points precede user-defined objects, and periods precede Access-defined ones, generally speaking. Be sure to use square brackets in your identifying expressions to maintain consistency and to make sure that Access always knows what you're referring to.

Q&A

Q Why bother to learn and use SQL?

A If you'll be using Access only for querying Access tables, there isn't any reason. SQL is a common query language used by professional database managers to query many different databases, and many large system databases need SQL to extract information. Access can provide a convenient front-end for these database systems, but most Access users aren't even aware that Access includes an SQL capacity. You can greatly extend Access's flexibility by learning SQL, though.

Q Can I enter lines such as `Forms!RedGreen![FirstName].Visible` directly in the Item line in the macro design grid instead of using the Expression Builder?

A Yes. The reason to use the Expression Builder is to make sure you don't make an error by typo. It's easy to make one, like this:

```
Forms![RebGreen]![FirstName].Visible
```

If you entered that line, the macro would misfire. A typo like RebGreen for RedGreen is easy to make and difficult to spot.

Q Can I use the On Click property with controls other than command buttons?

A Yes. Any control having an On Click property can respond to mouse clicks like command buttons. Most people think of command buttons when they think of clicking, though.

Workshop

Here's where you can test and apply the lessons you learned today.

Quiz

Possible answers to these questions are given in Appendix A.

1. Look at the way Exercise 23.2 had you enter the Caption property for the cmdExit button—`E&xit`—in step 5. Now look at the way the button appears in Design or Form View. What do you suppose the ampersand (&) does?

2. If the View option for the Switchboard.OpenReportCards macro was changed to Print, what do you suppose would happen if you ran the macro?

3. What does the period do in a macro name?

4. The word *Not* works as a criterion in queries, but won't work in mathematical expressions. How can you specify a Not or Not Equal To operator in an Access expression? Hint: *Not* is the same as "not equal to."

Put Access into Action

1. Start a new macro and enter `Close` as a macro action.

2. Click in the Action Arguments section. Pull down the Object Type combo box and enter `Form` as an object type.

24

3. Click in the Object Name section and enter `TabbedStudentPersonal` as an object name. This form is part of the sample data.

4. Close the macro, saving it as `macTabbedStudentPersonal`.

5. Open the TabbedStudentPersonal form in Design View. Place a command button in the footer section toward the right side of the form. Name the button `cmdCloseForm` and give it the caption `&Close Form`.

6. Assign the macro macTabbedStudentPersonal to the On Click property for this button.

7. Choose File|Save to save your changes, then switch to Form View.

8. Click the new command button. Did it work as you anticipated?

9. Reopen the form in Form View and press Alt+C. What happened? Why do you suppose it happened?

The Access Way

If you'd like to see something interesting, try this. Create a simple macro with one action—close the TabbedStudentPersonal form if you don't have the macro already made. A macro, macDragMe, that does this is part of the sample data. Open the StudentPersonalData form in Design View. Maximize it so it takes up the entire screen area, then press F11 to open the Database window. Click on the Macros tab and find the macro you just made. Click on that name and drag it to the form's footer section. (See Figure 24.31.) Switch to Form View and try the new command button.

In some ways, Access makes things almost *too* easy. After all, database programming is supposed to be a challenge, right?

For the Adventurous

1. Open the macBeeper macro in Design View.

2. Click on the OpenForm line in the Action column.

3. Find the Where Action Argument. Modify this property to open the form only when the displayed record has "Tirilee" for a first name. If you're stuck, see Appendix A for the solution.

Figure 24.31.

Drag-and-drop programming.

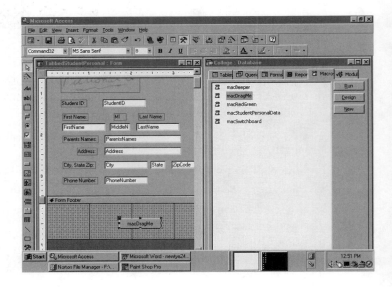

DAY
13

A.M.

25 Everything You Need to Know About Programming

P.M.

26 Programming Made Easy with Visual Basic

Chapter **25**

Everything You Need to Know About Programming

If you're thinking, "Everything…?" you've got good reason to be skeptical. This chapter has a rather grandiose title, one it probably can't live up to fully. However, consider this:

☐ Programming in Access is subject to the 80:20 rule: 80 percent of everything you need to do is contained in 20 percent of the scope of Access programming.

☐ The balance of programming knowledge in Access relates to advanced topics, such as manipulating or addressing Windows itself, multiuser applications, and manipulating the JET database engine directly. These topics, although important, interest only a limited number of professional developers. Several good books cover them, but this book doesn't try to.

Most of what people need to do when programming Access boils down to handling these few circumstances, which are covered in this morning's chapter:

☐ Springing into action upon an event

☐ Sensing a value and optionally manipulating it

☐ Error trapping

This chapter presents one example for each technique. In addition to these topics, there's the broad topic of OLE, or ActiveX controls, but it's large enough to warrant its own chapter: Chapter 27, "ActiveX: The Next Generation of OLE Controls."

Obviously, no example can come close to including every nuance that can crop up for each of these techniques, but you should be able to extrapolate from the specific examples here to the general case and then back to what applies to your specific needs.

Reacting to an Event

You saw how you can conditionally respond to an event in Chapter 24, "More Macro Magic," when you constructed a macro to open a message box reminding registration about the Roy Wilkens scholarship for African-American students. You can do the same thing using Visual Basic with greater clarity and an increased number of options.

Take a look at Figure 25.1. This is a form named frmCafeteriaBalance that's part of the sample data. At this point, it's still under construction.

Figure 25.1.

A form under construction.

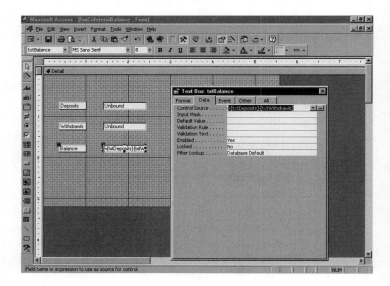

25

This is a simplified example with all the unnecessary elements stripped away for the sake of clarity. This form shows each student's cafeteria account balance. In a working example, you'd also have fields for (at least) the StudentID, name, and past balance. Also, a working example would pull the data from a query, but here you'll enter it in the two unbound text boxes, txtDeposits and txtWithdrawls. The example has been shortened so you can see clearly how things work; a "real" working example would have to be more complex, detracting from the focus of this example.

The purpose of this example is to alter the color characteristics of the text box showing the balance. The Balance text box changes color depending on the student's cafeteria balance.

The way to do this (well, one way) is to create a routine that, when certain events happen, examines the value of the control txtBalance and alters its colors accordingly. Figure 25.2 shows the code that does this.

Figure 25.2.

The code stripped of comments and error trapping.

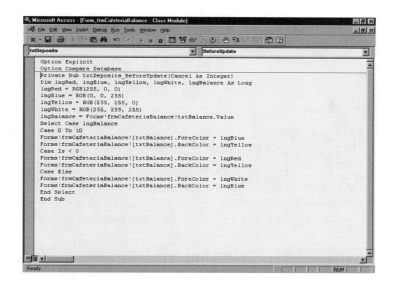

The Access Way

The code shown in Figure 25.2 has no error handling. Like other elements of this example, it has been left out intentionally for the sake of clarity. Since one of the benefits of using Visual Basic in Access is to trap errors, a real-world application written without at least a rudimentary trap isn't a good idea. Later in this chapter, you'll learn about errors and their traps.

Figure 25.3 is the same code as in Figure 25.2, but this time includes full remarks so you can follow the program's logic.

Figure 25.3.

The code with comments put back in.

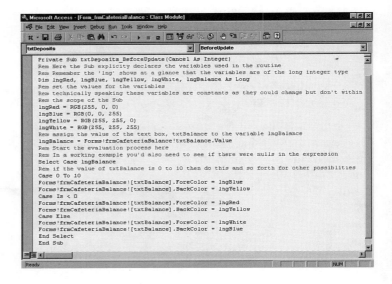

You can probably make better sense of the code shown in Figure 25.3 if you open the event procedure and examine it within Access because remarks (at least) are color-coded.

The code shown in Figures 25.3 "fires" when the form loads or when the AfterUpdate event triggers in either control, txtDeposits or txtWithdrawls. To see the code, open the form in Design View, open the Properties list box, click on the Event tab, then click on the [Event Handler] entry to bring up the three-dot button. Click that button and you'll be taken right to the code, as shown in Figure 25.3.

To try this for yourself, switch to Form View and enter differing amounts in either of the top two controls. After you press Enter or Tab to leave the control, Access examines the resulting sum in the txtBalance control and colors it according to the rules in the code. Try entering a negative number in both the top controls. What happens? Welcome to the world of a computer programmer, where you have to anticipate what your users will do.

Is That It?

The preceding example shows the essentials of responding to events and changing properties at runtime. Naturally, the scope of the events and properties you can respond to and alter are enormous, but these steps outline the generic solution to this problem:

25

1. Determine what you want to base your action on, such as the value of a control's contents.

2. Decide what event will trigger the examination—FormLoad, AfterUpdate, Change, something else?

4. Try to anticipate anything your users will do and make sure your routine will handle it.

3. If your actions are conditional, then tell Access what to do when it finds differing conditions (Select Case, If...Then...Else).

How Can I Learn All These Keywords?

In a way, you shouldn't. Once you have the generic solution down, you can always open up online help, look up the specific topic you're interested in (often with an example you can copy), and refresh your memory or learn something new. Figure 25.4 shows part of the online help when queried about the ForeColor keyword. The figure shows part of the sample Visual Basic code supplied with this topic.

Figure 25.4.

An entry from online help with sample code. Even if you have no idea how to set the ForeColor property for an Access object, you can learn it by reading the help text and example code. After you've absorbed the information, you can copy and paste the example code from the help system to your application.

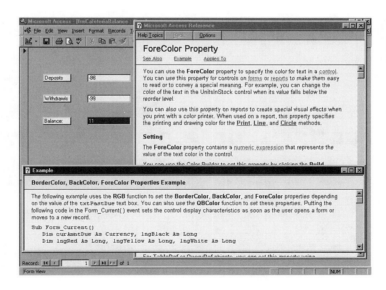

Are you surprised that the code fragment looks quite similar to the sample in the book? Well, you shouldn't be. The *lng* prefix for variables declared as Long Integer is widely accepted Access practice. As to the rest—well, there are only so many ways you can make ham and beans. If you open the online help to the place in Figure 25.4, you'll see the example uses If...Then...Else rather than Select Case. Either one works all right, but most people prefer If...Then...Else for short statements and Select Case for longer ones.

Don't knock yourself out trying to memorize all the properties for all the different controls. There's no need—that's what online help is for. Instead, focus on learning the generic solutions for each situation you'll run into, then use Access's help system to find the specific answers you need to write your code. Don't be shy about copying Microsoft's sample code and inserting your own control names and variables for Microsoft's. That's what the Edit|Replace entry in the code window is for. (See Figure 25.5.)

Figure 25.5.

Edit\Replace—a programmer's best friend after Copy/Paste.

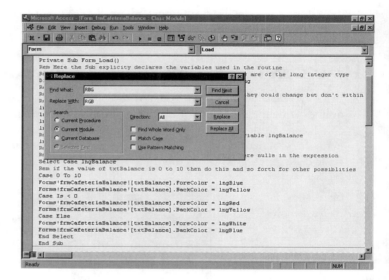

Functions, or General Procedures

The previous section dealt with Visual Basic procedures called *subs*. A *sub procedure* is called into action in response to some event. You use sub procedures when you want to do something, but they have certain limitations. First, you can't use a sub in an expression (actually, it'd make little sense), and a sub can't return a value. This section shows you how to create procedures called *functions* that can do both. If you're a bit hazy on subs and functions, that's all right; this section illustrates the differences.

Before you begin a more complex example, though, look at the basic steps for using a much simpler one that creates a general procedure, or function, that will accept data and return the thing you want. For example, if you wanted to create a function that would return the hypotenuse of any right triangle, you would follow these steps:

1. First, you need a formula—in this case, it's $a^2 + b^2 = c^2$.

2. Next, you have to determine what inputs you'll get. Assume you'll know *a* and *b*.

25

3. In a new or existing module, declare the function, telling Access what data type the inputs will be and what data type the function will return. Remember to use appropriate placeholders for each input. Here's one possible way to declare this function:

```
Function Hypotenuse(intSideOne as Integer, intSideTwo as Integer) as
Integer
```

4. Create the Visual Basic code from the equation or formula.

```
Hypotenuse = intSideOne ^2 + intSideTwo ^ 2
```

5. Now you just need to place the function in your application, specify where it'll get its inputs, and place its return.

That's it. Now for something a little more complicated.

The following example takes input (arguments) from three fields—Principal, Interest, and Years—and calculates the payment to amortize a loan having those factors. Most of the examples you see that accept arguments use only one argument. This is a more complex example, but it won't be too tough to follow. The payoff for not going for the simplest example is that after you catch on to what's to follow, you won't have any trouble creating either simple or complex functions of your own.

This example creates a function that will, when fed the user-supplied numbers, calculate the payment amount. As in the hypotenuse function, the first thing you need is a formula. Here it is:

$$\text{Payment} = \frac{(\text{Present Value})(\text{Rate})}{1 - \left[\frac{1}{(1 + \text{Rate})} \right]^{\text{Periods}}}$$

Now it's time to declare it to Access. Keep in mind that this function will take three arguments, each of which is of a different data type. Here are the three arguments with their data types:

Argument	Data Type
PresentValue	Currency
Interest	Double
Years	Integer

In addition, the overall function will return a value that has the data type of Currency. Keep in mind that these data types under discussion are the same as the data types you declared when you created tables.

This will be a function that can be called from anywhere in the application, so start a new module. To declare this function, first give it a name, then add in placeholders for each argument it will take along with their data types; finally, tell Access the overall data type this function will return. Complex? Look at Figure 25.6, which shows the start of this function-making process.

Figure 25.6.

Starting a function. The underscore (_) at the end of the third line is a line-continuation character that allows a long line to fit on one screen.

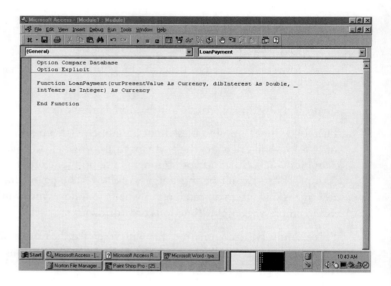

The argument placeholders are curPresentValue, dblInterest, and intYears for the current value of the loan, the interest rate, and the years of the loan, respectively. Note that the placeholders have data types of Currency, Double, and Integer, respectively, but the function LoanPayment has its own data type, Currency. What this means is that Access will treat the LoanPayment argument as a currency value, interest as a double-precision number, and length of the loan as an integer. The function itself will return a value of the Currency type.

If you are getting slightly boggled at this point, cheer up—this is the worst of it. The rest is much smoother sailing. Also, as you go through this example, these concepts will become clearer.

If you're following along, start a new module (click on the Modules tab, then New). Enter the following on the screen you see:

```
Function LoanPayment(curPresentValue As Currency, dblInterest As Double,
intYears As Integer) As Currency
```

Press Return. When you do so, Access will create a new function and your screen will look like Figure 25.7.

Figure 25.7.

The new function underway.

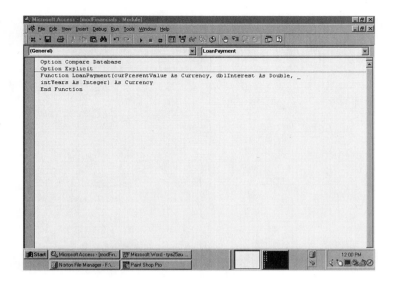

You probably can't see the entire function on one screen without the line-continuation character used in Figure 25.6. The line-continuation character in Visual Basic is a space followed by an underscore.

The next task is to duplicate the function of the payment equation in the function. First, you need to declare (type or Dim) two variables that will convert the years arguments to months and also change the yearly interest rate to a monthly one. This is because the output of the function should be the monthly payment, but both the term of loans and interest rates are traditionally given in years. Figure 25.8 shows the statement to type or Dim these variables.

Note that you can Dim variables on one line, but this example uses two for clarity and also because that's the way it's been done in previous examples.

Now you'll create the action that will do the yearly-to-monthly conversion. In the case of periods, you multiply by 12; for interest, you divide by 12. (See Figure 25.9.)

In other words, a mortgage with a yearly rate of 12 percent for 30 years will have a monthly rate of 1 percent and 360 payment periods.

There's nothing left but to re-create the equation with the existing variables. (See Figure 25.10.)

Figure 25.8.

The variables to convert yearly numbers to monthly.

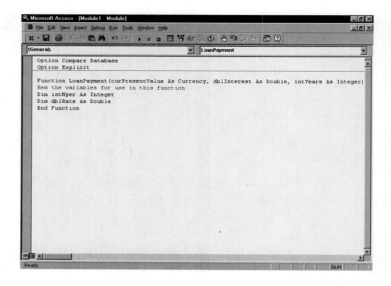

Figure 25.9.

Changing from yearly to monthly values in the function.

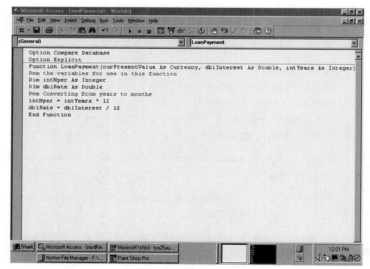

Figure 25.10.

The actual equation reproduced in Visual Basic.

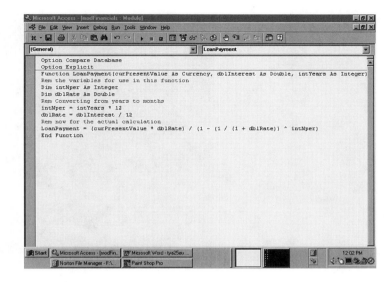

That's it for coding. If you've been following along and want to save this module, do so now, giving it an appropriate name. You'll find this function as part of the module modFinancials in the sample data.

The Access Way

As in previous examples, this function lacks error handling for the sake of clarity and simplicity. This isn't a good idea in your real-world applications, though.

Using the Function

Now that you have the function, it's time to see how to use it. This example uses a simple unbound form with fields for the three arguments—Principal, Interest, Term—and for the function's return, the payment.

If you're following along, create a new unbound form. To do this, click on the Forms tab, click the New button, then click OK with the Design View option selected and no query or table in the combo box. Add four unbound text box controls. Of course, you could use a form bound to a table or query rather than an unbound one.

Name the controls txtPrincipal, txtInterest, txtTerm, and txtPayment. If you want, change the control's labels to reflect these changes. Figure 25.11 shows the results of these steps.

25

Figure 25.11.

A form to show off the function.

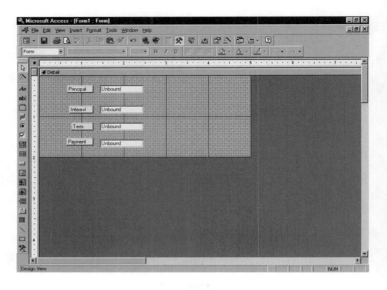

The point is to add numbers to the unbound text boxes for principal, interest, and term in years, and then see the payment show up in the final text box, txtPayment. To do this, add the following as the Control Source for the txtPayment unbound text box:

```
=LoanPayment([txtPrincipal],[txtInterest],[txtTerm])
```

This will take the values in the three text boxes and "feed" them to the function, LoanPayment. Your screen should look like Figure 25.12.

Figure 25.12.

Entering the function as a Control Source.

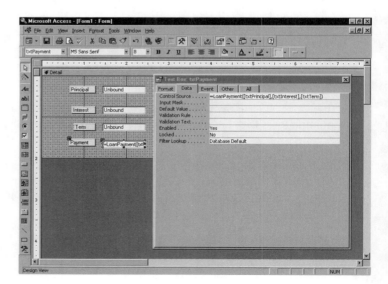

> **The Access Way**
>
> The placeholder names in this function—`curPresentValue`, `dblInterest`, and `intYears`—aren't the same as the text box names feeding into this function, `txtPrincipal`, `txtInterest`, and `txtTerm` from this form, but they don't have to be (obviously).
>
> The placeholder names in the function declaration are just that—placeholders—and nothing more. In this function, you must supply all three arguments—one for each placeholder. Access does, however, allow you to declare certain placeholders optional by prefixing them with the keyword `optional`. For more information on this, search online help.

There's nothing more to do, so switch to Form View. Initially, your Payment text box will be in an error condition because it's confused about being fed null information from the other text fields. Enter appropriate numbers for the principal, interest, and term of the loan. Figure 25.13 shows the form in action after clearing the error condition.

Figure 25.13.

The loan calculator in action.

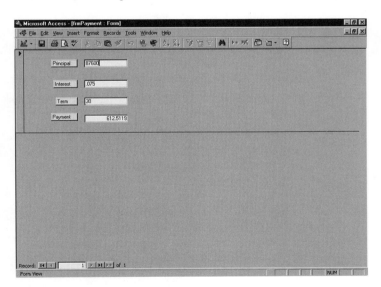

25

Be sure to enter the interest rate as a decimal when entering numbers for your payment calculator to grind away on.

The Access Way

This function is missing two important elements. The first is a checker to make sure all the "feeding" fields have data in them before the function tries to fire. This is as simple as adding an If...Then...Else statement to the function. If you prefer, you can do the same thing by creating default data for the form.

That's not all, though. If you're in an adventurous mood, enter a zero for the interest rate. Since the function uses this number as a divisor, Access will immediately enter an error condition, as shown in Figure 25.14.

Surely you don't want your users to see such messages, but think—it's conceivable that a user will enter a zero for interest rate, either in error or as an experiment. In this particular case, you can forestall having your users scared by error messages, such as the one in Figure 25.14, either by creating an error-trapping routine of your own or by entering >0 as a Validation Rule for this field, as shown in Figure 25.15. If you don't mind a little extra work and want your applications to run well, do both.

Figure 25.14.

A scary error condition.

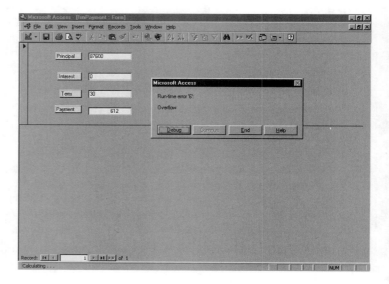

Figure 25.15.

One way to eliminate the error condition shown in Figure 25.14.

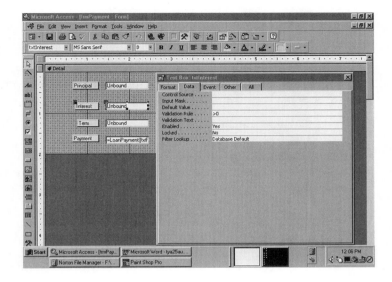

If you want to save your work, do so now. You'll find the form for doing payment calculations as part of the sample data as frmPayment.

Making a Function Summary

The section immediately preceding this one is the type many find difficult, as it requires a lot of code entry. Most people make seemingly insignificant typos when entering functions that prevent them from running. This is particularly distressing when starting out because you have no way of knowing if the function's failure is due to a typo or to your programming error. If you got through the section all right, you are unusual.

If you, like most, made some errors, got frustrated, or even resorted to dropping the whole thing and using the sample data, that's all right. This was a complex example to show differing data types at work together. Don't give up! To keep you going, here's some good news for you. Making your own functions is easier than following any book's because you're in charge of your own naming conventions and the direction of the programming.

Even if you didn't catch all the nuances of this example, but at least followed the general principles outlined in this section, you've gained quite a bit of insight into making your own custom functions, as well as passing arguments back and forth from your applications to modules. The ability to create functions such as LoanPayment() is what distinguishes an Access expert from an intermediate user. If you followed the previous example, you've crossed that line—congratulations!

25

Error Trapping

When distributing a program, expect the unexpected. Your users will constantly find interesting ways to bollix up your fine application—even ways you'd never anticipate. This is the reason software vendors like Microsoft engage in extensive beta or external testing. Even so, bugs slip by and into shipping products.

Take the last part of the LoanPayment() function as an example. If this were your application, you could have anticipated some error conditions, such as the new form popping up with blank fields, and performed an IsNull test for those fields. But what about those situations you don't anticipate? These are called *runtime errors* and you can address them even if you can't anticipate the specific errors that will occur.

Error trapping means anticipating that some errors, or a specific error, will occur and gracefully handling them (or it). The generic way to handle errors in Visual Basic is the following:

1. Give Access a hint as to what to do (or where to go to) when it stumbles on an error. Usually this means including an On Error statement in your function with a label to jump to.

2. Create a routine that comes alive when an error happens. This routine will probably differ, depending on the type of error. Some developers have generic error trap libraries for errors with things in common.

Looks simple, and, in concept, it is. The only complex part is creating custom routines for specific errors; then you must know the return codes for those specific errors.

Take a look at Figure 25.16. This is a sub procedure generated by a wizard with an error handle. This sub simply closes a form. You can see that in the third line: DoCmd Close. Here's the sub with added comments so you can follow the wizard's logic:

```
Sub cmdQuit_Click()
Rem Where to jump to when an error occurs. Err_cmdQuit_Click is a label
On Error GoTo Err_cmdQuit_Click

Rem if no error, do it
    DoCmd.Close

Rem jump to here after error message box or fall through to here if no error
Exit_cmdQuit_Click:
Rem exit the sub
    Exit Sub

Rem here is the label to jump to in the event of an error
```

```
Err_cmdQuit_Click:
    MsgBox Err.Description
    Resume Exit_cmdQuit_Click

End Sub
```

Now for specifics. Say you want to construct an error handler for the function created in the previous section. The first thing to do is add an `On Error` statement and a label to jump to in case an error happens. Here's one example of such a statement:

```
On Error Goto TroublesVille
```

Figure 25.16.

A generic error handler.

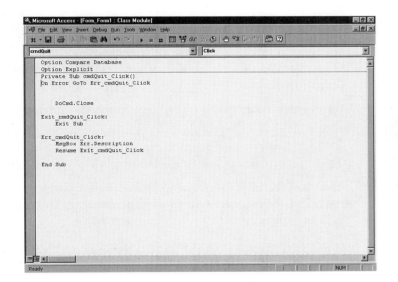

The next thing to is to construct the error handler. You could just create a generic handler for all circumstances as shown in Figure 25.16, or you can include some custom touches. Since you've seen that users entering zero for an interest rate is a possibility, handle that potential error specially. First add a label to jump to:

```
TroublesVille:
```

Remember to add a colon as a suffix on any identifier you want to make a label.

Now create the error handler itself. Look in Access's online help and you'll see the error number for Overflow is 6, and Divide by Zero is 11. Here's a simple `If...Then` statement to follow the label TroublesVille:

```
If Err.Number = 11 Or Err.Number = 6 Then
    Divide = Null
Else
    MsgBox "I've hit an unanticipated error"
End If
Resume Next
```

Access is internally aware of what error condition it finds itself facing. To take advantage of this, the `If...Then` statement asks whether the errors are either 6 or 11. If so, it nullifies the divide operation. However, other errors can happen; in those cases, the user will see a message box with the message "I've hit an unanticipated error." In all cases, Access will execute the `Resume Next` statement, which instructs it to move to the statement following the one that caused the problem.

There's only one thing left to do. If this code was to be entered into the `LoanPayment` function, you want to make sure it doesn't fire unless there's an error condition. If you placed the following code at the end of the function (really the only practical place), it'd execute every time, error or not:

```
LoanPayment = curPresentValue * dblRate / (1 - (1 / (1 + dblRate)) ^ intnper)
```

Effectively then, you'd be executing your error handler every time the function ran. This would cause great confusion to users and Access—the latter because Access would wonder why it found a `Resume Next` statement when there was no error.

Therefore, you need to exit gracefully after the last working line of your function to prevent the error handler from handling the vaporous error. Doing this is as simple as adding the following statement:

```
Exit Function
```

after this one:

```
LoanPayment = curPresentValue * dblRate / (1 - (1 / (1 + dblRate)) ^ intnper)
```

And that's about it.

Error-Trapping Summary

Like other topics in this chapter, this has been a quick dash through errors and their handling in Visual Basic. You now have the basics down, but there are many "devils" in the details. Keep in mind:

- ☐ If you're going to bother writing code (or generating it with a wizard) include error-trapping routines.
- ☐ You can create generic error trappers to paste into your functions and subs. You don't need to customize each one from the ground up.

☐ Include custom error-handling routines for specific errors you figure have a reasonable chance of happening.

☐ As with so much else in Access, don't bother to memorize the error numbers for each error. Instead, use online help and save your memory for remembering your wife's birthday, your anniversary, and so forth.

Morning Summary

Programming Access yields to the 80/20 rule which means that 80 percent of what you need to do resides within 20 percent of the total Access information store. Mostly what you will need to do using Visual Basic within your Access applications boils down to feeding information from your applications to Visual Basic for some manipulation.

This morning's example showed how you can define a small algebraic calculation (a function) in Visual Basic. Using an Access form you can enter several numbers then feed them in their proper place to that function and have Access return the results of the calculation on the form.

The trick to using Visual Basic from within Access is to keep it small and simple. Make your code as modular as possible. Be sure to test all parts of it using known data before trying to assemble all the parts into a huge whole. Keep in mind that one minute testing is worth 10 minutes debugging.

25

Chapter **26**

Programming Made Easy with Visual Basic

This lesson covers the following topics:

- [ ] When to use Visual Basic
- [ ] Making a custom function
- [ ] Variables, loops, and other programming concepts
- [ ] Identifiers
- [ ] Message boxes
- [ ] Input boxes

Visual Basic (technically, Visual Basic for Applications, or VBA) is the fully functional programming language for the Access database program. Using it is more difficult than using Access itself or the macro extensions of Access. Microsoft has made it a design goal that using Access shouldn't require programming in Basic for most database chores. However, some tasks simply require its use.

Programming in Basic

This chapter is heavy on discussion and is tough going in spots because it covers a lot of theory in a short amount of time. Chapter 25, "Everything You Need to Know About Programming," expands on this theory with some concrete examples. If you find yourself a bit overwhelmed here, don't despair—it might be because you skipped over Chapter 25 or need some time for the information to sink in. These aren't easy topics, so give yourself plenty of time with them.

When To Use Visual Basic

You use Visual Basic when nothing else will do the job. Here are some examples of those situations:

- ☐ You need to create a custom function that's not possible (or practical) through an expression.

- ☐ You need to get complex input from your user. Macros and parameter queries allow simple data input, but these tools are limited to a single-input data line with an OK and Cancel button. You need Visual Basic for a more complex input.

- ☐ You need to perform a conditional loop. Macros cannot, for example, use loops like the WHILE...WEND loop. WHILE...WEND means WHILE (a certain condition exists perform a certain task and) WEND (end when the condition fails to exist or ends).

- ☐ You need to trap errors; if an error occurs when the macro is running, the results can be unpredictable. Writing Visual Basic code (VBA) makes it possible to determine what to do when an unexpected error occurs; those who use your applications will appreciate this.

- ☐ You need to use Dynamic Data Exchange (DDE), allowing data to be exchanged on-the-fly with other Windows-based applications. This means a second application can process your data in real-time.

- ☐ You need to invoke Windows API (Application Programming Interface). The Windows API is a library of functions used to interact with the Windows environment. This extends the already powerful Access environment.

26

Custom Functions

You've seen several built-in Access functions such as Now() and Sum() in previous chapters. As you design your forms, you might find yourself repeatedly typing in a long, calculated expression. Rather than continue to do this, you could create a custom function that does the same thing. In a module, you'd type something like this:

```
Function Repeat(AnyField)
Repeat = That long expression
End Function
```

In this case, the name of the function is Repeat. It will apply to some field represented by AnyField, and the entry That long expression is the long expression you're converting to a custom function.

This is similar to elementary algebra. One of the first things you learn with algebra is to use letter symbols to replace certain numeric quantities. For example, you might read the following in algebra:

```
Let A = 2+3+4+5
```

If you then saw the following expression, you'd understand that the quantity B is equal to 17:

```
B = A + 3
```

In the preceding code example, you take the long expression and assign it to the function Repeat.

Complex Input

Macros have to work with what they find already entered into Access. You can't poke new information into them when they run. In some cases, you might want to have your user enter information during a database operation or put it into jargon at runtime. You've seen how queries can act on user-entered parameters, but by using Visual Basic, you can go further. You can develop a program that asks users for information, then executes an action based on what they enter.

Conditional Loops

A conditional loop executes, or fails to execute, a particular action until some other condition exists. Using macro conditions you can, in some cases, test to see whether a certain thing is true and act accordingly. That's a *static test*—it checks once to see whether something's true and moves on. Say you want to get a user input, test to see whether it's between 1 and 35, and then take different actions depending on whether the input's from 1 to 10, 11 to 21, 22 to 30, or 31 to 35. Doing this in Visual Basic is quite easy.

26

You might force macros to test these conditions, but the process is rather laborious. However, you can't use a macro to get a runtime user input to test.

The Event-Driven Model

In the past, database programming languages—for example, one that comes with the MS-DOS dBASE family of products, such as dBASE III—executed procedurally, from top to bottom. Visual Basic, on the other hand, is event-driven, meaning it responds to events usually caused by users. The examples used in this lesson respond to the event of a pushed button. They could just as easily respond to form events such as On Exit, On Enter, On Open, and so forth.

What's the Difference?

Programs using traditional procedural programming languages like Pascal or dBASE III execute outside the user's control. Once started, a procedural program just goes, following its own programmed path unless a hard interrupt ends its run, stopping only occasionally to either display a message or get some user-supplied information. The program and programmer are in control.

Windows programs, however, are all independent processes that can be started and stopped by the user at just about any point. As event-driven programs, they respond to the user's needs or actions. Actions such as clicking the mouse, moving a cursor into a field, pressing a button on a form, loading a form, and exiting a field are all events that can trigger any action you care to program into the event.

You've Already Done One

In Chapter 24, "More Macro Magic," you created a routine that responded to a control's contents. The macro then either posted a message box or didn't. Note that there would never have been a message box if the event of exiting an updated control had happened.

26

Identifiers

Visual Basic uses the same identifier syntax that Access macros do. The following line of code checks to see whether the contents of the control `Test Field`, embedded in the form `Test Form`, equal less than the value of `10`:

```
If Forms![Test Form]![Test Field] < 10 Then...
```

If so, Visual Basic executes the line following the word `Then`.

Annotating Code

Unless you create the simplest functions and subroutines, you should annotate your code with remarks. Remarks or annotations don't execute with your code; instead, they enable you or others to know what a particular segment of code is supposed to do. Remarks are a nuisance when you create code, but they're invaluable when you need to come back to the code weeks or months later to do some maintenance or alter the code to serve a slightly different purpose. Remarks also help others to follow your coding logic.

Do	Don't

DO use comments well. If you program Access for others, you have an ethical responsibility to use remarks extensively in your Visual Basic and macro code. Not doing so might make the code you write inaccessible, and your customer might need to modify or rewrite what you've created. Failing to add remarks to your code, thus making it difficult or impossible for someone else to modify, is similar to a car dealer putting a combination lock on a car's hood so that only dealership personnel can perform maintenance on the engine.

DON'T fall into the trap of not adding remarks while writing the code with the excuse that you'll come back to it later. That time rarely comes, and if it does, you might have forgotten what remarks need to be made.

26

You insert remarks (usually called comments) into your code by starting them with either the keyword `REM` or a single quotation mark. Look at the following code fragments:

```
Rem This example demonstrates remarks in Visual Basic
If Sales > Expenses THEN '> symbol means greater than
```

The first line uses the `REM` statement to tell Access, "Don't execute anything on this line." Similarly, line two uses the single quote (`'`) after the statement. The single quote mark says "Don't execute anything on this line after the quote mark."

A Question of Style

Its critics say Basic is a difficult-to-maintain programming language, but the problem is caused more by the way people use it than by anything inherent in the language itself. Three traps people fall into are cramming too many instructions on one line, not adding remarks, and using nondescriptive labels. Each trap makes the code much more difficult to understand than if separate instructions were each given on separate lines, the code had remarks added liberally, and variables had descriptive labels. Basic doesn't care if each instruction gets its own line, if remarks exist, or if variables have long names. Code Example One and Code Example Two execute identically:

Code Example One

```
Dim A As Integer:Dim B(0 To 50):GoSub X1
```

Code Example Two

```
Dim DepartmentNumber As Integer 'Department Number is a whole number or integer
REM Each Department has no more than 50 people.
Dim NumberOfEmployees(0 To 50)
GoSub Initialize 'Go to initialization routines
```

In Code Example One, the programmer crams all the code on one line and fails to either add remarks to the code or use descriptive labels. Code Example Two uses separate lines, descriptive labels, and plenty of remarks. Which one do you think will be clearer if this programmer or another one needs to return in three months to modify this code snippet?

The Access Way

Don't worry if you can't follow these code snippets. They're here only to illustrate principles. Actual instructions for using Visual Basic's vocabulary follow this conceptual introduction. In the preceding case, the `Dim` code word is a holdover from early Basic days. It's short for "dimension" and was first used to tell the computer how much storage space to reserve for a particular array. *Array* is computer talk for a matrix, so the following line means "computer, reserve enough space for 51 entries in a matrix under the name `NumberOfEmployees`":

```
Dim NumberOfEmployees(0 To 50)
```

Visual Basic uses the `Dim` statement for more than arrays. It also tells Access the type of variable; this line, for example, tells Access that `DepartmentNumber` will be a whole number or an integer:

```
Dim DepartmentNumber As Integer
```
If you're new to computer programming, you might have some trouble understanding some of these concepts. Just plow on until you start working the examples
later on, then many of these abstractions will come into focus.

Functions, Declarations, and Subs

Visual Basic is composed of three building blocks: function procedures, declarations, and sub
procedures.

The declarations section of a Visual Basic module globally defines constants, variables, and
data types for later use in subs and functions. A global declaration is valid for the entire scope
of the Visual Basic module but not valid across different modules. Visual Basic, like many
Basics, allows implicit declarations. This is terrible programming practice and is the prime
reason Basic has a bad reputation among professional programmers. You can force Visual
Basic to error on implicit declarations by adding the following line in the module's
declarations section:

```
Option Explicit
```

The Access Way

Access 97, by default, declares the `Option Explicit` argument as part of the general
declarations for a new module.

26

The Access Way

A module is a collection of at least one Visual Basic function, declaration, or sub
(although a declaration without a sub or function doesn't make much sense).
Modules appear in the Database window, but when calling functions or subs, you
use the function or sub name, not the name of the module.

What's This Implicit/Explicit Business All About?

Unless you're an experienced programmer, the preceding section might seem a little difficult to follow, so this section offers some explanation. When writing programming code, you assign names to variables and constants.

Variables are values that can change during the code's execution; *constants* are values that can't change during code execution. A constant could be the value of an interest rate, declared as

```
Const conInterestRate = .08750
```

in the declarations section. Then the following code line would multiply the value .0875 with the variable varMyInterest:

```
varMyInterest = 100 * InterestRate
```

Variables change depending on program code or user input. In the preceding example, you don't ask your user for a value of varInterestRate—you declare it. In the example used in the following section, varGotUserNumber is a variable because its value depends on user input.

Danger in Variable Land

Take a look at the way the following code snippet works. Access displays a message box with the title "Implicit Variable Demo." It then sets zero as the value for the variable varDefvalue, takes input from the user, and triples it in the last line. If you have some difficulty following the logic of this code snippet, look up INPUTBOX in the online help system. However, this code will not run correctly because of a typo:

```
Prompt = "Enter the number you want to triple" 'sets msg
Mtitle = "Implicit Variable Demo" ' Title of msgbox.
varDefvalue = 0 ' set a default value to zero
varGotUserNumber = InputBox(Prompt, MTitle, varDefvalue)
REM Get a number using an input box.
varGotUserNnmber = varGotUserNumber * 3 'What's wrong here?
```

If you're a careful reader, you might have spotted the error. The intent of this code is to triple a number specified by a user. The number entered by the user is given the variable label varGotUserNumber by the program in line four. The last line is supposed to change the variable to three times the user-entered amount, but it doesn't. In other words, the intent of this code is for the variable varGotUserNumber to be equal to three times the value entered by the user.

There's a minor typo that throws a giant-sized monkey wrench in this code. The programmer mistyped the variable name varGotUserNumber as varGotUserNnmber in the last line. This means that the variable varGotUserNumber will contain the original amount given by the user, and a new variable, varGotUserNnmber, implicitly declared, will contain the triple value of varGotUserNumber.

26

NOTE

> This lesson uses a lot of jargon specific to computer programming. Terms like declarations, variables, constants, code, function, array, and subs are familiar if you've programmed a computer before, but might be vague concepts at this point if you haven't. Rather than worry about memorizing the exact definitions now, continue along and, with use, these terms will become clear. If you forget a definition now, look it up in the glossary or use Access's online help.

If the programmer later uses the value of varGotUserNumber in a calculation, the calculation will come out wrong. Can you imagine the gravity of this error if this final calculation is critical?

Had the programmer used the Option Explicit instruction in the declarations section of this module and then declared GotUserNumber as a type of variable, Visual Basic would have complained when it hit the GotUserNnmber word because that variable hadn't been declared previously by using a Dim statement.

Function Procedures

Procedures create functions for use in Access tables, forms, queries, reports, and macros. Other Access objects, such as forms, can call these functions, once they're made. Here's a section of an Access function to determine the commission amount:

```
Function WhatRate(SalesValue)
If SalesValue > 10000 THEN
WhatRate = .05
Else
WhatRate = .025
End If
```

Note the variables SalesValue and CommissionRate were declared appropriately in the declarations section of the module holding this function; however, the entire declarations section isn't shown here so you can focus only on the subject.

Sub Procedures

Sub procedures are identical to function procedures except they can be called only by other subs or functions and can't return a value to the caller. In the preceding example, the value CommissionRate is returned by the procedure, and the function itself is called by a form event. Subs are used for housekeeping chores within modules. Most of the time, you'll be using function procedures rather than subs.

26

Use subs for altering values already contained in calling functions or implicit within Access itself. Access uses subs as event procedures when you've used a wizard to create a control.

A Simple First Code Example

The first code exercise is simplicity itself, but it demonstrates basic programming concepts and how to tie a Visual Basic function to a form object.

Exercise 26.1. Tie a Visual Basic function to a form control.

This exercise links a new function to a form control.

1. Launch Access. Open the College database, if necessary. Click the Modules tab, then click New. Access moves you to a screen like the one in Figure 26.1.

Figure 26.1.

Starting a new Visual Basic module in Access.

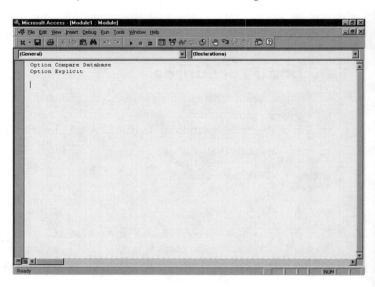

Before moving on, take a look at the space just below the toolbar. There are two combo boxes; the one on the left lists Objects and the one on the right lists Procedures. The righthand combo box has (Declarations) showing, which means you're in the declarations section of this yet-to-be-named module. When you pull down the combo box, you'll see that the only entry is (Declarations) because you've yet to add a function or sub to this module. Later on, when you have several functions or subs in a module, these combo boxes will help you navigate between them.

26

> **The Access Way**
>
> Access modules can contain many functions or subs, just as macros can; for example, one macro at the database level might contain many named macros. If you have a series of related procedures, contain them within a module rather than have a new module for each procedure. This makes them easier to get to. Also, related procedures might have code in common. Having them in the same place will make copying and pasting easier.

Back to the screen. Run your cursor over the buttons on the toolbar to familiarize yourself with each one's function. Don't worry if many of them seem unfamiliar; also, you'll notice that some are inactive at this point.

> **The Access Way**
>
> The `Option Compare Database` declaration is an Access-exclusive part of the Visual Basic for Applications language. This declaration tells Visual Basic to use string compares according to the order of database. The default for compares in Visual Basic is Text, which is a case-sensitive compare. This may or may not match the rest of the database containing the module, so Microsoft gave Access the exclusive database option for string comparisions.

2. Position the cursor back to where it was in the module (right under the `Option Explicit` declaration) by clicking at the cursor's original place. Next, without moving the cursor, enter the following:

```
Function DisplayMessage()
```

When you press the Enter key, Access scans the line, realizes you're trying to define a new function with the name `DisplayMessage`, and moves you to a function design area. (See Figure 26.2.)

3. Note that the righthand combo box now contains your new function. Pull down the combo box to see the two entries that have been added: (Declarations) and `DisplayMessage`. Click (Declarations), and Access moves you back up to the declarations section of the module. Pull down the combo box again and click `DisplayMessage`. Access takes you back to the function design area. This is how you navigate in a module.

26

Figure 26.2.

Starting a new function is as easy as typing it into a module.

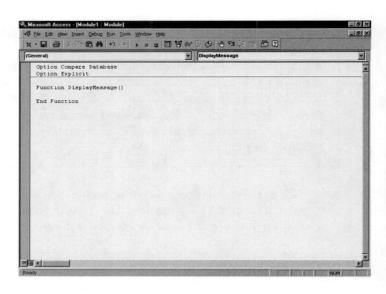

4. This function simply displays the message I'm a computer programmer at a button press. Add the following line right below the Function DisplayMessage() line:

```
MsgBox "I'm a computer programmer"
```

Your screen should now look like Figure 26.3.

Figure 26.3.

Entering the executing code within a function.

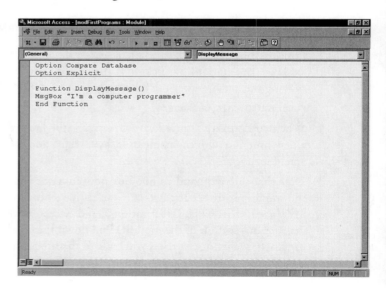

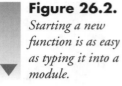

5. Choose File|Close from the menu. When Access asks whether you want to save the changes to the module, click Yes and save it under the name modFirstPrograms. That's the name of the module in the sample data. This example used a function that is overkill as it returned nothing. A sub procedure would have served equally well.

A Place to Show Off

You need a place to demonstrate the new function. Exercise 26.2 puts it into use and also shows you how to vary it.

Exercise 26.2. Using the function.

1. Click the Forms tab in the Database window and choose New. Don't bind the form to any table or query, and choose Design View rather than a wizard. Make sure that the toolbox is showing, but that the wizard isn't selected. Click the Command Button tool and draw a command button in the detail section of the form. (See Figure 26.4.)

Figure 26.4.

A place to attach a function.

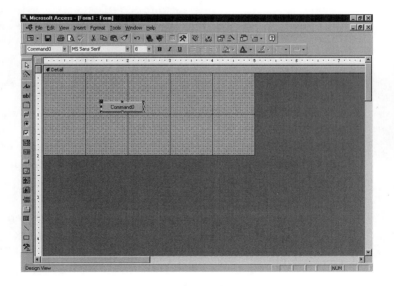

2. Open the Properties list box and find the On Click property. Enter =DisplayMessage() on the line next to On Click. (See Figure 26.5.)

The Access Way

If you were assigning a macro called DisplayMessage to the On Click property of this command button, you'd enter `DisplayMessage` at the On Click property line. Because `DisplayMessage` is a function written in Visual Basic, you have to indicate this to Access. The syntax of starting the property with an = and ending with a () tells Access to look for `DisplayMessage` as a function in a Visual Basic module.

Figure 26.5.

Entering the new function.

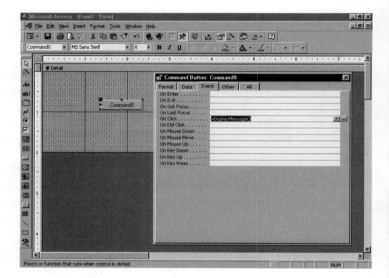

3. Switch to Form View and click the command button. When you do, the form should bring up the message box shown in Figure 26.6.

4. Now to modify the function. Click OK to close the message box. Close the form, saving it as `TempForm`. Return to the module by clicking the Module tab in the Database window. Highlight the modFirstPrograms module (if necessary) and click the Design button. Pull down the Procedure combo box and select the `DisplayMessage` function or just click in it—it should be visible on your screen. Modify the second line to match the following:

```
MsgBox "I'm a computer programmer", 65, "Progress in Access"
```

Your screen should now look like Figure 26.7.

26

Figure 26.6.

The running function as it responds to the On Click event of the command button.

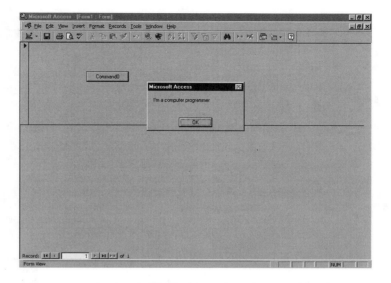

Figure 26.7.

The modified code that will change the message box.

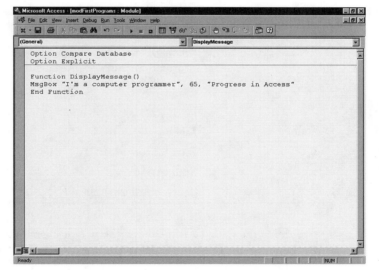

A message box takes three parameters separated by commas: the message, the display type, and the title. The parameter 65 added to the line in the second place tells Access to alter the message box to one having an Information Message icon and two buttons: OK and Cancel. Message boxes in Access have three numerically set properties: button count/type, icon type, and default button. Table 26.1 gives these values.

Table 26.1. Message box properties.

Button Type/Number	
Value	**Meaning**
0	Display OK button
1	Display OK and Cancel buttons
2	Display Abort, Retry, and Ignore buttons
3	Display Yes, No, and Cancel buttons
4	Display Yes and No buttons
5	Display Retry and Cancel buttons

Icon	
Value	**Meaning**
0	No icon
16	Critical message icon
32	Warning (query) icon
48	Warning (message) icon
64	Information icon

Default	
Value	**Default Button**
0	First button
256	Second button
512	Third button

Adding the value 65 as the message box type changes the message box to one having the properties of 64 + 1. Refer to the preceding table; you'll see that 64 gives you the Information icon and 1 gives you two buttons, OK and Cancel. Adding the string "Progress in Access" as the final property changes the message box's title to one saying Progress in Access.

5. Close and save this module. Open the TempForm in Form View and click its single button. Your three-parameter message box is done. (See Figure 26.8.)

26

Figure 26.8.
The modified message box in operation on a form.

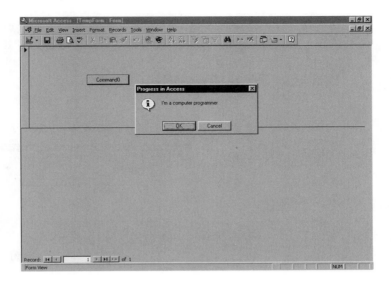

Congratulate yourself—you've just entered the ranks of Visual Basic programmers! Click OK or Cancel and close this form. The finished form is part of your sample data under the TempForm name.

Passing Variable Parameters

Remember, one of the reasons you might need to code in Visual Basic is to get more user input than just a parameter query. The following exercise adapts the message box from Exercise 26.2 to accept user-defined criteria for use in a message box display.

The chief tool for getting user input in Visual Basic is the Inputbox function, which is similar to the Messagebox function, but with three significant differences:

☐ You need to choose the right Inputbox function, depending on whether you want a variant or a string returned.

☐ An Inputbox passes its contents to a variable.

☐ You can place an Inputbox anywhere on the screen.

Defining a Global Type

The section "Functions, Declarations, and Subs" in this chapter mentions declaring variables. The message box example used no variables, so no declarations were needed. An input box requires an implicit or explicit variable declaration because Visual Basic uses it to capture user input and move it to the message box.

26

Because you'll be using only one variable in Exercise 26.3, it's slight overkill to explicitly declare just one variable; however, it's never too early to learn good programming practice.

Exercise 26.3. Declaring variables.

1. From the Database window, click on the Modules tab, then the modFirstPrograms module, and finally the Design button. (See Figure 26.9.)

Figure 26.9.
Getting ready to make some declarations.

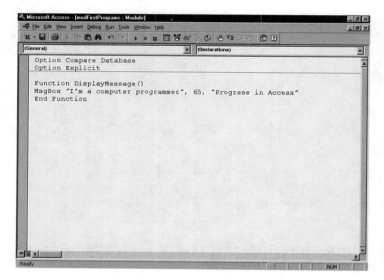

2. Click the Procedures View button at the lower-left corner of the status bar. This lets you add new lines to the General part of the declarations section. Enter `Option Explicit` on the first empty line, if it's not there already, and `Dim Response As String` on the last line of the declarations section.

The Access Way

The line `Dim Response As String` can, and usually does, appear in a function or sub rather than in the general declarations section. The example declared it in general just to show it can be done.

Remember `Option Explicit` forces you to declare variables before using them. The line `Dim Response As String` declares there will be a variable with the name `Response` and it will be a string. See Table 26.2 for some other types of Visual Basic variables.

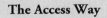

The Access Way

You can have two basic views of the module window, depending on how you like to work. Choose between the two views by clicking the buttons Procedure View or Full Module View in the status bar. The screens in this exercise switch between these views to clarify the process of making the module.

Table 26.2. Visual Basic variable types.

Type	Meaning
String	Alphanumeric and nonprinting characters. Strings represent literally. The string 1234 represents the literal figures 1, 2, 3, and 4. The numeric 1234 represents the value 1,234 in the decimal system.
Long	Whole numbers from –2,147,483,648 to 2,147,483,647.
Integer	Whole numbers from –32,678 to 32,676.
Single	Single-precision floating-point data type. Uses less storage space than Double.
Currency	A high-precision data type optimized for monetary transactions. Use this data type for critical calculations, such as accrued interest.
Double	A general-purpose high-precision floating point.
User Defined	One you dream up.
Variant	The default Access data type used for undeclared data types.

The Access Way

Of course, there are other types of Access objects. The subject's very wide in scope, but much of the discussion's an advanced topic not relevant to an intermediate-level book such as *Teach Yourself Access 97 in 14 Days*. Search online help for complete coverage of this topic.

3. Pull down the Procedure combo box and click DisplayMessage to move to the procedure. If you're in Full Module View, you can just click on the function. Enter

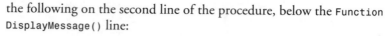

the following on the second line of the procedure, below the `Function DisplayMessage()` line:

```
Response = InputBox$("Enter a Message", "Input Box Demo", "I choose noth-
ing")
```

Next, modify the third line like this:

```
MsgBox Response, 65, "Progress in Access"
```

Your screen should now look like Figure 26.10.

Figure 26.10.

Input box code added to the function.

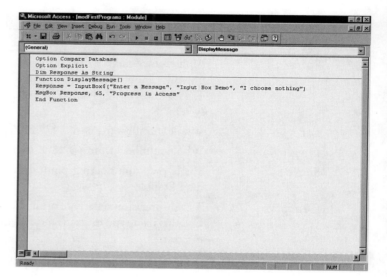

4. Close the module, saving the changes.

Open the TempForm form in Run mode, if it's not there already, and click the command button. Access displays the input box shown in Figure 26.11.

5. Enter anything that comes to mind on the input line; the example uses `Programming is Easy After All!` Click OK. Access runs the message box with your line included. (See Figure 26.12.)

Figure 26.11.

The input box springing into action at the click of a command button.

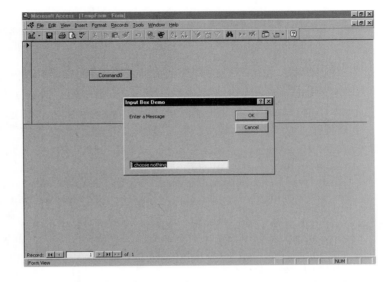

Figure 26.12.

The message box with the input box's contents.

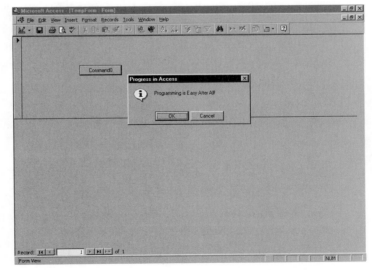

How It Worked

Examine the second line of code in the DisplayMessage() function:

```
Response = InputBox$("Enter a Message", "Input Box Demo", "I choose nothing")
```

The first word is Response, which is the variable you declared as a string type in this module's declarations section. This part of the line tells Access where to store what you enter in the input box. In this case, Access stores the string in a variable called Response.

The rest of the line just defines the input box. The first part, InputBox$, tells Access to use an input box. The $ part of the InputBox$ statement tells Access the input box will return a string type variable. Had this read InputBox, Access would have expected a variant type of variable. Using InputBox$ is another example of good programming practice, rather than dire necessity.

The next part, "Enter a Message", is the prompt for the input box. "Input Box Demo" is the title of the input box, and "I choose nothing" is the default value for the input box. If you didn't enter a string in the input box but just clicked OK, Access would have displayed I choose nothing in the message box. Click Cancel to close the input box.

Additionally, the InputBox$ parameters could have included x and y positions for the input box; these placement parameters are numbers representing how far in twips the coordinate position of the input box should be from the upper-left corner of the Access screen.

The Access Way

A *twip* is a real unit of measure in the computer world; it equals 1/1440 of an inch. There are about 575 twips in a centimeter. Another interesting unit of measure in the computer world is a *Mickey*, which measures mouse actions.

Close the form, saving any changes you've made. Return to the module, making it active, and close it, saving the changes.

Day Summary

When the Customize dialog box is visible you can add, move, or delete buttons from any toolbar. Also, by using the customize process, you can create custom buttons, change the look of new or built-in buttons, and change the balloon help attached to your own buttons.

Access has been carefully designed so that no programming is necessary in most cases. However, it also includes both macros and Visual Basic. Most people find programming

Access macros much easier than using Visual Basic because Access steps you through the macro process, but there are times you'll need to use Access's supplied Basic programming language.

Visual Basic as a language has been criticized by professional programmers as a sloppy language. However, that's an unfair characterization. It has great flexibility that permits possible sloppiness that would be impossible with more structured languages like Pascal. By using good programming practices, you can create good Visual Basic code that's easily maintained as well as you can with any other language.

An important thing to remember when programming in Visual Basic is to use the `Option Explicit` statement in the declarations section of a module. This forces you to declare variables before using them. Using `Option Explicit` prevents you from inadvertently implicitly declaring variables by making the inevitable typo. One of the options in Access is to make `Option Explicit` the default for modules. Figure 26.13 shows the option in the Modules tab of the Options dialog box.

Figure 26.13.

The check box to make `Option Explicit` *the default.*

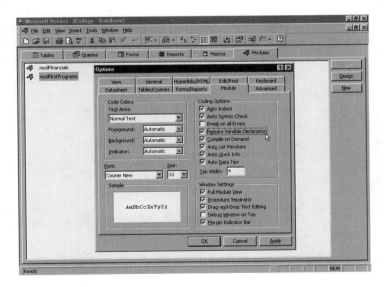

Another thing to remember is to annotate your code with remarks. You define a remark by starting a Basic statement with the `REM` keyword or the single quote. The examples in this lesson were too simple to require remarks, but if your procedures or declarations grow to more than 10 lines or so, or if you feel your programming logic isn't obvious, make sure to use a liberal number of remarks.

These examples created a new function, `DisplayMessage()`, for use anywhere in the College database. It's a simple function, but it also demonstrates the fundamentals of Visual Basic programming.

Q&A

Q Can I use a function I created in Visual Basic in a macro?

A Yes. Use the `RunCode` macro action and specify the function you want to run, along with any parameters the function needs.

Q I've heard Basic is a bad language to use because it's so full of `GoTo` branches. How true is this? Should I avoid `GoTos` when I program?

A This is a preposterous charge against Basic. Sure, some people misuse `GoTo` statements to create spaghetti-like code that's quite difficult to follow, much less maintain, but all programming languages need to have some branching. It's not the use of branching routines, but the misuse of them that's the problem. There are just as many bad practices committed when using other languages, such as FORTRAN or C, as there are in Basic.

It's true that Basic is a bit freer, though, and will let you go much further astray than "tight" languages, such as Pascal or Modula. As with any kind of freedom, the freedom Basic allows you must be practiced with responsibility.

As soon as you start doing high-power Visual Basic programming, you'll need some branching, and there's no reason to avoid the `GoTo` statements. The first thing to keep in mind when creating these structures is to annotate in a remark where the jump goes, why it jumps, and where it will jump back to. The second thing is to clearly label where you're jumping to. This statement, for example, isn't terribly clear:

```
Goto A
```

This one, however, is much better:

```
Goto DoSortRoutine
```

The third thing to remember is to avoid jumping to another jump. The following is just about impossible to understand after it's written:

```
Goto Animate
...
Animate:
Goto SectionEight
....
SectionEight:
Goto DoItNow
DoItNow:
```

The fourth rule is to jump to labels, which are descriptive words followed by a colon, rather than line numbers. Jumping to line numbers is a practice particularly fraught with danger.

Finally, use `GoTos` only when you can't use more structured statements, like these:

```
If...Then...Else; For...Next; Select Case; Do...Loop
```

Q **Is there some way to use Visual Basic to put pictures on command buttons?**

A You can do this, but you don't need Visual Basic. With the button highlighted in Design View, open the Properties list box for the tool and find the Picture property. Just enter the full path for the bitmap you want to include on the button on this line. For example, if you wanted to place the picture `c:\windows\skylight.bmp` in the button shown in TempForm, enter `c:\windows\skylight.bmp` on the line to the right of the property Picture. Make sure to include the entire path for your bitmapped picture when trying this trick. You also can click the ellipsis button and browse for the picture.

Q **What's the button limit for a toolbar?**

A You can place as many buttons as you have room for. Don't overdo it, though, because too many buttons make it difficult to find any.

Workshop

Here's where you can test and apply the lessons you learned today.

Quiz

Possible answers to these questions are given in Appendix A.

1. Say you have the following statement in the declarations section of an Visual Basic module:

   `Dim I as String`

   You also have this statement in a procedure:

   `Dim Interest As Double`

   Will `Interest` be a string or a double-precision floating-point type when used in the procedure?

2. If you want to execute a loop 10 times, should you use a macro or a module?

3. Would you use Visual Basic to create a custom menu on a form?

4. When would you use the Currency data type in Visual Basic? What's the disadvantage of using this data type?

5. How do you create a remark in Visual Basic code?

26

Put Access into Action

1. Start a new module.

2. Declare two string and one integer data types. The two strings will be a title and a message in a message box; the integer will be the message box type.

3. Create a new function, Chapter26(), with three input box lines to give the user an opportunity to enter a message box title, message box message, and message box type.

4. Add a message box function to the user-defined function that will display a message box, using the criteria from the input boxes.

5. Add placement parameters for each of the input boxes. Search online help for the exact syntax to do this. Close the module, saving it as ProgrammingExercise.

6. Open TempForm in Design View.

7. Attach your custom function to the On Click property of the command button.

8. Test the function by switching to Form View and clicking the button.

9. Close the form and module. You can discard the changes, if you like; neither the module nor the function is part of the sample data.

DAY 14

A.M.

27 ActiveX: The Next Generation of OLE Controls

P.M.

28 Access and the World Wide Web

Chapter **27**

ActiveX: The Next Generation of OLE Controls

This morning's lesson covers the following topics:

- [ ] What are ActiveX and OLE?
- [ ] Registering ActiveX controls
- [ ] Using OLE to link other office applications
- [ ] Using ActiveX controls
- [ ] Using older controls and performance considerations

Using OLE Controls

The two easiest ways to program Access both avoid programming. No, that statement is neither an oxymoron nor a paradox. It's the plain truth. You've seen one way to program Access without programming by using wizards. The trend in all programming from Access to C++ is to have wizards or prebuilt objects remove the laborious and repetitive grunt work from coding. Many professional programmers protest that they use neither, but don't believe them. Even if that's true, why should you bother reinventing everything?

Access 2 was the first commercial application able to use the new OLE custom controls. They were a new specification that, from a user standpoint, were a superset over the original VBX standards.

A Computer Legend

The VBX control (now evolved to the ActiveX control specification), which lets a user add functions to a program with little or no programming, arrived with Visual Basic—the program. VBX is what made Visual Basic the success it has become. Other similar programs, such as those from Borland, preceded or came at the same time as Visual Basic, but they lacked VBXs. The VBX specification launched a huge industry and assured Visual Basic's market leadership where it remains today.

Legend has it that the programmers at Microsoft didn't intend to include VBX support in Visual Basic, but that it was included at the insistence of Bill Gates himself.

ActiveX and the older OLE controls are known collectively as OCXs—from their traditional file extension. After the release of Access 2, Microsoft widened the specification for OCXs, which made Access 2 somewhat out of date in this area. Access 97 goes far in playing catch-up. Today Microsoft has renamed controls with the OCX extension from OLE controls to ActiveX.

The change of label reflects an expansion of purpose. Once OLE controls were only 32-bit extensions of the older VBX controls, aimed at programming ease and the eventual emergence of an object-oriented operating system. The idea of the latter is component-based applications that you can buy OLE or OCX controls for to extend the basic core functioning of your programs. Today, with the expansion of the Internet, Microsoft has extended OLE controls to include the capability to plug these controls into Internet objects—usually Web pages.

Registering ActiveX Controls

Before you use ActiveX controls in Access or any other application, you need to register them in your Windows registry. You can do this several ways:

1. Use a custom REG script.
2. Run the vendor's setup program, which not only copies the OCX (ActiveX) control to your system, but also registers it ready for use.
3. Manually register the control by editing the registry.
4. Manually register the control by telling Access to do the work.

Of these, only options 2 and 4 are realistic from a standpoint of spending your time profitably. Figure 27.1 shows a complex REG script. Writing this or manually editing the registry to include these values is obviously a tedious task you want to avoid.

Figure 27.1.

A complex REG file, a script for updating or adding to a Windows registry.

Any ActiveX controls you buy should come with a setup program. At the very least, there should be a REG file already created. If you see the former, just run the setup program and it will register the controls for you. If you have the latter, just double-click on the REG file from Explorer and let Windows do all the work for you.

From time to time, Windows might lose its registry entries for an ActiveX control. This will surely happen if you reinstall Windows clean or if you make an error editing the registry. In these cases, you'll have to re-register your ActiveX controls to get them to work again. You can do this by running setup for the controls, double-clicking on the REG files for the controls if they exist, or using Access's built-in registration routine.

27

To see Access's routine, choose Tools|ActiveX Controls from the menu. Your screen should look like Figure 27.2. Click on the control you want to register, then click the Register... button.

Figure 27.2.

Asking Access to register your ActiveX controls.

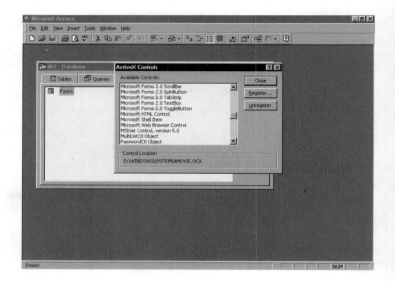

Using OLE to Link or Embed Office Documents

You can combine different Microsoft Office applications in many ways. How you choose to do so depends on the results you need and the method you prefer. Chapter 28, "Access and the World Wide Web," covers how to publish some Access objects to HTML documents. Such documents can be opened in Microsoft Office applications or by using a Web browser, such as Internet Explorer.

Take a look at Figures 27.3 through 27.7. They show a sequence in which a document in Word 97 gets converted to a scrap on the desktop and subsequently to an embedded object on an Access form. The captions explain the sequence.

Figure 27.3.

To create a scrap, highlight a file or part of a file, then drag it to the desktop.

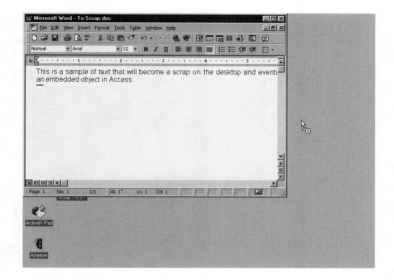

Figure 27.4.

Windows converts the dragged file or part of the file to a scrap and labels it as such on the desktop.

27

Figure 27.5.

Dragging the scrap from the desktop to the Access form embeds it there.

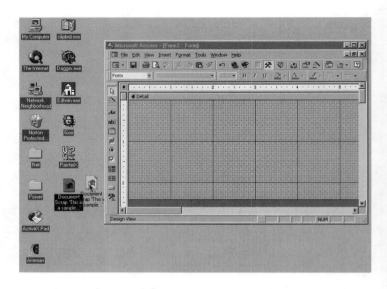

Figure 27.6.

Dropping the scrap on the form places it there.

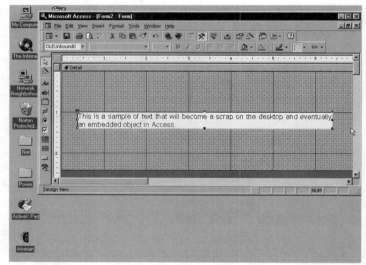

Figure 27.7.

The finished embedding in Form View shows what a scrap or any other embedded object looks like in a running form.

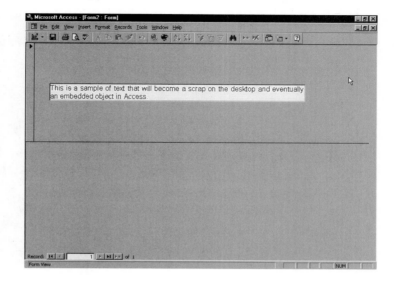

The finished embedded object shown in Figure 27.7 can be edited in Word by double-clicking on the object in Design View.

Office 97 actually makes the entire process easier than even the preceding sequence. There's a standard menu entry for using other Office applications from within Access.

Say you want to do some numeric analysis on a table or query in Access that's beyond the functions built into Access. Any business chore you need to do is probably within Excel 97's capabilities, so wouldn't it be nice to be able to call on that when you need to? As you're probably guessing, you can.

Figure 27.8 is the table PressureData from the sample data. It was the one used to demonstrate top queries. To use Excel's analytic tools, follow Figures 27.8 through 27.10. The captions explain the sequence.

27

Figure 27.8.

A table with much numeric data can present analysis difficulties for Access's built-in functions.

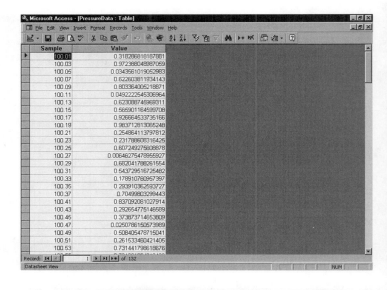

Figure 27.9.

The Tools\Office Links menu selection brings up a set of choices, depending on which Office components you have installed.

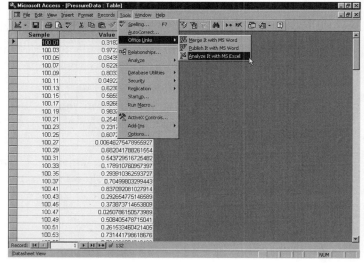

Figure 27.10.

Clicking on the Excel choice launches Excel and creates a worksheet with the table or query's name; it also creates the file on disk.

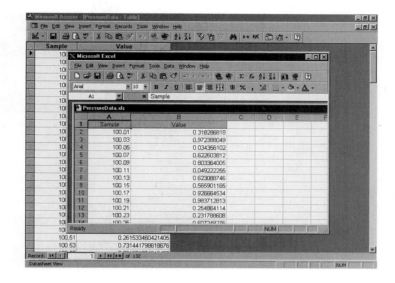

Duplicating a table or query into Excel, then, is as simple as making a menu choice. In a similar way, Excel lacks Access's management tools, so it can use Access's facilities with similar menu choices. For example, the Data menu in Excel 97 has the View MS Access Form entry that lets you use a previously created Access form to enter data into Excel.

Live Links

You can also link a live Excel workbook (or any other OLE-enabled application) into an Access object. Figures 27.11 through 27.14 show one of several sequences to create a live OLE link to another application—again, Excel 97. This example could have used any fully OLE-enabled application, however.

27

Figure 27.11.

Add a Bound Object Frame object to a form for a place to insert the OLE object.

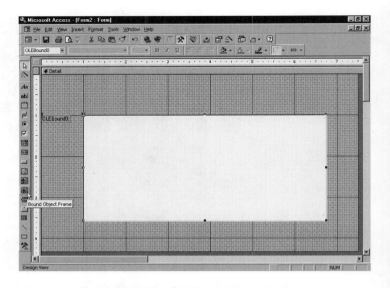

Figure 27.12.

Switch to Form View and choose Insert\Object from the menu.

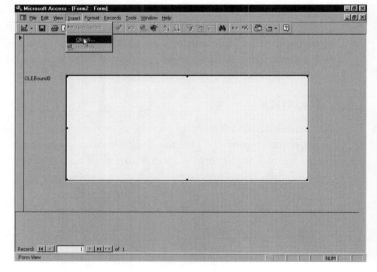

27

Figure 27.13.

This brings up a dialog box where you can choose which type of OLE object (from all those registered) to insert and determine whether it exists on file or you want to create a new one. This demonstration uses an Excel Worksheet and the New option.

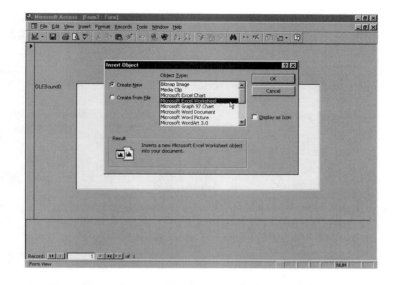

Figure 27.14.

Clicking OK returns to Form View with the new worksheet as part of the form.

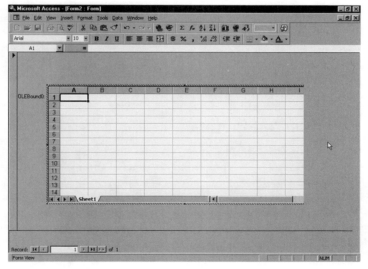

27

You can use this worksheet in a form, just as you would any other worksheet. When this new control has the focus, your menu and toolbars change to reflect that you're working within Excel. Contrast Figure 27.15 with 27.14. Figure 27.15 has a new control inserted in the form to show how the menu and toolbars differ depending on which control, the Access native one or the one linked to Excel, has the focus.

Figure 27.15.

The menu bars and toolbars of the host application will change when activating an OLE link.

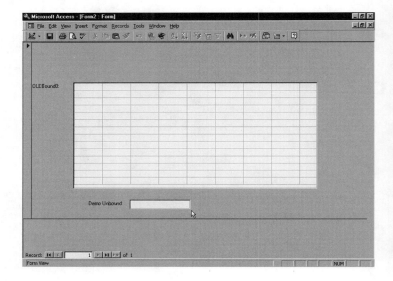

There's Much More

The few examples in this chapter just barely scratch the surface of how you can use OLE to create compound documents within Microsoft Office or with any other OLE-enabled application. Lack of space prevents even a basic discussion of the different combinations and permutations available to you, the Office user.

That's all this chapter has room for when it comes to linking to other Office applications and creating compound documents. Most of the essentials can be discovered by looking at the toolbars in Microsoft Office 97 applications, exploring the menus, or, if you get in desperate straits, checking the online help.

27

Using ActiveX Controls

ActiveX controls or OCXs are special DLL applications you can include in your Access applications. Take a look at Figure 27.16. How long do you think it took the programmer to include the calendar as part of the form?

Figure 27.16.

Including a calendar in a form by using an ActiveX control.

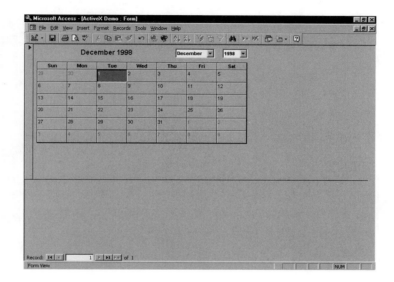

The answer, if you haven't guessed it, is about 10 seconds. What you see in Figure 27.16 is an ActiveX control from Microsoft called the Calendar Control 8, part of Access 97. If you don't have this control in your ActiveX list, run Setup again to choose Add-Remove Components. Select the Calendar Control check box and let Setup do the rest.

Not only does this custom control display a calendar, but form fields (controls) can respond to the dates on the control. You can, for example, set dates on your form by clicking on calendar dates. Obviously, trying to do this by programming Access manually would be a chore.

All ActiveX controls have properties, methods, and events, just like any other control. Naturally, they vary depending on the control's purpose. Because of the specialized nature of ActiveX controls, you'll often find properties very different from those you'd expect to see applying to the standard controls in the Access toolbox.

Figure 27.17 shows the addition of two command buttons that scroll through the months on the form shown in Figure 27.16. Figure 27.18 shows the Visual Basic code behind the On Click event for the Next Month> command button.

27

Figure 27.17.
Adding command buttons that let users scroll through the months.

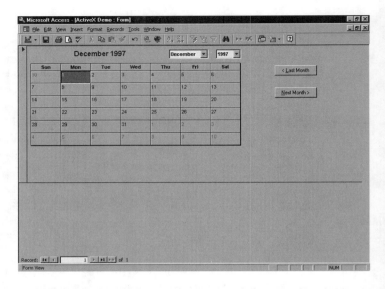

Figure 27.18.
One line of code is all it takes to control the calendar in the form.

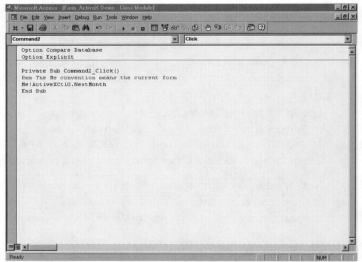

To learn about the methods, events, and properties of ActiveX controls, open their help files.

No Help Here

Each ActiveX control comes with its own help file. Access itself has no specific information on the methods, properties, or events for a particular ActiveX control. Even though Access uses illustrations of its Calendar control for its generic discussion of ActiveX controls, you won't find specific tips for the control in the general help file. Seek help either from the vendor's manuals or from the supplied online help file. In the case of the Calendar control, the control's name is MSCAL.OCX and the help file is MSCAL.HLP. Double-clicking on the help file from Explorer brings up the help file.

ActiveX Properties

Using custom controls is similar to using the controls that come with Access (such as text boxes). You add the controls, set properties either in Design View or during runtime (or both), and optionally program them to handle events.

Many custom controls have extra property sheets that add to their flexibility and complexity. Figure 27.19 shows the standard Properties list box for the Calendar control, and Figure 27.20 shows the special properties dialog box for this control. Note the similarity of the entries. If you have the Calendar control installed on a form, you can see the dialog box in Figure 27.20 by right-clicking on the control in Design View, then choosing Calendar Object|Properties from the menu.

Figure 27.19.

The standard Properties list box for the Calendar control.

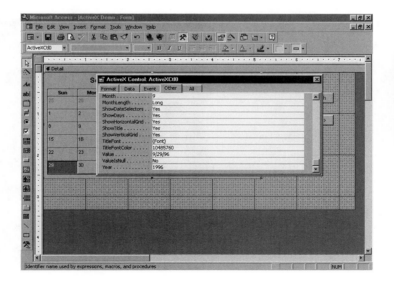

Figure 27.20.

The custom properties dialog box from the right-click menu of the control itself.

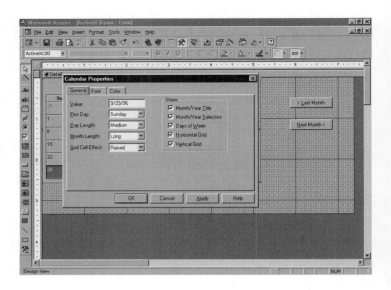

Changing properties in either property box will affect both. You can change these properties, such as the date displayed, by using Visual Basic or, in some cases, macros.

Using the Calendar control is so much easier than figuring out dates by yourself. Figure 27.21 shows an unbound text box, called txtEnterDate, added to the form used for these examples. Enter any date in this box, and the Calendar control will switch to this date. Figure 27.21 has the date 12/1/2018 entered and the calendar has obligingly switched to this date. Figure 27.22 shows the code that makes this magic act possible.

Figure 27.21.

Add a text box to a form and you can program the calendar to move to any date entered in this box.

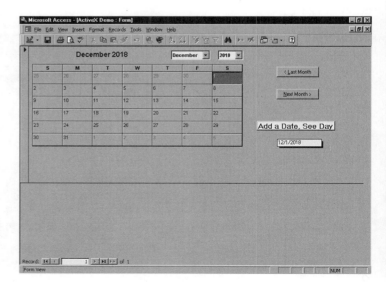

Figure 27.22.

The code that will examine the date in a text box and update the calendar control to that date.

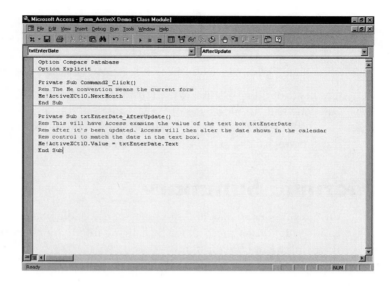

That's it! Programming and manipulating custom controls like the ActiveX Calendar control is that easy.

Older Controls and Performance Considerations

For the past several years, the specification for custom controls has been a moving target. Microsoft itself hasn't fully standardized a universal container for its applications. Vendors have, therefore, had to choose between universality of use and feature sets when making their controls. Often, in the past, they've settled on features, which has left many controls useless or only partly useful under Access.

There are two ways you can determine whether a control works under Access:

- [ ] Ask the vendor and hope for an honest reply
- [ ] Test them yourself

The good news is that most controls made to the OCX or ActiveX specification work at least partly in Access. The part that works is usually the most important, and the part that doesn't usually won't adversely affect the whole. More good news is that the controls that work worse are generally those related to data control, which is inherent in Access so it's redundant in any potential control. Most of the new controls you'll want to use work fine.

27

There's a down side to including ActiveX controls in your applications. They slow down your application and increase its overhead. The amount of parasitic drag from an ActiveX control is greater than if you hand-coded stuff like the calendar form in Visual Basic, but the trade-off is slight performance degradation for greater ease in programming.

The key to deciding whether to use a custom control is your target market. If you have a strong base, one with 16 megabytes of RAM assured in the typical machine, it's safe to use these controls. If your target market is slight, watch out. You might push the performance mark down past what's tolerable—only you can decide.

Morning Summary

OLE is an industry standard for linking or embedding objects in documents. It also acts as an interapplication protocol for exchanging information, expanding what the older DDE (Dynamic Data Exchange) did.

Windows NT, 95, and 97 are OLE-enabled operating systems, and Office 97 is an OLE-enabled suite of applications, so all work together well. Using Office 97 under any appropriate operating system enables you to easily share and exchange information between applications. You can also create compound documents, in which more than one application created objects in the final document.

ActiveX controls are an extension of the OLE custom control specification that was, in turn, an extension of the VBX control type. Using ActiveX controls in Access can extend the usefulness of your applications with very little or no programming effort.

Chapter 28

Access and the World Wide Web

This afternoon, you'll learn about the following:

☐ How the World Wide Web works

☐ Converting a table/query to an HTML document

☐ Static and dynamic Web objects

☐ Publishing a form/report to an HTML document for Web viewing

☐ Hyperlinks to other Microsoft Office documents plus other non-Microsoft applications if they're so enabled.

☐ Hyperlinks to Web documents in forms/reports

How the World Wide Web Works

The World Wide Web (or just Web) is a part of the Internet. It was initially a way to publish and view hypertext documents online. Online viewing has two main benefits: First, you don't need to use up your own disk space for these files, and second, the hyperlinks to other documents let you jump to those documents while you're online. In essence, the Web is a huge library of hypertext documents.

You've seen Access's online help system; documents on the Web operate similarly. You can jump from document to document by hyperlink (embedded link to an external reference), and the documents contain illustrations or graphics.

It wasn't long before the Web grew to include multimedia objects as well as hypertext. Although the early pioneers of the Web probably take a jaundiced view of the animation, sounds, and even real-time audio now available on the Web, there's no doubt that these new developments have caught the public's imagination.

With the spread of the Web over the Internet, corporations discovered that this technology could be used for their internal needs. What followed was the growth of *intranets*, which is the Internet Web technology (for the most part) behind a firewall or security screen. Unlike the Internet, which is mostly public, intranets are for internal use by those authorized by the corporation or other publishing entity.

Besides the hypertext and multimedia extensions to the Web, the basic service extends to other Internet services, such as FTP, WAIS, Gopher, Usenet, and so on. These extensions to the Web are well beyond the scope of this short chapter, but there are many fine books available that do go into this topic in detail.

How Do I Get There?

The fundamental protocol of the Web is HTTP—Hypertext Transfer Protocol. To view and interact with Web documents, you need three things:

1. An Internet connection capable of HTTP support.
2. A way for your computer to connect with the Internet. This is generally a Winsock (or TCP/IP layer)for your network. Windows 95/97, NT, and later have a Microsoft-supplied ability to connect to the Internet through either a LAN or dial-up (modem) connection.
3. A browser that can interpret HTTP. There are many browsers on the market, but the two dominant ones are Netscape Navigator and Microsoft Internet Explorer. The latter is a Microsoft product and the browser shown for the screens in this chapter.

The basic language of the Web is HTML—Hypertext Markup Language. HTML is a subset of SGML, or Standard General Markup Language. HTML *does not* describe page layout. What it does is supply formatting information and let the browser handle the actual layout because the makers of Web documents (that will be you soon) have no idea what system or browsers will be used to view their Web documents. Figure 28.1 shows an HTML page viewed through a browser.

Figure 28.1.

A Web page belonging to an obscure software company, shown through the Internet.

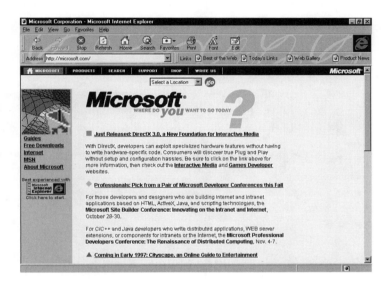

Microsoft Access 97 is Web-enabled, so you can use it to publish objects to the Web for all to see. Access 97, when used with Windows NT's IIS (Internet Information Server) can also create dynamic Web pages that let users view, edit, and do other database chores online through the Web. You can also embed hyperlinks in Access objects that let you link them to other Office documents. You can link the following, as well as many other objects, to other documents:

- ☐ Office 97 documents on your local computer
- ☐ Office 97 documents on an intranet
- ☐ Office 97 documents on the Internet
- ☐ HTML documents on your local computer
- ☐ HTML documents on an intranet
- ☐ HTML documents on the Internet

28

What Is a Web Page?

Web pages are plain text with embedded tags. Additions such as embedding Java programs, VBScript, or ActiveX controls add considerably to what Web pages can do, but basically, Web pages are just text with tags. Figure 28.2 shows a simple Web page that uses Notepad as an editor. Keep in mind that to make a Web page, you must save such documents as plain ASCII text, not in a word processor's native format. Keep that in mind, if you want to edit in a program like Word 97.

> **Tip of the Iceberg**
>
> There's much more to Web publishing than what's covered in this chapter, but lack of space prevents an in-depth discussion.

Figure 28.2.

Making a Web page manually using an editor, in this case, Notepad.

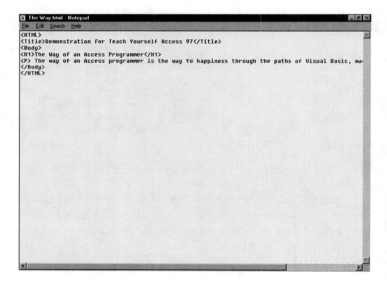

Figure 28.3 shows the page from Figure 28.2 in a browser. Note how the browser, Internet Explorer, mapped (or parsed) the tags. The title line appears in the title bar of the browser. The heading (<H1>), or Heading One, is the heading, and the line following the <P> tag makes up a paragraph. In HTML, the slash means the end of a tag. So <H1> means to start a line formatted as Heading One, and </H1> means End Heading One here. The document shown in Figures 28.2 and 28.3 is part of the sample data under the name The Way.HTML.

Figure 28.3.

The page from Figure 28.2 shown in Internet Explorer. This is what the page would look like over an Internet or intranet connection.

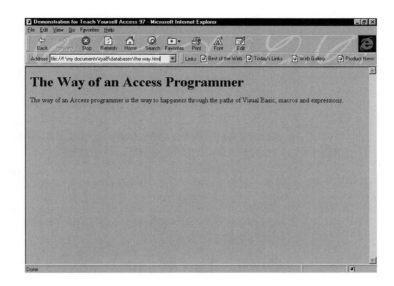

How Can I Do That?

You can always make your HTML pages manually, but since you own Office 97 Professional (with Access 97), Microsoft has taken all the hard work out. Essentially, all you need to do is create the objects you want to put out on the Web, then tell Access to publish them as a Web object.

Converting a Table/Query to an HTML Document

After you've converted any object, such as a datasheet, table, or query, to an HTML document, the only factor determining whether users can get to it on the Internet, an intranet, or over a LAN (or a local machine, for that matter) is where you place it.

You might think that publishing an Access object to an HTML page makes little sense over a LAN or intranet, since presumably you could give users rights to see the original object itself. Here are a few reasons to publish to an HTML document:

☐ People seeing your data won't be able to alter the actual data in the database since the HTML page isn't linked to the database. Database security is 100 percent because the users won't get near the real data.

☐ HTML is plain text, so it won't add much to net traffic load. You also don't need Access or any of its parts to look at HTML, which simplifies distribution.

28

☐ You can add fancy formatting to HTML documents easily and quickly.

☐ People are familiar with using browsers, so they won't need any training, as they might with Access.

☐ There are no licensing issues.

Still, ultimately the decision is yours. You can distribute Access applications without buying more copies of Access or by using the Office Developers' Edition for Office 97. Of course, if your organization uses Office 97 Professional, all the people in your organization already have Access 97, so your distribution task is simplified. Even if your organization is all Office 97, the world at large has a few stubborn holdouts, so for Internet publication, HTML can't be beat.

Creating an HTML document from any datasheet is as simple as following your nose through a wizard.

Exercise 28.1. The Publish to the Web Wizard.

EXERCISE

1. Figure 28.4 shows a simple query, qryBirthdays, that's part of the sample data. If you want to follow along, create an identical or similar query based on the StudentPersonalDOB (or just StudentPersonal) table. The end document will be published on the college Web site as a list of all the students, their birthdays, and their e-mail addresses.

Figure 28.4.

A simple query in Datasheet View.

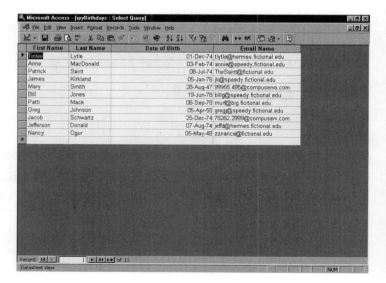

28

2. Close the query if you have it open, and move to the Database View (press F11).

3. Choose File|Save as HTML from the menu. Access responds by bringing up a wizard, as shown in Figure 28.5.

Figure 28.5.

Starting a wizard that will convert a datasheet to an HTML document.

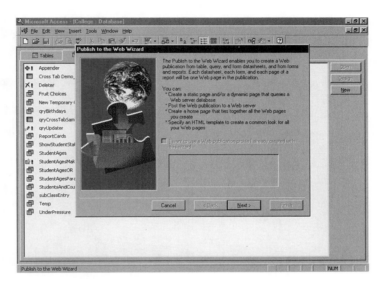

4. Click the Next> button to move past the wizard's introduction. Now you'll need to tell the wizard which objects to include in the publishing wizard as shown in Figure 28.6.

Figure 28.6.

Choosing which objects to include in the Publish to the Web Wizard.

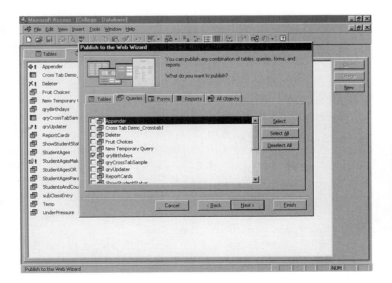

28

Include as many objects as you want to publish to the Web in this dialog box. This example used only the sample query, qryBirthdays. Click Next> to bring up a text box where you can add a template to your page. A *template* is a standard for HTML pages, such as background or logos. You can use your own templates or those supplied by Microsoft. This example uses no templates, so click the Next> button. Figure 28.7 shows the place in the wizard where you can include a template.

Figure 28.7.

You can choose a template for your Web page. This is a handy way to create a standard look for your pages.

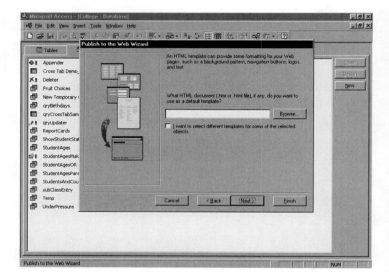

5. The next dialog box is probably the most critical one in the wizard. Here you tell the wizard whether you want to publish a dynamic (able to be edited) or static (fixed data) page. In the case of a dynamic page, you have the choice between the old HTX/IDC format or the new ActiveX ASP format. This example creates a static page for data display only, so it left the top option button as the selection. (See Figure 28.8.) Click Next>.

6. The next dialog box allows you to store your finished Web page in any location you have rights to. There are three choices: You can publish locally, you can publish to your local hard disk (or LAN volume), or you can use the built-in FTP transfer to publish to a new Web site or one already set up. This example published to a local site. Unless you have a Web site, this is your only option. Keep in mind that you can always publish locally, then transfer the file(s) to a Web site. You don't have to do this directly from the Access wizard. Figure 28.9 shows you the screen with the target options.

Figure 28.8.

Choosing between a dynamic page or a static page.

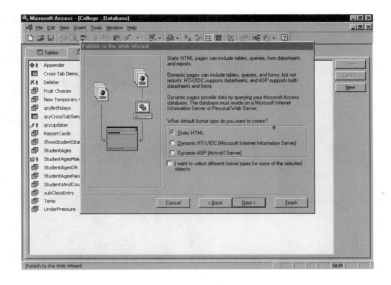

Figure 28.9.

The wizard lets you publish locally or to a Web site.

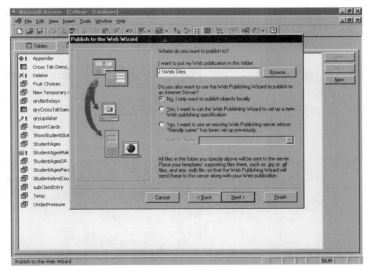

7. You are then given two other dialog box choices. The first asks if you want to create a home page for your Web publication, and the second asks if you want to create a template from this publication. This example declined both offers, but feel free to experiment with both—they're useful options. When you come to the end of the wizard or your interest, click the Finish button to make the HTML document. Figure 28.10 displays the finished HTML document shown in Internet Explorer.

28

Figure 28.10.

The finished HTML document accurately reflects the data in the original query.

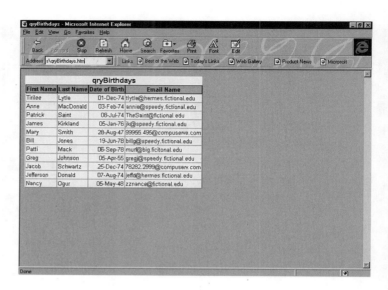

Figure 28.11 shows the HTML page inside Word for Windows 97, showing the HTML source for this page. The reason for the complex formatting is the display's table nature, which requires a lot more instructions for the browser to parse.

Figure 28.11.

The HTML source code for the document created in the exercise.

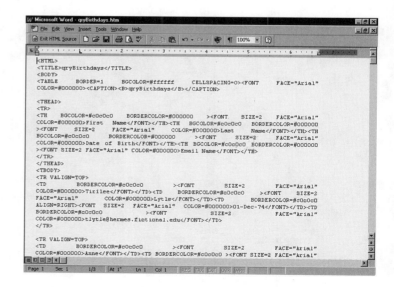

28

Publishing a Form/Report to an HTML Document for Web Viewing

There isn't much difference publishing a form statically to the Web and, in reality, no difference in output, either, than a datasheet. Naturally, the form will modify the displayed data according to the expressions and property settings for the form, but you'll get a datasheet look after you're done.

If you think about it, you'll realize using a datasheet for display is the only reasonable solution to static publishing to the Web. If you wanted Access to output the forms to a page that looks like the form, it would need to create a new page for each record in the bound table or query. This would be cumbersome for small datasets, such as the one in the College database; it would be impossible for even modest-sized ones, such as the vendors for a small company. Since Access can hold millions of records, a form published to the Web might have millions of pages—a clear impossibility. Figure 28.12 shows a Web page derived from the ClassSignUp form published to a Web document; it was made using the wizard in the same way as the qryBirthdays done in Exercise 28.1.

Figure 28.12.

A form published to the Web, viewed in Word for Windows 97.

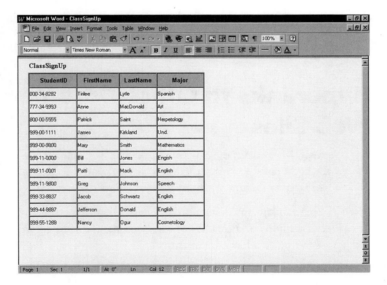

Something pretty cool happens if you publish a multipage document to the Web. Figure 28.13 is the ClassCards report published to the Web and viewed in Internet Explorer.

28

Figure 28.13.

Multipage reports show up as multipage documents on the Web, complete with hyperlinks to other parts of the document.

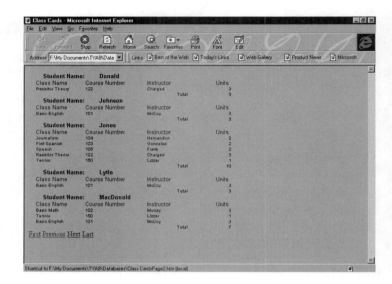

Take a look at the bottom of the display shown in Figure 28.13. You see the four words First, Previous, Next, and Last; they're hyperlinks to other parts of this document. The words refer to pages in this Web "page." Since ClassCards went on for two pages, there are two pages you can hyperlink to when this page is open in any browser-capable program .

Hyperlinks to Office Documents or to Web Sites

Access 97 has added the capability to create link fields to documents on your local machine, your LAN or WAN, plus the Web. In fact, you can place a link in a table, query, form, or report to any document that you have rights to access or open.

Placing a link to any document on a network, the Internet, or your local machine is identical. Because I know that readers of this book have at least a local machine, Exercise 28.2 shows how to link to a local document.

Keep in mind that linking to nonlocal documents is exactly the same as the method shown in Exercise 28.2, except you'd alter the UNC or URL to the nonlocal document.

28

> **The Access Way**
>
> *UNC* stands for Universal Naming Convention. It's the standard way to refer to a document locally or across a network. The convention looks like this: `\\server\[path]`. Therefore, a file called Jennifer located in the subdirectory Nancy on the server Tirilee would look like this in UNC: `\\tirilee\nancy\jennifer`.
>
> Similarly, the UNC for the local file Jennifer located in the Nancy subdirectory of drive C: would be `C:\Nancy\Jennifer`.
>
> *URL* stands for Universal Resource Locator and it's the way to locate documents and other resources on the Web. The address `http://www.microsoft.com` is the URL for the Microsoft Corporation's home page. The http part tells the browser (or other searcher) that the address uses Hypertext Transfer Protocol. The balance of the address is the specific address for Microsoft's site.

There are three basic ways to include hyperlinks in Access:

- ☐ Add a field with the Hyperlink data type in a table. This field will then appear in forms, reports, and queries.
- ☐ Add a label to a form or report and set the Hyperlink property to a UNC or a URL.
- ☐ Add a command button to a form and set the Hyperlink property to a UNC or a URL.

Exercise 28.2 adds a hyperlink to a command button to a form.

Exercise 28.2. The command button hyperlink.

1. Figure 28.14 shows a table with a Hyperlink data type field. This table, StudentPersonal is part of the sample data and one that you should be familiar with by now. To jump to any URL or UNC entered in this field, you just need click on the field and Access jumps to that document. In addition to highlighting the URL or UNC address, Access's cursor changes to the conventional hand when passed over such an address. Figure 28.14 shows the hand cursor over one of the URLs in the StudentPersonal table.

2. The following exercise jumps to a specific place in a Word 97 document. This document, `Linker.doc`, is part of the sample data. (See Figure 28.15.) It's nothing more than a series of paragraphs with the words "Not Here" and one paragraph with the line "Here is the place you should have landed on!" There's a bookmark, LandingZone, at that one different line. Figure 28.15 shows the bookmark and the target line in the target file.

28

Figure 28.14.
*A table with a
hyperlink as part of
a data field.*

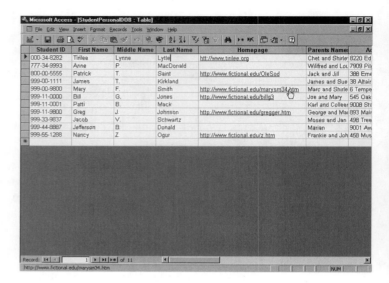

Figure 28.15.
*A document to
jump to from
within an Access
form.*

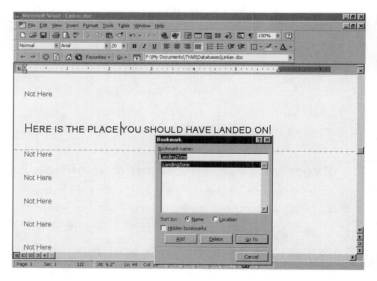

3. Launch Access if necessary and open either the College database or another one.
   Open a form in Design View or start a new form and open it in Design View. This
   exercise uses the TabbedStudentPersonal form.

4. Add a command button to your form. You could also have added a label or chosen Insert|Hyperlink from the menu. That menu choice puts a label on the form rather than a command button. Figure 28.16 shows a command button added, the Properties list box opened to the Format tab, and the Caption property altered to read Word Document.

Figure 28.16.

Adding an object on the form to house the link.

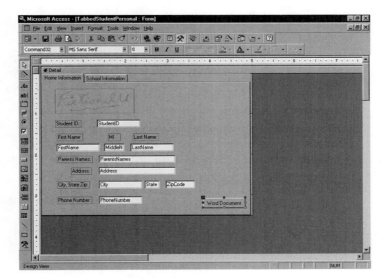

To add the link, edit the Hyperlink property on the Format tab. The Hyperlink property should contain the URL or the UNC. The Hyperlink SubAddress will hold the bookmark to jump to within the opened document. Figure 28.17 shows the hyperlink added that's right for one local machine. If you're following along, you'll need to add the right UNC for your setup. The Hyperlink SubAddress is the bookmark name in the document. In this case, it's LandingZone, as shown in Figure 28.15.

5. Note how Access altered the appearance of the Caption as soon as you told it this button is a link to a UNC.

6. Switch to Form View and click the command button you just made. Access will open Word 97, load the document Linker.doc, and jump to the LandingZone bookmark. Figure 28.18 shows the form in Form View, and Figure 28.19 shows the result of clicking the command button.

28

Figure 28.17.

Adding the Hyperlink address (UNC) and the Hyperlink SubAddress (bookmark) to the properties for this command button.

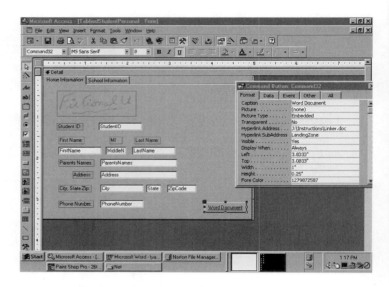

Figure 28.18.

The command button hyperlink ready for action.

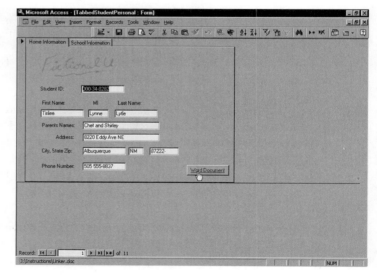

7. To return to your Access form, click the Back button in the Web toolbar in Word 97, as shown in Figure 28.20.

8. You can also browse for a UNC or URL. To do this, click the builder button on the Hyperlink property for an object. Figure 28.21 shows the Browse for UNC or URL dialog box open.

Figure 28.19.
You can not only open a document, but also jump to a bookmark (or anchor) within that document.

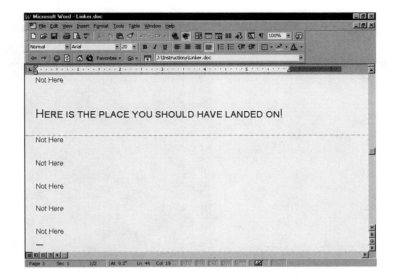

Figure 28.20.
The path back to the Access form.

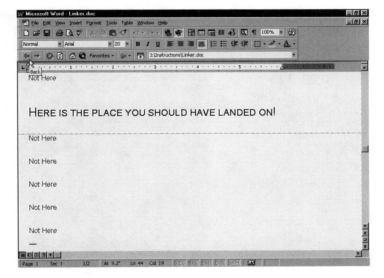

28

Figure 28.21.

If you prefer, you can browse for a UNC or URL.

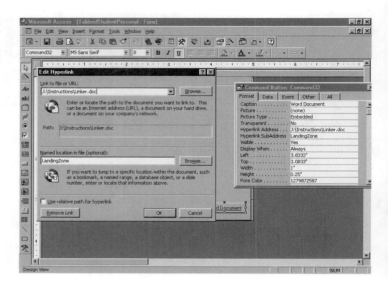

Using URLs is no different from using UNCs. Figure 28.22 shows the TabbedStudentPersonal form with a label added that has a hyperlink to a URL; Figure 28.23 displays the results of clicking on that label.

Figure 28.22.

A tab form with a label containing a hyperlink to a Web URL.

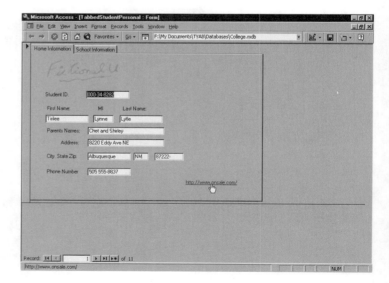

Figure 28.23.

Click on the URL hyperlink and Access, along with Windows, takes you for an express ride to that Web site.

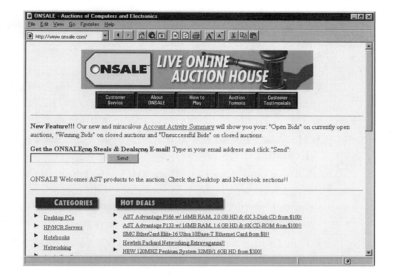

Day Summary

The Web started as a protocol for hypertext documents on the Internet. Today, the Web and Web-like institutions exist on domains as small as a single computer, on a LAN to a WAN to an intranet, and even on the Internet itself. The original limits of hypertext documents are being expanded as the Web encompasses multimedia extensions.

You can publish tables, queries, forms, and reports from their native Access format to the HTML format used on the Web. Once converted to HTML, your documents become detached from their underlying data, but become available to anyone with a browser. You don't need Access to view such documents. In fact, you don't even need a computer. You just need a Web appliance to see such documents.

Access can include links to documents or other resources in forms, tables, queries, and reports. You can add such links either by specifying a field as having the Hyperlink data type or by including a label or command button on a form or report with its property set to a UNC or URL.

Using OLE or ActiveX controls or both greatly enhances the scope of what you can do in Access. In some cases, you might be able to program what an ActiveX control does, but not easily. Using OLE, you can exchange data and objects with other OLE-enabled applications.

28

Q&A

Q Do I need a TCP/IP protocol to link to documents on my local machine or LAN?

A If your LAN is TCP/IP, you need the layer. Otherwise, you don't need anything more than whatever is your default protocol. This is often NetBEUI for Windows 95/97. You need no protocol whatsoever for local links.

Q How do I install the TCP/IP layer so I can use Dial Up networking in my hyperlinks?

A Open the Add-Remove Programs applet from the Control Panel. Click on the Windows Setup tab, then find the Communications check box. Click the Details button, then the Dial Up Networking check box. You will need your Windows 95/97 distribution disks or CD-ROM to perform the task.

Q Can I jump to a place in an Excel 97 workbook?

A Yes. Say you want to jump to a range named Sales for a worksheet named Colorado in a file called `Finance.xls`. Enter the path to the file as the Hyperlink property and enter `Colorado!Sales` for a Hyperlink SubAddress property.

Q I bought a set of ActiveX controls. The manual talks about a property sheet I can't find after I place the control on an Access form. Is it a defective control?

A Depends on your definition of "defective." This control is only partly enabled under Access. It will probably run fine under Visual Basic 4 or later.

Q I am getting complaints that my HTML documents look oddly formatted when viewed by some of my users. What's up?

A Browsers vary as to how they display the data they format. The best way to ensure that your pages look like you hope they will is to make sure all your target viewers use one browser, such as Internet Explorer. Failing that, you can modify your HTML pages to be as simple as possible, or you can view them with all the possible browsers your target market will use. The latter method is tedious, but it's the path chosen by many Web page developers. This problem will naturally go away as the world migrates to one or two browsers from the dozens now in use.

Workshop

Here's where you can test and apply what you have learned today.

Quiz

Possible answers to these questions are given in Appendix A.

1. What does ASP format mean when publishing to the Web?
2. In what format is an HTML file?
3. Is HTML a page description language like PostScript?
4. How do you insert an ActiveX control into an Access form?
5. Which of the following does an ActiveX control have: methods, properties, events?
6. Why does Access output HTML files with the extension HTM rather than HTML?

Put Access into Action

1. Create a new form within or outside `College.mdb` (it makes no difference).
2. Insert the ActiveX Calendar control.
3. Add two command buttons to your form.
4. Program those two buttons so that, when clicked, they jump the calendar one year ahead and one year back, respectively.
5. Close the form, saving it if you want to.

28

APPENDIXES

Quiz Answers

Answers for Day 1

1. Compact setups don't include the wizards, which most find very useful for making Access applications.
2. A double-pointed arrow.
3. Locate its menu choice and click it.
4. The status bar and tooltips.
5. Yes. This is a new feature for Access 97 only. It does not apply to older versions of the program.

Answers for Day 2

1. Click the Tables tab, then click the New button.
2. Sales to Customers.
3. It saves time and effort.
4. 255.
5. 64 characters and spaces.
6. Its name will be shortened (truncated).

Answers for Day 3

1. In both cases, it changes into a bar with two opposite-pointing arrows.
2. No.
3. Yes.
4. Yes, you can override default properties without special considerations.
5. No.
6. To help users enter and read field data. It also is a form of data validation.

Answers for Day 4

1. The field changes its color scheme to the opposite of normal. For example, if normal is black on white, highlighted fields will be white on black.
2. The hand cursor.
3. A thin, double-faced arrow.
4. No.
5. Click on one, then press shift and click on the other.
6. Use a marquee selection; that is, click and drag to surround the fields. You can also use the Shift+click method for contiguous controls.

Answers for Day 5

1. The linking together of more than one. In Access the link usually refers to field contents.
2. Yes.
3. Once.
4. In the Page Footer band.
5. Yes. Other than some minor slowdown (usually unnoticeable), there are no adverse consequences.
6. Grid X and Grid Y properties.
7. None. This was a trick question.

Answers for Day 6

1. The equals (=) sign.
2. To positively indicate to Access that you mean a field. Also, to be able to include white spaces in a field name when it's used in an expression.
3. `Sum()`.
5. You can bind reports only to tables or queries.
6. A list box and a text box.
7. No.

Answers for Day 7

1. Control Source.
2. Row Source.
3. No. Access will view the criterion January as being a Text data type, not a Date/Time one, so it won't make any match.
4. Limit to List.
5. After January 31, 1997.

Answers for Day 8

1. No, no. These changes are permanent unless you have a backup of the database to restore from.
2. Yes.
3. Changing the sort order from descending to ascending will alter whether Access selects the bottom or top of any percentage in a query.

4. Yes.

5. Yes.

6. Yes.

7. Individual fields.

Answers for Day 9

1. Queries.

2. No.

3. A different table.

4. The same table(s).

5. Click on the Data tab of the Properties list box.

6. The entries on the Link Child Field and Link Master Field need to be for the linked fields, in this case the SSN field.

7. Run them as select queries first.

Answers for Day 10

1. No. Many vary, depending on control types.

2. Picture Tiling property.

3. `Sub cmdNextRecord_Clack ().`

4. `Like "Ka"` won't let either Kaplan or Kramer through. `Like "Ka*"` will allow Kaplan but not Kramer.

Answers for Day 11

1. The phrase to the left of the colon will be the column's title or label.

2. Yes.

3. Yes.

4. No.

5. Change the width through the Properties list box settings or by selecting the line width choices from within the Formatting toolbar when the line or rectangle has the focus.

6. Group fields have the same icon in the Sorting and Grouping list box as the Sorting and Grouping toolbar button.

Answers for Day 12

1. The & in a caption tells Access that the character that follows, in this case the x, is the hotkey for this control. Pressing Alt+hotkey when the form is active gives this control the focus; in this case, it's the same as a click and you'll exit the form.

2. The Report Cards report would print to the printer rather than show on the screen.

3. Separate the macro name from the macro itself

4. Use the greater than and less than symbols in combination (<>).

For the Adventurous

1. The line to enter in the Where property is [FirstName]="Tirilee".

Answers for Day 13

1. Double. Access will view I and Interest as separate variables.

2. Use a module or code behind forms (some say code within forms) to do looping. Macros won't loop.

3. No. You can use the Customize facility to make custom bars—menu bars or toolbars. In addition, Access 97 supports making custom menus through macros, so they will be backward-compatible with previous versions of Access and older programming habits.

4. When calculating monetary fields that require a great deal of precision, such as recursive interest calculations. The disadvantage of this data type is the amount of overhead it adds to your application. Use when you need to, but not otherwise.

5. Preface the remark with the REM keyword or a single quote (').

Answers for Day 14

1. ASP is an Access object published in the form of an ActiveX control.

2. Plain ASCII—that is, straight text.

3. No. HTML is text with tags. The tags themselves are also nothing but text. The browser does the page formatting based on the tags and the bracketed text.

4. Choose object from the Insert menu or use the ActiveX button in the toolbox.

5. ActiveX controls have them all.

6. DOS and Windows 3.1 aren't long filename-enabled and will be foxed by any extension longer than three characters.

APPENDIX

B

Exercise Guide/
Quick Reference

Exercise 2.1. Introduction to the Office Assistant.

The Office Assistant is Microsoft's new implementation of artificial intelligence (AI) in an online help system. This exercise gives you a quick tour of how you can use the Office Assistant to find information within the online help system. Like so many things in a visual tool like Access, you can learn how to use the new Office Assistant best by trying it out. This exercise serves as an introduction.

Exercise 2.2. Creating a new database.

This exercise teaches you how to create a new database.

Exercise 2.3. Using a wizard to make a new table.

This exercise shows you how to make a table using a wizard.

Exercise 2.4. Help with Help.

Sometimes the help you need can't be found through the Office Assistant or by using wizards. In those cases, such as how to use a particular function, you'll likely use Access's online help system. This exercise steps you through some parts of Access's online help.

Exercise 3.1. Creating the new database.

Before you can start any database project, you need a new database to store database objects. This exercise gets you moving in the right direction.

Exercise 3.2. Creating the StudentPersonal table.

This exercise creates the first table for the book's sample database.

Exercise 4.1. Modifying a table.

Nobody plans perfectly. Many times you'll design a table only to realize that either a particular field's data type is wrong, or you included a field you shouldn't have, or left one out you need. In all these cases, you'll need to modify an existing table design, the purpose of this exercise.

Exercise 4.2. Adding a field to an existing table.

You can easily add a field to an existing Access database. This exercise shows you how to go about adding the field Ethnicity to the StudentPersonal table.

Exercise 4.3. Creating a table without a wizard.

As valuable as the wizards are, it's important for you to know how to accomplish these tasks on your own. This exercise teaches you how to create a table without a wizard.

Exercise 4.4. Creating a one-to-many link.

Often, you want to be sure you can enter many records that correspond to another single record. A relationship where one record can be linked to many is called, not surprisingly, a one-to-many relationship. Making sure a record exists in the table on the one side before any records can be entered in the many side is called referential integrity. This exercise demonstrates how to create a one-to-many link.

Exercise 5.1. Entering data directly into a table.

Tables in and of themselves do nothing. It's the data they can store that's the heart of your database project. Entering data into a table is as simple as typing it in. This exercise shows how you create your first record using Access.

Exercise 5.2. Adding an input mask.

This exercise demonstrates a level of data accuracy by creating an input mask for data entry.

Exercise 5.3. Changing the field order of a table.

Sometimes you aren't happy with the field order you've created. This exercise shows you how to move fields to different positions.

Exercise 5.4. Changing the apparent field order.

When you change the field order in the field design grid, you also change the order in which the fields appear in the Datasheet View. You can make changes in the Datasheet View that won't change the field order in the Database Design View, however, as this exercise shows.

Exercise 5.5. Changing apparent field widths and heights.

The Field Size property for text fields determines the capacity of the fields, but doesn't affect how wide they're shown in the Datasheet View. Naturally that leaves some fields appearing too small while others are too wide in the Default Datasheet View. As this exercise demonstrates, changing apparent field sizes from Access's default in the Datasheet View is quite simple.

Exercise 6.1. Setting a Default Field property.

Our fictional college is in northern Illinois, and most of the students are from Illinois. Therefore, it makes sense for us to set a default value to IL for the state field in our StudentPersonal table. This exercise shows how it's done.

Exercise 6.2. Setting the Data Validation field property.

In many cases you'll want to limit field entries to one or a certain array of selections. One way to do this in Access is to set the Data-Validation field property. This exercise isn't an optimal use of the Data-Validation property, but working through this and reviewing the table of data-validation examples will give you a good idea of this field property's use.

Exercise 6.3. Making a data validation error message.

Access has a standard error message box for data validation problems. Many times you'll want to create your own custom message box.

Exercise 7.1. An instant form.

This exercise demonstrates how easily Access handles the job of making a simple data-entry form.

Exercise 7.2. Using a wizard to make a form.

This exercise teaches you how to use Access's built-in wizard capabilities to create a form.

Exercise 7.3. Resizing a form control.

To make all the fields or form controls fit on one screen conveniently, you need to both alter the size of some overly wide ones and then move some of them up from the bottom of the form. Keep in mind that the terms field control and form control, or just control, refer to the same thing. This exercise demonstrates how to manipulate these controls.

Exercise 7.4. Moving form controls.

This exercise moves two controls with their labels so the entire form fits on one screen.

Exercise 7.5. Marquee selections.

Often you'll want to act on several controls at once. This exercise teaches you how to choose several controls quickly and easily by using a marquee selection.

Exercise 7.6. Using the Formatting toolbar.

This exercise covers how to alter the appearance of form elements with the Formatting toolbar.

Exercise 8.1. The simple query.

This exercise constructs a simple query in Access.

Exercise 8.2. Sorting in a query.

This exercise demonstrates how to make your queries more effective by sorting the data they retrieve.

Exercise 8.3. A criteria query.

Access queries also perform the very important function of extracting subsets of your data. This exercise shows how to convert the general query made in Exercises 9.1 and 9.2 into one with a criterion.

Exercise 8.4. Variations of criteria.

Access has a wide variety of criteria you can enter into a query. Using a little imagination and some knowledge, you can extract your data in almost any manner you can think of. This exercise goes into some variations on the criteria theme.

Exercise 8.5. ORs and ANDs in criteria.

This exercise illustrates the distinction between logical ORs and ANDs in queries.

Exercise 9.1. A two-table query.

This exercise shows how you construct a simple two-table query.

Exercise 9.2. The three-table query.

This exercise refines the query from Exercise 9.1, including information about course title and credit hours.

Exercise 10.1. The basic report.

This exercise creates a report that prints out students' names and addresses.

Exercise 10.2. Modifying a report.

This exercise covers deleting and rearranging fields in a report.

Exercise 10.3. Making mailing labels.

This exercise demonstrates the Label Wizard.

Exercise 11.1. Field expressions in reports.

This exercise will replace the first and third lines of the report's detail area with expressions that automatically size to fit the field's data.

Exercise 11.2. A grouped and totaled report.

This exercise creates a report showing all the courses all the students are signed up for, plus it adds up the course load to show the total credit hours for each student.

Exercise 11.3. Adding report elements.

The only elements missing from the report created in Exercise 11.2 are a label for students' last names and some detail to show the current course load for each student. This exercise shows you how to add these elements.

Exercise 12.1. A form with combo boxes.

All the controls on your previously made forms have been text boxes. These allow data entry and basic editing within them. List and combo boxes are two handy controls for data entry. A list box shows a list of values you can scroll through. A combo box is a combination of a list box and a text box. It has a place to enter data and a drop-down list that works identically to the list box.

Exercise 12.2. Manual combo box programming.

This exercise uses a combo box for the CourseNumber field. If you prefer the list box, you could use that for this application as well.

Exercise 12.3. The tabbed form.

One of the most interesting inclusions in Access 97 is the new tab control. This will allow you to easily create forms that look like the tabbed dialog boxes Microsoft uses throughout Office 97. This exercise shows you how easy it can be to include this control in your forms.

Exercise 13.1. Modifying an existing table.

This short exercise adds a new field to the StudentPersonal table to hold either a 1, 2, or 3 that will correspond with a student status.

Exercise 13.2. Creating and programming the option group.

The purpose of this exercise is to make room on the StudentPersonalData form for the new option group and then to install the option group on it.

Exercise 13.3. Embedding a graphic in a form.

This exercise creates a logo for the fictional college and embeds it in the StudentPersonalData form.

Exercise 14.1. Adding a Date field to a table.

This exercise adds a Date field to the StudentPersonal table and examines how Access can present date information.

Exercise 14.2. Date criteria.

This exercise simply shows how you can use dates as criteria for queries.

Exercise 14.3. Date math and expression (developer-defined) fields.

This exercise dynamically calculates the age of each student in years. Dynamic calculation means the computer fetches the current date and does the age calculation based on that date and the fixed value of the student's birthday.

Exercise 15.1. A different criteria demonstration.

This exercise shows the parallels between criteria and parameters in queries.

Exercise 15.2. The parameter query.

This exercise constructs a simple parameter query and demonstrates its operation.

Exercise 15.3. Wildcard parameter queries.

This exercise shows how to use wildcards in parameter queries.

Exercise 15.4. The range parameter query.

This exercise shows how to create a parameter query that will return a range of values.

Exercise 15.5. The make table action query.

This exercise shows how to convert a query from a select query to a simple action query. This action query creates a new table containing the query's output.

Exercise 16.1. The delete query.

This exercise demonstrates the delete action query.

Exercise 16.2. Compacting a database.

This exercise shows how to compact a database and the results of doing so.

Exercise 16.3. The append query.

This query extracts records from the AppendMe table and appends them to the Student'sCurrentClasses table. You will need the AppendMe table from the sample data to complete this exercise. If it currently doesn't exist as part of your data, either enter the table's data now or include this table from the sample set you acquired following the directions in Appendix E.

Exercise 16.4. Update queries.

This exercise creates an update query that looks for any ZIP codes meeting the criterion of 38990 and changes them to 38989.

Exercise 16.5. The crosstab query.

This exercise creates two crosstabs—one showing the sum of the dollars and one showing the frequency of sales.

Exercise 17.1. Making the subform's query.

This short exercise creates a query to bind to the new subform.

Exercise 17.2. The form with subform.

This exercise uses a wizard to create a form with a subform.

Exercise 18.1. Field control properties.

This exercise fully demonstrates Link field control properties.

Exercise 18.2. Locked and Enabled properties.

This exercise demonstrates the use and limitations of the Locked and Enabled properties.

B

Exercise 18.3. Filter by selection.

The exercise shows how to apply data filters by selection. Keep in mind that you can design and change filters when a form is running. This isn't a task done at design time.

Exercise 19.1. Record manipulation.

This exercise shows you how you can make controls that scroll through records.

Exercise 19.2. Another command button.

This exercise creates a command button that moves up one record at a time.

Exercise 20.1. Record selectors and navigation buttons.

The purpose of this exercise is to demonstrate the use of record selectors and navigation buttons in forms.

Exercise 20.2. Changing the tab order.

This exercise shows how to alter the tab order in a form and eliminate controls from being in the tab order.

Exercise 20.3. Altering a subform.

This exercise shows how to alter the properties of a subform.

Exercise 20.4. Graphics elements in forms.

The purpose of this exercise is to show some uses for graphics calculation elements in forms and how their properties affect their appearance.

Exercise 21.1. Calculation expressions in queries.

This exercise shows how to construct a moderately complex query containing a mathematical expression.

Exercise 21.2. Grouping and sorting in reports.

This exercise manually creates a grouped report with several expressions and a secondary sort order.

Exercise 22.1. Calculation expressions in reports.

This exercise demonstrates how to create calculations in reports. The technique shown is identical to the technique used for forms. All the material in this exercise applies to forms also.

Exercise 22.2. Graphics elements in reports.

This exercise adds some graphics to the ReportCards report.

Exercise 22.3. A dynamic control.

This exercise places an option button on the report card that evaluates a student's weighted grade point average and visibly indicates if it merits inclusion on the dean's list.

Exercise 23.1. The macro design grid.

This exercise shows the macro design grid and constructs a simple macro.

Exercise 23.2. The switchboard or menu form.

This exercise constructs a simple unbound form that acts as a switchboard for the College database.

Exercise 23.3. The compound macro.

This exercise designs a compound macro for use in the Switchboard form.

Exercise 23.4. Activating the form.

This exercise attaches the macros to the command buttons.

Exercise 24.1. Conditional message box macro.

This macro evaluates the contents of the Ethnicity field when a new student is registered and responds accordingly.

Exercise 24.2. Attaching macros.

This exercise edits the On Click property for cmdCloseForm, causing it to point to the right macro, and attaches the Scholarship macro to the proper event.

Exercise 24.3. The form.

This exercise creates a very simple form with four controls. Two of the controls respond to events by altering the other two's control properties by a macro. Each macro in this exercise is multiline and represents an increase in complexity in several areas.

Exercise 24.4. Control property macros.

This exercise creates one macro containing two macro names. When called by its command button, this macro changes the label's Visible properties.

Exercise 24.5. Putting it all together.

This exercise attaches the macros done in Exercise 24.4 to controls in the RedGreen form.

Exercise 26.1. Tie a Visual Basic function to a form control.

This exercise links a new function to a form control.

Exercise 26.2. Using the function.

This exercise attaches the new function to a form control.

Exercise 26.3. Declaring variables.

This exercise demonstrates the use of variables.

Exercise 28.1. The Publish to the Web Wizard.

Access 97 can publish many of its objects to be either static or dynamic objects on the World Wide Web. This exercise steps you through this process.

Exercise 28.2. The command button hyperlink.

In Access 97 you can include URLs and UNCs as part of your data. You can also include those addresses as part of your forms that will, in effect, make those addresses (this includes anything on the Web) part of your application. This exercise shows you how you can integrate a Web address into your application.

APPENDIX

C

The Toolbox Illustrated

Microsoft Access stores the tools, or controls, used to design database objects in a specialized toolbar called the toolbox. This appendix provides an explanation of each tool and an illustration of the toolbox for easy reference.

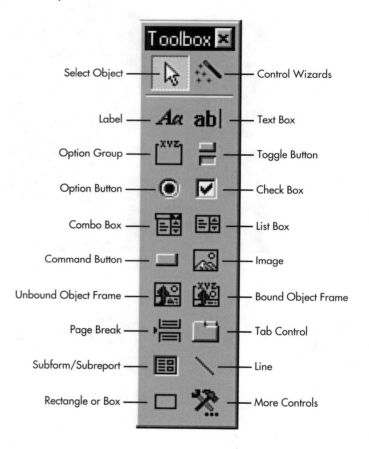

Select Object: Click this to return to the pointer cursor. The pointer cursor is used to make selections either on the design grid or from menus, the toolbox, or a toolbar.

Control Wizards: With Control Wizards on, any control you create will automatically be created with a wizard. With Control Wizards off, you can create the control without the help of a wizard.

Label: Use this tool to create a label. Use labels for decoration, instructions, or field identification.

Text Box: The Text Box tool or control holds text. This is one of the most flexible tools in Access. Text boxes can be used for data entry or display, or to hold calculated fields.

Option Group: An option group holds other tools—such as option buttons, check boxes, or toggle buttons—in a group. Only one control within an option group can be chosen at a time.

Toggle Button: A toggle button toggles between being selected and unselected at the click of a mouse button. It's a good control for Yes/No fields.

Option Button: Also called radio buttons, option buttons are similar in function to check boxes and toggle buttons. An option button is selected and deselected at the click of the mouse button.

Check Box: Another toggle-type tool that's changed from selected to deselected with a mouse click.

Combo Box: A combo box is a text box grafted to the top of a list box and tied to the list. Using a combo box, you can choose from a list as you can with a list box, or enter a value not on the list as you can in a text box.

List Box: A list box presents a list of entries from a field in a table or query. You cannot enter your own value or edit values from the list.

Command Button: A command button carries out a set of programmed instructions when clicked. In Access, the most common use for command buttons is to execute macros.

Image: A control to display a static graphic; that is, one that won't change during runtime.

Unbound Object Frame: Displays an OLE object that's not stored in an Access database.

Bound Object Frame: Displays an OLE object stored in an Access database.

Page Break: This tool inserts a page break.

Tab Control: Used to create tabbed forms that conform to the Windows 95/97 user-interface guidelines.

Subform/Subreport: Used to add a subform or subreport to a form or report, respectively.

Line: Used to draw lines on a form or report.

Rectangle or Box: Used to create squares or rectangles on a form or report.

More Controls: Brings up a selection list of ActiveX (OCX) custom controls.

APPENDIX

D

Access Toolbars

Figure D.1.

The Database toolbar.

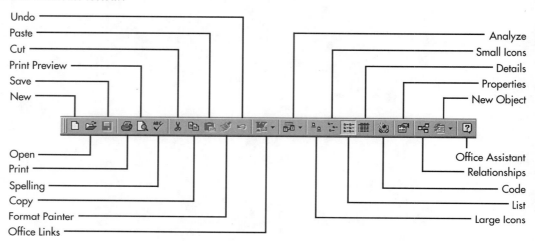

Undo
Paste
Cut
Print Preview
Save
New

Analyze
Small Icons
Details
Properties
New Object

Open
Print
Spelling
Copy
Format Painter
Office Links

Office Assistant
Relationships
Code
List
Large Icons

Figure D.2.

The Table Design toolbar.

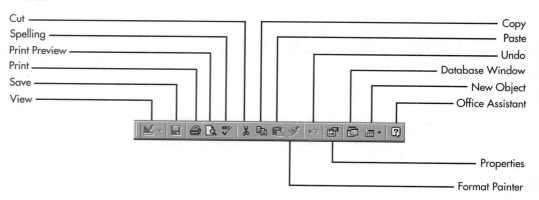

Cut
Spelling
Print Preview
Print
Save
View

Copy
Paste
Undo
Database Window
New Object
Office Assistant

Properties
Format Painter

Figure D.3.

The Table Datasheet toolbar.

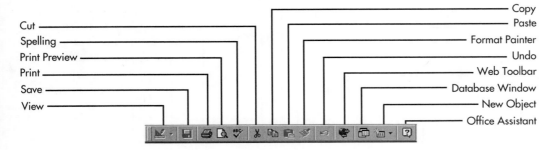

Cut
Spelling
Print Preview
Print
Save
View

Copy
Paste
Format Painter
Undo
Web Toolbar
Database Window
New Object
Office Assistant

Figure D.4.

The Query Datasheet toolbar.

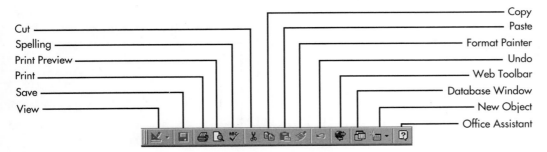

Cut
Spelling
Print Preview
Print
Save
View

Copy
Paste
Format Painter
Undo
Web Toolbar
Database Window
New Object
Office Assistant

D

Figure D.5.

The Query Design toolbar.

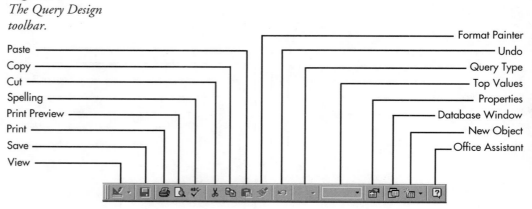

Figure D.6.

The Form View toolbar.

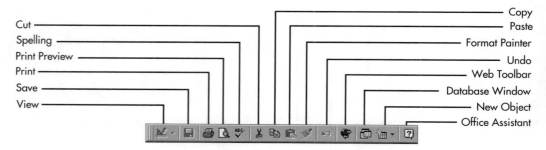

Figure D.7.

The Form Design toolbar.

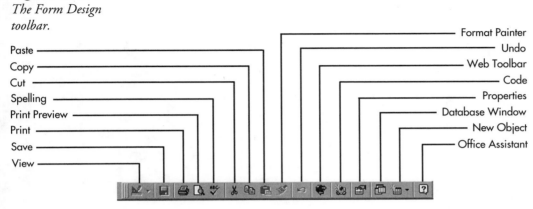

Format Painter
Paste
Undo
Copy
Web Toolbar
Cut
Code
Spelling
Properties
Print Preview
Database Window
Print
New Object
Save
Office Assistant
View

Figure D.8.

The Formatting (Form and Report Design) toolbar.

Align Left
Align Center
Underline
Align Right
Italic
Fill/Back Color
Bold
Font/Fore Color
Font Size
Line/Border Color
Font
Line/Border Width
Object
Special Effect

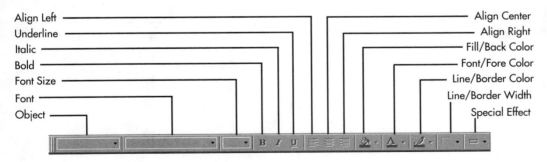

Figure D.9.

The Print Preview toolbar.

Multiple Pages
Two Pages
One Page
Zoom
Print
View

Zoom Control
Close
Office Links
Database Window
New Object
Office Assistant

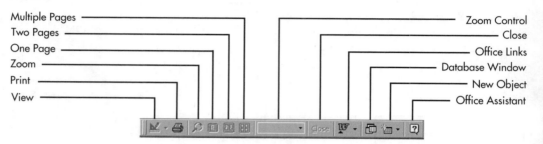

Figure D.10.

The Report Design toolbar.

Paste
Copy
Cut
Spelling
Print Preview
Print
Save
View

Format Painter
Undo
Web Toolbar
Code
Properties
Database Window
New Object
Office Assistant

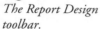
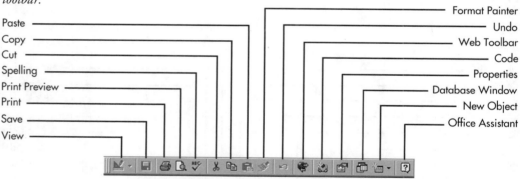

Figure D.11.

The Macro toolbar.

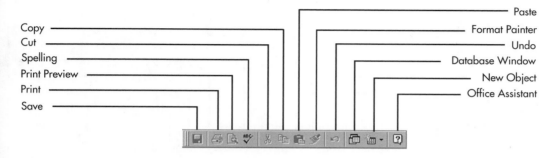

Figure D.12.

The Module toolbar.

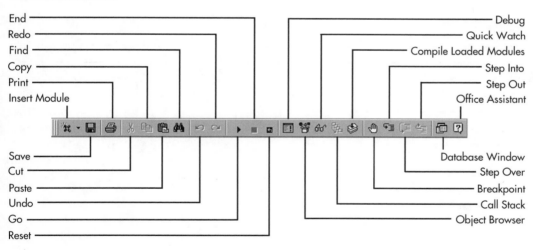

Figure D.13.

The Relationships toolbar.

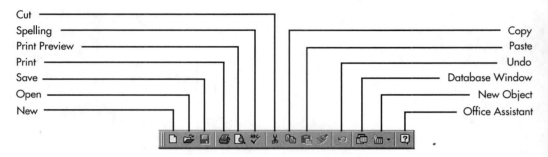

Cut
Spelling
Print Preview
Print
Save
Open
New

Copy
Paste
Undo
Database Window
New Object
Office Assistant

Figure D.14.

The Formatting (Datasheet) toolbar.

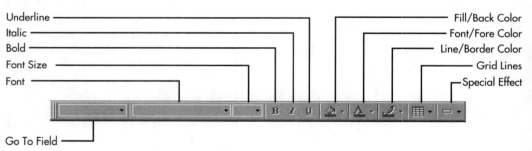

Underline
Italic
Bold
Font Size
Font

Fill/Back Color
Font/Fore Color
Line/Border Color
Grid Lines
Special Effect

Go To Field

Figure D.15.

The Web toolbar.

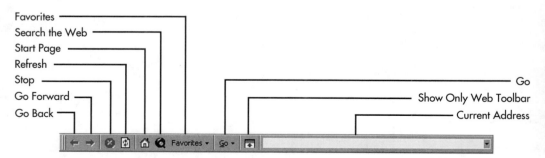

Favorites
Search the Web
Start Page
Refresh
Stop
Go Forward
Go Back

Go
Show Only Web Toolbar
Current Address

Figure D.16.

The Filter/Sort toolbar.

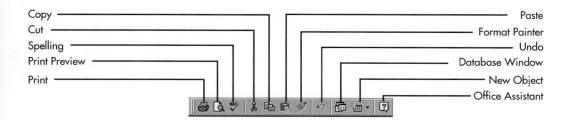

Copy —————————————————————————————————— Paste
Cut —————————————————————————————————— Format Painter
Spelling —————————————————————————————————— Undo
Print Preview —————————————————————————————— Database Window
Print —————————————————————————————————— New Object
                                                    —— Office Assistant

APPENDIX
E

The Sample Data

The Sample Data

One of the easiest methods to teach is to have you follow along with a real-world example. In this book you partially develop a database for a fictitious college. This appendix lists all the data you need to follow the exercises in this book. You can save hours of typing, however. This entire database is available on CompuServe and on the Internet.

To access the sample data on CompuServe, type GO SAMS. Look in the database library for the file tya97.exe.

The URL where the sample date may be found on our site is this:

ftp://ftp.mcp.com/pub/sams/books/969-6/tya97.exe.

For Access-specific information on our site, use this URL:

http://www.mcp.com/sams/workshops/access-ws.html

StudentPersonal

StudentID:	999-11-0000
FirstName:	Bill
MiddleName:	G.
LastName:	Jones
ParentsNames:	Joe and Mary
Address:	545 Oak Street
City:	Chicago
State:	IL
ZipCode:	39844
PhoneNumber:	(317) 555-9875
Major:	English
EmailName:	billg@speedy.fictional.edu
Ethnicity:	Anglo
Homepage:	http://www.fictional.edu/billg
StudentStatus:	1
Notes:	Hobbies include woodworking and skiing

StudentID:	999-00-9800
FirstName:	Mary
MiddleName:	F.
LastName:	Smith

ParentsNames:	Marc and Shirley
Address:	6 Tempest Way
City:	Cairo
State:	IL
ZipCode:	35854
PhoneNumber:	(317) 555-9038
Major:	Mathematics
EmailName:	99955.495@compuserve.com
Ethnicity:	Indian
Homepage:	http://www.fictional.edu/marysm34.htm
StudentStatus:	2
Notes:	On full scholarship
StudentID:	999-11-9800
FirstName:	Greg
MiddleName:	J.
LastName:	Johnson
ParentsNames:	George and Martha
Address:	893 Main St.
City:	Daytona
State:	IL
ZipCode:	35888
PhoneNumber:	(317) 555-2983
Major:	Speech
EmailName:	gregj@speedy.fictional.edu
Ethnicity:	Black
Homepage:	http://www.fictional.edu/gregger.htm
StudentStatus:	1
Notes:	Honor society candidate
StudentID:	999-55-1288
FirstName:	Nancy
MiddleName:	Z.
LastName:	Ogur
ParentsNames:	Frankie and Johnny
Address:	458 Mustang Way
City:	Scofield
State:	IL
ZipCode:	65899-5871
PhoneNumber:	(317) 555-8745
Major:	Cosmetology

E

EmailName:	zznance@fictional.edu
Ethnicity:	Anglo
Homepage:	http://www.fictional.edu/z.htm
StudentStatus:	3
Notes:	Minor in nail painting

StudentID:	999-33-9837
FirstName:	Jacob
MiddleName:	V.
LastName:	Schwartz
ParentsNames:	Moses and Jan
Address:	498 Tree Street
City:	Cairo
State:	IL
ZipCode:	35888
PhoneNumber:	(304) 555-9827
Major:	English
EmailName:	78282.2999@compuserve.com
Ethnicity:	Anglo
Homepage:	
StudentStatus:	1
Notes:	A fast swimmer

StudentID:	000-34-8282
FirstName:	Tirilee
MiddleName:	Lynne
LastName:	Lytle
ParentsNames:	Chet and Shirley
Address:	8220 Eddy Ave NE
City:	Albuquerque
State:	NM
ZipCode:	87222
PhoneNumber:	(505) 555-8837
Major:	Spanish
EmailName:	tlytle@hermes.fictional.edu
Ethnicity:	Anglo
Homepage:	
StudentStatus:	1
Notes:	A wild woman for sure!

StudentID:	999-44-8887
FirstName:	Jefferson
MiddleName:	B.

LastName:	Donald
ParentsNames:	Marian
Address:	9001 Avenue A
City:	Skokie
State:	IL
ZipCode:	34922
PhoneNumber:	(309) 555-9911
Major:	English
EmailName:	jeffd@hermes.fictional.edu
Ethnicity:	Black
Homepage:	
StudentStatus:	3
Notes:	Full academic scholarship
StudentID:	777-34-9993
FirstName:	Anne
MiddleName:	P.
LastName:	MacDonald
ParentsNames:	Wilifred and Louise
Address:	7909 Pilgrim Ct.
City:	Cairo
State:	IL
ZipCode:	32998
PhoneNumber:	(309) 555-8899
Major:	Art
EmailName:	annie@speedy.fictional.edu
Ethnicity:	Anglo
Homepage:	
StudentStatus:	1
Notes:	Fast learner
StudentID:	999-00-1111
FirstName:	James
MiddleName:	T.
LastName:	Kirkland
ParentsNames:	James and Sue
Address:	38 Altair Way
City:	Skokie
State:	IL
ZipCode:	34883
PhoneNumber:	(312) 555-8272
Major:	Und.

E

EmailName: jk@speedy.fictional.edu
Ethnicity: Anglo
Homepage:
StudentStatus: 1
Notes: A space cadet

StudentID: 999-11-0001
FirstName: Patti
MiddleName: B.
LastName: Mack
ParentsNames: Karl and Colleen
Address: 9008 State Street
City: Champas
State: IL
ZipCode: 31288
PhoneNumber: (312) 555-9900
Major: English
EmailName: murf@big.fictional.edu
Ethnicity: Black
Homepage:
StudentStatus: 1
Notes:

StudentID: 800-00-5555
FirstName: Patrick
MiddleName: T.
LastName: Saint
ParentsNames: Jack and Jill
Address: 388 Emerald Way
City: Cork
State: IL
ZipCode: 35887
PhoneNumber: (317) 555-8794
Major: Herpetology
EmailName: TheSaint@fictional.edu
Ethnicity: Anglo
Homepage: http://www.fictional.edu/OleSod
StudentStatus: 1
Notes: Wears robes

AppendMe

StudentID: 777349993
CourseNumber: 101
Completed:
Grade:

StudentID: 777349993
CourseNumber: 150
Completed:
Grade:

StudentID: 777349993
CourseNumber: 102
Completed:
Grade:

StudentID: 999110000
CourseNumber: 150
Completed:
Grade:

StudentID: 999110000
CourseNumber: 122
Completed:
Grade:

StudentID: 999110000
CourseNumber: 105
Completed:
Grade:

StudentID: 999110000
CourseNumber: 103
Completed:
Grade:

AvailableClasses

CourseNumber: 101
Class Name: Basic English
Department Name: English
Section Number: 4
Instructor: McCoy

Term:	2-94
Units:	3

CourseNumber:	102
Class Name:	Basic Math
Department Name:	Mathematics
Section Number:	1
Instructor:	Murray
Term:	2-94
Units:	3

CourseNumber:	103
Class Name:	First Spanish
Department Name:	Language
Section Number:	2
Instructor:	Gonzalez
Term:	2-94
Units:	2

CourseNumber:	104
Class Name:	Journalism
Department Name:	English
Section Number:	1
Instructor:	Hernandon
Term:	2-94
Units:	2

CourseNumber:	105
Class Name:	Speech
Department Name:	Speech
Section Number:	1
Instructor:	Frank
Term:	2-94
Units:	2

CourseNumber:	202
Class Name:	Accounting
Department Name:	Business
Section Number:	1
Instructor:	Guffsaton
Term:	2-94
Units:	3

CourseNumber:	302
Class Name:	Physical Chemistry
Department Name:	Chemistry
Section Number:	1
Instructor:	Eiffler
Term:	2-94
Units:	3

CourseNumber:	150
Class Name:	Tennis
Department Name:	Physical Education
Section Number:	1
Instructor:	Lizzer
Term:	2-94
Units:	1

CourseNumber:	121
Class Name:	Basic circuits
Department Name:	Engineering
Section Number:	2
Instructor:	Shockly
Term:	2-94
Units:	3

CourseNumber:	203
Class Name:	Composition
Department Name:	English
Section Number:	1
Instructor:	Mauffler
Term:	2-94
Units:	3

CourseNumber:	223
Class Name:	Political Talking
Department Name:	Speech
Section Number:	1
Instructor:	Reagan
Term:	2-94
Units:	3

E

CourseNumber: 330
Class Name: Organic Chemistry
Department Name: Chemistry
Section Number: 1
Instructor: Curie
Term: 2-94
Units: 3

CourseNumber: 122
Class Name: Resistor Theory
Department Name: Engineering
Section Number: 1
Instructor: Charged
Term: 2-94
Units: 3

CourseNumber: 130
Class Name: Statistics
Department Name: Mathematics
Section Number: 2
Instructor: Counter
Term: 2-94
Units: 3

CompletedCourses

StudentID: 999009800
CourseNumber: 104
Completed: Yes
Grade: b

StudentID: 999448887
CourseNumber: 101
Completed: Yes
Grade: c

StudentID: 999119800
CourseNumber: 101
Completed: Yes
Grade: a

StudentID: 999339837
CourseNumber: 101
Completed: Yes
Grade: b+

StudentID: 000348282
CourseNumber: 101
Completed: Yes
Grade: c+

StudentID: 777349993
CourseNumber: 102
Completed: Yes
Grade: f

StudentID: 777349993
CourseNumber: 150
Completed: Yes
Grade: a

StudentID: 777349993
CourseNumber: 330
Completed: Yes
Grade: c+

StudentID: 999110000
CourseNumber: 102
Completed: Yes
Grade: d

StudentID: 999110000
CourseNumber: 150
Completed: Yes
Grade: b

StudentID: 999110000
CourseNumber: 122
Completed: Yes
Grade: c+

StudentID: 999110000
CourseNumber: 330
Completed: Yes
Grade: a+

StudentID: 999110000
CourseNumber: 302
Completed: Yes
Grade: b

StudentID: 000348282
CourseNumber: 102
Completed: Yes
Grade: a

StudentID: 000348282
CourseNumber: 103
Completed: Yes
Grade: b+

StudentID: 777349993
CourseNumber: 104
Completed: Yes
Grade: c+

Demo_Crosstab1

Sale Number: 1
Salesman: Smith
Category: Canoes
Sale Value: $30.00

Sale Number: 2
Salesman: Jones
Category: Yachts
Sale Value: $30,000.00

Sale Number: 3
Salesman: Doe
Category: Canoes
Sale Value: $500.00

Sale Number: 4
Salesman: Smith
Category: Canoes
Sale Value: $100.00

Sale Number:	5
Salesman:	Doe
Category:	Boats
Sale Value:	$5,000.00

Sale Number:	6
Salesman:	Jones
Category:	Canoes
Sale Value:	$300.00

Sale Number:	7
Salesman:	Doe
Category:	Yachts
Sale Value:	$40,000.00

Sale Number:	8
Salesman:	Smith
Category:	Canoes
Sale Value:	$100.00

Sale Number:	9
Salesman:	Jones
Category:	Boats
Sale Value:	$5,000.00

Sale Number:	10
Salesman:	Doe
Category:	Boats
Sale Value:	$4,500.00

Sale Number:	11
Salesman:	Jones
Category:	Yachts
Sale Value:	$400.00

Sale Number:	12
Salesman:	Smith
Category:	Yachts
Sale Value:	$2,000.00

Sale Number:	13
Salesman:	Jones
Category:	Canoes
Sale Value:	$500.00

Sale Number:	14
Salesman:	Doe
Category:	Boats
Sale Value:	$325.00

Fruit Choices

| Name: | Paul |
| Fruit: | Apple |

| Name: | Sam |
| Fruit: | Pear |

| Name: | Paul |
| Fruit: | Pear |

| Name: | Laine |
| Fruit: | Peach |

| Name: | Laine |
| Fruit: | Pear |

| Name: | Paul |
| Fruit: | Cherry |

| Name: | Mark |
| Fruit: | Cherry |

| Name: | Mark |
| Fruit: | Apple |

| Name: | Mark |
| Fruit: | Banana |

| Name: | Paul |
| Fruit: | Plum |

Fruits

| Name: | Paul |
| Fruit: | Apple |

| Name: | Sam |
| Fruit: | Pear |

| **Name:** | Paul |
| **Fruit:** | Pear |

| **Name:** | Laine |
| **Fruit:** | Peach |

| **Name:** | Laine |
| **Fruit:** | Pear |

| **Name:** | Paul |
| **Fruit:** | Cherry |

| **Name:** | Mark |
| **Fruit:** | Cherry |

| **Name:** | Mark |
| **Fruit:** | Apple |

| **Name:** | Mark |
| **Fruit:** | Banana |

| **Name:** | Paul |
| **Fruit:** | Plum |

| **Name:** | |
| **Fruit:** | Cherry |

| **Name:** | |
| **Fruit:** | Kiwi |

| **Name:** | |
| **Fruit:** | Lime |

GradeValues

| **Grade:** | a+ |
| **GradeValue:** | 4.5 |

| **Grade:** | a |
| **GradeValue:** | 4.0 |

| **Grade:** | b+ |
| **GradeValue:** | 3.5 |

| **Grade:** | b |
| **GradeValue:** | 3.0 |

| Grade: | c+ |
| GradeValue: | 2.5 |

| Grade: | c |
| GradeValue: | 2.0 |

| Grade: | d+ |
| GradeValue: | 1.5 |

| Grade: | d |
| GradeValue: | 1.0 |

| Grade: | f |
| GradeValue: | 0.0 |

StudentStatusLookup

| StudentStatus: | 1 |
| StatusName: | Full-Time |

| StudentStatus: | 2 |
| StatusName: | Part-Time |

| StudentStatus: | 3 |
| StatusName: | Visiting |

| StudentStatus: | 4 |
| StatusName: | Non-Degree |

GLOSSARY

The following is a list of Access or database terms used in *Teach Yourself Access 97 in 14 Days*. For a complete Access glossary, search online help under the category "Glossary."

action query   A query that performs actions when run.

ActiveX control   Newer term for OLE custom controls, part of the COM object model. Using ActiveX controls, you can greatly extend the functionality of your Access applications with little or no programming. An object you can insert in a form. The Calendar control used in an exercise in this book is an ActiveX control. After doing the exercise, you'll have a feel for ActiveX controls and how to incorporate them into your applications. (See Object Linking and Embedding.)

array   A finite set of variables sharing a common name and data type.

binding   Telling Access what table, query, or field a particular control, form, or report is linked to.

bound object   A control in a form or report that's linked to an underlying table or query.

check box   A control with two states: on (`true`) or off (`false`). Can be part of an option group.

code   Usually source code. These are the instructions that you type in to write a computer program; these lines of instructions are then compiled or interpreted into machine instructions that the computer can execute.

combo box   A control that combines both a list box and a text box.

concatenation   The chaining together of separate elements.

constant   A name assigned to a data storage location. Constants cannot change their value during code execution.

crosstab query   A query that performs a numerical process at its intersections. This query can also show summary information.

database   An orderly collection of data.

Database window   The view of your database where you can see its object collection.

Datasheet View   A window showing information in a grid.

declaration   A section of a module (Basic code) where, among other things, you declare the default data type for variables.

Design View   The mode in which an Access developer designs or changes the design of a table, form, report, or module.

function   A procedure that returns a value. Compare with subs.

group Records bunched according to a common criterion. Example: a report with records grouped according to the year in a selected date field.

information Data collected into a database.

input mask A mask (think of a screen) that allows the entry of only certain characters and can supply literal characters of its own. Most people use input masks as placeholders for formatted entries such as SSN, phone numbers, ZIP codes, and so forth.

Label tool A control for inserting unbound text into a form or report.

list box A control giving you a list of choices.

module Visual Basic code (VBA) containing one or more subs and procedures with one global declarations section.

normalize To decompose data into logical groups.

null An empty field or the end of the data set.

Object Linking and Embedding (OLE) Using OLE with Windows, you can embed an object created in one application in another. An example of OLE is a voice annotation made with the Windows Sound System embedded in a Word for Windows document. The sound object appears in the Word document as a microphone icon. When you click the icon, the document calls the Windows Sound System to play the sound. ActiveX is an extension of OLE controls. (See ActiveX.)

option button A button that can be on (true) or off (false).

option group A control with check boxes, radio buttons, or toggle buttons. Users can choose any one, but not more than one, control within the group.

primary key (field) A field that uniquely identifies a record in a table. Access orders (sorts or indexes) a table by primary key. A primary key value can't be duplicated in the same table nor can the field identified as primary key be null (blank).

Query by Example (QBE) A visual way to construct your queries using Access's query design grid. Using QBE, you drag the fields you want to query from a list box to the design grid and then optionally give Access an example of criteria to narrow the selection.

radio button A control with two toggled states: on (true) or off (false). Another name for an option button.

referential integrity The existence of a related value or attribute in a database depends upon another identical value or attribute.

relationship An association between two data tables in a database.

row source The source of an Access object's data.

sort   The order records appear in a database. For example, a table sorted in an ascending alphabetical sort would start with the As and move through the Zs.

SQL   Pronounced sequel, this stands for Structured Query Language. Certain relational database systems use this language for queries. Access can connect to many of these database systems and uses SQL extensively internally, too. When you use Access to construct a query for an attached or connected SQL table, you can create the query using normal Access QBE methods and Access translates your query to proper SQL syntax. You can also use SQL to construct queries and as the Control Source property for forms and reports.

sub   A procedure not returning a value. Compare with function.

text box   A control that accepts text entry and editing.

toolbar   A menu shortcut tool that appears directly under the menu bar. Although most people call this bar the button bar, it's officially called the toolbar by Microsoft.

unbound object   A control in a form or report that isn't linked to an underlying table or query.

variable   A name assigned to a data storage location. Variables can change value during code execution.

INDEX

Symbols

' (apostrophes), 571
* (asterisks), 321
\ (backslashes), 79
[ ] (brackets), 213, 247
: (colons), 563
& (concatenation operator), 214
... (ellipsis), 410
= (equals sign)
    criterial expressions, 155
    field expressions, 212
    operators, 279
! (exclamation points), 80, 540-541

\> (greater-than signs)
    greater-than operator, 279, 395
    \> buttons, 26
    \>\> buttons, 19, 44
< (less-than operator), 279, 395
( ) (parentheses), 482
. (periods), 540-541
(pound signs), 155
80:20 rule (programming), 547

A

A shortcut key, 59
accessing
    help systems, 28
    WWW (World Wide Web), 614-615
acNext command, 411
Action combo box, 502
action queries, 301-302
    defined, 684
    running, 302
activating
    combo boxes, 237
    list boxes, 237
    Office Assistant, 18

Activating the form exercise,
512-514
ActiveX controls, 596, 607
Access support, 611
Calendar, 607
defined, 684
disadvantages of, 612
enabling, 632
help files, 609
properties, 607-611
registering, 597-598
ActiveX Controls command
(Tools menu), 598
Add button, 62
Add Table dialog box, 62
Add-Remove Programs
applet, 632
Adding a Date field to a
table exercise, 268-270
Adding a field to a table
exercise, 52-55
Adding an input
mask exercise, 78-79
Adding report elements
exercise, 218-219
After Update property, 524
AfterUpdate events, 550
Align command (Format
menu), 139
aligning
fields, 192
form controls, 139
text boxes, 483
Alphanumeric fields, 46
Alt+X key combination, 515
Altering a subform exercise,
425-426
ampersands (&), concatenation
operators, 214
AND queries, 156-159
parameters, 346
Another command button
exercise, 405
answers to quizzes
day 1, 638
day 2, 638
day 3, 638
day 4, 638

day 5, 639
day 6, 639
day 7, 639
day 8, 639-640
day 9, 640
day 10, 640
day 11, 640
day 12, 641
day 13, 641
day 14, 641
API (Windows application
programming interface),
invoking, 568
apostrophes ('), 571
apparent field orders,
changing, 83-85
Append command (Query
Type menu), 321
Append dialog box, 321
append queries, 317-318
creating, 319-324
defined, 316
Append query exercise,
319-323
AppendMe table, 672-673
applications
linking (OLE), 603-606
macros, 496
benefits of, 496
creating, 501-505
arguments, 553
declaring, 553-557
Option Explicit, 573
placeholders, 554
naming, 559
arithmetic expressions,
evaluating, 481-482
arranging toolbars, 10
arrays, 572, 684
artifical fields, 346
ascending sorts (queries),
149
assigning
control defaults, 434
field properties, 68
properties, 138
Border Style, 425
Default Field, 98-100

Default Value, 360
Force New Page, 462
Group Footer, 472
Locked, 385-386
Navigation Buttons, 425
Tab Stop, 423-424
Validation Rule,
101-102
wizards, 376
associating fields, 363
asterisks (*), 321
wildcard characters, 153
Attaching macros exercise,
523-524
attaching macros to
controls, 536-540
forms, 512-515, 522-524
Auto Expand property, 232
auto expanding combo boxes,
231-232
AutoForm, 113-114
closing, 119
opening, 114
AutoForm button, 114
AutoFormat command
(Format menu), 438
autoformatting forms, 438
AutoNumber fields, 47
properties, 95
AvailableClasses table,
673-676
average values, calculating,
475, 481
Avg( ) function, 481

B

Back button, 45, 628
Back Color button, 430
background images, 440
backslashes (\), 79
bands
creating, 472
Detail, resizing, 207
Group Header, 216
Page Footer, 189
Page Header, 188
Report Header, 188

Basic report exercise, 184-186
Beeper macro, constructing, 501-505
Between criteria expressions, 155
Between...AND operators, 298
binding, 684
    combo boxes to tables, 235
    option groups, 259
    tables to fields, 208
blank fields, testing, 481
blank rows, inserting, 254
Bold button, 238
boldface, applying, 238
Border Color button, 431
Border Style property, 425
Border Width button, 430
borders
    colors, 431
    styles, 425
    widths, 430
bound controls, 127
Bound Object Frame tool, 655
bound objects, 684
Box tool, 655
brackets ([ ]), 247
    in expressions, 213
branching (conditional), 518-521
breaking form/subform links, 382
Browse button, 413
browsers, 614
    display differences, 632
Build button, 412
builder buttons, 78
built-in functions
    Avg( ), 481
    Count( ), 481
    DateAdd( ), 481
    dateDiff( ), 281, 481
    IIF( ), 481
    IsNull( ), 481
    Left( ), 481
    Now( ), 189, 481
    NZ( ), 481
    Sum( ), 472-473

buttons
    >, 26
    >>, 19, 44
    Add, 62
    AutoForm, 114
    Back, 45, 628
    Back Color, 430
    Bold, 238
    Border Color, 431
    Border Width, 430
    Browse, 413
    Build, 412
    builder buttons, 78
    Cancel, 7, 233
    Change Option, 4
    Close, 187
    cmdExit, 505
    command buttons
        events, 407
        icons, 412-414
        naming, 403
    Create, 64
    Current Database, 302
    Datasheet View, 80, 270
    Delete Row, 53
    Design, 50, 128
    Design View, 78
    Details, 74
    F/T, 260
    Field List, 139, 225, 455
    Find, 386
    Find First, 387
    Finish, 27, 45, 365, 621
    Form View, 229
    icons, 402
    Insert Field, 53
    New, 43, 56
    New Database, 22, 40
    New Object, 113
    New Object AutoForm, 263
    Next>, 26, 44, 363
    Open Database, 74
    option
        defined, 685
        labeling, 258
    option buttons, 489
    Personal, 24
    Primary Key, 60

    Print, 187
    Print Preview, 193
    Procedures View, 584
    Properties, 193, 258
    properties, 582
    Query Type, 321
    radio buttons, 685
    Register, 598
    Rename Field, 26
    Restore Window, 370
    Run, 147, 178, 276, 290, 356
    Sample Preview, 460
    Save, 151
    Search, 19
    Show Table, 176, 450
    Sort Ascending, 394-395
    Sort Descending, 395
    Sorting and Grouping, 215, 458, 472
    Special Effect, 141, 430, 436
    toggle buttons, 655
    tooltips, 9-10
    View Selection, 118
bytes (field sizes), 97

C

calculated fields, 490
Calculating expressions in reports exercise, 471-478
calculations
    arithmetic hierarchy, 481-482
    averages, 475, 481
    calculated fields, 490
    dates/time intervals, 279-282, 481
    errors, identifying, 475-477
    expressions, 471-478
    field-size numbers, 98
    GPAs (grade point averages), 475
    sums, 472-473
    times, 284
    weighted values, 454, 478

Calendar Control (ActiveX), 607-610

Calendar Object menu, Properties command, 609

Cancel button, 7, 233

Caption property, 85, 187, 242, 258

captions (tabbed forms), creating, 242

Cartesian products, 200

case-sensitivity, SQL (Structured Query Language), 314

centering
    controls (subforms), 425
    text boxes, 483

Change Option button, 4

changing
    ActiveX properties, 610
    apparent field orders, 83-85
    control properties, 380-382
        macros, 527-535
    default controls, 434
    error messages, 103
    fields
        order of, 82-85
        types, 48, 106
        widths/heights, 86
    query types, 312-314
    tab orders, 420-424

Changing field widths and height (exercises), 86

Changing the apparent field order exercise, 84

Changing the field order of a table exercise, 82-83

Changing the tab order exercise, 421-424

Check Box tool, 655

check boxes, 684

checkered-flag icons, 26, 45

choosing fields, 26

circular expressions, 480

Class Entry form, navigation buttons, 418

ClassSignUp form, 377
    subforms, 378

click( ) function, 411

clicking the mouse, On Click property, 407-408

Close button, 187

Close command (File menu), 27, 61, 64, 119, 194, 505, 579

closing
    Access, 32
    AutoForm, 119
    floating list boxes, 128
    forms, 126
    tables, 27, 55, 61

cmd prefix, 403

cmdExit button, 505, 514

cmdNextRecord buttons, creating, 400-403

cmdOpenClassEntry command button, 512

cmdOpenReportCards control, 513

cmdPreviousRecord buttons, creating, 405

code, defined, 684

colons (:), 563

colors
    borders, 431
    lines, 431

Column command (Insert menu), 66

Column Count property, 237

Column Widths property, 237

columns (tables)
    duplicating, 342
    inserting, 66
    moving, 84, 271
    zooming, 520

Combo Box tool, 226, 655

Combo Box Wizard, 224-229
    starting, 227

combo boxes, 88, 224
    activating, 237
    auto expanding, 231-232
    binding to tables, 235
    creating
        Combo Box Wizard, 224-229
        manually, 232-235
    defined, 684

fields, 229
    multicolumn, 231
    properties
        Auto Expand, 232
        Column Count, 237
        Column Widths, 237
        Format, 235
        Input Mask, 235
        Limit to List, 232
        List Width, 237
        Row Source, 234
    sizing, 284

Command Button control, 401

Command button hyperlink exercise, 625-628

Command Button tool, 508, 579, 655

Command Button Wizard, 401-403

command buttons
    defined, 655
    events, 407
        procedures, 410-412
    icons, 412-414
    images, adding, 591
    naming, 403
    properties
        ControlTip Text, 405
        On Click, 407-408
        Picture, 412-414
    scrollbars, creating, 400-405

commands
    acNext, 411
    Calendar Object menu, Properties, 609
    Copy menu, Paste, 529
    Database Utilities mn, Compact Database, 315
    DoCmd, 411
    Edit menu
        Cut, 138, 381
        Duplicate, 530
        Go To, 116
        Replace, 552
        Select All, 138, 386
        Select Report, 193
        Undo, 130, 137
    Exit, 411

File menu
    Close, 27, 61, 64, 119, 194, 505, 579
    Exit, 32
    Open, 50, 74
    Page Setup, 200
    Save, 66
    Save As, 174, 219
    Save as HTML, 619
Filter menu, Filter By Form, 387
Form menu, New, 120
Format menu
    Align, 139
    AutoFormat, 438
    Send to Back, 483
    Set Control Defaults, 434
    Snap To Grid, 139
Help menu, Content and Index, 18, 28
Insert menu
    Column, 66
    Date and Time, 437
    Hyperlink, 627
    Object, 604
    Row, 268
Layout menu, Snap to Grid, 427
Layout View menu
    Page Header/Footer, 247
    Report Header/Footer, 247
MsgBox, 412
Options menu
    Keep Help on Top, 21
    Show System Objects, 74
Query menu
    Delete, 310
    Make Table, 301
    Select Query, 312
Query Type menu, Append, 321
Records menu, Filter, 387
Save As menu, Export, 509
Start menu, Programs, 7
Toolbars menu, Customize, 13

Tools menu
    ActiveX Controls, 598
    Database Utilities, 315
    Options, 135, 439
    Relationships, 62, 176, 450
    Toolbars, 13
View menu
    Condition, 518
    Datasheet, 80
    Grid, 456
    Macro Names, 518
    Properties, 523
    Tab Order, 421
Window menu
    Tile Horizontally, 370
    Tile Vertically, 370
comments
    commenting tables, 58
    usage tips, 571
    Visual Basic, 571
Compact Database command (Database Utilities menu), 315
Compact layout option, 185
Compact option (Access installation), 6
compacting databases, 314-316
CompletedCourses table, 446
    sample data, 676-678
Compound macro exercise, 509-511
concatenation
    defined, 684
    fields, 211
Condition command (View menu), 518
conditional branching, 518-521
conditional loops, 569-570
Conditional message box macro (listing), 518-521
constants
    declaring, 574
    defined, 684

constructing queries
    actions, 301-302
    append, 316-324
    crosstab, 335-344
    delete, 308-313
    expressions, 448-454
    multitable, 169-173, 176-180
    parameters, 292
    ranges, 296-300
    simple, 144-147
    top, 324-329
    update, 329-334
    wildcards, 294
container forms,
    sizing, 427-428
    specifying, 363
Content and Index command (Help menu), 18, 28
context-sensitive help systems, 408-410
control properties, changing, 527-535
Control property macros exercise, 532-535
Control Source property, 208, 212, 259, 473
    editing, 218
    Row Source property, compared, 247
Control Wizards, 654
    disabling, 233
    enabling, 226
controls (forms), 112, 124
    Access identifiers, 540-541
    Active, enabling, 632
    ActiveX, 596, 607, 612, 684
        Access support, 611
        Calendar, 607
        help files, 609
        properties, 607-611
        registering, 597-598
    aligning, 139
    bound, 127
    centering, 425
    Command Button, 401
    defaults, setting, 434

deleting, 138
dragging, 258
duplicating, 529
dynamic, 485
    inserting, 485-486
    programming, 487
formatting, 140-142
grouping, 136-138
Image, 244
inserting, 139
labels, moving, 134
macros, attaching, 536-540
moving, 132-135
naming, 473
OLE (object linking and
    embedding), 596, 685
properties, 125, 138, 375-377
    changing, 380-382
    Enabled, 383-384
    Link Child Fields, 366,
        378
    Link Master Fields, 366
removing, 425
reordering, 15
scrollbars, creating, 400-405
sizing, 127-131
unbound, 127
unlocking, 508
VBX, 596
ControlTip Text property, 405
converting
    forms to HTML, 623-624
    image formats, 262
    reports to HTML, 623-624
    tables to HTML, 617-622
Copy menu, Paste command,
    529
Count( ) function, 481
Create button, 64
creating
    combo boxes
        Combo Box Wizard,
            224-229
        manually, 232-235
    controls
        dynamic, 485-486
        scrollbars, 400-405
    databases, 22-23, 40-41

error handlers, 562-564
field labels, 218
fields, 52
forms, 112
    AutoForm, 113-114
    combo boxes, 224
    Form Wizard, 119
    image controls, 244
    layouts, 433-434
    manually, 123
    subforms, 360-365,
        370-373
    tabbed, 240-243
    templates, 439
    unbound, 434
hyperlinks, 625-628
input boxes, 583-588
input masks, 78-79
list boxes, 232-235
macros, 501-505
mailing labels, 194-195
menu forms, 506-509
    macros, 509-514
option groups, 252
queries
    actions, 301-302
    append, 316-324
    crosstab, 335-344
    delete, 308-313
    expressions, 448-454
    parameters, 292
    ranges, 296-300
    subforms, 356-359
    top, 324-329
    update, 329-334
    wildcards, 294
records, 74-76
reports, 184
    Report Wizard, 184-186
subforms
    drag and drop, 370-373
    Main/Subform Wizard,
        360-364
tables, 42-45
    Datasheet View, 64-66
    fields, 43-44
    links, 62-64
    manually, 55-61

    Table Wizard, 24-27,
        42-45
Creating a new database
    exercise, 22-23
Creating a one-to-many link
    exercise, 62
Creating a table without a
    wizard exercise, 56-61
Creating the new database
    exercise, 40-41
Creating the StudentPersonal
    table exercise, 43-45
Creating/programming the
    option group exercise,
    256-260
criteria queries, 152-159
    constructing, 151
    dates, 276-278
        calculations, 279-282
        expressions, 280-282
    running, 152
    syntax, 155
        <Date( ), 156
        = (equal sign), 155
        AND, 156-159
        Between, 155
        In, 156
        Left( ), 156
        Like( ), 156
        Not, 156
        OR, 156-159
        usage tips, 153
        Year( ), 156
cross-references (help system),
    410
crosstab queries, 336-339
    advantages of, 341
    creating, 335-339
    defined, 335, 684
    forms, 347
    multiple operatives, 341-344
    subtotals, compared, 347
    updating, 347
Crosstab Query exercise,
    336-339
Ctrl+' key combination,
    354, 358

Ctrl+A key combination,
138-140
Ctrl+F6 key combination,
512
Ctrl+N key combination, 22
Ctrl+V key combination,
158, 217, 382, 458
Ctrl+X key combination,
158, 217, 381, 458
Ctrl+Z key combination, 130
Currency fields, 47
  properties, 95
currency variable types, 585
Current Database option
  button, 302
cursors
  double-sided arrows, 128,
    134
  hand-shaped, 132
Custom install option (Access
  installation), 5
Customize command (Toolbars
  menu), 13
Customize dialog box, 13
customizing
  design grids, 147, 193
  error messages, 103
  functions, 569
  menu bars, 11-15
  status bars, 32
  subforms, 424-428
  toolbars, 10-15, 32
Cut command (Edit menu),
  138, 381

D

data
  editing, 160
  entering, 122
  ranges (queries), 296-300
  sample table data
    AppendMe, 672-673
    AvailableClasses, 673-676
    CompletedCourses,
      676-678
    Demo_Crosstab1,
      678-680

    Fruit Choices, 680
    Fruits, 680-681
    GradeValues, 681-682
    StudentPersonal,
      668-672
    StudentStatusLookup,
      682
  validating
    error messages, 103
    input masks, 80-82
    lookups, 88-89
data criteria queries, 155
Data fields, 270
data integrity, 92
Data properties, 377
data types
  changing, 106
  fields, 46-48
    AutoNumber, 47
    changing, 48
    Currency, 47
    Date/Time, 46
    Hyperlink, 47, 625
    Lookup Wizard, 47
    Memo, 47
    Number, 46
    OLE Object, 47, 262
    Text, 46
    Yes/No, 47
  properties, 92, 97
    defaults, 98
Data validation error message
  exercise, 103
data-entry forms, creating,
  113-114
Database toolbar, 658
Database Utilities command
  (Tools menu), 315
Database Utilities menu,
  Compact Database com-
  mand, 315
Database windows, 24, 240,
  684
databases, 38
  compacting, 314-316
  creating, 22-23, 40-41
  defined, 684
  designing, 39, 61

efficiency of, 39, 447, 471
forms
  advantages, 112
  AutoForm, 113-114
  closing, 126
  controls, 124-125
  creating, 112
  Form Wizard, 119
  layout, 120
  naming, 120
  navigating, 115-119
naming, 22-23, 41
objects, 61
opening, 50, 74
planning, 38-40
queries, 268
  actions, 301-302
  advantages, 268
  append queries, 316-324
  changing types of,
    312-314
  crosstab queries, 335-344
  dates, 276-282
  delete queries, 308-313
  expressions, 447-454
  parameters, 289-292
  ranges, 296-300
  repeating, 477
  select queries, 301
  SQL (Structured Query
    Language), 312
  top queries, 324-329
  update queries, 329-334
  updating, 477
  wildcards, 294
records
  finding, 386-392
  relationships, 354-355
structures, 369
tables, 40
  closing, 27, 61
  creating, 42-45, 55-59, 61
  hiding, 74
  linking, 56, 61-64
  matching, 62
  modifying, 50
  naming, 26, 44
  querying, 144

relationships, 61-62
validating, 62
see also records
Datasheet command (View menu), 80
Datasheet View, 74
defined, 684
tables, 64-66
moving columns, 271
reordering fields, 83-85
Datasheet View button, 80, 270
datasheets, 262
Date and Time command (Insert menu), 437
Date criteria exercise, 276-278
<Date( ) criteria expressions, 156
Date fields
formats, 273-274, 284
changing, 275
inserting, 268-270
invalid entries, 273-274
date( ) function, 281
Date math and expression fields exercise, 279-280
Date/Time fields, 46
benefits of, 68
properties, 94, 104
dateAdd( ) function, 481
datediff( ) function, 281, 284, 291, 481
DateOfBirth fields, 281
dates
criteria queries, 155-156
inserting, 437
intervals between, calculating, 481
notations, 276
queries, 276-278
calculations, 279-282
expressions, 279-282
DDE (Dynamic Data Exchange), 568
Decimal Places property, 105
declarations
defined, 684
implicit, 573

declaring
constants, 574
functions, 552-553, 561
arguments, 553-557
input boxes, 588
key fields, 59
variables, 555, 574-575
Declaring variables exercise, 584-586
default controls, changing, 434
Default Field properties, 98
assigning, 98-100
default properties
assigning, 98
message boxes, 582
Default Value property, 360
Default View property, 425
defining
constants, 574
functions, 552-553, 561
arguments, 553-557
input boxes, 588
key fields, 59
variables, 555, 574-575
Del key, 308
Delete command (Query menu), 310
Delete key, 50, 138
delete queries, 308, 312
creating, 309-313
Delete query exercise, 309-313
Delete Row button, 53
deleting
fields, 50, 207
form controls, 138
query fields, 175
records, 106, 308
Demo_Crosstab1 table, 678-680
Design button, 50, 128
design grids
customizing, 193
macros, 501-505
queries, 145-146
Criteria rows, 151
customizing, 147
Sort rows, 149

Design View, 56
defined, 684
exiting, 270
fields, reordering, 82
grids, 131
Design View button, 78
designing
databases, 39, 61
forms, 120
subforms, 355
desktop hot spots, 12-13
Detail bands, resizing, 207
Details button, 74
dialog boxes
Add Table, 62
Append, 321
Customize, 13
Expression Builder, 532
Find in Field, 386
Join Properties, 465
Print Setup, 489
Prototype label, 199
Relationships, 63
Table Properties, 74
Table Wizard, 26
Different criteria demonstration exercise, 290
Dim statements, 555, 572-573
disabling Control Wizards, 233
displaying
form controls, 160
help topics, 19, 30
labels, 532
message boxes, 579-583
running sums (reports), 201
DisplayMessage( ) function, 577
exercise, 579-583
Distinctrow keyword, 312
docking
menu bars, 12-13
toolbars, 12-13
DoCmd actions, 411
attaching, 439
help system, 439

documents
embedding, 598-603
hyperlinks, 624-628
linking, 598-603
live links, 603-606
double field-size numbers, 97
double variables, 585
**double-sided arrow cursors,
128, 134**
down scrollbars, creating, 400
**drag-and-drop, creating
subforms with, 370**
dragging
controls, 258
toolbars, 10
**Duplicate command (Edit
menu), 530**
duplicating
columns, 342
controls, 529
dynamic controls, 485
inserting, 485-486
programming, 487
**Dynamic controls exercise,
485-487**
**Dynamic Data Exchange
(DDE), 568**
dynamic pages, 620

E

Edit menu commands
Cut, 138, 381
Duplicate, 530
Go To, 116
Replace, 552
Select All, 138, 386
Select Report, 193
Undo, 130, 137
Edit mode, 190, 238
editing
form data, 160
functions, 580
properties, 218
queries, 147-148
records, 77
reports, 187-193

ellipsis (...) icons, 410
embedding
images in forms, 262-265,
429-433
lines, 431
rectangles, 429-431
MS Office documents,
598-603
**Embedding a graphic in a form
exercise, 262-265**
**Enabled property, setting,
383-384**
enabling
ActiveX controls, 632
Control Wizards, 226
**Enforce Referential Integrity
option, 64**
**enforcing referential integrity,
64, 224**
**Entering data directly into a
table exercise, 74-76**
entering form data, 122
equal signs (=)
criterial expressions, 155
field expressions, 212
operators, 279
**error messages, customizing,
103**
errors
runtime, 562
trapping, 562-568
functions, 560
macros, 503
Esc key, 80, 508
**evaluating expressions,
481-482**
Event properties, 377
**event-driven programming,
570**
events, 407
AfterUpdate, 550
DoCmd actions, attaching,
439
OnClick, 411-412
OnError, 411
procedures, 410-412

responding to
macros, 548
Visual Basic, 548-551
triggering, 551
**Excel documents, linking to
Access, 603-606**
exclamation points (!), 80
identifiers, 540-541
executing macros, 525-527
exercises
Activating the form, 512-514
Adding a Date field to a table,
268-270
Adding a field to a table,
52-55
Adding an input mask, 78-79
Adding report elements,
218-219
Altering a subform, 425-426
Another command button,
405
Append query, 319-323
Attaching macros, 523-524
Basic report, 184-186
Calcuating expressions in
reports, 471-478
Changing field widths and
height, 86
Changing the apparent field
order, 84
Changing the field order
of a table, 82-83
Changing the tab order,
421-424
Command button hyperlink,
625-628
Compacting a database, 315
Compound macro, 509-511
Conditional message box
macro, 518-521
Control property macros,
532-535
Creating a new database,
22-23
Creating a one-to-many
link, 62
Creating a table without a
wizard, 56-61

Creating and programming the option group, 256-260

Creating the new database, 40-41

Creating the StudentPersonal table, 43-45

Criteria queries, 151-152

Crosstab Query, 336-339

Data validation error message, 103

Date criteria, 276-278

Date math and expression fields, 279-280

Declaring variables, 584-586

Delete query, 309-313

Different criteria demonstration, 290

DisplayMessage( ) function, 579-583

Dynamic controls, 485-487

Embedding a graphic in a form, 262-265

Entering data directly into a table, 74-76

Expressions in queries, 448-454

Field control properties, 380-382

Field expressions in reports, 206-211

Filter by selection, 391-392

Form, 528-531

Form creation, 113-114

Form with combo boxes, 224-229

Form with subform, 360-364

Graphic elements in forms, 429-431

Graphic elements in reports, 483-485

Grouped and totaled report, 215-217

Grouping and sorting in reports, 455-462

Help with Help, 28-32

Locked and Enabled properties, 383-386

Macro design grid, 501-505

Making a table action query, 301-302

Making mailing labels, 195-198

Making the subform's query, 356-359

Manual combo box programming, 233-235

Marquee selections, 136-137

Modifying a report, 187-193

Modifying a table, 50

Modifying an existing table, 254-255

Moving form controls, 132-135

Office Assistant introduction, 18-20

ORs and ANDs in criteria, 156-158

Parameter query, 292

Publish to the Web Wizard, 618-622

quick reference, 644-652

Range parameter query, 298

Record manipulation, 400-404

Record selectors/navigation buttons, 418-419

Resizing a form control, 128-131

sample data
    AppendMe, 672-673
    AvailableClasses, 673-676
    CompletedCourses, 676-678
    Demo_Crosstab1, 678-680
    Fruit Choices, 680
    Fruits, 680-681
    GradeValues, 681-682
    StudentPersonal, 668-672
    StudentStatusLookup, 682

Setting a Default Field property, 98-100

Setting the Data Validation property, 101-102

Simple queries, 144-147

Sorting in a query, 149

Switchboard or menu form, 506-509

Tabbed form, 240-243

Three-table query, 176-180

Tie a VB function to form controls, 576-579

Two-table query, 169-172

Using a wizard to make a table, 24-27

Using the Formatting toolbar, 140-142

Variations of criteria, 153

Wildcard parameter queries, 294

Exit command (File menu), 32, 411

Exit macros, 511

exiting
    Access, 32
    Design View, 270
    Edit mode, 190, 238
    forms, 505
    functions, 564
    subprocedures, 411
    Zoom mode, 454

expanding combo boxes, 231-232

Export command (Save As menu), 509

Expression Builder, 540-542

Expression Builder dialog box, 532

expressions, 199, 447-448
    calculating, 471-478
    circular, 480
    creating, 448-454
    date queries, 279-282
    efficiency, 471
    evaluating, 481-482
    fields, 205-211
    in-query, 471
    inserting, 456
    placement, 471
    syntax, 214
        concatenation (&), 214
        equal signs (=), 213
        FirstName fields, 213

space characters, 213
Trim( ), 213
**Expressions in queries exercise,
448-454**
**extensions (filename), .mdb,
23, 41**

F

F/T option button, 260
F1 shortcut key, 18, 56, 408
**F11 shortcut key, 474, 477,
509**
F4 shortcut key, 270
F5 shortcut key, 116
**Field control properties
exercise, 380-382**
field expressions, 205-211
concatenation (&), 214
equal signs (=), 213
FirstName fields, 213
Trim( ), 213
**Field expressions in reports
exercise, 206-211**
**Field List button, 139, 225,
455**
**Field Property New Number
option, 47**
**Field Size property, 85,
104-105**
field templates, 77
benefits of, 80-82
creating, 78-79
data validation, 80-82
defined, 685
exclamation points (!), 80
format, 79
placeholders, 79
fields
adding to queries, 145-146
aligning, 192
associating, 363
binding to tables, 208
choosing, 26
combo boxes, 229
concatenating, 211
creating, 43-44, 52

data types, 46-48
AutoNumber, 47
changing, 48, 106
Currency, 47
Date/Time, 46
Hyperlink, 47
Lookup Wizard, 47
Memo, 47
Number, 46
OLE Object, 47
selecting, 54-57
Text, 46
Yes/No, 47
Date
data formats, 275
inserting, 268-270
invalid entries, 273-274
deleting, 50, 207
highlighting, 50
inserting, 52-55, 361
key fields, 57
defining, 59
identifying, 62
labels, moving, 216
linking, 382, 448
naming, 52, 58
properties, 92, 97
Caption, 85
Decimal Places, 105
Default Field, 98-100
defaults, 98
Field Size, 85, 104-105
Format, 104
Required, 104
setting, 68
Validation Rule, 101-102
removing from queries,
174-175
renaming, 44
reordering
Datasheet View, 83-85
Design View, 82-83
selecting, 383
sizes, 97
sizing, 59, 128-131, 190-191,
206-211
benefits, 87
rows, 85-86

widths, 85-86
StudentStatus, 255
see also controls
File menu commands
Close, 27, 61, 64, 119, 194,
505, 579
Exit, 32
Open, 50, 74
Page Setup, 200
Save, 66
Save As, 174, 219
Save as HTML, 619
file names
databases, 23
long, 24, 42
.mdb extension, 23, 41
**Filter By Form command
(Filter menu), 387**
**Filter by selection exercise,
391-392**
**Filter command (Records
menu), 387**
**Filter menu, Filter By Form
command, 387**
Filter/Sort toolbar, 665
filtering searches, 389-390
by selection, 391-392
Find button, 386
Find First button, 387
Find in field dialog box, 386
finding records
Filter by Form command,
387-390
Filter by Selection command,
391-392
Find button, 386-387
**Finish button, 27, 45,
365, 621**
**FirstName fields (mailing
labels), 195, 213**
Fixed property, 478
flat files, 39
floating help systems, 21
**floating list boxes, closing,
128**
fonts
boldface, applying, 238
mailing labels, 195

footers, 188-189
  group footers, 460
Force New Page property, 462
Forecolor keyword, 551
Form creation exercise,
  113-114
Form Design toolbar, 661
Form exercise, 528-531
Form menu, New command,
  120
Form View button, 229
Form View toolbar, 660
Form with combo boxes
  exercise, 224-229
Form with subform exercise,
  360-364
Form Wizard, 119
Format menu commands
  Align, 139
  AutoFormat, 438
  Send to Back, 483
  Set Control Defaults, 434
  Snap To Grid, 139
Format property, 104, 235,
  377, 478
formatting
  autoformat option, 438
  controls, 140-142
  Date fields, 273-275
Formatting toolbar, 140-142
  illustrated, 661-664
Formatting toolbar exercise,
  140-142
forms
  advantages, 112, 160
  autoformatting, 438
  background images, 440
  ClassSignUp, 377-378
  closing, 126
  combo boxes, 224
    activating, 237
    auto expanding, 231-232
    Combo Box Wizard,
      224-229
    manual programming,
      232-235
    multicolumn, 231
    sizing, 284

controls, 124
  aligning, 139
  bound, 127
  deleting, 138
  displaying, 160
  formatting, 140-142
  grouping, 136-138
  inserting, 139
  labels, 134
  moving, 132-135
  properties, 138, 375-377
  sizing, 127-131
  unbound, 127
converting to HTML,
  623-624
creating, 112
  AutoForm, 113-114
  Form Wizard, 119
  Main/Subform wizard,
    360-364
  manually, 123
data entry, 122
dates, inserting, 437
dragging and dropping, 370
exiting, 505
fields, 120
  associating, 363
frmCafeteriaBalance, 548
images, 428-429
  controls, 244
  embedding, 262-265,
    429-433
  icons, 414
labeling, 238
layouts, 120, 363, 433-434
linked, 363
list boxes, 224
  activating, 237
  defined, 685
  manual programming,
    232-235
macros
  attaching, 522-524
  executing, 525-527
menus, creating, 506-509
naming, 120

navigating
  Go To menu, 116
  keyboard shortcuts, 116
  navigation buttons,
    418-419
  scrollbars, 115
  toolbars, 118-119
OLE objects, inserting, 438
option groups
  benefits of, 253-254
  creating, 252
  defined, 251
  option values, 260
PictureStudentPersonal, 265
properties
  Caption, 242
  Default View, 425
  Link Master Fields, 378
  Navigation Buttons, 419
  Picture, 414
  Record Selectors, 419
  setting, 125
  Tab Stop, 423-424
  viewing, 125
queries, binding, 369
records
  finding, 386-392
  record selectors, 418-419
  sorting, 394
reports, compared, 184
security, 160
  Enabled property,
    383-385
  Locked property, 385-386
special effects
  raised graphics, 437
  sunken graphics, 436
subforms, 354, 369
  creating, 360-365,
    370-373
  customizing, 424-428
  designing, 355
  efficiency of, 395
  linking, 378-379, 395
  naming, 355
  planning, 361
  queries, 355-356, 359,
    368

sizing, 427-428
specifying, 363
synchronizing, 366
tabbed, 239
    adding/removing pages,
        243
    creating, 240-243
    tab order, 420-424
templates, 439
times, inserting, 437
unbound
    advantages of, 284
    creating, 434
fractions, entering, 106
frmCafeteriaBalance form, 548
Fruit Choices query, 464
Fruit Choices table, 680
Fruits table, 680-681
functions, 575
applying, 558-559
arguments, 553
    placeholders, 554
Avg( ), 481
click( ), 411
Count( ), 481
customizing, 569
date( ), 281
DateAdd( ), 481
dateDiff( ), 281, 284,
    291, 481
defined, 552, 684
defining, 552-553, 561
    arguments, 553-557
DisplayMessage( ), 577-583
editing, 580
error-trapping, 560
exiting, 564
IIF( ), 481
Inputbox( ), 583
IsNull( ), 481
Left( ), 481
LoanPayment( )
    applying, 557-559
    declaring, 554-557
    error-trapping, 562-564
Ltrim( ), 213
Mid( ), 481
Now( ), 189, 481

NZ( ), 481
placeholders, 559
Repeat( ), 569
Right( ), 481
Rtrim( ), 213
Sum( ), 472-473
syntax, 580
Trim( ), 213, 247
tying to objects, 576-579
unbound, 557-559

G

global options, 135
**Globally Unique Identifiers
    (GUIDs), 97**
**Go To command (Edit
    menu), 116**
Go To menu commands, 116
GoTo statements, 590
**GPAs (grade point averages),
    calculating, 475**
GradeValue table, 476
GradeValues table, 446
displaying, 450
efficiency of, 447
opening, 477
sample data, 681-682
**Graphic elements in forms
    exercise, 429-431**
**Graphic elements in reports
    exercise, 483-485**
graphics
converting, 262
embedding, 262-265
forms, 428-429
    background images, 440
    controls, 244
inserting, 429-433
    in forms, 428-429
    in reports, 483-485
    lines, 431
    rectangles, 429-431
sending to back, 483
**greater-than operator (>),
    279, 395**
green cross icons, 323

**Grid command (View menu),
    456**
grids, 131
customizing, 193
macro design, 501-505
queries, 145-146
    customizing, 147
Group Footer property, 472
Group Header bands, 216
Group On property, 458
**group-aligning form controls,
    139**
**Grouped and totaled report
    exercise, 215-217**
grouping
controls, 136-138
reports, 215-217, 455-462
**Grouping and sorting in
    reports exercise, 455-462**
groups
average values, calculating,
    475
defined, 685
option groups
    binding, 259
    creating, 252
    defined, 251-252
    inserting, 256
    uses, 253-254
**GUIDs (Globally Unique
    Identifiers), 97**

H

<H1> HTML tag, 616
hand-shaped cursors, 132
**handlers (error), creating,
    562-564**
headers, 188
group headers, 460
**Help menu, Content and
    Index command, 18, 28**
Help systems
accessing, 18, 28, 56
ActiveX controls, 609
context-sensitive, 408-410
cross-references, 410

floating, 21
Help Topics window, 29
keywords, 551
Office Assistant, 18-21
    activating, 18
    searching, 19
properties, 408-410
searching, 30
tooltips, 9-10
topics
    displaying, 20, 30
    indexing, 29
Help Topics window, 29
Help with Help exercise,
28-32
hiding tables, 74
Hierarchy (arithmetic),
481-482
highlighting fields, 50
hot spots (desktop), 12-13
controls, 128
HTML (HyperText Markup
Language), 615
Access conversions
    forms, 623-624
    reports, 623-624
    tables, 617-622
advantages of, 617
pages, storing, 620
tags
    <H1>, 616
    <P>, 616
templates, 620
HTTP (HyperText Transfer
Protocol), 614
Hyperlink command (Insert
menu), 627
Hyperlink
data type, 625
fields, 47
property, 97, 625-627
hyperlinks, 614, 624
inserting, 625-628
HyperText Markup Language,
see HTML

I

icons, 402
command buttons, 412-414
forms, 414
green crosses, 323
properties (message boxes),
    582
identifiers, 571
macros, 540-541
identifying
blank fields, 481
key fields, 62
IDs, Replication IDs, 97
if...then statements, 564
IIF( ) function, 481
Image control, 244
Image tool, 655
images
converting, 262
embedding, 262-265
forms, 428-429
    background images, 440
    controls, 244
inserting, 429-433
    in forms, 428-429
    in reports, 483-485
    lines, 431
    rectangles, 429-431
sending to back, 483
implicit declarations, 573
In( ) criteria expressions, 156
in-query expressions, 471
Increment property, 47
indexing help topics, 29
information, defined, 685
inner joins, 463
input boxes
creating with Visual Basic,
    583-588
defining, 588
positioning, 588
titling, 588
Input Mask Builder Wizard, 78
Input Mask property, 235

input masks, 77
benefits, 80-82
creating, 78-79
data validation, 80-82
defined, 685
exclamation points (!), 80
format, 79
placeholders, 79
Input-mask Field property, 80
Inputbox( ) function, 583
Insert Field button, 53
Insert menu commands
Column, 66
Date and Time, 437
Hyperlink, 627
Object, 604
Row, 268
inserting
blank rows (tables), 254
columns, 66
dates in forms, 437
dynamic controls, 485-486
expressions, 456
fields in queries, 26, 52-55,
    146, 361
    Date, 268-270
    unbound, 208, 211
form controls, 139
graphics in forms, 428-433
hyperlinks, 625-628
images in reports, 483-485
OLE objects in forms, 438
option groups, 256
rows, 268
time displays in forms, 437
installing
Access 97, 4-6, 32
TCP/IP software, 632
integers, 585
field sizes, 97
Internet, 614
intranets, 614
invoking Windows API
(application programming
interface), 568
IsNull( ) function, 481

J-K

join lines, arranging, 450
Join Properties dialog box, 465
joins, 463
  inner, 463
  outer, 464-467

**Keep help on top command
  (Options menu), 21**
Keep Together property, 458
key combinations
  Alt+X, 515
  Ctrl+', 354, 358
  Ctrl+A, 138-140
  Ctrl+F6, 512
  Ctrl+N, 22
  Ctrl+V, 158, 217, 382, 458
  Ctrl+X, 158, 217, 381, 458
  Ctrl+Z, 130
  Shift+F2, 103, 209, 279, 454,
    473, 478, 520, 535
key fields, 57
  defining, 59
  identifying, 62
keys
  Del, 308
  F1, 56, 408
  F11, 474, 477, 509
  F4, 270
  primary, 685
keywords, 551-552
  Distinctrow, 312
  Forecolor, 551
  help system, 551
  optional, 559
  REM, 571

L

Label tool, 218, 654, 685
Label Wizard, 195
  creating mailing labels,
    195-198
  printing mailing labels, 199

labeling
  forms, 238, 242
  text boxes, 472
  option buttons, 258
labels, 134
  cutting, 458
  displaying, 532
  field labels
    creating, 218
    moving, 216
  forms, 238, 242
  mailing labels
    creating, 194-195
    fields, 195
    printing, 199-201
    sizing, 200
    sorting, 197
  moving, 134
  pasting, 458
  text boxes, 472
languages
  HTML (HyperText Markup
    Language), 615
    Access conversions,
      617-624
    advantages of, 617
    pages, storing, 620
    tags, 616
    templates, 620
  SGML (Standard Generalized
    Markup Language), 615
  SQL (Structured Query
    Language), 237, 496-500
    advantages of, 541
    applications, 500-501
    defined, 686
  Visual Basic, 568
    advantages of, 568
    code styles, 572
    comments, 571
    complex input, 569
    constants, 574
    Dim statement, 572-573
    events, 570
    functions, 569, 575
    GoTo statements, 590
    identifiers, 571
    loops, 569-570

    modules, 573
    sub-procedures, 575-576
    variables, 574-575
Last Name property, 85
**LastName fields (mailing
  labels), 85, 195**
  grouping, 216
launching Access, 7, 32
layout changes, 87
  saving, 106
**Layout menu, Snap to Grid
  command, 427**
Layout View menu commands
  Page Header/Footer, 247
  Report Header/Footer, 247
layouts
  forms, 363, 433-434
  reports, 482-485
**Left( ) criteria expressions,
  156**
Left( ) function, 481
**less-than operators (<), 279,
  395**
**Like( ) criteria expressions,
  156**
Limit to List property, 232
Line tool, 431, 655
**lines, embedding in forms,
  431**
**Link Child Field property,
  395**
**Link Child Fields property,
  366, 378**
link fields, 58
  displaying, 171
**Link Master Field property,
  395**
**Link Master Fields property,
  366, 378**
linked forms, 363
linking, 382
  fields, 448
  forms with subforms,
    378-379
  MS Office documents,
    598-603
    live links, 603-606
  tables, 56, 61-64, 450
  Web documents, 624-628

List Box tool, 655
list boxes, 224, 655
　　activating, 237
　　creating, 232-235
　　defined, 685
List Width property, 229, 237
live links, 603-606
lng variable prefix, 551
LoanPayment( ) function
　　applying, 557-559
　　declaring, 554-557
　　error-trapping, 562-564
Locked and Enabled properties
　　exercise, 383-386
Locked property, setting,
　　385-386
long filenames, 24, 42
long integers, 97
long variables, 585
Lookup properties, 88
Lookup Wizard fields, 47
lookups, 88-89
loops, 568-570
Ltrim( ) function, 213

M

macBeeper macro, 501-505
Macro design grid exercise,
　　501-505
Macro Names command
　　(View menu), 518
Macro toolbar, 663
macros, 496
　　Access identifiers, 540, 541
　　actions, 501
　　attaching to
　　　　controls, 536-540
　　　　forms, 512-515, 522-524
　　benefits of, 496
　　columns, zooming, 520
　　conditional branching,
　　　　518-521
　　control properties, 527-535
　　creating, 501-505
　　design grids, 501-505
　　error traps, 503

executing, 525-527
Expression Builder, 540
functions, 590
macBeeper, 501-505
macStudentPersonalData,
　　519-521
menu forms, 509-514
naming, 509-511, 518
macStudentPersonalData
　　macro, 519-521
mailing labels
　　creating, 194
　　fields, 195
　　fonts, 195
　　printing, 199-201
　　sizing, 200
　　sorting, 197
Main/Subform Wizard
　　forms
　　　　creating, 361-366
　　　　layouts, 363
　　　　opening, 360
Make Table command (Query
　　menu), 301
Making a table action query
　　exercise, 301-302
Making mailing labels exercise,
　　195-198
Making the subform's query
　　exercise, 356, 359
Manual combo box
　　programming exercise,
　　233-235
marquee selections, 136-137
Marquee selections exercise,
　　136-137
masks (input), 77
　　benefits, 80-82
　　creating, 78-79
　　data validation, 80-82
　　defined, 685
　　exclamation points (!), 80
　　format, 79
　　placeholders, 79
matching
　　tables, 62
　　words (queries), 156

mathematical calculations
　　arithmetic hierarchy, 481-482
　　averages, 475, 481
　　calculated fields, 490
　　dates/time intervals, 279-282,
　　　　481
　　errors, identifying, 475-477
　　expressions, 471-478
　　field-size numbers, 98
　　GPAs (grade point averages),
　　　　475
　　sums, 472-473
　　times, 284
　　weighted values, 454, 478
maximizing windows, 75, 113
.mdb filename extensions,
　　23, 41
Me expressions, 540
Memo fields, 47
　　properties, 93
menu bars, 9
　　customizing, 11-15
　　docking, 12-13
menu forms, 509-514
message boxes
　　displaying, 579-583
　　properties
　　　　buttons, 582
　　　　defaults, 582
　　　　icons, 582
Mickeys, 588
Mid( ) function, 481
mistakes, undoing, 130
models (programming),
　　event-driven, 570
modes, 77
　　Edit, 190
modFirstPrograms file, 579
Modifying a report exercise,
　　187-193
Modifying a table exercise, 50
Modifying an existing table
　　exercise, 254-255
Module toolbar, 663
modules, 573, 577
　　defined, 685
　　starting, 554
mouse clicks, On Click
　　property, 407-408

moving
columns, 271
controls, 132-135, 258
fields, 82-83
labels, 216
toolbars, 10
Moving form controls exercise, 132-135
MSCAL.OCX, 609
MsgBox command, 412
multicolumn combo boxes, 231
multitable queries
constructing, 169-173
running, 172, 178

N

Name property, 473
naming
command buttons, 403
controls, 473
databases, 22, 41
fields, 44, 52
link fields, 58
files, 42
forms, 120
macros, 509-511, 518
placeholders (functions), 559
subforms, 355
tables, 26, 44, 184
navigating, 55, 59
Access
menu bars, 9, 13-15
title bars, 8
toolbars, 9-15
forms
Go To menu, 116
keyboard shortcuts, 116
scrollbars, 115
toolbars, 118-119
records, 402
navigation buttons, 418
removing, 418-419
Navigation Buttons property, 425
New button, 43, 56

New command (Form menu), 120
New Database button, 22, 40
New Object AutoForm button, 263
New Object button, 113
Next> button, 26, 44, 363
NextRecord command buttons, creating, 400-403
nonrelational databases, 39
normalization, 685
Not criteria expressions, 156
NOT queries, 161
Notes control, 132
Now( ) function, 189, 481
null values, 685
Number fields, 46, 255
limitations, 69
properties, 94, 97-98
Decimal Places, 105
Field Size, 104-105
field size, 97-98
NZ( ) function, 481

O

Object command (Insert menu), 604
object linking and embedding, *see* **OLE**
objects
bound, 684
OLE (object linking and embedding), 283-284
selecting, 188
unbound, 686
OCXs, *see* **ActiveX**
Office Assistant, 18-21, 32
activating, 18, 28
searching, 19
Office Assistant introduction exercise, 18-20
OLE (object linking and embedding)
controls, 596
defined, 283, 685
live links, 603-606

objects, 283-284
inserting, 438
see also ActiveX
OLE Object fields, 47, 262
OnClick events, 411-412, 607
OnClick property, 407-408, 542
OnError events, 411
OnTop property, 21
one-to-many relationships, 62
OnError statements, 562
Open command (File menu), 50, 74
Open Database button, 74
OpenForm macros, 510
opening
databases, 50, 74
tables, 477
OpenReport macros, 510
operators
AND, 298
Between...AND, 298
concatenation (&), 214
equality (=), 279
greater-than (>), 279, 395
less-than (<), 279, 395
optDeansList option button, 518
Option Button tool, 252
option buttons
defined, 685
disadvantages, 489
labeling, 258
Option Compare Database declarations, 577
Option Explicit
arguments, 573
statements, 584
Option Group tool, 252, 655
Option Group Wizard, 257
option groups
advantages of, 253-254
binding, 259
creating, 252
defined, 251, 685
inserting, 256

properties
Caption, 258
Control Source, 259
Option Value, 258
Option Value property, 258
optional keyword, 559
Options command (Tools menu), 135, 439
options groups, 260
Options menu commands
Keep help on top, 21
Show System Objects, 74
OR queries, 156-161
parameters, 346
ordering tabs (forms), 420-424
Tab Order list box, 15
organizing databases, 40
ORs and ANDs in criteria (exercise), 156-158
outer joins, 464-467

P

<P> HTML tag, 616
Page Break tool, 655
Page Footer bands, 189
Page Header bands, 188
Page Header/Footer command (Layout View menu), 247
Page Setup command (File menu), 200
page sizes (reports), setting, 489
pages
footers, 188-189
headers, 188
storing, 620
WWW (World Wide Web), 616
parameter queries, 290
advantages of, 289-290
creating, 292
limitations, 300
ranges, 296-300
running, 290-291
wildcards, 294
Parameter query exercise, 292

parentheses ( ), 482
Paste command (Copy menu), 529
performance issues, ActiveX controls, 612
periods (.), 540-541
Personal button, 24
Picture property, 412-414, 591
PictureStudentPersonal form, 265
placeholders
arguments, 554
input masks, 79
planning
databases, 38-40
forms, 361
positioning input boxes, 588
pound signs (#), 155
prefixes
cmd, 403
lng, 551
PresentValue arguments, 553
PressureData table, 324
previewing reports, 460
PreviousRecord control buttons, creating, 405
Primary Key button, 60
primary keys
defined, 685
specifying, 44
Print button, 187
Print Preview button, 193
Print Preview mode, 198
Print Setup dialog box, 489
printing
mailing labels, 194, 199-201
reports, 187
private subprocedures, 411
procedures, 410-412, 569, 575-583
exiting, 411
private, 411
sub-procedures, 575-576
see also functions
Procedures View button, 584
programming techniques, 547-548
dynamic controls, 487
error-trapping, 562-565

event-driven, 570
events, 548
functions, 552
applying, 558-559
arguments, 553
defining, 552-557, 561
exiting, 564
unbound, 557-559
keywords, 551, 552
subprocedures, 552
see also languages
programs, Setup, 4
Programs command (Start menu), 7
properties
Access identifiers, 540-541
After Update, 524
assigning, 125, 376
Auto Expand, 232
Border Style, 425
Caption, 187, 242, 258
changing, 380-382
Column Count, 237
Column Widths, 237
Control Source, 208, 212, 259
control properties, 527-535
ControlTip Text, 405
Decimal Places, 105
Default Field, 98-100
Default Value, 360
Default View, 425
defaults, assigning, 98
Enabled, 383-384
Field Size, 85, 104-105
fields, 85
Fixed, 478
Force New Page, 462
Format, 104, 235, 478
Group Footer, 472
Group On, 458
help systems, 408-410
Hyperlink, 625-627
Input Mask, 235
Keep Together, 458
Limit to List, 232
Link Child Field, 395
Link Child Fields, 366, 378

Link Master Field, 395
Link Master Fields, 366, 378
List Width, 229, 237
Locked, 385-386
Name, 473
Navigation Buttons, 419, 425
On Click, 407-408, 542
Option Value, 258
Picture, 412-414, 591
Record Selectors, 419
Required, 104
Row Source, 234
Running Sum, 201
Selection Behavior, 135
Tab Stop, 423-424
viewing, 125
Visible, 528
Properties button, 193, 258
Properties command
    Calendar Object menu, 609
    View menu, 523
Properties list box, 92
Property list box, 377
protocols
    HTTP (HypterText Tranfer
      Protocol), 614
    TCP/IP (Transmission
      Control Protocol/Internet
      Protocol), 632
**Prototype label dialog
box, 199**
**Publish to the Web Wizard,
618-622**
publishing (WWW), 616
    Access documents
      forms, 623-624
      reports, 623-624
      tables, 617-622
    benefits of, 617-618

Q

QBE (Query by Example), 685
queries, 160, 167, 268, 359
    action queries, 684
    actions, 301-302
    advantages, 268

AND, 346
append queries, 317-318
    creating, 319-324
    defined, 316
changing types of, 312-314
criteria, 151-156
    <Date( ), 156
    = (equality operator), 155
    AND, 156-159
    Between, 155
    In, 156
    Left( ), 156
    Like( ), 156
    matches, 156
    Not, 156
    OR, 156-159
    Year( ), 156
criterial, 153
crosstab queries, 336, 339
    advantages, 341
    creating, 335-339
    defined, 335, 684
    forms, 347
    multiple operatives,
      341-344
    updating, 347
dates, 276-278
    calculations, 279-282
    expressions, 279-282
delete queries, 308, 312
    creating, 309-313
design grids, 145-146
    Criteria rows, 151
    customizing, 147
    Sort rows, 149
    editing, 147-148
expressions, 447-448, 454
    circular, 480
    creating, 450-454
    inserting, 456
fields, removing, 174-175
forms, 368
functions of, 143-144
joins, 463
    arranging join lines, 450
    inner, 463
    outer, 464-467
limitations, 200

links, 450
multitable
    constructing, 169-173
    running, 172
    three-table, 176-180
    two-table, 169-172
OR, 346
parameters, 290
    advantages of, 289-290
    creating, 292
    limitations, 300
    ranges, 296-300
    wildcards, 294
QBE (Query by Example),
    685
querying, 471
re-queries, triggering, 477
relationships, 450
running, 147, 276, 290,
    356, 477
select, 301, 309
ShowStudentStatus, 260
simple, 144-147
sorting, 148-151
SQL (Structured Query
    Language), 312, 496-500
tables, adding, 176-180
top queries, 324
    advantages, 328-329
    creating, 325-328
update queries, 329-334
updating, 477
wizards, 168
**Query by Example (QBE),
685**
**Query Datasheet toolbar,
659**
Query Design toolbar, 660
Query menu commands
    Delete, 310
    Make Table, 301
    Select Query, 312
Query tab, 144
Query Type button, 321
**Query Type menu, Append
command, 321**

quick reference to exercises,
  644-652
quizzes
  day 1, 33
    answers, 638
  day 2, 69
    answers, 638
  day 3, 107
    answers, 638
  day 4, 161-162
    answers, 638
  day 5, 201
    answers, 639
  day 6, 248
    answers, 639
  day 7, 284-285
    answers, 639
  day 8, 348
    answers, 639-640
  day 9, 396
    answers, 640
  day 10, 440
    answers, 640
  day 11, 491
    answers, 640
  day 12, 542
    answers, 641
  day 13, 591
    answers, 641
  day 14, 633
    answers, 641

R

radio buttons, 685
raised graphics, 437
Random property, 47
Range parameter query
  exercise, 298
ranges (queries), 296-300
reacting to events
  macros, 548
  Visual Basic, 548-551
Record manipulation exercise,
  400-404
record selectors (forms), 418
  removing, 418-419

Record selectors and
  navigation buttons exercise,
  418-419
records
  creating, 74-76
  data integrity, 92
  data types, 92, 97-98
  deleting, 106, 308-313
  editing, 77
  finding
    Filter by Form command,
      387-390
    Filter by Selection
      command, 391-392
    Find button, 386-387
  groups, 214, 685
  input masks, 77
    benefits of, 80-82
    creating, 78-79
    data validation, 80-82
    exclamation points (!), 80
    format, 79
    placeholders, 79
  navigating, 402
    Go To menu, 116
    keyboard shortcuts, 116
    toolbars, 118-119
  relationships, 354
  sorting, 394
Records menu, Filter com-
  mand, 387
Rectangle tool, 429, 655
rectangles
  embedding in forms, 429-431
  special effects, 436
recursive calculations, 98
RedGreen macro, 532
referencing controls, 473
referential integrity, 62, 224,
  685
REG scripts, 597
Register button, 598
registering ActiveX controls,
  597-598
relational databases, 38
  compacting, 314-316
  creating, 22-23, 40-41
  defined, 684

designing, 39, 61
efficiency of, 39, 447, 471
forms
  advantages, 112
  AutoForm, 113-114
  closing, 126
  controls, 124-125
  creating, 112
  Form Wizard, 119
  layout, 120
  naming, 120
  navigating, 115-119
naming, 22-23, 41
objects, 61
opening, 50, 74
planning, 38-40
queries, 268
  actions, 301-302
  advantages, 268
  append queries, 316-324
  changing types of,
    312-314
  crosstab queries, 335-344
  dates, 276-282
  delete queries, 308-313
  expressions, 447-454
  parameters, 289-292
  ranges, 296-300
  repeating, 477
  select queries, 301
  SQL (Structured Query
    Language), 312
  top queries, 324-329
  update queries, 329-334
  updating, 477
  wildcards, 294
records
  finding, 386-392
  relationships, 354-355
structures, 369
tables, 40
  closing, 27, 61
  creating, 42-45, 55-61
  hiding, 74
  linking, 56, 61-64
  matching, 62
  modifying, 50
  naming, 26, 44

querying, 144
relationships, 61-62
validating, 62
see also records
relationships, 61, 354-355
defined, 685
one-to-many, 62
queries, 450
updating, 347
**Relationships command
(Tools menu), 62, 176, 450**
Relationships dialog box, 63
Relationships toolbar, 664
REM keyword, 571
removing
controls, 425
fields from queries, 174-175
navigation buttons, 418-419
record selectors, 418-419
Rename Field button, 26
renaming fields, 44
reordering
controls, 15
fields, 82
Datasheet View, 83-85
Design View, 82, 83
Tab Order list box, 15
tabs (forms), 420-424
Repeat( ) function, 569
**Replace command (Edit
menu), 552**
Replication IDs, 97
Report Design toolbar, 662
Report header bands, 188
**Report Header/Footer
command (Layout View
menu), 247**
**Report Print Preview toolbar,
662**
Report Wizard
creating reports, 184-186
usage tips, 194
ReportCards report, 462, 470
reports, 184
controls, 485-487
converting to HTML,
623-624

creating, 184-186
editing, 187-193
expressions
calculating, 471-478
field, 205-211
syntax, 213-214
fields
aligning, 192
deleting, 207
sizing, 190-191, 206-211
footers, 188
forms, compared, 184
grouping, 215-217, 455-462
headers, 188
images, embedding,
262-265, 483-485
labeling, 218
layouts, 482-485
page sizes, specifying, 489
previewing, 460
printing, 187
properties
Force New Page, 462
Group Footer, 472
Group On, 458
Keep Together, 458
running sums, displaying,
201
sorting, 455-462
subreports, 490
zooming, 193
re-queries, triggering, 477
Required property, 104
**reregistering ActiveX controls,
597**
rerunning queries, 477
reserved words, 551-552
resizing
Detail bands, 207
fields, 190-191
benefits of, 87
rows, 85-86
widths, 85-86
form controls, 127-131
query design grids, 147
subforms, 427-428
toolbars, 11

**Resizing a form control
exercise, 128-131**
resolutions, 114
responding to events
macros, 548
Visual Basic, 548-551
Response variable, 588
Restore Window button, 370
restoring
toolbars, 11
windows, 370
restricting searches
Filter by form command,
387-390
Filter by Selection command,
391-392
Right( ) function, 481
**Row command (Insert menu),
268**
Row Source property, 234
Control Source property,
compared, 247
defined, 685
rows (fields), 85
blank, 254
inserting, 268
queries design grids
Criteria, 151
Sort, 149
sizing, 85-86
Rtrim( ) function, 213
**Run button, 147, 178, 276,
290, 356**
RunCode macro, 590
running
macros, 525-527
queries, 147, 276, 356
action queries, 302
criteria, 152
multitable, 172, 178
parameter queries, 290
Running Sum property, 201
running sums, displaying, 201
runtime errors, 562

S

sample data
   AppendMe, 672-673
   AvailableClasses, 673-676
   CompletedCourses, 676-678
   Demo_Crosstab1, 678-680
   Fruit Choices, 680
   Fruits, 680-681
   GradeValues, 681-682
   StudentPersonal, 668-672
   StudentStatusLookup, 682
**Sample Fields list box, 24,
   43-44**
Sample Preview button, 460
Sample Tables list box, 24
**Save As command (File
   menu), 174, 219**
**Save as HTML command
   (File menu), 619**
**Save As menu, Export com-
   mand, 509**
Save button, 151
**Save command (File
   menu), 66**
saving layout changes, 106
screen resolutions, 114
scrollbars, 115
   creating, 400-405
   scrolling, 59, 115
Search button, 19
searching
   databases, 387-392
   help systems, 30
   Office Assistant, 19
security (forms), 160
   Enabled property, 383-385
   Locked property, 385-386
**See Also entries (Help system),
   410**
**Select All command (Edit
   menu), 138, 386**
Select Object tool, 654
select queries, 301, 309
**Select Query command
   (Query menu), 312**
**Select Report command
   (Edit menu), 193**

SELECT statements, 498
selecting
   controls, 136-138
   fields, 54-57, 383
   objects, 188
   views, 585
**Selection Behavior property,
   135**
**Send to Back command
   (Format menu), 483**
**Set Control Defaults command
   (Format menu), 434**
**Setting a Default Field
   property exercise, 98-100**
**Setting the Data Validation
   property exercise, 101-102**
Setup program, 4
**SGML (Standard Generalized
   Markup Language), 615**
**Shift+F2 key combination,
   103, 209, 279, 454, 473,
   478, 520, 535**
shortcut keys, 116
   A, 59
   Del, 308
   Esc, 80
   F1, 18, 408
   F11, 474, 477
   F4, 270
   F5, 116
   Y, 59
**Show System Objects com-
   mand (Options menu), 74**
Show Table button, 176, 450
ShowGreen macro, 535
**ShowStudentStatus queries,
   260**
simple queries
   constructing, 144-147
   design grids, 145-147
   exercise, 144-147
   Simple Query Wizard, 168
   sorting, 148-151
Simple Query Wizard, 168
Single Form view, 418
single variables, 585

sizing
   combo boxes, 284
   fields, 59
      benefits of, 87
      reports, 206-211
      rows, 85-86
      widths, 85-86
   form controls, 127-131
   mailing labels, 200
   subforms, 427-428
   toolbars, 11
**Snap To Grid command,
   131, 192**
   Format menu, 139
   Layout menu, 427
software
   browsers, 614
      display differences, 632
   TCP/IP (Transmission
      Control Protocol/Internet
      Protocol), 632
   Winsock, 614
**Sort Ascending button,
   394-395**
Sort Descending button, 395
sort orders, 686
sorting
   mailing labels, 197
   queries, 148-151
   records, 394
   reports, 455-462
   sort orders, 686
   tables, 394
**Sorting and Grouping button,
   215, 458, 472**
space characters, 213
special effects
   raised graphics, 437
   sunken graphics, 436
**Special Effects button, 141,
   430, 436**
specifying subforms, 363
**SQL (Structured Query
   Language), 237, 496-500**
   advantages, 541
   applications, 500-501
   case-sensitivity, 314
   defined, 686

queries, 312
statements
    SELECT, 498
    WHERE, 499
SQL View, 327
Standard Generalized Markup
  Language, 615
Start menu, Programs
  command, 7
starting
    Access, 7, 32
    Combo Box wizard, 227
    modules, 554
statements
    Dim, 555, 572-573
    GoTo, 590
    OnError, 562
    Option Explicit, 584
    SELECT, 498
    WHERE, 499
static pages, 620
static tests, 569
status bars, customizing, 32
strings, 585
Structured Query Language,
  see **SQL**
StudentAgesMakeTable
  queries, 302
StudentCurrentCourses table,
  224
StudentID Footer bands,
  creating, 472
StudentNumber field, 50
StudentPersonal table
    creating, 43-45
    data, 81, 99
    Date fields, inserting,
      268-270
    naming, 44
    querying, 144
    sample data, 668-672
StudentPersonalPicture table,
  262
StudentPersonalPictures table,
  263
Students and Classes.mdz
  databases, 55

StudentsAndCourses query,
  215
StudentStatus fields, 255
StudentStatusLookup table,
  260
    sample data, 682
sub-procedures, 575-576
Subform/Subreport tool, 655
subforms, 354, 369
    controls, 425
    creating, 360-365
        drag-and-drop, 370-373
        Main/Subform Wizard,
          360-364
    customizing, 424-428
    designing, 355
    efficiency of, 395
    layouts, 363
    linking, 378-379, 395
    naming, 355
    planning, 361
    properties
        Border Style, 425
        Navigation Buttons, 425
    queries, 355-359, 368
    sizing, 427-428
    specifying, 363
    synchronizing, 366
subprocedures
    defined, 552, 686
    exiting, 411
    private, 411
subreports, 490
subtotals, 347
Sum( ) function, 472-473
sums, calculating, 472-473
    see also mathematical
      calculations
sunken graphics, 436
super-VGA resolution, 114
switchboard forms
    creating, 506-509
    macros, 509-514
Switchboard or menu form
  exercise, 506-509
synchronizing forms with
  subforms, 366, 378-379

T

Tab Control tool, 655
Tab Order command (View
  menu), 421
Tab Order list box, reordering,
  15
Tab Stop property, 423-424
Tabbed form exercise,
  240-243
tabbed forms, 239
    captions, 242
    creating, 240-243
    option groups, inserting, 256
    pages, adding/removing, 243
    tab order, changing, 420-424
TabbedStudentPersonal form,
  255-256
TabControl, 239-240
Table Datasheet toolbar, 659
Table Design toolbar, 658
Table Properties dialog
  box, 74
Table Wizard, 24-27
    creating tables, 24-27, 42-45
    selecting, 43
Table Wizard dialog box, 26
tables, 40
    binding to fields, 208
    closing, 27, 55, 61
    columns, 66
    combo boxes, 88
        binding, 235
    commenting, 58
    CompletedCourses, 446
    converting to HTML,
      617-622
    creating, 42-45
        Datasheet View, 64-66
        fields, 43-44
        manually, 55-61
        Table Wizard, 24-27,
          42-45
    data
        editing, 77
        entering, 74-76
        input masks, 77-82

integrity, 92
validating, 88-89
fields
    adding, 268-270
    choosing, 26
    creating, 52
    data types, 46-48
    deleting, 50
    highlighting, 50
    inserting, 52-55
    key fields, 57
    moving, 82-85
    naming, 52
    properties, 68, 92-98
    sizing, 59
GradeValue, 476
GradeValues, 446
    displaying, 450
    efficiency, 447
    opening, 477
hiding, 74
linking, 56, 61-64, 450
matching, 62
modifying, 50
naming, 26, 44, 184
PressureData, 324
querying, 144
    actions, 301-302
    date criteria, 276
    delete queries, 308-313
    expressions, 447-454
    parameters, 289-292
    ranges, 296-300
    wildcards, 294
records, 74-76
    deleting, 106, 308
    navigating, 402
referential integrity, 224
relationships, 61, 354
    defined, 685
    one-to-many, 62
    updating, 347
rows, inserting, 268
sorting, 394
StudentCurrentCourses, 224
StudentPersonalPicture, 262
StudentPersonalPictures, 263
StudentStatusLookup, 260

validating, 62
see also queries
tags (HTML), 616
TCP/IP (Transmission Control Protocol/Internet Protocol), 632
templates
    forms, 439
    HTML (HyperText Markup Language), 620
Text Box tool, 208, 218, 654
text boxes
    aligning, 483
    defined, 686
    properties
        Control Source, 473
        Fixed, 478
        Format, 478
    unbound, labeling, 472
Text fields, 46, 255
    efficiency of, 58
    inserting, 208, 211
    properties, 93, 97
    unbound, 470
three-table queries
    constructing, 176-180
    running, 178
three-table query exercise, 176-180
Tie a VB function to form controls exercise, 576-579
Tile Horizontally command (Window menu), 370
Tile Vertically command (Window menu), 370
tiling windows, 370
times
    calculations, 284
    inserting, 437
title bars, 8
titling input boxes, 588
toggle buttons, 89, 655
toolbars, 9, 118-119
    arranging, 10
    buttons, 591
    customizing, 13-15, 32
    Database, 658
    defined, 686

docking, 12-13
Filter/Sort, 665
Form Design, 661
Form View, 660
Formatting, 140-141
    illustrated, 661, 664
limitations, 591
Macro, 663
Module, 663
Query Datasheet, 659
Query Design, 660
Relationships, 664
Report Design, 662
Report Print Preview, 662
restoring, 11
sizing, 11
Table Datasheet, 659
Table Design, 658
title bars, 11
tooltips, 9-10
Toolbars command (Tools menu), 13
Toolbars menu, Customize command, 13
tools, 654
    Bound Object Frame, 655
    Box, 655
    Check Box, 655
    Combo Box, 226, 655
    Command Button, 508, 579, 655
    Control Wizards, 654
    Image, 244, 655
    Label, 218, 654, 685
    Line, 431, 655
    List Box, 655
    Option Button, 252
    Option Group, 252, 655
    Page Break, 655
    Rectangle, 429, 655
    Select Object, 654
    Subform/Subreport, 655
    Tab Control, 655
    TabControl, 239-240
    Text Box, 208, 218, 654
    Toggle Button, 655
    Unbound Object Frame, 655

Tools menu commands
ActiveX Controls, 598
Database Utilities, 315
Options, 135, 439
Relationships, 62, 176, 450
Toolbars, 13
tooltips, 9-10
top queries, 324
advantages, 328-329
creating, 325-328
trapping errors, 562-565, 568
functions, 560
macros, 503
triggering
events, 551
re-queries, 477
Trim( ) function, 213, 247
twips, 588
**two-headed arrow cursors,
  128, 134**
**two-table query exercise,
  169-172**
txtWeightedGPA field, 487
Typical install option, 5

U

**Unbound Object Frame tool,
  655**
unbound objects, 686
controls, 127
Name property, 473
forms
advantages of, 284
creating, 434
functions, 557-559]
text boxes
Control Source properties,
  473
labeling, 472
text fields
advantages, 470
inserting, 208, 211
**UNC (Universal Naming
  Convention), 47, 625**
underlines, inserting, 483

**Undo command (Edit menu),
  130, 137**
undoing mistakes, 130, 137
unitary forms, 395
**Universal Naming Convention
  (UNC), 47, 625**
**Universal Resource Locators
  (URLs), 625**
unlocking controls, 508
up scrollbars, creating, 405
update queries, 329
creating, 330-334
defined, 329
updating
field relationships, 347
queries, 347, 477
**URLs (Universal Resource
  Locators), 625**
user interface (Access)
menu bars, 9
customizing, 13-15
title bars, 8
toolbars, 9
customizing, 13-15
docking, 12-13
moving, 10
restoring, 11
sizing, 11
user-defined variables, 585
**Using a wizard to make a table
  exercise, 24-27**

V

validating data
error messages, 103
input masks, 80-82
records, 88-89
tables, 62
Validation Rule property,
  101-102
**Validation Rule property,
  101-102**
values
message box properties, 582
NULL, 685

variables, 574
declaring, 555, 574-575,
  584-586
defined, 686
types, 585
variants, 585
**Variations of criteria exercise,
  153**
VB, *see* **Visual Basic**
VBX controls, 596
View menu commands
Condition, 518
Datasheet, 80
Grid, 456
Macro Names, 518
Properties, 523
Tab Order, 421
View Selection button, 118
viewing properties, 125
views, 77, 456
changing, 118
Datasheet, 74, 684
Design, 270, 684
selecting, 585
Single Form, 418
SQL (Structured Query
  Language), 327
Zoom, 103
Visible property, 528
Visual Basic, 568
advantages of, 568
code styles, 572
commands
acNext, 411
DoCmd, 411
Exit, 411
MsgBox, 412
comments, 571
inserting, 571
usage tips, 571
complex input, 569
constants, 574
events, 407, 570
identifiers, 571
input boxes
creating, 583-586, 588
positioning, 588
titling, 588

loops, 569-570
message boxes, creating, 579-583
modules, 573
procedures, 410-412
    functions, 569, 575-583
    sub-procedures, 575-576
SQL (Structured Query Language) queries, 500
statements
    Dim, 572-573
    GoTo, 590
    REM, 571
variables, 574
    declaring, 574-575, 584-586
    types, 585
VBX controls, 596
see also functions

W

Web, *see* WWW
weighted values, calculating, 454, 478
WHERE statements, 499
widening fields, 86
Wildcard parameter queries exercise, 294
wildcards
    asterisks (*), 153
    queries, 294
Window menu commands
    Tile Horizontally, 370
    Tile Vertically, 370
windows
    Database, 24, 240, 684
    Help Topics, 29
    maximizing, 75, 113
    restoring, 370
    tiling, 370
Windows API (application programming interface), invoking, 568
Winsock, 614

wizards, 21
    benefits of, 21
    Combo Box, 227
    Command Button, 401-403
    Control
        disabling, 233
        enabling, 226
    Input Mask Builder, 78
    Label, 195-198
    Main/Subform
        forms, 361-366
        opening, 360
    Option Group, 257
    Publish to the Web, 618
    Report, 184-186, 194
    Simple Query, 168
    Table Wizard, 24-27, 43
workshop exercises
    day 1, 33
    day 2, 70
    day 3, 107-108
    day 4, 162-163
    day 5, 202
    day 6, 248
    day 7, 285-286
    day 8, 349
    day 9, 396
    day 10, 440-441
    day 11, 492
    day 12, 542-543
    day 13, 592
    day 14, 633
WWW (World Wide Web), 614
    accessing, 614-615
    browsers, 614
    protocols, 614
    publishing, 616
        Access forms, 623-624
        Access reports, 623-624
        Access tables, 617-622
        benefits of, 617-618
    sites, 616

X-Y-Z

Y key, 59
Year( ) criteria expressions, 156
Yes/No fields, 47
    properties, 96

Zoom view, 103
    exiting, 454
zooming, 103
    columns, 520
    reports, 193

Access 97 Unleashed, Second Edition

Dwayne Gifford, et al.

Microsoft's Access has become one of the most accepted standards of database management for personal computers. The *Unleashed* series format makes it easy for database programmers new to Access as well as current users to quickly find the information they need. This complete reference includes instructions for programming Access and integrating the database with the Internet along with advanced techniques for working with tables, queries, forms, and data. The CD-ROM contains Access utilities and applications and an electronic Access reference library.

Price: $49.99 USA/$70.95 CDN
ISBN: 0-672-30983-1   1,100 pages

Alison Balter's Mastering Access 95 Development, Premier Edition

Alison Balter

This collection of the most concise and valuable information of Access 95 development shows readers how to solve simple and complex Access programming problems. Covers tables, forms, queries, reports, advanced VBA techniques, objects, properties, debugging, and more—a library of functions and skills that readers can use in all of their development projects. CD-ROM includes source code from the book and powerful utilities.

$49.99 USA/$70.95 CDN
ISBN: 0-672-30944-0   800 pages

World Wide Web Database Developer's Guide

Swank & Kittle

This book teaches readers how to quickly and professionally create a database and connect it to the Internet. Real-world database problems and solutions illustrate how to manage information. Readers discover how to use HTML, Java, and the newest Netscape 2.0 features to organize their information. CD-ROM included.

$59.99 USA/$84.95 CDN
1-57521-048-7   800 pages

Teach Yourself Microsoft Office 97 in 24 Hours

Greg Perry

An estimated 22 million people use Microsoft Office, and with the new features of Office 97, much of that market will want the upgrade. To address that market, Sams has published a mass-market version of its best-selling *Teach Yourself* series. This entry-level title includes many illustrations, screen shots, and a step-by-step plan to learning how to use each Office product and how to use them together. Readers learn how to create documents in Word that include hypertext links to files created with one of the other Office products.

$19.99 USA/$28.95 CDN
ISBN: 0-672-31009-0   450 pages

Web Site Developer's Kit with Microsoft Resources

James Townsend, et al.

Geared toward business professionals, MIS professionals, and power users, this book presents the information necessary to create and/or integrate database systems, incorporate SQL functionality, and provide complex information systems on the World Wide Web using Microsoft tools. Teaches how to design and build sophisticated databases and connect them to the World Wide Web. Includes coverage of security, large database access, using WINCGI, and the Microsoft Network as well as hot new products like Internet Studio, Internet Information Server, and Catapult. CD-ROM includes databases by the author, third-party utilities, and various tools.

$49.99 USA/$70.95 CDN
1-57521-095-9   784 pages

Web Publishing Unleashed, Professional Reference Edition

William Stanek, et al.

This all-new, updated edition combines coverage of all Web development technologies in one volume. It now includes entire sections on JavaScript, Java, VBScript, and ActiveX, plus expanded coverage of developing multimedia Web sites, adding animation, developing intranet sites, designing pages and sites, and much more! Includes a 200-page reference section. CD-ROM includes a selection of HTML, Java, CGI, and scripting tools for Windows/MAC, plus Sams.net Web Publishing Library and electronic versions of top Web publishing books.

$59.99 USA/$84.95 CDN
1-57521-198-X 1,200 pages

Developing Intranet Applications with Java

Jerry Ablan

Developers learn the intricacies of Java intranet development, including how to create interactive databases with sound and animation. CD-ROM includes source code from the book and powerful Java utilities.

$49.99 USA/$70.95 CDN
1-57521-166-1   528 pages

Microsoft SQL Server 6.5 DBA Survival Guide, Second Edition

Mark Spenik & Orryn Sledge

Updated to cover new features such as the new transaction wizard, this book will turn a mediocre administrator into an effective, skilled leader in charge of a well-tuned RDBMS. Time-saving techniques show how to maximize the Microsoft SQL Server. Teaches how to implement day-to-day preventive maintenance tasks. CD-ROM contains scripts and time-saving programs from the book.

$49.99 USA/$67.99 CDN
0-672-30959-9   912 pages

Add to Your Sams Library Today with the Best Books for Programming, Operating Systems, and New Technologies

The easiest way to order is to pick up the phone and call

1-800-428-5331

between 9:00 a.m. and 5:00 p.m. EST.
For faster service please have your credit card available.

ISBN	Quantity	Description of Item	Unit Cost	Total Cost
0-672-30983-1		Access 97 Unleashed, Second Edition (Book/CD-ROM)	$49.99	
0-672-30944-0		Alison Balter's Mastering Access 95 Development, Premier Edition (Book/CD-ROM)	$49.99	
1-57521-048-7		World Wide Web Database Developer's Guide (Book/CD-ROM)	$59.99	
0-672-31009-0		Teach Yourself Microsoft Office 97 in 24 Hours	$19.99	
1-57521-095-9		Web Development with Microsoft Resources (Book/CD-ROM)	$49.99	
1-57521-198-X		Web Publishing Unleashed, Professional Reference Edition (Book/CD-ROM)	$59.99	
1-57521-166-1		Developing Intranet Applications with Java (Book/CD-ROM)	$49.99	
0-672-30959-9		Microsoft SQL Server 6.5 DBA Survival Guide, Second Edition (Book/CD-ROM)	$49.99	

❑ 3 ½" Disk

❑ 5 ¼" Disk

Shipping and Handling: See information below.

TOTAL

Shipping and Handling: $4.00 for the first book, and $1.75 for each additional book. Floppy disk: add $1.75 for shipping and handling. If you need to have it NOW, we can ship product to you in 24 hours for an additional charge of approximately $18.00, and you will receive your item overnight or in two days. Overseas shipping and handling adds $2.00 per book and $8.00 for up to three disks. Prices subject to change. Call for availability and pricing information on latest editions.

201 W. 103rd Street, Indianapolis, Indiana 46290

1-800-428-5331 — Orders   1-800-835-3202 — FAX   1-800-858-7674 — Customer Service

Book ISBN 0-672-30969-6

A VIACOM SERVICE

The Information SuperLibrary™

Bookstore

Search

What's New

Reference

Software

Newsletter

Company Overviews

Yellow Pages

Internet Starter Kit

HTML Workshop

Win a Free T-Shirt!

Macmillan Computer Publishing

Site Map

Talk to Us

CHECK OUT THE BOOKS IN THIS LIBRARY.

You'll find thousands of shareware files and over 1600 computer books designed for both technowizards and technophobes. You can browse through 700 sample chapters, get the latest news on the Net, and find just about anything using our massive search directories.

All Macmillan Computer Publishing books are available at your local bookstore.

We're open 24-hours a day, 365 days a year.

You don't need a card.

We don't charge fines.

And you can be as LOUD as you want.

The Information SuperLibrary

http://www.mcp.com/mcp/   ftp.mcp.com